CAREER SELECTOR 2001

CAREER SELECTOR 2001

James C. Gonyea

President
Gonyea and Associates, Inc.

Copyright © 1993 James C. Gonyea

All rights reserved.

No part of this book may be reproduced in any form, by photostat, microfilm, xerography, or any other means, or incorporated into any information retrieval system, electronic or mechanical, without the written permission of the copyright owner.

All inquires should be addressed to:
Barron's Educational Series, Inc.
250 Wireless Boulevard
Hauppauge, New York 11788

Library of Congress Cataloging in Publication Data

International Standard Book No. 0-8120-1453-7

Library of Congress Cataloging in Publication Data

Gonyea, James C.
    Career Selector 2001/James C. Gonyea.
        p.   cm.
    Includes bibliographical references.
    ISBN 0-8120-1453-7
    1. Vocational guidance. 2. Job descriptions. I. Title.
    II. Title: Career selector two thousand one.
    HF5381.G577 1992
    650.14—dc20
                                                                      92-32711
                                                                       CIP

PRINTED IN THE UNITED STATES OF AMERICA

56   5100   9876543

Dedication

Career Selector 2001 is dedicated to the many individuals who are confused about a career direction and, as a result, have yet to realize their full human potential. The journey to the right career begins with an understanding of your personality style and those occupations that match. *Career Selector 2001* will guide you on that journey.

To Pam and Korie—the two best choices I ever made!

Table of Contents

	Page
Acknowledgements	viii
Preface	ix
Chapter 1 Purpose of *Career Selector 2001*	1
Chapter 2 Career Planning for the Year 2001 and Beyond	3
Career Planning in the Year 2001	3
Career Management Skills for the Future	4
Chapter 3 Excuse Me, But Before We Begin, I Have a Few Questions ...	5
Chapter 4 Checklists of Things to Do	9
Task 1: Identifying Possible Career Options	9
Work Groups	10
List of Possible Career Options	24
Additional Career Options	25
Task 2: Choosing Your Work Preferences	25
Work Preference Categories	26
Work Preferences/Evaluation Guide	30
Task 3: Selecting a Career Direction	34
Task 4: Developing a Career Plan	37
Career Planning Guide	39
Chapter 5 501 Occupational Profiles	45
Chapter 6 Jobs of the Future	300
The Jobs	302
Jobs of the Future Evaluation Sheet	311
Appendixes	312
A. Additional Resources	313
B. Alphabetical Index of Job Titles	323
C. How to Select a Career Counselor	329
D. How to Use the DOT, GOE, and OOH Directories	333
About the Author	336

Acknowledgements

For their help in writing this book, I would like to thank the following individuals: Dr. Jamie Huntington-Meath for his work on the chapter dealing with jobs of the future, Wayne Gonyea for his editorial assistance during the early stage of development and continued personal support over the years, Dr. Kenneth Hoeltzel and Sonia Scheim for their professional assistance in shaping the content and format, Pam Gonyea for her assistance in compiling the 501 occupational profiles, and Max Reed for her editorial support throughout the entire writing process. Finally, a special note of thanks to Barron's Educational Series, Inc. for continued support and interest in my work and for the opportunity to write this book.

Preface

If you are unsure or confused about a career direction and wish to discover which of America's best occupations are right for you, *Career Selector 2001* can help you find the answer.

With library and bookstore shelves overflowing with career guidance books, you might ask why I have chosen to write *Career Selector 2001*. Surprisingly, there are several good reasons.

Most of the career guidance books deal with how to land a job rather than how to select a career direction. These books provide advice on how to find potential employers, write employment cover letters and resumés, prepare for and conduct job interviews, and other related matters. The authors often assume that readers have already determined which career they want to pursue, and now only need advice concerning how to get there. For those who are confused about a career direction, these books offer little help.

Of the books that do address the subject of how to select a career direction, the effectiveness of the guidance may range from poor to good. While most of these books do an adequate job of helping readers define their personality style—a necessary ingredient in career selection—many fail to guide readers in translating what they have learned about themselves into a career direction (i.e. a job title or titles). Since there exist over 13,500 occupations in our society and most individuals have little understanding of the nature of more than a handful of these occupations, it is understandable that many individuals still can not select a career direction after reading some of these self-help books.

As someone who has devoted his entire professional career—some twenty years plus—to the resolution of this problem, I am pleased to share with you a methodology that, if followed, can help you discover which occupations are best for you to pursue. This methodology is the system found in *Career Selector 2001*—and only requires about five to ten hours of your time to complete.

The guidance system found in *Career Selector 2001* has been tested, revised, and perfected by tens of thousands of users. It works if you follow the directions completely. In addition to offering a sound career decision-making system, *Career Selector 2001* is based upon data compiled on over 13,500 occupations. All data has been gathered by the U.S. Department of Labor, considered by many professional counselors to be one of the best and most accurate sources of occupational information.

Within this book are 501 occupational profiles to help you select a career direction from among the most popular occupations available today and for after the year 2001. Should you not find your career direction from those occupations profiled in this book, optional steps are included to help you compare your interests and work preferences to more than 13,000 additional occupations.

As a I write this book, the latest unemployment figures are tragic—nearly 10,000,000 people are out of work. The future projection is for even higher unemployment rates. Whether you're among the millions of unemployed forced to make a career change, or part of the employed group who want to change careers, you will find *Career Selector 2001* to be an invaluable guide to discovering a new career direction.

Those who use *Career Selector 2001* to discover a career direction, as well as professional counselors and others who use this book to guide individuals in career planning, are encouraged to write to the author (in care of the publisher) to share their suggestions for future revisions.

James C. Gonyea

CHAPTER 1

Purpose of *Career Selector 2001*

At first glance, the purpose of *Career Selector 2001* may seem obvious—to help you select a career direction or to quickly obtain information about a particular occupation. While this is true, this book can help you accomplish a much more important task.

Your happiness and success in life are, in great part, determined by the work you do. Choose the right career direction, one that is suited to your personality style, and your chances of happiness and success are increased. Choose the wrong career path, and you are more likely to experience dissatisfaction with yourself and life in general.

It's easy to understand that a flower placed in the wrong environment (*i.e.*, too little sunlight, water, or minerals from the earth) will not survive. The same analogy can be said for the type of work environment in which you place yourself. Put yourself into a work situation that does not match your personality style, and you, like the flower, may wither and die.

Selecting a suitable career path involves identifying occupations that match your personality—your interests, abilities, values, needs, and behavioral traits. Foremost in this matching process is the task of selecting occupations that will enable you to pursue your interests and use your abilities. Interest and ability in your work have a direct bearing on the level of success you can achieve. To succeed at any occupation requires hard work and dedication, and these can not be sustained for long if the work is boring, unfulfilling, or beyond your capabilities.

How often have you, or people you have known, longed for the end of the workday because you could no longer stand the work? It's tragic when you consider that millions of individuals go to work each day dreading the time they spend at work and looking forward to the hour when they are free to return home. Beyond the personal tragedy of such a situation is the loss in productivity our country suffers when people have little enthusiasm for their work. Further compounding this problem is the fact that many of these unhappy people do not know which occupations would be better to pursue. The outcome of such a situation is inevitable—unhappiness and lower productivity continue unnecessarily, often for years.

Which career options are best for you? Only you can answer this question, but *Career Selector 2001* can help by guiding you through a carefully designed program of career exploration, decision-making, and planning. Completing *Career Selector 2001* will help you discover which work activities hold the most promise for personal enjoyment and success for you. This objective, while less obvious than the first, is the real and most important purpose of this book. *Career Selector 2001* is your guide on a journey of self-discovery and personal enrichment—a journey well worth taking!

CHAPTER 2

Career Planning for the Year 2001 and Beyond

Career Planning in the Year 2001

Never before in history have more people been involved in career planning. Only a few decades ago, it was expected that you would have only one or two careers in your lifetime. Anything more was often seen as a sign of instability. Working for the same employer until retirement was encouraged and strongly rewarded. Today, however, it is rare to find anyone who continues to subscribe to this way of thinking.

Today, many individuals change careers as often as six times in the course of their lifetime—and this number is expected to increase as people live longer and as the attitudes regarding changing careers continue to become more liberal. Fewer employers today want their employees to remain with the company until they retire. Employees who remain with the same employer for many years are often less productive at the time when they are earning the highest salary. As a result, employers are more apt to dismiss employees in an effort to gain a more competitive, productive, and less expensive work force. For employees, the lesson to be learned here is obvious—protecting your career development and security requires the ability to change careers several times throughout life.

In addition to changing careers more often, many individuals today are quitting jobs to become traditional or home-based entrepreneurs. In fact, one of the hottest trends today is to work at home as a self-employed entrepreneur. According to LINK Resources Corporation, a New York-based research group, "...home workers now number 32.8 million" Americans. More employees and entrepreneurs are electing to work at home. This figure is up 22 percent from last year and is expected to climb dramatically. The corporate environment has lost its appeal for millions of workers who are attempting to reshape their work life to satisfy more fully their personal needs and preferences. It's possible that your next career—or one down the road—may be as a small business owner or even as a home-based entrepreneur.

Coupled with all the people who are making voluntary career changes are millions of individuals who are being forced to find a new line of work. With thousands of companies laying off employees as a result of mergers, downsizing, or economic hard times, many individuals have no choice but to change careers in order to secure new employment. It seems no occupational area is safe from layoffs. The armed forces are reducing their personnel needs, the federal government is cutting back on the number of employees it needs to run the government, and companies—both large and small—are trimming their payrolls in an effort to remain competitive. You can no longer count on an employer to provide your career security—it must come from your ability to adjust your career path when the time is necessary. *Career Selector 2001* can be a helpful guide when it's your turn to chart a new career direction.

Career Management Skills for the Future

If the above scenario does not convince you that you need to take more control of your career development, consider the following. The career direction you select will, more than anything else in life, determine your financial security, emotional well-being, and the financial and emotional security of those people who depend upon you.

In years past, few individuals bothered to develop personal financial management skills. The level of financial planning undertaken by most individuals amounted to no more than socking away money in a bank account in hopes that it would take care of their needs during retirement. As we know now, this type of financial planning is of questionable value today.

The need for managing your career is equally important. If you expect to succeed in tomorrow's workplace, you need to develop several career management skills, such as:

1. **Personality assessment**. The ability to identify your major interests, abilities, values, needs, and behavioral traits as evident from your life experiences.

2. **Career decision-making**. The ability to identify occupations that match your personality style—occupations that offer the most promise of enjoyment and success.

3. **Career planning**. The ability to determine which steps should be taken and in which order to reach your career goal(s).

4. **Job hunting**. The ability to identify potential employers who have a real need for your talent—to determine what it is that employers are doing and, therefore, need that you can provide.

5. **Persuasive communication**. The ability to communicate orally and in writing just what your employment value is and how it can be used by employers to help them more effectively realize their business goals and objectives.

6. **Negotiation**. The ability to present orally and in writing your position on various career and work-related matters, to communicate your ideas in such a way as to illustrate the wisdom of your suggestions as they relate to the achievement of the goals and objectives of your business or industry, and to persuade others to agree with your position.

7. **Industry and position analysis**. The ability to "read" and assess the current and projected status of your industry and occupational interests, to determine if your current career endeavor is viable, or whether a career change is necessary to maintain your career enjoyment and success.

Career Selector 2001 can help you develop skills 1–3 above and enable you to gain more control of your career direction and success.

CHAPTER 3

Excuse Me, But Before We Begin, I Have a Few Questions...

Before I begin the process of career guidance, either on an individual basis or within a group setting, I normally provide an opportunity for the client or clients to ask questions about what is about to occur. Without exception, I am always asked the following questions. Since the process of career guidance is foreign to most individuals, it is helpful to address these questions before we begin. Understanding what is about to occur can help you complete each task more effectively. Review these questions and answers to prepare yourself for selecting your own career direction.

Question: Who is the program designed for?

Answer: *Career Selector 2001* is ideally suited for:

- High school and college students who are about to make their first career decisions.
- Working adults who wish to change their career direction.
- Military service personnel who plan to transfer to the civilian workforce.

It may also be used as a resource tool by:

- Senior citizens who have retired but would like an enjoyable part-time career in line with their interests and skills.
- Career seekers and changers who have special needs and require careful career planning.
- Career counselors, guidance counselors, teachers, academic advisors, psychologists, and other professionals who help people select a career direction.

Question: Why is selecting a career direction often so difficult?

Answer: Choosing a career direction can be one of the most difficult decisions to make. You soon discover that career decision-making requires a variety of knowledge and skills, such as:

- A solid understanding of your personality style (i.e. interests, skills, values, needs, and behavioral traits).

- A solid understanding of occupations that *seem* to match your personality style.
- A decision-making system for determining which occupations best match your personality style.
- A career-planning system for determining which steps you should take and in which order to acquire the qualifications needed for the occupation you have chosen.
- The dedication and persistence to accomplish the many steps involved in the process of career decision-making and planning.

With the exception of the last item, these skills and knowledge are usually associated only with professional counselors who have years of experience. Unfortunately, most people do not seek the assistance of a professional career counselor when trying to determine a career direction and therefore have difficulty in planning their careers.

Using *Career Selector 2001* is an easy and effective way to obtain the professional guidance you need and to find the answer to the question, "Which career direction should I pursue?"

Question: What can I expect to accomplish?

Answer: By completing the *Career Selector 2001* system, you can expect to have a:

- greater self-awareness of your personality style, including information about your interests, skills, and preferences for various work attributes
- better understanding of how to identify the many occupational opportunities that exist in the American work society, and how to obtain information about these opportunities
- better understanding of how to select a career goal that is right for you
- clearer idea of which occupations may be appropriate as career goals for you and what steps you should take to reach those goals
- stronger sense that you are in control of your career development and that your career can be managed in a direction you prefer to travel

Question: What will I be expected to do?

Answer: To complete the *Career Selector 2001* program, you will complete four tasks:

- First, you will review a list of sixty-six work-related interest areas with 501 matching occupations and compile a list of those occupations you believe match your interests.
- Second, you will review a list of work preferences normally important to people when evaluating possible career options. You will be asked to select those preferences that are important to you.
- Third, you will compare your work preferences to each occupation on your career options list to determine how well each occupation matches your preferences. By determining which occupation(s) best match your interests and work preferences, you can determine which occupations may be best for you to pursue.
- Finally, you will develop a plan of action to follow to reach the career goal you have selected.

The tasks will be presented in the form of a "Checklist of Things to Do" to help you organize your work and monitor your progress as you complete the program.

Question: How does your system work?

Answer: The system incorporated into *Career Selector 2001* is a self-directed program of career guidance. This means that you are working indirectly with a professional career counselor in order to explore, evaluate, and select a career direction. The guidance normally provided by a counselor is built into the book—all you have to do is follow the directions carefully and completely to achieve the desired results.

Each task in the program is broken down into steps. The steps are then arranged in order from those that you should do first, to those you should complete last. Each task is presented in a checklist format. When you complete one step, you check it off and move on to the next step. Complete all steps, and you have completed the entire guidance program.

Question: How much time will this take?

Answer: While the time required to complete the program varies from one person to another, past experience with thousands of users indicates that you should be able to complete the entire program in about five to ten hours.

Question: What materials will I need?

Answer: Only a few materials are needed to complete the *Career Selector 2001* program. These resources include:

- This book.

- (Optional) A copy of the *Guide for Occupational Exploration* and the *Dictionary of Occupational Titles*. See Appendix D for information on where to obtain these materials.

- (Optional) A copy of several standard occupational literature sources, such as the *Occupational Outlook Handbook* or the *Encyclopedia of Careers and Vocational Guidance*. See Appendix A for information on where to obtain these materials.

- (Optional) Use of the *Career Analysis Service* to expand your list of possible career options. See Appendix A for information on how to use this service.

- (Optional) Assistance from a professional career counselor if you experience difficulty in selecting a career direction. See Appendix C for information on how to obtain career guidance assistance.

Question: Why does your system work?

Answer: *Career Selector 2001* has been used as an effective tool for career decision-making and planning. Its effectiveness is due to several factors:

- The program is based upon well-established guidance principles and techniques recognized by most career counselors as essential to the process of career decision-making and planning.

- The program incorporates extensive data on occupations as compiled by the U.S. Department of Labor—information that has no equal anywhere in the world.

- The system has been tested and perfected by tens of thousands of individuals.

- The system is sequential (step-by-step)—you complete one step at a time and only after you have completed the previous step. In addition, you control how fast you move through the program.
- The system is quantitative—you can actually determine a score for each occupation you are considering as a career goal in order to determine which occupations are best for you to pursue.
- This system uses a self-directed program of career guidance. With a self-directed system, you are in control and you make the decisions each step along the way. As a result, you are more likely to trust in the decisions you feel are correct and undertake the steps you identify as necessary to reach your new career goal.

Question: How can I increase my chances of success?

Answer: Of all the factors that are important in successfully completing this program, persistence is by far the most critical. Many people fail to achieve a better career simply because they were not willing to do the work necessary to select and plan for a new direction. After all, five to ten hours is not much to ask in exchange for a more enjoyable and rewarding career.

Now, let's take the first step!

CHAPTER 4

Checklists of Things to Do

In this section of *Career Selector 2001*, you will find four tasks that, when completed, will help you select a career direction in line with your personality and develop a step-by-step plan for reaching your new career goal.

You must complete the tasks in the order presented. Each task is broken down into several steps and arranged into a "Checklist of Things to Do" format. After completing the first step, check it off and move on to step two. Continue this procedure until all steps have been completed for each task. In this way you can monitor your progress, and you will always know where you are in the program and what your next step is.

Task 1: Identifying Possible Career Options

Purpose: Task 1 will help you identify occupations that match your interests. By completing this task, you will develop a list of occupations that may be possible career options for you. This list will be used as the starting point of your career exploration. The information you gather in this task is very important, as all other tasks in the *Career Selector 2001* program will require the use of this information.

To find career options, you will review sixty-six work groups. Collectively, these work groups represent the broad range of occupational activities found in the United States. Each work group contains a description and a list of sample occupations that you may find enjoyable if you are interested in the work group. As you come across occupations that are of interest, write them down for analysis later in the program.

Time: Task 1 can be completed in approximately 45–60 minutes.

Use a pencil to complete this task because you may wish to change your answers.

Checklist of Things to Do

__ 1. Review the first work group (1. Literary Arts) on Page 10. Read its description carefully and then review its list of sample occupations.

__ 2. Place a checkmark to the left of any occupation that seems interesting to you. List the name of any occupation you check and its page number on the "List of Possible Career Options" sheet at the end of this section (see Page 24).

Note: You may come across some occupational titles that you are unfamiliar with. If you want a brief description for any occupation, please note the page number to the right of the occupation in question. Then, turn to that page for a profile of the occupation and note its job description.

If you find no occupations that are interesting in work group 1, move on to work group 2.

__ 3. Repeat the above procedure for work groups 2 through 66.

__ 4. Read the section, "Additional Career Options" found at the very end of Task 1 on Page 25.

When you have completed Task 1, move on to Task 2.

Work Groups

1. Literary Arts—an interest in writing, editing, or directing the publication of prose or poetry.

Sample Occupations	Page	Sample Occupations	Page
__ Biographer	82	__ Playwright	224
__ Copy Writer	114	__ Screen Writer	256
__ Critic	118	__ Story Editor (Film/Radio/TV)	271
__ Editor, Film	134	__ Writer, Prose (Fiction/Nonfiction)	298
__ Editor, Publications	135		

2. Visual Arts—an interest in drawing, painting, photography, or in sculpture in clay, wood, or other materials.

Sample Occupations	Page	Sample Occupations	Page
__ Art Appraiser	67	__ Illustrator (Commercial)	170
__ Art Teacher	67	__ Interior Designer	175
__ Clothes Designer	105	__ Painter	213
__ Exhibit Artist (Museum)	142	__ Photographer	221
__ Floral Designer	151	__ Sculptor	257

Checklists of Things to Do 11

3. Performing Arts (Drama)—an interest in producing, directing, or performing in plays, television/radio/video programs, or motion pictures, or in teaching others how to act in such productions.

Sample Occupations	Page	Sample Occupations	Page
__ Actor	51	__ Dramatic Coach	131
__ Casting Director	95	__ Magician	190
__ Comedian	107	__ Narrator	203
__ Disk Jockey	128	__ Stage Director	267

4. Performing Arts (Musical)—an interest in playing a musical instrument, singing, or teaching or directing musicians or singers, or in composing or arranging musical compositions or concerts.

Sample Occupations	Page	Sample Occupations	Page
__ Choral Director	101	__ Musician	203
__ Composer	108	__ Orchestra Conductor	212
__ Music Director (Film/Radio/TV)	202	__ Singer	262
__ Music Teacher	202		

5. Performing Arts (Dance)—an interest in composing, performing a dance routine, or in teaching others how to dance.

Sample Occupations	Page	Sample Occupations	Page
__ Choreographer	101	__ Dancer	121
__ Dance Studio Manager	120	__ Dancing Instructor	121

6. Craft Arts—an interest in making, decorating, or repairing wooden, cloth, clay, stone, metal, or gemstone objects, or in decorating such objects to improve their look and visual appeal.

Sample Occupations	Page	Sample Occupations	Page
__ Aerial Photographer	53	__ Prop Maker (Film/Stage/TV)	235
__ Airbrush Painter	56	__ Sign Painter	261
__ Exhibit Builder (Museum)	143	__ Silversmith	261
__ Hand Engraver	162	__ Special Effects Specialist	265
__ Jeweler	179	__ Taxidermist	274
__ Make-Up Artist (Film/TV)	192		

7. Elemental Arts—an interest in entertaining people by announcing or performing acts at a carnival or amusement park, or by conducting person-to-person consultations with people to predict their future or to tell them other things about themselves.

Sample Occupations	Page	Sample Occupations	Page
__ Amusement Park Entertainer	58	__ Graphologist	161
__ Diver (Amusement)	129		

8. Modeling—an interest in posing before a camera to model clothes or other commercial products, or to appear before a live audience in a nonspeaking role, or in acting as a stand-in for an actor or actress.

Sample Occupations	Page	Sample Occupations	Page
__ Artists' Model	68	__ Extra (Film/Stage/TV)	143
__ Clothes Model	106	__ Modeling Instructor	200
__ Double (Film/TV)	130	__ Photographers' Model	221

9. Physical Sciences—an interest in studying nonliving things such as chemicals, rocks, metals, or the movements of the earth, stars, and planets, and developing theories based upon what you have learned.

Sample Occupations	Page	Sample Occupations	Page
__ Astronomer	69	__ Geologist (Petroleum)	159
__ Chemist	98	__ Mathematician	195
__ Environmental Analyst	140	__ Meteorologist	198
__ Geographer	159	__ Physicist	223

10. Life Sciences—an interest in studying plants, animals, and other living things to understand how they function, and to conduct research to improve the medical, health, and general living conditions of human beings.

Sample Occupations	Page	Sample Occupations	Page
__ Agronomist	55	__ Biologist	83
__ Animal Breeder	59	__ Botanist	86
__ Animal Scientist	60	__ Food Technologist	153
__ Biochemist	82	__ Zoologist	299

11. Medical Sciences—an interest in diagnosing and treating humans or animals who are ill or injured.

Sample Occupations	Page	Sample Occupations	Page
__ Acupuncturist	52	__ Psychiatrist	236
__ Anesthesiologist	59	__ Radiation Therapy Technologist	241
__ Chiropractor	100	__ Speech Pathologist	266
__ Dentist	125	__ Veterinarian	291
__ Physician (General Practitioner)	223		

12. Laboratory Technology—an interest in using laboratory equipment and techniques to perform tests in such fields as chemistry, biology, and physics, and to record your findings for use by such professionals as scientists, medical practitioners, and engineers.

Sample Occupations	Page	Sample Occupations	Page
__ Automobile-Laboratory Technician	74	__ Chemical-Laboratory Technician	97
__ Ballistics Expert	76	__ Criminalist	118
__ Biomedical Equipment Technician	83	__ Laboratory Assistant (Zoo)	181
__ Blood Laboratory Assistant	84	__ Ultrasound Technologist	289

Checklists of Things to Do   13

13. Managerial Work (Plants and Animals)—an interest in operating or managing a farm, ranch, fish hatchery, plant nursery, or other plant or animal business, including the breeding of plants or animals.

Sample Occupations	Page	Sample Occupations	Page
__ Farmer	145	__ Livestock Rancher	186
__ Fish Farmer	150	__ Logging Operations Inspector	188
__ Forester	155	__ Tree Surgeon	286
__ Landscape Gardener	181	__ Wildlife Control Agent	297

14. General Supervision (Plants and Animals)—an interest in supervising people (and often working alongside them) on farms, ranches, fish hatcheries, in forests, plant nurseries, or parks.

Sample Occupations	Page	Sample Occupations	Page
__ Cemetery Supervisor	95	__ Lawn/Tree Spray Service Supervisor	183
__ Dairy Farm Supervisor	120	__ Poultry Farm Supervisor	228
__ Forest Nursery Supervisor	155		
__ Forester Aide	156		
__ Insect/Disease Inspection Supervisor	172		

15. Animal Training and Service—an interest in training or caring for animals in pet shops, pet grooming parlors, animal testing laboratories, animal shelters, veterinary offices, animal obedience schools, kennels, or zoos.

Sample Occupations	Page	Sample Occupations	Page
__ Animal Caretaker	60	__ Dog Groomer	130
__ Animal Trainer	61	__ Horse Trainer	165
__ Aquarist	64		

16. Elemental Work (Plants and Animals)—an interest in working with your hands or with tools and equipment to perform strenuous tasks with plants or animals, usually outdoors on farms, ranches, logging camps, fish hatcheries, in forests, animal game preserves, off- or onshore in fishing boats, or in parks and gardens.

Sample Occupations	Page	Sample Occupations	Page
__ Animal Trapper	61	__ Livestock Farm Worker	186
__ Farm Machine Operator	144	__ Net Fisher	204
__ Forest Fire Fighter	154	__ Tree Planter	285
__ Landscape Laborer	182	__ Tree Pruner	286
__ Lawn Service Worker	182		

17. Safety and Law Enforcement—an interest in enforcing laws and regulations, investigating crimes, or supervising people who stop or arrest lawbreakers.

Sample Occupations	Page	Sample Occupations	Page
__ Chief Deputy Sheriff	99	__ Park Superintendent	215
__ Customs Patrol Officer	119	__ Police Chief	225
__ Detective	126	__ Police Officer	226
__ Fire Marshall	150	__ U.S. Special Agent	290

18. Security Services—an interest in fighting fires or protecting people, animals, or property in prisons, railroad cars and facilities, hotels, industrial plants, or amusement parks.

Sample Occupations	Page	Sample Occupations	Page
__ Bodyguard	85	__ Lifeguard	185
__ Correctional Officer	115	__ Park Ranger	215
__ Fire Fighter	149	__ Security Guard	258
__ Forest Fire Ranger	154		

19. Engineering—an interest in planning, designing, or directing the development or construction of buildings, bridges, roads, airports, dams, sewage systems, air-conditioning systems, mining machinery, or other structures or equipment.

Sample Occupations	Page	Sample Occupations	Page
__ Aeronautical Research Engineer	54	__ Electronics Research Engineer	138
__ Architect	66	__ Industrial Engineer	171
__ Chemical Test Engineer	98	__ Nuclear Engineer	206
__ Civil Engineer	102	__ Pollution Control Engineer	227

20. Managerial Work (Mechanical)—an interest in managing industrial processing or manufacturing plants; overseeing the delivery of utilities, communication, or transportation services; or supervising the operations of mining, petroleum, maintenance, or construction workers.

Sample Occupations	Page	Sample Occupations	Page
__ Appliance Service Supervisor	63	__ Sanitation Superintendent	254
__ Maintenance Superintendent	192	__ Solid-Waste Disposal Manager	265
__ Mine Superintendent	199	__ Technical Director (Radio/TV)	277
__ Production Superintendent	231		

21. Engineering Technology—an interest in technical tasks, such as making detailed drawings or work plans, measuring and preparing maps of land and water areas, operating complex communications equipment, inspecting buildings and equipment for structural, mechanical, or electrical problems; or scheduling and controlling production or transportation operations.

Sample Occupations	Page	Sample Occupations	Page
__ Air-Traffic Control Specialist	56	__ Petroleum Field Engineer	220
__ Architectural Drafter	66	__ Pollution Control Technician	227
__ Building Inspector	88	__ Radiographer	242
__ Navigator	204	__ Solar-Energy Systems Designer	264

22. Air and Water Vehicle Operation—an interest in operating a plane, ship, train, or in supervising people who operate such vehicles.

Sample Occupations	Page	Sample Occupations	Page
__ Commercial Airplane Pilot	107	__ Helicopter Pilot	163
__ Ferryboat Captain	146	__ Ship Pilot	259
__ Fishing Vessel Captain	151	__ Test Pilot	279
__ Flying Instructor	152		

Checklists of Things to Do 15

23. Craft Technology—an interest in performing highly skilled hand or machine work requiring special techniques, training, and experience at such locations as construction sites, shipyards, foundries, woodworking shops, machine shops, or automotive garages.

Sample Occupations	Page	Sample Occupations	Page
__ Automobile Body Repairer	73	__ Machinist	190
__ Bricklayer	87	__ Offset Press Operator	211
__ Carpenter	93	__ Paperhanger	214
__ Electrician	137	__ Plumber	225

24. Systems Operation—an interest in operating or maintaining equipment in systems which generate and distribute electricity, treat and pump water to customers, pump oil from oil fields to storage tanks, or provide telephone services to customers.

Sample Occupations	Page	Sample Occupations	Page
__ Boiler Operator	85	__ Hydroelectric Station Operator	169
__ Cable Maintainer (Light/Heat/Power)	91	__ Incinerator Plant Supervisor	170
		__ Stationary Engineer	268
__ Gas Dispatcher (Light/Heat/Power)	158	__ Water-Treatment Plant Operator	295

25. Quality Control (Mechanical)—an interest in inspecting buildings, utilities, and transportation equipment, or in evaluating methods, raw materials, or environmental conditions to ensure companies or organizations comply with federal, state, or local standards.

Sample Occupations	Page	Sample Occupations	Page
__ Automobile Repair Service Estimator	75	__ Dust Sampler (Mining)	132
		__ Petroleum Inspector	220
__ Bridge Inspector	87	__ Transmission Tester (Telephone)	284
__ Construction-Maintenance Inspector	111	__ Truck Safety Inspector	288

26. Land and Water Vehicle Operation—an interest in driving large or small trucks, delivery vans, locomotives, or small boats to transport materials, goods, or people.

Sample Occupations	Page	Sample Occupations	Page
__ Ambulance Driver	58	__ Motorboat Operator	201
__ Car Rental Vehicle Deliverer	92	__ Tractor-Trailer Truck Driver	283
__ Concrete-Mixing Truck Driver	110	__ Truck Driver (Light Deliveries)	287
__ Locomotive Engineer	187		

27. Material Control—an interest in ordering, receiving, storing, or shipping materials or products in such places as a factory, freight office, department store, restaurant, hospital or dry-cleaning plant.

Sample Occupations	Page	Sample Occupations	Page
__ Cargo Agent	93	__ Shipping & Receiving Clerk	260
__ Inventory Clerk	176	__ Stock Clerk	269
__ Material Coordinator	194	__ Warehouse Supervisor	294
__ Production Coordinator	230		

28. Crafts (Mechanical)—an interest in using your hands or hand tools to skillfully make, process, install, or repair materials, products, or structural parts, or to cook and prepare food.

Sample Occupations	Page	Sample Occupations	Page
__ Air-Conditioning Installer	55	__ Electrical Appliance Repairer	136
__ Audiovisual Technician	72	__ Medical Equipment Repairer	196
__ Blaster	84	__ Riveter	247
__ Cook	114		

29. Equipment Operation—an interest in operating heavy equipment and machines used in construction work, highway maintenance, mining, petroleum production, water transportation, or materials movement.

Sample Occupations	Page	Sample Occupations	Page
__ Bulldozer Operator	89	__ Log Loader	188
__ Concrete-Paving Machine Operator	110	__ Mechanical Shovel Operator	195
__ Construction Drill Operator	111	__ Rotary Oil Drill Operator	248
__ Front-End Loader Operator	156	__ Steam-Cleaning Machine Operator	269

30. Elemental Work (Mechanical)—an interest in performing any variety of manual tasks requiring little skill, such as moving materials, cleaning work areas, operating simple machines, or helping skilled workers.

Sample Occupations	Page	Sample Occupations	Page
__ Antenna Installer	62	__ Grip (Film/TV)	161
__ Construction Worker	112	__ Highway Maintenance Worker	163
__ Corrosion Prevention Metal Sprayer	115	__ Home Housekeeper	165
		__ Janitor	178

31. Production Technology—an interest in using special skills and knowledge of machines and processes to perform demanding and complex activities, such as setting up or operating machinery or doing precision handwork, or in supervising and training skilled workers.

Sample Occupations	Page	Sample Occupations	Page
__ Chemical Processing Supervisor	97	__ Machine Setup Worker	189
__ Computer Subassembly Supervisor	109	__ Numerical-Control Lathe Operator	206
__ Electrical Equipment Tester	136	__ Production Engine Repairer	230
__ Machine Operator	189	__ X-Ray Equipment Tester	298

32. Production Work—an interest in performing skilled hand or machine work to make or repair products, or to process materials in a factory setting.

Sample Occupations	Page	Sample Occupations	Page
__ Carpet & Rug Weaver	94	__ Precision Lens Grinder	229
__ Drill Press Operator	131	__ Radial-Arm Saw Operator	240
__ Ironworker Machine Operator	178	__ Sewing Machine Operator	259

33. Quality Control (Production)—an interest in inspecting, testing, weighing, sorting, or grading products and materials in manufacturing or processing plants.

Sample Occupations	Page	Sample Occupations	Page
__ Agricultural Shipping Inspector	54	__ Glass Inspector	160
__ Exhaust Emissions Inspector	142	__ Packing Materials Inspector	213
__ Final Inspector, Musical Instruments	147	__ Quality Control Food Technician	240
__ Finished Carpet Inspector	148	__ Welding Inspector	296

34. Elemental Work (Production)—an interest in using your hands, machines, hand tools, or other equipment to make products (which require little to moderate skill), to process materials in a factory setting, or in helping more skilled workers.

Sample Occupations	Page	Sample Occupations	Page
__ Finishing Machine Operator	149	__ Surgical Dressing Maker	272
__ Injection-Molding Machine Offbearer	172	__ Threading Machine Operator	280
__ Spinning Lathe Operator	266	__ Trimming Machine Operator	287

35. Administrative Detail (Clerical)— an interest in performing high-level clerical work requiring special skills and knowledge, or in performing management-related activities according to pre-established procedures.

Sample Occupations	Page	Sample Occupations	Page
__ Bank Loan Counselor	77	__ Secretary	257
__ Credit Analyst	117	__ Title Examiner	281
__ Office Manager	210	__ Town Clerk	283
__ School Attendance Officer	255		

36. Mathematical Detail (Clerical)—an interest in collecting, organizing, computing, and recording numerical information for use by higher skilled professionals who work in business and financial institutions.

Sample Occupations	Page	Sample Occupations	Page
__ Bank Collection Clerk	76	__ Insurance Claim Examiner (Clerk)	173
__ Billing Clerk	81	__ Mortgage Accounting Clerk	200
__ Bookkeeper	86	__ Payroll Clerk	218

37. Financial Detail (Clerical)—an interest in using basic arithmetic, keeping records, and answering customers' questions in banks, grocery stores, ticket booths, check-out counters, or other places where money is paid to or received from the general public.

Sample Occupations	Page	Sample Occupations	Page
__ Bank Teller	78	__ Post Office Clerk	228
__ Bill Collector	81	__ Store Cashier Checker	270
__ Cashier (Gambling Casino)	94	__ Ticket Agent	281
__ Check Cashier	96	__ Toll Collector	282

38. Oral Communications (Clerical)— an interest in talking with people in person, by telephone, or by using other types of communication equipment to give or obtain information.

Sample Occupations	Page	Sample Occupations	Page
__ Hospital Admitting Clerk	166	__ Reservations Agent (Airline)	246
__ Hotel Clerk	168	__ Skip Tracer	262
__ Radio Dispatcher (Fire Service)	241	__ Telephone Operator	
__ Receptionist	243	(Central Office)	279

39. Records Processing (Clerical)—an interest in preparing, reviewing, filing, distributing, and coordinating recorded information; checking records and schedules for accuracy; or in scheduling the activities of people or equipment.

Sample Occupations	Page	Sample Occupations	Page
__ Airline Crew Scheduler	57	__ Mail Carrier	191
__ Auto Club Travel Counselor	73	__ Microfilm Document Preparer	199
__ Classified Ad Clerk	103	__ News Assistant (Radio/TV)	205
__ Investigator (Utility Bill Complaints)	177	__ Office File Clerk	209

40. Clerical Machine Operation—an interest in using business machines to record or process data; to operate machines that type, print, sort, compute, send, or receive information.

Sample Occupations	Page	Sample Occupations	Page
__ Adding Machine Operator	52	__ Electronic Typeset Machine	
__ Bank Proof Machine Operator	78	Operator	138
__ Clerk-Typist	104	__ Typist	288
__ Computer Operator	108	__ Word-Processing Machine Operator	297

41. Clerical Handling—an interest in performing clerical duties that require little special training or skill, such as filing, sorting, routing, or delivering information, messages, or items to other people.

Sample Occupations	Page	Sample Occupations	Page
__ Coin-Machine Collector	106	__ Mailroom Supervisor	191
__ Delivery Person (In-town)	123	__ Office Files Supervisor	210

42. Sales Technology—an interest in selling technologically advanced products, such as industrial machinery, computers and data processing equipment, aircraft equipment, or pharmaceuticals; or in selling related services, such as industrial shipping, insurance, and advertising; or in advising people about how to use these products or services.

Sample Occupations	Page	Sample Occupations	Page
__ Buyer	90	__ Sales Rep (Data Processing	
__ Insurance Estate Planner	173	Services)	251
__ Insurance Sales Agent	174	__ Sales Rep (Dental/Medical	
__ Pawnbroker	217	Supplies)	252
__ Sales Agent (Financial Services)	249	__ Sales Rep (Livestock)	252
__ Sales Rep (Chemicals & Drugs)	250	__ Telephone Communication	
__ Sales Rep (Computers)	251	Consultant	278

Checklists of Things to Do 19

43. General Sales—an interest in selling or demonstrating products, or in soliciting orders for any number of products or services.

Sample Occupations	Page	Sample Occupations	Page
__ Auctioneer	71	__ Real Estate Sales Agent	243
__ Demonstrator	124	__ Sales Route Driver	253
__ Fund Raiser	157	__ Salesperson (General Merchandise)	253
__ Manufacturers' Representative	193	__ Salesperson (Household Appliances)	254
__ Membership Solicitor	197	__ Travel Agent	285

44. Vending—an interest in selling novelties, snacks, or other inexpensive items at stadiums, street fairs, in nightclubs and restaurants, or wherever crowds gather for entertainment or recreation.

Sample Occupation	Page
__ Vendor (Amusement/Sports Park)	291

45. Hospitality Services—an interest in providing basic personal services to help visitors, travelers, or customers get acquainted with and feel at ease in an unfamiliar setting, such as in a hotel or motel, restaurant, museum, retirement home, or on a plane, train, or boat; or in escorting or guiding people, planning or directing social activities, or caring for the safety or comfort of people.

Sample Occupations	Page	Sample Occupations	Page
__ Airplane Flight Attendant	57	__ Plant Guide	224
__ Funeral Attendant	157	__ Recreational Leader	244
__ Host	167	__ Sightseeing Guide	260
__ Hunting & Fishing Guide	169	__ Social Director	263

46. Barber and Beauty Services—an interest in cutting and styling hair or in providing a variety of related services to improve the appearance of people.

Sample Occupations	Page	Sample Occupations	Page
__ Barber	79	__ Hair Stylist	162
__ Cosmetologist	116		

47. Passenger Services—an interest in driving limousines, buses, taxis, or other vehicles to take people from one location to another; or in teaching or supervising people who operate such vehicles.

Sample Occupations	Page	Sample Occupations	Page
__ Bus Driver	89	__ Streetcar Operator	271
__ Chauffeur	96	__ Taxi Driver	273
__ Driving Instructor	132		

48. Customer Services—an interest in waiting on customers and accepting payment for purchases or services in such places as stores, recreational settings, and restaurants.

Sample Occupations	Page	Sample Occupations	Page
__ Automobile Rental Clerk	75	__ Personal Shopper	219
__ Bartender	79	__ Storage Facility Rental Clerk	270
__ Dealer (Gambling Establishment)	122	__ Tool & Equipment Rental Clerk	282
__ Fast-Foods Worker	146	__ Waiter (Bar)	293
__ Parking Lot Supervisor	216		

49. Attendant Services—an interest in providing basic personal services requiring little special knowledge or skill to assist travelers in such settings as hotels, motels, restaurants, or recreational facilities.

Sample Occupations	Page	Sample Occupations	Page
__ Bell Captain	80	__ Manicurist	193
__ Cafeteria Attendant	91	__ Masseur	194
__ Electrologist	137	__ Reducing Salon Attendant	245
__ Elevator Operator	139	__ Weight Reduction Specialist	295

50. Social Services—an interest in using special skills and advanced training to help people deal with and resolve their personal problems, on a one-to-one basis or in groups, in such areas as personal, social, educational, vocational, physical, or spiritual development.

Sample Occupations	Page	Sample Occupations	Page
__ Clergy Member	104	__ Probation & Parole Officer	229
__ Clinical Psychologist	105	__ School Psychologist	255
__ Counselor (Professional)	116	__ School Social Worker	256
__ Dean of Students (College)	123	__ Social Service Caseworker	263
__ Director of Placement (College)	128	__ Vocational Rehabilitation Counselor	292

51. Nursing, Therapy, and Specialized Teaching Services—an interest in caring for or treating people who are ill, have been injured, or are handicapped; or in training people to improve their physical and emotional well-being.

Sample Occupations	Page	Sample Occupations	Page
__ Art Therapist	68	__ Physical Therapist	222
__ Dental Hygienist	125	__ Radiologic Technologist	242
__ Dialysis Technician	127	__ Respiratory Therapist	246
__ Nurse (General Duty)	207	__ Teacher (Kindergarten)	275
__ Nurse (Licensed Practical)	207	__ Teacher (Preschool)	276
__ Occupational Therapist	209	__ Teacher (Special Needs Students)	277
__ Physical Education Instructor	222		

52. Child and Adult Care

—an interest in caring for the physical needs and welfare of very young or elderly persons or handicapped individuals, often performing tasks that they can not do for themselves; or in using special equipment and techniques to diagnose the health of individuals and in treating various ailments under the direction of a doctor or other health care professional.

Sample Occupations	Page	Sample Occupations	Page
__ Audiometrist	71	__ Mental Retardation Aide	198
__ Cardiopulmonary Technologist	92	__ Nurse's Aide	208
__ Dental Assistant	124	__ Nursery School Attendant	208
__ Emergency Medical Technician	139	__ Optometric Assistant	211
__ Hospital Orderly	167	__ Perfusionist	218

53. Mathematics and Statistics

—an interest in using advanced mathematics and statistics to solve problems, to analyze and interpret numerical data, and to conduct research to solve problems and help other professionals make decisions and plans.

Sample Occupations	Page	Sample Occupations	Page
__ Actuary	51	__ Programmer (Business)	233
__ Computer Software Technician	109	__ Programmer (Engineering/Science)	233
__ Engineering Analyst	140	__ Programmer (Information Systems)	234
__ Financial Analyst	148	__ Statistician	268
__ Information Scientist	171		

54. Educational and Library Services

—an interest in teaching students on the primary, elementary, secondary, or college level, in vocational or adult settings; or in cataloging and shelving books and performing other related services in a library.

Sample Occupations	Page	Sample Occupations	Page
__ Acquisitions Librarian	50	__ Librarian	184
__ Bibliographer	80	__ Library Technical Assistant	184
__ Children's Librarian	100	__ Teacher (Adult Education)	274
__ County Agricultural Agent	117	__ Teacher (Elementary)	275
__ Faculty Member (College/University)	144	__ Teacher (Secondary)	276
__ Home Economist	164	__ Vocational Training Instructor	292

55. Social Research

—an interest in gathering, studying, and analyzing information about individuals, groups, or entire societies to better understand human behavior as seen through their language, politics, lifestyle, customs, and cultural activities.

Sample Occupations	Page	Sample Occupations	Page
__ Anthropologist	62	__ Personnel Recruiter	219
__ Archaeologist	65	__ Political Scientist	226
__ Economist	133	__ Psychologist (Educational)	237
__ Historian	164	__ Psychologist (Industrial)	237
__ Intelligence Specialist	175	__ Sociologist	264
__ Job Analyst	179	__ Urban Planner	290

56. Law—an interest in providing legal advice and in representing clients in a court of law; in hearing and making decisions on court cases; in helping individuals and groups reach agreement over disputed matters; and in conducting investigations into legal matters.

Sample Occupations	Page	Sample Occupations	Page
__ Arbitrator	65	__ Paralegal Assistant	214
__ District Attorney	129	__ Patent Agent	217
__ Judge	180	__ Tax Attorney	273
__ Lawyer	183		

57. Business Administration—an interest in directing, through the use of lower-level personnel, all or part of the activities of a business or department, in setting policy, in making important decisions, and in delegating tasks to others to complete.

Sample Occupations	Page	Sample Occupations	Page
__ Association Executive	69	__ Department Manager	126
__ Bank President	77	__ Public Works Commissioner	239
__ Business Manager		__ Purchasing Agent	239
(College/University)	90	__ Sales Manager	250
__ City Manager	102		

58. Finance—an interest in planning, managing, analyzing, and making decisions about financial transactions, systems, and records that affect the operational success of companies, organizations, and individuals.

Sample Occupations	Page	Sample Occupations	Page
__ Accountant	49	__ Records Analyst Manager	244
__ Auditor	72	__ Risk & Insurance Manager	247
__ Budget Analyst	88	__ Securities Sales Agent	258
__ Insurance Underwriter	174		

59. Services Administration—an interest in setting policies and goals and then directing and managing, through the use of lower-level personnel, all or part of the activities of institutions and agencies that provide health, safety, recreation, and social services to the general public.

Sample Occupations	Page	Sample Occupations	Page
__ Athletic Director	70	__ Museum Curator	201
__ Director of Admissions	127	__ Public Health Educator	238
__ Financial Aid Officer	147	__ Volunteer Services Supervisor	293
__ Hospital Administrator	166	__ Welfare Director	296

60. Communications—an interest in writing, editing, translating, or reporting factual information in such facilities as radio and television stations, newspapers, or magazines and publishing firms.

Sample Occupations	Page	Sample Occupations	Page
__ Deaf Interpreter	122	__ Newswriter	205
__ Editor (Dictionary)	133	__ Reporter	245
__ Editor (News)	134	__ Technical Writer	278
__ Editorial Assistant	135	__ Translator	284
__ Interpreter	176		

61. Promotion—an interest in promoting the sale and use of products or services, soliciting membership and financial support for organizations and projects, or in influencing public opinion and support for various projects or causes.

Sample Occupations	Page	Sample Occupations	Page
__ Account Executive	49	__ Media Director	196
__ Advertising Manager	53	__ Membership Director	197
__ Fashion Coordinator	145	__ Promotion Manager	234
__ Foreign Service Officer	153	__ Public Service Director	238
__ Lobbyist	187		

62. Regulations Enforcement—an interest in investigating business practices, examining records, and inspecting materials, products, and work places to ensure they comply with established governmental standards and regulations and in imposing appropriate action upon those companies who fail to comply.

Sample Occupations	Page	Sample Occupations	Page
__ Chief Bank Examiner	99	__ Food & Drug Inspector	152
__ Consumer Affairs Director	112	__ Investigator	177
__ Customs Inspector	119	__ Safety Coordinator	249
__ Equal Opportunity Representative	141		

63. Business Management—an interest in directing and managing the operation of an establishment, such as a store, hotel, food service facility, warehouse, railroad or airline terminal, or automobile service station, by carrying out the policies and procedures as established by other individuals with higher authority.

Sample Occupations	Page	Sample Occupations	Page
__ Apartment Manager	63	__ Parts Manager	216
__ Funeral Director	158	__ Property Manager	235
__ Golf Club Manager	160	__ Theater Manager	280
__ Hotel/Motel Manager	168	__ Warehouse Manager	294

64. Contracts and Claims—an interest in negotiating contracts and in settling damage, personal injury, or loss claims for companies and individuals; or in helping buyers and sellers prepare contracts suitable to each party.

Sample Occupations	Page	Sample Occupations	Page
__ Athletic Manager	70	__ Literary Agent	185
__ Claim Examiner	103	__ Outdoor Advertising Leasing Agent	212
__ Contract Administrator	113	__ Property Utilization Officer	236
__ Contractor (Construction)	113		

65. Sports—an interest in participating in a professional sporting event, such as a football or baseball game, horse race, tennis match, automobile race, hockey game; or in training, coaching, or officiating a sporting event.

Sample Occupations	Page	Sample Occupations	Page
__ Automobile Racer	74	__ Professional Sports Scout	232
__ Jockey	180	__ Sports Instructor	267
__ Professional Athlete	231	__ Umpire	289
__ Professional Athletic Coach	232		

66. Physical Feats—an interest in entertaining audiences by performing unusual or daring acts that require special skill and training.

Sample Occupations	Page	Sample Occupations	Page
__ Acrobat	50	__ Rodeo Performer	248
__ Aquatic Performer	64	__ Stunt Performer	272
__ Equestrian	141		

List of Possible Career Options

Directions: List below the titles of those occupations you have identified from completing Task 1 that you believe match your interests and may be appropriate as a future career goal. Also list the page number where the profile for each occupation can be found.

1. Title: _____ Page _____
2. Title: _____ Page _____
3. Title: _____ Page _____
4. Title: _____ Page _____
5. Title: _____ Page _____
6. Title: _____ Page _____
7. Title: _____ Page _____
8. Title: _____ Page _____
9. Title: _____ Page _____
10. Title: _____ Page _____

Additional Career Options

After completing Task 1, you may find that you have developed a long or short list of career options. The length of your list depends upon how many interests you have. If you have six or more career options, then you are ready to move on to Task 2. However, if you have fewer than six options, you may wish to consider identifying additional career options before moving ahead to the next task.

Career Selector 2001 has given you an opportunity to evaluate 501 occupations, but there are many more occupations that exist. In fact, there are over 13,500 occupations that belong to the above sixty-six work groups. Therefore, if your list of occupational options is short, you may want to explore further, using any of the options below to identify additional career options:

1. Obtain a copy of the *Guide for Occupational Exploration* and check the listing of occupational titles associated with the work groups that you found to be interesting in Task 1. Refer to Appendix D for more information regarding how to find and use this publication.

2. Use a commercial service to analyze your work group interest selections, as well as other information about your preferences for various work situations, and to provide you with a list of job titles that match your interests, skills, and work preferences. Refer to Appendix A (Computerized Career Guidance Services) for more information regarding these services.

3. Complete a career interest inventory. An interest inventory is a multiple-choice question-and-answer device used by career counselors to help individuals clarify their interests and identify related occupations. Refer to Appendix A (Vocational/Career Assessment Instruments) for more information regarding the use of a career interest inventory.

Add any new occupational options you find from using the above resources to your List of Possible Career Options. When completed, move on to Task 2.

Task 2: Choosing Your Work Preferences

Purpose: Now that you have prepared a list of possible career options, you are ready to decide which of these occupations are best for you to pursue. To do this, you will evaluate each occupation on your list to see how well each matches various "work preferences" that are important to you. Those occupations that have the highest number of matches are those that you should seriously consider as possible careers. This evaluation and decision-making will actually take place in Task 3. In Task 2 you will simply determine which work preferences are important to you.

The eight work preference categories presented in this task have been developed by the U.S. Department of Labor as a means of describing the similarities and differences between occupations. The descriptions of each category are based primarily on government data, but revised by the author to be more useful to individuals involved in career exploration and planning.

Time: Task 2 can be completed in approximately 30–45 minutes.

Use a pencil to complete this task because you may wish to change your answers.

> ## Checklist of Things to Do
>
> __ 1. Review the first work preference category (Aptitudes) below.
>
> __ 2. Follow the directions to determine which of its answer options are important for you.
>
> __ 3. Place your answer(s) on the Work Preferences/Evaluation Guide found on pages 30 and 31 at the end of this section.
>
> __ 4. Repeat the above procedure for all remaining work preference categories.

When you have completed Task 2, move on to Task 3.

Work Preference Categories

1. Aptitudes

Each occupation requires a certain degree of aptitude or skill in order to successfully do the work. Review the list of Aptitudes below. On the Work Preferences/Evaluation Guide circle whether you want your future occupation to require of you a High (H), Moderate (M), or Low (L) level of each aptitude. If you have no preference for a particular aptitude, do not rate it. If you have no preference for *any* of the aptitudes, skip this item entirely and move on to the next work preference category.

Note: Trying to assess your preferred level of each aptitude often depends on how competent you think you are in that aptitude. For some, this is an easy task, for others it is very difficult. If you have difficulty assessing your aptitudes, you may wish to have them tested. Contact your local State Employment Service and ask to schedule a time when you can take the General Aptitude Test Battery (GATB). The test will produce a score for each of the eleven aptitudes below. In some cases, the testing is free; in other cases a minimal fee is required.

The eleven aptitudes are:

- **Intelligence**—the ability to think critically, to reason logically and analytically, to understand complex and abstract ideas.

- **Verbal**—the ability to use the English language effectively, in both writing and speaking.

- **Numerical**—the ability to understand and use advanced mathematical concepts and operations.

- **Spatial**—the ability to visualize forms and objects clearly in your "mind's eye" without actually seeing them in real life; to be able to "see" the inside of objects, flip them around, open them up—all in your mind's eye.

- **Form Perception**—the ability to spot quickly and easily pertinent details or information in objects, pictures, charts, or graphs.

- **Clerical Perception**—the ability to spot quickly and easily pertinent details or information in written or printed materials.

Checklists of Things to Do **27**

- **Motor Coordination**—the ability to coordinate your eyes, hands, and fingers quickly and accurately to perform a function or task.
- **Finger Dexterity**—the ability to move your fingers quickly and accurately to perform some function or task.
- **Manual Dexterity**—the ability to move your hands quickly and accurately to perform some function or task.
- **Eye/Hand/Foot Coordination**—the ability to move your eyes, hands, and feet together quickly and accurately to perform a function or task.
- **Color Discrimination**—the ability to perceive colors or shades of colors quickly and accurately in objects or printed materials.

2. **Data**

Every occupation requires you to deal with data or information to some degree. Review the three levels of data found below and circle on the Work Preferences/Evaluation Guide the level (High, Moderate, or Low) you wish your future occupation to require of you. If you have no preference, skip this category entirely and move on to the next work preference category.

- **High Data Involvement (H)**—A high level means you prefer to be extensively involved in the compilation, analysis, interpretation, and use of data or information. You would like this type of activity to be the main focus or function of your occupation.
- **Moderate Data Involvement (M)**—A moderate level means you are willing to compile and use data or information to help you accomplish your work, but you prefer not to be involved in the higher levels of data compilation and analysis. You also prefer that data and information not be the main focus or function of your occupation.
- **Low Data Involvement (L)**—A low level means you prefer to have little or no involvement with the use of information or data in your occupation.

3. **People**

Every occupation requires you to deal with people to some degree. Review the three levels found below and circle on the Work Preferences/Evaluation Guide the level (High, Moderate, or Low) you wish your future occupation to require of you. If you have no preference, skip this category entirely and move on to the next work preference category. Note, however, that these classifications refer to the degree of *intimacy* that exists between people, as opposed to the degree of *interaction*.

- **High People Involvement (H)**—A high level means you prefer, as the main focus of your occupation, to be intimately and extensively involved in working with people. You would be in a position of authority and, as a high-ranking professional, responsible for helping people. You could be engaged in such activities as mentoring, teaching, negotiating, supervising, or counseling. You might also be involved with people from an administrative or management position. The subject matter of your involvement could be in such areas as personal and social development, educational and career planning, spiritual development, legal protection, business development, family planning, or health care.
- **Moderate People Involvement (M)**—A moderate level means you are interested in working with and helping people as the main focus of your work, but not to the same high degree as described above. You prefer to work more in an assisting,

coordinating, or helping manner, sometimes alongside other, higher-ranking professionals, to aid people in meeting their needs and/or in solving their problems.
- **Low People Involvement (L)**—A low level means you prefer to have only marginal or no contact or interaction with people, and that people will have little or no bearing on your occupation and you on theirs.

4. **Things**

Every occupation requires you to deal with things to some degree. Review the three levels found below and circle on the Work Preferences/Evaluation Guide the level (High, Moderate, or Low) you wish your future occupation to require of you. If you have no preference, skip this category entirely and move on to the next work preference category.

Note: Machinery and tools as used below may be interpreted to mean such items as computers, typewriters, telephones, duplicating machines, etc., as well as the kind of machines and tools commonly found in factory and construction settings.

- **High Things Involvement (H)**—A high level means you prefer your job to center around and depend upon the use of machinery or tools, and that these machines or tools will be the main focus or function of your occupation.
- **Moderate Things Involvement (M)**—A moderate level means you do not mind using some machinery or tools to accomplish your work, as long as the use of such machinery or tools is not the main focus of your occupation.
- **Low Things Involvement (L)**—A low level means you prefer to have little use or need for machinery or tools in your occupation.

5. **Salary Range**

Gives an approximation of the salary you might expect to receive in a given position.

6. **Opportunity Outlook**

Indicates what you may expect in the way of future opportunities in each field.

7. **Environmental Conditions**

Every occupation exposes you to certain kinds of environmental conditions. Review the list of nine environmental conditions below. On the Work Preferences/Evaluation Guide, check those conditions that are important to you. If you have no preference for a particular condition, do not check it. If you have no preference for *any* of the conditions, skip this category entirely and move on to the next work preference category.

- I prefer to work inside (indoors) only.
- I prefer to work outside (out of doors) only.
- I prefer to work both inside and outside.
- I must avoid extremely cold work environments.
- I must avoid extremely hot work environments.
- I must avoid wet and humid work environments.
- I must avoid work environments where loud noises or vibrations are present.
- I must avoid work environments where physical hazards are present.
- I must avoid work environments where atmospheric dangers, such as fumes, odors, etc. are present.

8. **Physical Demands**

Each occupation will demand of you some level of physical performance or exertion. Review the list of six physical demands below. On the Work Preferences/Evaluation Guide, check those demands that *you do not want*. If you have no preference for a particular demand, do not rate it. If you have no preference for *any* of the demands, skip this category entirely and move on to the next work preference category.

I can not work where...
- Lifting heavy objects is required.
- Climbing or balancing is required.

- Stooping, kneeling, crouching, or crawling is required.
- Reaching, handling, fingering, or feeling is required.
- Talking or hearing is required.
- Seeing is required.

9. Temperaments

Each occupation requires certain temperaments (behavioral traits) in order to accomplish the work. Review the list of temperaments below. On the Work Preferences/Evaluation Guide, check those temperaments that best describe how you prefer to work. If you have no preference for a particular temperament, do not check it. If you have no preference for *any* of the temperaments, skip this category entirely and move on to the next work preference category.

When working, I prefer to...
- Work alone or apart from other people.
- Direct, control, or plan the work activities of others.
- Interpret the feelings and ideas of other people.
- Influence the actions and beliefs of other people.
- Make judgments based on sensory, judgmental criteria which can not be proven one way or another.
- Make judgments based on measurable, verifiable facts which can be proven.
- Deal with people beyond the level of simply giving and receiving information.
- Perform repetitive work (the same work over and over again).
- Perform under stressful, pressure-packed, or in emergency situations.
- Attempt to attain set limits, tolerances, or standards set by other people.
- Perform a variety of tasks all at the same time or one right after another.

10. Vocational Preparation

Each occupation requires some length of preparation in order to learn the techniques, acquire the necessary information, and develop the capability for *average* performance. For some occupations, the length of preparation may only last a few hours; for other occupations it may take more than ten years to complete. Preparation may include not only the time spent in a formal training program but also the time spent on the job to translate the training into an average level of performance. The formal training phase of the preparation period (if one is required) may be completed on the job, in a vocational, technical, or business school, or at a college or university. Typically, the longer the preparation time, the more likely it is that part of the preparation will include a formal college education.

Review the nine vocational preparation levels below. On the Work Preferences/Evaluation Guide, write in the number of the *longest* level you would be willing to complete, have already completed, or are currently involved in completing in order to prepare for your future occupation. Select only one level. If you have no preference, skip this category entirely.

The longest length of preparation I am willing to complete, or have completed, or am about to complete is...

Number	Length	Number	Length
1	From 1 to 3 hours	6	From 1 to 2 years[1]
2	From 1 to 30 days	7	From 2 to 4 years[2]
3	From 1 to 3 months	8	From 4 to 10 years[3]
4	From 3 to 6 months	9	Over 10 years[3]
5	From 1/2 to 1 year		

[1]This level usually includes a one- or two-year college education.
[2]This level usually includes a four-year college education.
[3]These levels usually include a graduate and/or doctoral program after completing four years of college.

Work Preferences/Evaluation Guide

(This form may be photocopied)

CAREER OPTIONS		1	2	3	4	5	6

Aptitudes

		1	2	3	4	5	6
Intelligence	H M L						
Verbal	H M L						
Numerical	H M L						
Spatial	H M L						
Form	H M L						
Clerical	H M L						
Motor	H M L						
Finger	H M L						
Manual	H M L						
Eye/Hand/Foot	H M L						
Color	H M L						

Data/People/Things

		1	2	3	4	5	6
Data	H M L						
People	H M L						
Things	H M L						

Environmental Conditions

	1	2	3	4	5	6
Work inside only						
Work outside only						
Work inside and outside						
Avoid cold environments						
Avoid hot environments						
Avoid wet/humid environments						
Avoid noises/vibrations						
Avoid physical hazards						
Avoid atmospheric dangers						

Checklists of Things to Do 31

	1	2	3	4	5	6
Physical Demands						
Can not lift heavy objects						
Can not climb/balance						
Can not stoop, kneel, etc.						
Can not reach, finger, etc.						
Can not talk or hear						
Can not see						
Temperament						
Work alone						
Direct others						
Interpret feelings						
Influence others						
Decide based on senses						
Decide based on facts						
Deal with people						
Perform repetitive work						
Perform under stress						
Attain set limits						
Perform various tasks						
Vocational Preparation Level [ ]						
Additional Factors						
_____						
_____						
_____						
_____						
Total Matches						

Career Goal(s)   1st place   _____

2nd place   _____

3rd place   _____

Work Preferences/Evaluation Guide

(Example of completed form)

CAREER OPTIONS		1 Counselor	2 Faculty Member	3 Architect	4 Programmer	5 Historian	6
Aptitudes							
(Intelligence)	(H) M L	✓✓	✓✓	✓✓	✓✓	✓✓	
Verbal	(H) M L	✓	✓		✓	✓	
Numerical	H (M) L	✓				✓	
Spatial	H M L						
Form	H M L						
Clerical	H (M) L			✓			
Motor	H M L						
Finger	H M L						
Manual	H M L						
Eye/Hand/Foot	H M L						
Color	(H) M L						
Data/People/Things							
(Data)	(H) M L	✓✓	✓✓	✓✓	✓✓	✓✓	
People	(H) M L	✓	✓				
Things	H M (L)	✓	✓			✓	
Environmental Conditions							
✓ Work inside only		✓	✓	✓	✓	✓	
Work outside only							
Work inside and outside							
Avoid cold environments							
Avoid hot environments							
Avoid wet/humid environments							
Avoid noises/vibrations							
✓ Avoid physical hazards		✓	✓	✓	✓	✓	
✓ Avoid atmospheric dangers		✓	✓	✓	✓	✓	

Checklists of Things to Do 33

	1	2	3	4	5	6
Physical Demands						
✓ Can not lift heavy objects	✓	✓	✓	✓	✓	
Can not climb/balance						
Can not stoop, kneel, etc.						
Can not reach, finger, etc.						
Can not talk or hear						
Can not see						
Temperament						
Work alone						
✓ Direct others	✓	✓		✓		
✓ Interpret feelings	✓					
✓ Influence others	✓	✓	✓			
✓ Decide based on senses	✓	✓	✓		✓	
Decide based on facts						
✓ Deal with people	✓	✓	✓			
Perform repetitive work						
Perform under stress						
Attain set limits						
Perform various tasks						
Vocational Preparation Level [8]	✓	✓	✓		✓	
Additional Factors						
(Salary at least $35,000)		✓	✓	✓	✓	
Future Outlook - excellent				✓	✓	
Professional Setting	✓	✓	✓	✓	✓	
Total Matches	19	18	16	13	15	

Career Goal(s)
- 1st place: Counselor
- 2nd place: Faculty Member
- 3rd place: Programmer

Task 3: Selecting a Career Direction

Purpose: The purpose of Task 3 is to guide you in evaluating each of the occupations on your List of Possible Career Options to determine which occupations best match your work preferences. One of the underlying principles of this guidance system is the belief that those occupations that best match your interests and work preferences are the ones you should seriously consider when selecting a career goal.

To evaluate an occupation, review its profile (found in Chapter 5). Using the Work Preferences/Evaluation Guide, you will then determine how well the occupation can satisfy each of your work preferences. Each time the occupation matches one of your work preferences, you will place a checkmark on the Guide. After evaluating all work preferences, you will then add up the number of checkmarks to see how well the occupation matches all of your preferences.

By repeating this procedure with all occupations on your List of Possible Career Options, and by noting which occupations receive the highest total scores, you can determine which occupations are best for you to pursue as a career goal.

Time: Variable, depending upon the number of occupations on your List of Career Options. Average evaluation time is ten to twenty minutes per occupation.

A sample Work Preferences/Evaluation Guide can be found on pages 32 and 33, complete with answers to illustrate how this form may be completed. Use a pencil to complete this task as you may wish to change your answers.

Checklist of Things to Do

1. Review the list of work preferences on your copy of the Work Preferences/Evaluation Guide (see pages 30–31). Circle (or highlight with a magic marker) those items that are most important to you—the ones that must be matched or satisfied by your future occupation. Be selective. Only mark the "must satisfy" items!

2. Note the title of the first occupation listed on your copy of the List of Possible Career Options (see page 24).

3. Write the name of your first occupation in Column 1 (Career Options) on the Work Preferences/Evaluation Guide.

4. Flip to the appropriate page in *Career Selector 2001* where the profile for your occupation can be found and read the profile. Check your List of Possible Career Options or the alphabetical list of occupational titles (Appendix B) if you are unsure of the page number of your first occupation's profile. *Note:* If your first occupation is not listed in *Career Selector 2001* (i.e., you derived it from some other source), then use any of the occupational directories listed in Appendix A to learn more about the nature of your occupation. See Appendix A to learn how to obtain and use these directories.

5. Rate how well the occupation matches your work preferences.
   Start with Aptitudes. Check the profile of your occupation to determine the required level of each aptitude. Whenever the required level of a particular aptitude matches the level you prefer for that same aptitude, place a checkmark to the right of that aptitude in the column for the occupation. Repeat this procedure for each aptitude.
   Note: If the required level of a particular aptitude matches the level you prefer and is one of your "must satisfy" aptitudes, place two checkmarks to the right of that item. In this way, "must satisfy" items will have more bearing on the total score for a particular occupation than factors that are less important to you.

Note: How do you rate the occupation if it requires a level of a particular aptitude below the level you prefer? If you are willing to accept an occupation that requires less of an aptitude than the level you prefer, then mark it as a match. If you are not willing to accept such a situation, do not mark it as a match.

Note: If the directories you are using to learn more about your first occupation do not indicate whether they can satisfy a particular work preference of yours, then you may have to use your own best judgment or contact a career counselor for advice. See Appendix C to learn how to obtain career guidance assistance.

__ 6. Rate the remaining work preferences in the same manner as you did Aptitudes, keeping in the mind the conditions as outlined in the three Notes above.

At this point in the evaluation process, you have determined how well the characteristics of your first occupation match your work preferences. However, there may be other work preferences (not listed in this book) that may be important to you and, therefore, should now be taken into consideration. For example, when thinking about your future occupation, you may be concerned about such factors as:

- salary
- benefits
- hours of work
- future employment outlook
- advancement opportunities
- training options
- locations of employment
- positive and negative working conditions
- type of co-workers
- current availability of employment openings
- other (please specify) _____
- other (please specify) _____
- other (please specify) _____

If any of these additional work preferences are important to you and should be taken into consideration when evaluating an occupation, follow directions 7 and 8 below. If none of these additional work preferences are important, move directly to direction number 9 below and proceed from there.

__ 7. Write the names of the additional work preferences that are important to you on the Work Preferences/Evaluation Guide under the heading, "Additional Factors."

__ 8. Use the occupational directories listed in Appendix A to determine if your first occupation can satisfy your additional work preferences. See Appendix A to learn how to obtain and use these directories.

Read any information you can find about your first occupation, and determine how well it can match your additional work preferences. Place a checkmark in the same manner as you did when evaluating the regular work preferences whenever the occupation can satisfy one of your additional preferences.

___ 9. After comparing and rating all work preferences, count up the total number of checkmarks that you have placed in the column for occupation number 1.
Place this number in the "Total Matches" box at the bottom of the column for occupation number 1.

___ 10. Repeat steps 1–9 above for all occupations listed on your List of Possible Career Options. Make sure you write in the total score (matching number of checkmarks) for each occupation.

___ 11. Note the occupations that have received the three highest scores. These occupations best match your interests and work preferences. For all practical purposes, you are probably looking at the occupations that are best for you to pursue.

___ 12. Decide which of these occupations you want to pursue as a career goal. Also decide which two alternative career options would be best for you if, for some reason, you are unable to pursue your first choice.
Note: If you are still unable to select a career goal, don't panic or give up! This situation does happen. Review the list below to see if you have missed any step in the program. If so, return to that step and complete it thoroughly.

- Did you carefully review all sixty-six work groups?
- Did you use the optional career exploration strategies as mentioned on Page 25 to expand your list of career options?
- Did you carefully select only those work preferences that are important to you?
- Did you evaluate accurately how well each occupation on your List of Possible Career Options matches your work preferences, including your additional work preferences?
- Did you accurately add the number of checkmarks for each occupation listed on the Work Preferences/Evaluation Guide?

If you believe you have properly completed all the items above, and if you are still uncertain about a career direction, then professional career counseling is recommended. See Appendix C for information concerning how to find and use a career guidance service. Bring your copy of *Career Selector 2001* along with you to help your counselor understand what progress you have made so far in selecting a career direction.

___ 13. List your 1st, 2nd, and 3rd place career goals at the bottom of the Work Preferences/Evaluation Guide.

You are now ready to move on to Task 4.

Task 4: Developing a Career Plan

Purpose: The purpose of Task 4 is to guide you in identifying the steps you should take to reach your new career goal. By first examining your career goal to determine what qualifications are normally required, and then by examining your own qualifications, you can determine what steps you should take to realize your goal. By then arranging the steps in sequential order, from those you should complete first to those you should complete last, and by assigning a completion date for each step, you will have a personalized, step-by-step plan of action for reaching your goal.

Developing a career plan is an essential task in achieving your career objective. Some people, after selecting a career goal, fail to reach it because they elect not to develop a plan. There is a tendency at this step to move ahead as quickly as possible. While this is understandable, it can be dangerous!

Considering that you have invested much time and energy in determining a career direction and the importance of selecting an appropriate goal, it seems only wise that you should now take a little extra time to develop an effective plan of action. Most travelers realize that a good road map is an essential tool for successfully reaching their destination. The same "road map" is necessary in achieving your career destination.

In preparing your career plan, you may need to refer to several sources of occupational information to find the required information. These may be the same sources you used in a previous step when you were evaluating various career options. See Appendix A for a listing of occupational directories.

Time: approximately 3 hours.

Use a pencil to complete this task because you may wish to change your answers.

Checklist of Things to Do

___ 1. On the Career Planning Guide (see pages 39–44 at the end of this section), in the section labeled, Career Goal, write in the title of the occupation you wish to pursue.

___ 2. Required Qualifications. In this section, list the qualifications normally required or recommended for entrance into your chosen career goal for each of the following factors:

- areas of knowledge
- abilities and skills
- personal characteristics, traits, or qualities
- educational training
- employment experience
- other factors

    If you plan to enter the occupation at the "entry" level, list only the qualifications required or recommended for entry level workers. If you plan to enter the occupation at the "experienced" level, then list only those qualifications.

    It is recommended that you consult the occupational directories as listed in Appendix A to obtain the above information for your career goal.

___ 3. Missing Qualifications. In this section, list the qualifications (as identified in Step 2 above) for each factor that you *do not* currently possess.

> ____ 4. **Task Analysis.** In this section, list the various kinds of activities, for each factor, you could undertake to develop any missing qualification.
>
>   If you are unsure as to what you could do to develop missing qualifications, discuss this section with a professional career counselor. See Appendix C for information regarding how to find a career counseling service.
>
> ____ 5. **Trouble Shooting and Problem Solving.** In this section, list the obstacles (problems) for each factor you believe you may encounter in attempting to develop any missing qualification.
>
> ____ 6. **Summary.** Review the information you have collected in the above steps. Decide what step you should undertake first to reach your new career goal. Describe that step to the right of Step 1 under the column heading What Needs to Be Done?.
>
>   To the right of Step 1 (What Needs to Be Done?), list a Starting and Ending Date for Step 1.
>
>   To the right of the Starting and Ending Dates, list the Obstacle(s) you expect to encounter in completing Step 1.
>
>   To the right of Obstacles, list the Resources you will call upon should any obstacle occur.
>
> ____ 7. Repeat the procedure as outlined above for all other steps you believe should be taken to reach your career goal. Make sure your steps are in sequential order: 1st, 2nd, 3rd, and so on.

You should review your completed plan with a professional career counselor if at all possible. This will help ensure that you have identified all necessary steps, that you have put your steps in the proper order, and that you have adequately prepared yourself to undertake each step.

You are now ready to implement your plan. To reach your new career goal, complete Step 1, Step 2, and so on until all steps have been completed. Be flexible as you attempt to complete each step. Allow for changes along the way. Seek additional advice whenever you have a question or when an unforeseen event occurs that may threaten your plan. And above all, motivate yourself to complete each step. You now have a path to follow to realize a more enjoyable and successful career. The one factor most likely to prevent you from reaching your career goal is you.

Good luck and best wishes for a new and more exciting and rewarding career!

Career Planning Guide

Career Goal: _____

Required Qualifications

   Areas of Knowledge

   Abilities and Skills

   Personal Characteristics, Traits, or Qualities

   Educational Training

   Employment Experience

   Other Factors

Missing Qualifications

Areas of Knowledge

Abilities and Skills

Personal Characteristics, Traits, or Qualities

Educational Training

Employment Experience

Other Factors

Task Analysis

Areas of Knowledge

Abilities and Skills

Personal Characteristics, Traits, or Qualities

Educational Training

Employment Experience

Other Factors

Trouble Shooting and Problem Solving

Areas of Knowledge

Abilities and Skills

Personal Characteristics, Traits, or Qualities

Educational Training

Employment Experience

Other Factors

Summary

Step	What Needs to Be Done?	Starting/Ending Dates	Obstacles	Resources
1.				
2.				
3.				
4.				
5.				

Summary

Step	What Needs to Be Done?	Starting/Ending Dates	Obstacles	Resources
6.				
7.				
8.				
9.				
10.				

CHAPTER 5

501 Occupational Profiles

In this chapter, you will find profiles on 501 occupations representing many of America's most popular career options. The purpose of these profiles is to provide you with basic occupational information to aid you in selecting a career goal.

The occupations presented in this chapter are in alphabetical order. To quickly find a particular occupation, simply flip through the pages noting the titles at the top, or check the Index of Job Titles found in Appendix B for the correct page number. Some occupations have, in the past, had separate title designations for men and women—actor/actress, for example. In the interest of language trends in today's society, the unisex terms (referring to both genders) are used wherever appropriate in this book.

The occupations profiled represent about 90 percent of all the work actually being conducted in America. Since most Americans work in these occupations, they may be defined as the most "popular" and "realistic" employment opportunities available. It is very likely that you will find your career direction among these options. However, as pointed out earlier, this is not the sum total of all occupations. In reality, there exists more than 13,500 occupations. Most people work in fewer than 1,000 of these occupations, so you can see how specialized some occupations are, and how few people actually work in those specialized occupations.

The information presented in these profiles can be best used in conjunction with the steps outlined in Tasks 1, 2, and 3.

Each profile contains the following information:
1. Occupational title
2. The occupation's DOT (Dictionary of Occupational Titles) number
3. The occupation's GOE (Guide for Occupational Exploration) number
4. A brief description of the occupation. Job descriptions are general in nature and represent activities *commonly* found for each occupation. Actual job situations may or may not include the activities listed here, and may or may not include additional activities *not* listed here.
5. The level (High, Moderate, or Low) of Aptitude required in each of the following skill areas:

- Intelligence
- Verbal
- Numerical
- Spatial
- Form Perception
- Clerical Perception
- Motor Coordination
- Finger Dexterity
- Manual Dexterity
- Eye/Hand/Foot Coordination
- Color Discrimination

6. The level (High, Moderate, or Low) of involvement with each of the following factors:
   - Data
   - People
   - Things

7. Salary: the typical annual income earned by experienced workers. Salary may be expressed as a singular amount or as a range from low to high.
   Caution: Entry-level positions usually offer lower salaries. For some occupations, the difference between entry-level and experienced-level salaries may be considerable. The salaries quoted here should be used as general guidelines. Within every occupational field, salaries may vary considerably from one employer to another depending upon your experience and level of responsibility, your work performance, industry averages, economic well-being of the employer, union strength, and geographical location. The salaries listed here are intended to be general guidelines, and those that you encounter in your job search may be somewhat higher or lower.

8. Opportunity outlook for the future: the expected growth rate of the occupation over the next ten to fifteen years. Rates are expressed as:
   - 35% growth
   - 25–34% growth
   - 14–24% growth
   - 5–13% growth
   - 0–4% growth or decline
   - 5% decline

   Caution: The predictions quoted here are based upon extensive analysis of current trends and conditions. Any change in these trends and conditions may result in an increase or decrease in the future need for employees in any occupation affected by the changes.

9. The Environmental Conditions that you are likely to encounter in the occupation, such as:
   - Inside work only
   - Outside work only
   - Inside and outside work
   - Extremely cold work environment
   - Extremely hot work environment
   - Wet and humid work environment
   - Presence of loud noises and vibrations
   - Presence of physical hazards
   - Presence of atmospheric dangers such as fumes, odors, etc.

10. The Physical Demands that will more than likely be required in the occupation, such as:
    - Strength
        - Sedentary—little or no lifting
        - Light—lifting of no more than 20 pounds
        - Moderate—lifting of no more than 50 pounds
        - Heavy —lifting of no more than 100 pounds
        - Very Heavy—lifting of more than 100 pounds
    - Climbing or balancing
    - Stooping, kneeling, crouching, or crawling
    - Reaching, handling, fingering, or feeling
    - Talking or hearing
    - Seeing

    Note to individuals with physical limitations: If an occupation in which you are interested requires a physical ability that you believe you lack or possess only at a minimal level, don't automatically rule it out as a possible career option. Many employers provide physically challenged employees with special services and equipment to help them accomplish their work. Also, it is against the law for any employer to discriminate against people who are physically challenged when considering them for employment. Therefore, if you are interested in a particular occupation that seems to call for physical capabilities beyond those you possess, talk to a career counselor to find out if optional resources exist that can enable you to function in the occupation. Your expectations, however, should be realistic.

11. The Temperaments (behavioral traits) that have been identified as important in achieving success in the occupation, such as:
    - Working alone or apart from others
    - Directing, controlling, or planning the work of others
    - Interpreting the feelings and ideas of others
    - Influencing the actions and beliefs of others
    - Making decisions based upon senses and feelings
    - Making decisions based upon facts
    - Dealing with people beyond giving and receiving information
    - Performing repetitive tasks
    - Performing under stressful, pressure-packed, or emergency conditions
    - Attempting to attain set limits, tolerances, or standards
    - Performing a variety of tasks

12. The Vocational Preparation level representing the amount of time normally required to develop an average level of competency in the occupation. The levels include:

- 1–3 hours
- 1–30 days
- 1–3 months
- 3–6 months
- 1/2–1 year
- 1–2 years[1]
- 2–4 years[2]
- 4–10 years[3]
- Over 10 years[3]

Source of the data

The information used to prepare each occupational profile was obtained from data compiled by the U.S. Department of Labor. For items 7 and 8, additional information was extracted from private industry reports, classified help-wanted announcements, government publications, and research conducted by the author.

Accuracy of the data

The data used to prepare each profile represents the most comprehensive and accurate source of information available on occupations. Hundreds of occupational researchers and many years of research time were required to compile this data. Information was synthesized to produce a view of a typical occupation. The occupations that you personally encounter may present characteristics different from those presented here.

As accurate as the data may be, it is not without fault. Consequently, a thorough analysis of the data was undertaken and some editing was done to bring it in line with the realities of today's world of work. Readers are encouraged to seek additional information whenever they encounter information that seems suspicious or inconsistent with their observations and experiences.

---

[1] This level usually includes a one- or two-year college education.
[2] This level usually includes a four-year college education.
[3] These levels usually include a graduate and/or doctoral program after the completion of a four-year college education.

Account Executive

DOT = 164.167-010   GOE = 11.09.01

Plans, coordinates, and directs the advertising campaigns of business clients using an advertising agency.

Aptitudes:
Intelligence	High
Verbal	High
Numerical	Moderate
Spatial	Moderate
Form Perception	Moderate
Clerical Perception	Moderate
Motor Coordination	Low
Finger Dexterity	Low
Manual Dexterity	Low
Eye-Hand-Foot Coordination	Low
Color Discrimination	Moderate

Data = High   People = Low   Things = Low

Salary Range:
$20,000–$120,000

Opportunity Outlook:
25–34% growth

Environmental Conditions:
Inside

Physical Demands:
Sedentary—little or no lifting
Talking or hearing required

Temperaments:
Directing, controlling, or planning the work of others
Dealing with people beyond giving and receiving information
Influencing the actions and beliefs of others
Making decisions based upon senses and feelings
Interpreting the feelings and ideas of others

Vocational Preparation:
4–10 years

Accountant

DOT = 160.167-010   GOE = 11.06.01

Prepares records of income and expenses for individuals or companies, such as balance sheets, profit and loss statements, and income tax records, and determines the financial condition of the individual or company.

Aptitudes:
Intelligence	High
Verbal	High
Numerical	High
Spatial	Low
Form Perception	Low
Clerical Perception	High
Motor Coordination	Low
Finger Dexterity	Low
Manual Dexterity	Low
Eye-Hand-Foot Coordination	Low
Color Discrimination	Low

Data = High   People = Low   Things = Low

Salary Range:
$17,000–$80,000

Opportunity Outlook:
25–34% growth

Environmental Conditions:
Inside

Physical Demands:
Sedentary—little or no lifting
Talking or hearing required

Temperaments:
Directing, controlling, or planning the work of others
Making decisions based upon senses and feelings
Making decisions based upon facts
Attempting to attain set limits

Vocational Preparation:
4–10 years

Acquisitions Librarian

DOT = 100.267-010   GOE = 11.02.04

Selects and orders books, periodicals, films, and other materials for a library.

Aptitudes:
Intelligence	High
Verbal	High
Numerical	High
Spatial	Low
Form Perception	Low
Clerical Perception	High
Motor Coordination	Low
Finger Dexterity	Low
Manual Dexterity	Low
Eye-Hand-Foot Coordination	Low
Color Discrimination	Low

Data = High   People = Low   Things = Low

Salary Range:
$23,400–$44,500

Opportunity Outlook:
5–13% growth

Environmental Conditions:
Inside

Physical Demands:
Light—lifting of no more than 20 pounds
Talking or hearing required
Stooping, kneeling, crouching, or crawling required
Reaching, handling, fingering, and feeling required

Temperaments:
Performing a variety of tasks
Making decisions based upon senses and feelings
Making decisions based upon facts

Vocational Preparation:
4–10 years

Acrobat

DOT = 159.247-010   GOE = 12.02.01

Entertains audiences by performing difficult and spectacular feats, such as leaping, tumbling, and balancing, alone or as a member of a team.

Aptitudes:
Intelligence	Moderate
Verbal	Moderate
Numerical	Low
Spatial	High
Form Perception	Moderate
Clerical Perception	Low
Motor Coordination	High
Finger Dexterity	High
Manual Dexterity	High
Eye-Hand-Foot Coordination	High
Color Discrimination	Low

Data = Mod   People = Mod   Things = Low

Salary Range:
Varies

Opportunity Outlook:
25–34% growth

Environmental Conditions:
Inside

Physical Demands:
Very Heavy—lifting of over 100 pounds
Climbing or balancing required
Stooping, kneeling, crouching, or crawling required
Talking or hearing required
Seeing required

Temperaments:
Performing a variety of tasks
Dealing with people beyond giving and receiving information
Interpreting the feelings and ideas of others

Vocational Preparation:
1/2–1 year

Actor

DOT = 150.047-010   GOE = 01.03.02

Portrays a role in a dramatic or comedy production to interpret a character or present a characterization to an audience.

Aptitudes:
Intelligence	High
Verbal	High
Numerical	Low
Spatial	Moderate
Form Perception	Moderate
Clerical Perception	Low
Motor Coordination	Low
Finger Dexterity	Low
Manual Dexterity	Low
Eye-Hand-Foot Coordination	Moderate
Color Discrimination	Low

Data = High   People = Mod   Things = Low

Salary Range:
$12,000–several million dollars

Opportunity Outlook:
35% growth or more

Environmental Conditions:
Inside and outside

Physical Demands:
Light—lifting of no more than 20 pounds
Talking or hearing required

Temperaments:
Interpreting the feelings and ideas of others
Making decisions based upon senses and feelings
Dealing with people beyond giving and receiving information
Performing under stressful, pressure-packed, or emergency conditions
Performing a variety of tasks

Vocational Preparation:
2–4 years

Actuary

DOT = 020.167-010   GOE = 11.01.02

Applies knowledge of mathematics, probability, statistics, principles of finance, and business to develop policies and plans for solving problems in such areas as life and health insurance, social services, casualty insurance, annuities, and pension programs.

Aptitudes:
Intelligence	High
Verbal	High
Numerical	High
Spatial	Low
Form Perception	Moderate
Clerical Perception	High
Motor Coordination	Low
Finger Dexterity	Low
Manual Dexterity	Low
Eye-Hand-Foot Coordination	Low
Color Discrimination	Low

Data = High   People = Low   Things = Low

Salary Range:
$28,300–$61,900

Opportunity Outlook:
25–34% growth

Environmental Conditions:
Inside

Physical Demands:
Sedentary—little or no lifting
Seeing required

Temperaments:
Directing, controlling, or planning the work of others
Making decisions based upon facts
Attempting to attain set limits

Vocational Preparation:
4–10 years

Acupuncturist

DOT = 079.271-010   GOE = 02.03.04

Using ancient knowledge of acupuncture and modern medical findings, inserts needles of various lengths into patients at locations of the body that are known to be effective to relieve symptoms of disease or illness.

Aptitudes:
Intelligence	High
Verbal	High
Numerical	Moderate
Spatial	High
Form Perception	High
Clerical Perception	Moderate
Motor Coordination	High
Finger Dexterity	Moderate
Manual Dexterity	Moderate
Eye-Hand-Foot Coordination	Low
Color Discrimination	Moderate

Data = High   People = Low   Things = High

Salary Range:
$20,000–$100,000+

Opportunity Outlook:
25–34% growth

Environmental Conditions:
Inside

Physical Demands:
Light—lifting of no more than 20 pounds
Reaching, handling, fingering, or feeling required
Talking or hearing required
Seeing required

Temperaments:
Making decisions based upon senses and feelings
Making decisions based upon facts

Vocational Preparation:
2–4 years

Adding Machine Operator

DOT = 216.482-014   GOE = 07.06.02

Computes details of business transactions using knowledge of arithmetic and the use of an electrically powered or lever-operated adding machine that automatically performs addition and subtraction and records the results on paper tape.

Aptitudes:
Intelligence	Moderate
Verbal	Low
Numerical	Moderate
Spatial	Low
Form Perception	Low
Clerical Perception	Moderate
Motor Coordination	Moderate
Finger Dexterity	Moderate
Manual Dexterity	Low
Eye-Hand-Foot Coordination	Low
Color Discrimination	Low

Data = Mod   People = Low   Things = Mod

Salary Range:
$9,500–$20,000

Opportunity Outlook:
14–24% growth

Environmental Conditions:
Inside

Physical Demands:
Sedentary—little or no lifting
Reaching, handling, fingering, and feeling required
Seeing required

Temperaments:
Performing repetitive tasks
Attempting to attain set limits

Vocational Preparation:
1–3 months

Advertising Manager

DOT = 164.117-010   GOE = 11.09.01

Plans, directs, and executes the advertising policies of an organization, department, or company.

Aptitudes:
Intelligence	High
Verbal	High
Numerical	High
Spatial	Moderate
Form Perception	Low
Clerical Perception	Low
Motor Coordination	Low
Finger Dexterity	Low
Manual Dexterity	Low
Eye-Hand-Foot Coordination	Low
Color Discrimination	Low

Data = High   People = High   Things = Low

Salary Range:
$20,300–$78,500

Opportunity Outlook:
35% growth or more

Environmental Conditions:
Inside

Physical Demands:
Sedentary—little or no lifting
Talking or hearing required

Temperaments:
Performing a variety of tasks
Directing, controlling, or planning the work of others
Dealing with people beyond giving and receiving information
Making decisions based upon senses and feelings

Vocational Preparation:
4–10 years

Aerial Photographer

DOT = 143.062-014   GOE = 01.06.01

Photographs segments of earth and other subject material from aircraft to produce pictures used in surveying, mapping, volumetric surveying, or related purposes.

Aptitudes:
Intelligence	High
Verbal	Moderate
Numerical	Moderate
Spatial	High
Form Perception	High
Clerical Perception	Low
Motor Coordination	Moderate
Finger Dexterity	Moderate
Manual Dexterity	Moderate
Eye-Hand-Foot Coordination	Low
Color Discrimination	High

Data = High   People = Low   Things = Mod

Salary Range:
$24,814–$37,273

Opportunity Outlook:
14–24% growth

Environmental Conditions:
Inside and outside
Presence of loud noises and vibrations
Presence of physical hazards

Physical Demands:
Light—lifting of no more than 20 pounds
Reaching, handling, fingering, and feeling required
Seeing required

Temperaments:
Making decisions based upon senses and feelings
Attempting to attain set limits

Vocational Preparation:
2–4 years

Aeronautical Research Engineer

DOT = 002.061-026   GOE = 05.01.01

Conducts research in the field of aeronautics to assist aeronautical engineers in the development of aircraft and space materials, systems, and vehicles.

Aptitudes:
Intelligence	High
Verbal	High
Numerical	High
Spatial	High
Form Perception	Moderate
Clerical Perception	Moderate
Motor Coordination	Moderate
Finger Dexterity	Moderate
Manual Dexterity	Moderate
Eye-Hand-Foot Coordination	Low
Color Discrimination	Moderate

Data = High   People = Low   Things = High

Salary Range:
$31,412–$93,514

Opportunity Outlook:
14–24% growth

Environmental Conditions:
Inside

Physical Demands:
Light—lifting of no more than 20 pounds
Talking or hearing required

Temperaments:
Performing a variety of tasks
Directing, controlling, or planning the work of others
Making decisions based upon senses and feelings
Making decisions based upon facts
Attempting to attain set limits

Vocational Preparation:
4–10 years

Agricultural Shipping Inspector

DOT = 801.667-010   GOE = 06.03.02

Examines agricultural equipment, such as tractors, combines, and balers, for surface defects, prior to shipment to buyers.

Aptitudes:
Intelligence	Moderate
Verbal	Low
Numerical	Low
Spatial	Moderate
Form Perception	Low
Clerical Perception	Low
Motor Coordination	Low
Finger Dexterity	Low
Manual Dexterity	Low
Eye-Hand-Foot Coordination	Low
Color Discrimination	Low

Data = Low   People = Low   Things = Low

Salary Range:
$29,000 (average)

Opportunity Outlook:
25–34% growth

Environmental Conditions:
Inside

Physical Demands:
Light—lifting of no more than 20 pounds
Reaching, handling, fingering, and feeling required
Seeing required

Temperaments:
Making decisions based upon senses and feelings
Attempting to attain set limits

Vocational Preparation:
3–6 months

Agronomist

DOT = 040.061-010 GOE = 02.02.02

Conducts experiments and investigations into field-crop problems and develops new methods of growing crops to secure more efficient production, higher yields, and improved nutritional quality.

Aptitudes:
Intelligence	High
Verbal	High
Numerical	High
Spatial	Low
Form Perception	Low
Clerical Perception	Moderate
Motor Coordination	Low
Finger Dexterity	Moderate
Manual Dexterity	Moderate
Eye-Hand-Foot Coordination	Low
Color Discrimination	Low

Data = High   People = Low   Things = High

Salary Range:
$42,000 (average)

Opportunity Outlook:
25–34% growth

Environmental Conditions:
Inside and outside

Physical Demands:
Light—lifting of no more than 20 pounds
Reaching, handling, fingering, and feeling required
Seeing required

Temperaments:
Directing, controlling, or planning the work of others
Making decisions based upon senses and feelings
Making decisions based upon facts

Vocational Preparation:
4–10 years

Air-Conditioning Installer

DOT = 827.464-010 GOE = 05.10.04

Installs window or central air-conditioning units in private residences and small business establishments.

Aptitudes:
Intelligence	Moderate
Verbal	Low
Numerical	Low
Spatial	Moderate
Form Perception	Moderate
Clerical Perception	Low
Motor Coordination	Moderate
Finger Dexterity	Moderate
Manual Dexterity	Moderate
Eye-Hand-Foot Coordination	Low
Color Discrimination	Low

Data = Mod   People = Low   Things = Mod

Salary Range:
$13,050–$38,750

Opportunity Outlook:
14–24% growth

Environmental Conditions:
Inside and outside

Physical Demands:
Heavy—lifting of no more than 100 pounds
Climbing or balancing required
Reaching, handling, fingering, and feeling required
Talking or hearing required
Seeing required

Temperaments:
Making decisions based upon senses and feelings
Making decisions based upon facts
Attempting to attain set limits

Vocational Preparation:
3–6 months

Air-Traffic Control Specialist

DOT = 193.162-018   GOE = 05.03.03

Controls airplane traffic at and within vicinity of an airport according to established procedures and policies to prevent collisions and to minimize delays arising from air-traffic congestion.

Aptitudes:
Intelligence	High
Verbal	Moderate
Numerical	Moderate
Spatial	Moderate
Form Perception	Moderate
Clerical Perception	Moderate
Motor Coordination	Low
Finger Dexterity	Moderate
Manual Dexterity	Moderate
Eye-Hand-Foot Coordination	Low
Color Discrimination	Moderate

Data = High   People = Low   Things = Mod

Salary Range:
$21,000–$47,200

Opportunity Outlook:
5–13% growth

Environmental Conditions:
Inside

Physical Demands:
Light—lifting of no more than 20 pounds
Reaching, handling, fingering, and feeling required
Talking or hearing required
Seeing required

Temperaments:
Performing a variety of tasks
Performing under stressful, pressure-packed, or emergency conditions
Making decisions based upon senses and feelings

Vocational Preparation:
4–10 years

Airbrush Painter

DOT = 741.684-018   GOE = 01.06.03

Coats, decorates, glazes, retouches, or tints articles, such as fishing lures, toys, dolls, pottery, artificial flowers, greeting cards, and household appliances, using an airbrush.

Aptitudes:
Intelligence	Moderate
Verbal	Low
Numerical	Low
Spatial	Moderate
Form Perception	Moderate
Clerical Perception	Low
Motor Coordination	Moderate
Finger Dexterity	Moderate
Manual Dexterity	Moderate
Eye-Hand-Foot Coordination	Low
Color Discrimination	Moderate

Data = Low   People = Low   Things = Mod

Salary Range:
Varies

Opportunity Outlook:
Not available

Environmental Conditions:
Inside
Presence of atmospheric dangers such as fumes, odors, etc.

Physical Demands:
Light—lifting of no more than 20 pounds
Reaching, handling, fingering, and feeling required
Seeing required

Temperaments:
Making decisions based upon facts
Attempting to attain set limits

Vocational Preparation:
1/2–1 year

Airline Crew Scheduler

DOT = 215.362-010 GOE = 07.05.01

Compiles duty rosters of flight crews and maintains records of crew members' flying time for scheduled airline flights.

Aptitudes:
Intelligence	Moderate
Verbal	Moderate
Numerical	Moderate
Spatial	Low
Form Perception	Moderate
Clerical Perception	Moderate
Motor Coordination	Low
Finger Dexterity	Moderate
Manual Dexterity	Low
Eye-Hand-Foot Coordination	Low
Color Discrimination	Low

Data = Mod   People = Low   Things = Mod

Salary Range:
Not available

Opportunity Outlook:
Not available

Environmental Conditions:
Inside

Physical Demands:
Sedentary—little or no lifting
Reaching, handling, fingering, and feeling required
Seeing required

Temperaments:
Performing repetitive tasks

Vocational Preparation:
1/2–1 year

Airplane Flight Attendant

DOT = 352.367-010 GOE = 09.01.04

Performs a variety of personal services conducive to the safety and comfort of airline passengers during a flight, such as greeting passengers, verifying tickets, serving food and drinks, and assigning seats.

Aptitudes:
Intelligence	Moderate
Verbal	Moderate
Numerical	Moderate
Spatial	Low
Form Perception	Low
Clerical Perception	Moderate
Motor Coordination	Moderate
Finger Dexterity	Low
Manual Dexterity	Moderate
Eye-Hand-Foot Coordination	Moderate
Color Discrimination	Low

Data = Mod   People = Mod   Things = Low

Salary Range:
$13,000–$35,000

Opportunity Outlook:
35% growth or more

Environmental Conditions:
Inside
Presence of loud noises and vibrations
Presence of physical hazards

Physical Demands:
Moderate—lifting or no more than 50 pounds
Climbing or balancing
Stooping, kneeling, crouching, or crawling required
Talking or hearing required
Seeing required

Temperaments:
Performing a variety of tasks
Performing repetitive tasks

Vocational Preparation:
1–3 months

Ambulance Driver

DOT = 913.683-010   GOE = 05.08.03

Drives an ambulance to transport sick, injured, or convalescent persons to and from hospitals and other medical facilities.

Aptitudes:
Intelligence	Moderate
Verbal	Low
Numerical	Low
Spatial	Moderate
Form Perception	Low
Clerical Perception	Low
Motor Coordination	Moderate
Finger Dexterity	Low
Manual Dexterity	Moderate
Eye-Hand-Foot Coordination	Moderate
Color Discrimination	Low

Data = Low   People = Low   Things = Mod

Salary Range:
$14,000–$20,000

Opportunity Outlook:
14–23% growth

Environmental Conditions:
Inside and outside
Presence of loud noises and vibrations
Presence of physical hazards

Physical Demands:
Very Heavy—lifting of over 100 pounds
Reaching, handling, fingering, and feeling required
Seeing required

Temperaments:
Dealing with people beyond giving and receiving information
Performing under stressful, pressure-packed, or emergency conditions

Vocational Preparation:
3–6 months

Amusement Park Entertainer

DOT = 159.647-010   GOE = 01.07.03

Entertains an audience in an amusement park by exhibiting special skills, such as fire-eating, hypnotism, snake charming, or sword swallowing.

Aptitudes:
Intelligence	Moderate
Verbal	Moderate
Numerical	Low
Spatial	Low
Form Perception	Low
Clerical Perception	Low
Motor Coordination	Low
Finger Dexterity	Low
Manual Dexterity	Low
Eye-Hand-Foot Coordination	Low
Color Discrimination	Low

Data = Low   People = Mod   Things = Low

Salary Range:
Varies

Opportunity Outlook:
Not available

Environmental Conditions:
Inside and outside

Physical Demands:
Light—lifting of no more than 20 pounds
Reaching, handling, fingering, and feeling required
Talking or hearing required

Temperaments:
Dealing with people beyond giving and receiving information
Interpreting the feelings and ideas of others

Vocational Preparation:
Up to 30 days

Anesthesiologist

DOT = 070.101-010   GOE = 02.03.01

Administers anesthetics (special gas mixtures) to render hospital patients insensible to pain during a surgical, obstetrical, or other form of medical procedure.

Aptitudes:
Intelligence	High
Verbal	High
Numerical	High
Spatial	High
Form Perception	High
Clerical Perception	Moderate
Motor Coordination	Moderate
Finger Dexterity	High
Manual Dexterity	High
Eye-Hand-Foot Coordination	Low
Color Discrimination	Moderate

Data = High   People = High   Things = High

Salary Range:
$150,000 (average)

Opportunity Outlook:
14–24% growth

Environmental Conditions:
Inside

Physical Demands:
Light—lifting of no more than 20 pounds
Reaching, handling, fingering, and feeling required
Talking or hearing required
Seeing required

Temperaments:
Making decisions based upon senses and feelings
Making decisions based upon facts
Dealing with people beyond giving and receiving information

Vocational Preparation:
4–10 years

Animal Breeder

DOT = 041.061-014   GOE = 02.02.01

Develops systems for breeding desirable characteristics in animals, such as improvement in strength, maturity rate, disease resistance, and meat quality and quantity.

Aptitudes:
Intelligence	High
Verbal	High
Numerical	High
Spatial	Moderate
Form Perception	Moderate
Clerical Perception	Low
Motor Coordination	Moderate
Finger Dexterity	Moderate
Manual Dexterity	Low
Eye-Hand-Foot Coordination	Low
Color Discrimination	Low

Data = High   People = Low   Things = High

Salary Range:
$20,000–$48,500

Opportunity Outlook:
14–24% growth

Environmental Conditions:
Inside and outside

Physical Demands:
Light—lifting of no more than 20 pounds
Reaching, handling, fingering, and feeling required
Seeing required

Temperaments:
Performing a variety of tasks
Directing, controlling, or planning the work of others
Making decisions based upon facts
Attempting to attain set limits

Vocational Preparation:
4–10 years

Animal Caretaker

DOT = 410.674-010   GOE = 03.03.02

Performs a variety of duties to care for animals, such as mice, canaries, guinea pigs, dogs, and monkeys on farms and in other facilities, such as kennels, pounds, animal hospitals, and laboratories.

Aptitudes:
Intelligence	Moderate
Verbal	Moderate
Numerical	Low
Spatial	Low
Form Perception	Low
Clerical Perception	Low
Motor Coordination	Moderate
Finger Dexterity	Moderate
Manual Dexterity	Moderate
Eye-Hand-Foot Coordination	Low
Color Discrimination	Low

Data = Low   People = Low   Things = Mod

Salary Range:
$7,500–$20,000

Opportunity Outlook:
35% growth or more

Environmental Conditions:
Inside and outside
Presence of physical hazards

Physical Demands:
Moderate—lifting of no more than 50 pounds
Reaching, handling, fingering, and feeling required
Seeing required

Temperaments:
Performing a variety of tasks
Attempting to attain set limits

Vocational Preparation:
3–6 months

Animal Scientist

DOT = 040.061-014   GOE = 02.02.01

Conducts research in the selection, breeding, feeding, management, and marketing of beef and dual-purpose cattle, horses, mules, sheep, dogs, goats, and pet animals.

Aptitudes:
Intelligence	High
Verbal	High
Numerical	High
Spatial	High
Form Perception	High
Clerical Perception	Moderate
Motor Coordination	Moderate
Finger Dexterity	High
Manual Dexterity	High
Eye-Hand-Foot Coordination	Low
Color Discrimination	Low

Data = High   People = Low   Things = High

Salary Range:
$19,000–$48,800

Opportunity Outlook:
14–24% growth

Environmental Conditions:
Inside and outside

Physical Demands:
Moderate—lifting of no more than 50 pounds
Reaching, handling, fingering, and feeling required
Seeing required

Temperaments:
Performing a variety of tasks
Making decisions based upon facts
Directing, controlling, or planning the work of others
Attempting to attain set limits

Vocational Preparation:
4–10 years

Animal Trainer

DOT = 159.224-010   GOE = 03.03.01

Trains animals to obey commands, compete in shows, or perform tricks to entertain an audience.

Aptitudes:
Intelligence	Moderate
Verbal	Moderate
Numerical	Low
Spatial	Moderate
Form Perception	Low
Clerical Perception	Low
Motor Coordination	Moderate
Finger Dexterity	Low
Manual Dexterity	Moderate
Eye-Hand-Foot Coordination	Moderate
Color Discrimination	Low

Data = Mod   People = Mod   Things = Mod

Salary Range:
$10,000–$100,000

Opportunity Outlook:
5–13% growth

Environmental Conditions:
Inside and outside
Wet and humid work environment
Presence of physical hazards

Physical Demands:
Light—lifting of no more than 20 pounds
Stooping, kneeling, crouching, or crawling required
Reaching, handling, fingering, and feeling required
Talking or hearing required

Temperaments:
Directing, controlling, or planning the work of others
Dealing with people beyond giving and receiving information
Performing under stressful, pressure-packed, or emergency conditions
Making decisions based upon senses and feelings

Vocational Preparation: 1–2 years

Animal Trapper

DOT = 461.684-014   GOE = 03.04.03

Traps animals for pelts, live sale, bounty, or to relocate them in other areas where they may live a safer or more healthy life.

Aptitudes:
Intelligence	Moderate
Verbal	Low
Numerical	Low
Spatial	Low
Form Perception	Moderate
Clerical Perception	Low
Motor Coordination	Moderate
Finger Dexterity	Moderate
Manual Dexterity	Moderate
Eye-Hand-Foot Coordination	Moderate
Color Discrimination	Moderate

Data = Low   People = Low   Things = Mod

Salary Range:
Not available

Opportunity Outlook:
Not available

Environmental Conditions:
Outside
Wet and humid work environment

Physical Demands:
Heavy—lifting of no more than 100 pounds
Climbing or balancing
Stooping, kneeling, crouching, or crawling required
Reaching, handling, fingering, and feeling required
Seeing required

Temperaments:
Performing a variety of tasks
Making decisions based upon senses and feelings

Vocational Preparation:
1/2–1 year

Antenna Installer

DOT = 823.684-010   GOE = 05.12.16

Installs antennas for radio or television receiving sets, usually on rooftops, for private individuals or companies.

Aptitudes:

Intelligence	Moderate
Verbal	Low
Numerical	Low
Spatial	Moderate
Form Perception	Moderate
Clerical Perception	Low
Motor Coordination	Moderate
Finger Dexterity	Moderate
Manual Dexterity	Moderate
Eye-Hand-Foot Coordination	High
Color Discrimination	Low

Data = Low   People = Low   Things = Mod

Salary Range:
$11,000–$24,900

Opportunity Outlook:
5–13% growth

Environmental Conditions:
Outside
Presence of physical hazards

Physical Demands:
Moderate—lifting of no more than 50 pounds
Climbing or balancing
Stooping, kneeling, crouching, or crawling required
Reaching, handling, fingering, and feeling required

Temperaments:
Performing repetitive tasks
Attempting to attain set limits

Vocational Preparation:
3–6 months

Anthropologist

DOT = 055.067-010   GOE = 11.03.03

Conducts comparative studies to learn about the distribution, origin, evolution, and races of humans, the cultures they have created, and their distribution and physical characteristics.

Aptitudes:

Intelligence	High
Verbal	High
Numerical	Moderate
Spatial	High
Form Perception	High
Clerical Perception	Low
Motor Coordination	Low
Finger Dexterity	Low
Manual Dexterity	Low
Eye-Hand-Foot Coordination	Low
Color Discrimination	Low

Data = High   People = Low   Things = Low

Salary Range:
$16,200–$67,800

Opportunity Outlook:
35% growth or more

Environmental Conditions:
Inside and outside

Physical Demands:
Light—lifting of no more than 20 pounds
Reaching, handling, fingering, and feeling required
Talking or hearing required
Seeing required

Temperaments:
Making decisions based upon senses and feelings
Making decisions based upon facts

Vocational Preparation:
4–10 years

Apartment Manager

DOT = 186.167-018   GOE = 11.11.01

Manages an apartment house complex or development for owners or a property management firm, shows prospective tenants apartments and explains rental terms, and carries out renting of apartments.

Aptitudes:
Intelligence	Moderate
Verbal	Moderate
Numerical	Moderate
Spatial	Low
Form Perception	Low
Clerical Perception	Moderate
Motor Coordination	Low
Finger Dexterity	Low
Manual Dexterity	Low
Eye-Hand-Foot Coordination	Low
Color Discrimination	Low

Data = High   People = Mod   Things = Low

Salary Range:
$14,600–$72,800

Opportunity Outlook:
25–34% growth

Environmental Conditions:
Inside

Physical Demands:
Light—lifting of no more than 20 pounds
Talking or hearing required
Seeing required

Temperaments:
Performing a variety of tasks
Making decisions based upon senses and feelings
Making decisions based upon facts

Vocational Preparation:
1–2 years

Appliance Service Supervisor

DOT = 187.167-010   GOE = 05.02.06

Coordinates the activities of a repair service department within a gas or electric appliance distributor or sales company.

Aptitudes:
Intelligence	Moderate
Verbal	Moderate
Numerical	Moderate
Spatial	High
Form Perception	Moderate
Clerical Perception	Moderate
Motor Coordination	Low
Finger Dexterity	Low
Manual Dexterity	Low
Eye-Hand-Foot Coordination	Low
Color Discrimination	Low

Data = High   People = Low   Things = Low

Salary Range:
$16,000–$33,600

Opportunity Outlook:
5% decline or more

Environmental Conditions:
Inside

Physical Demands:
Light—lifting of no more than 20 pounds
Talking or hearing required
Seeing required

Temperaments:
Directing, controlling, or planning the work of others
Making decisions based upon facts
Dealing with people beyond giving and receiving information
Performing a variety of tasks

Vocational Preparation:
2–4 years

Aquarist

DOT = 449.674-010   GOE = 03.03.02

Attends and cares for fish and other aquatic life in aquarium exhibits in museums, public aquariums, and aquatic research facilities.

Aptitudes:
Intelligence	Moderate
Verbal	Moderate
Numerical	Low
Spatial	Moderate
Form Perception	Moderate
Clerical Perception	Low
Motor Coordination	Moderate
Finger Dexterity	Moderate
Manual Dexterity	Moderate
Eye-Hand-Foot Coordination	Low
Color Discrimination	Low

Data = Low   People = Low   Things = Mod

Salary Range:
$15,000 (average)

Opportunity Outlook:
4% growth or decline

Environmental Conditions:
Inside and outside
Wet and humid work environment

Physical Demands:
Light—lifting of no more than 20 pounds
Stooping, kneeling, crouching, or crawling required
Reaching, handling, fingering, and feeling required
Seeing required

Temperaments:
Performing a variety of tasks
Making decisions based upon facts

Vocational Preparation:
3-6 months

Aquatic Performer

DOT = 159.347-014   GOE = 12.02.01

Performs water-ballet routines to entertain an audience, using synchronized swimming techniques.

Aptitudes:
Intelligence	Moderate
Verbal	Moderate
Numerical	Low
Spatial	High
Form Perception	High
Clerical Perception	Low
Motor Coordination	High
Finger Dexterity	Moderate
Manual Dexterity	Moderate
Eye-Hand-Foot Coordination	High
Color Discrimination	Low

Data = Mod   People = Mod   Things = Low

Salary Range:
Varies

Opportunity Outlook:
Not available

Environmental Conditions:
Inside and outside
Wet and humid work environment

Physical Demands:
Moderate—lifting of no more than 50 pounds
Climbing or balancing required
Reaching, handling, fingering, and feeling required

Temperaments:
Performing a variety of tasks
Dealing with people beyond giving and receiving information
Making decisions based upon senses and feelings

Vocational Preparation:
1/2-1 year

Arbitrator

DOT = 169.107-010   GOE = 11.04.03

Attempts to settle disputes between individuals or groups of individuals in an effort to bind both parties to specific terms and conditions of a labor contract that is fair and equitable to both parties.

Aptitudes:
- Intelligence — High
- Verbal — High
- Numerical — Moderate
- Spatial — Low
- Form Perception — Low
- Clerical Perception — Moderate
- Motor Coordination — Low
- Finger Dexterity — Low
- Manual Dexterity — Low
- Eye-Hand-Foot Coordination — Low
- Color Discrimination — Low

Data = High   People = High   Things = Low

Salary Range:
$17,500–$99,900

Opportunity Outlook:
25–34% growth

Environmental Conditions:
Inside

Physical Demands:
Sedentary—little or no lifting
Talking or hearing required

Temperaments:
Directing, controlling, or planning the work of others
Influencing the actions and beliefs of others
Making decisions based upon senses and feelings
Dealing with people beyond giving and receiving information
Performing under stressful, pressure-packed, or emergency conditions

Vocational Preparation:
4–10 years

Archaeologist

DOT = 055.067-018   GOE = 11.03.03

Attempts to reconstruct the activities of extinct cultures, especially preliterate cultures, by digging up their artifacts, classifying each object, and by preparing reports depicting the daily life and cultural activities of those individuals who left the artifacts behind.

Aptitudes:
- Intelligence — High
- Verbal — High
- Numerical — Moderate
- Spatial — High
- Form Perception — High
- Clerical Perception — Low
- Motor Coordination — Low
- Finger Dexterity — Low
- Manual Dexterity — Low
- Eye-Hand-Foot Coordination — Low
- Color Discrimination — Low

Data = High   People = Low   Things = Low

Salary Range:
$16,200–$67,800

Opportunity Outlook:
0–4% growth or decline

Environmental Conditions:
Inside and outside
Extremely hot work environment
Wet and humid work environment

Physical Demands:
Light—lifting of no more than 20 pounds
Reaching, handling, fingering, and feeling required
Talking or hearing required
Seeing required

Temperaments:
Making decisions based upon senses and feelings
Making decisions based upon facts

Vocational Preparation:
4–10 years

Architect

DOT = 001.061-010 GOE = 05.01.07

Prepares designs of new or remodeled buildings and homes including specifications for spatial requirements, materials, equipment needed, estimated costs, and building time.

Aptitudes:
Intelligence	High
Verbal	High
Numerical	High
Spatial	High
Form Perception	High
Clerical Perception	Moderate
Motor Coordination	Low
Finger Dexterity	Moderate
Manual Dexterity	Moderate
Eye-Hand-Foot Coordination	Low
Color Discrimination	Moderate

Data = High   People = Low   Things = High

Salary Range:
$17,900–$100,000+

Opportunity Outlook:
14–24% growth

Environmental Conditions:
Inside

Physical Demands:
Light—lifting of no more than 20 pounds
Reaching, handling, fingering, and feeling required
Talking or hearing required
Seeing required

Temperaments:
Influencing the actions and beliefs of others
Making decisions based upon senses and feelings
Dealing with people beyond giving and receiving information

Vocational Preparation:
4–10 years

Architectural Drafter

DOT = 001.261-010 GOE = 05.03.02

Prepares drawings of architectural and structural features of a home or office building showing all dimensions and specifications, for use by other people who will follow the drawing to actually complete the construction.

Aptitudes:
Intelligence	High
Verbal	Moderate
Numerical	High
Spatial	High
Form Perception	High
Clerical Perception	High
Motor Coordination	High
Finger Dexterity	High
Manual Dexterity	High
Eye-Hand-Foot Coordination	Low
Color Discrimination	Low

Data = High   People = Low   Things = High

Salary Range:
$15,400–$41,600

Opportunity Outlook:
0–4% growth or decline

Environmental Conditions:
Inside

Physical Demands:
Sedentary—little or no lifting
Reaching, handling, fingering, and feeling required
Seeing required

Temperaments:
Making decisions based upon facts
Attempting to attain set limits

Vocational Preparation:
2–4 years

Art Appraiser

DOT = 191.287-014   GOE = 01.02.01

Examines works of art, such as paintings, sculpture, and antiques, to determine their authenticity and value.

Aptitudes:
Intelligence	High
Verbal	High
Numerical	Low
Spatial	Moderate
Form Perception	High
Clerical Perception	Low
Motor Coordination	Low
Finger Dexterity	Low
Manual Dexterity	Low
Eye-Hand-Foot Coordination	Low
Color Discrimination	High

Data = High   People = Low   Things = Low

Salary Range:
Not available

Opportunity Outlook:
Not available

Environmental Conditions:
Inside

Physical Demands:
Light—lifting of no more than 20 pounds
Seeing required

Temperaments:
Making decisions based upon senses and feelings
Making decisions based upon facts
Attempting to attain set limits

Vocational Preparation:
4-10 years

Art Teacher

DOT = 149.021-010   GOE = 01.02.01

Instructs students in the basic methods and techniques of painting, sketching, design, and sculpture as a means of helping them improve their artistic ability and deepen their appreciation of art.

Aptitudes:
Intelligence	High
Verbal	High
Numerical	Low
Spatial	High
Form Perception	High
Clerical Perception	Low
Motor Coordination	Moderate
Finger Dexterity	High
Manual Dexterity	Moderate
Eye-Hand-Foot Coordination	Low
Color Discrimination	High

Data = High   People = High   Things = High

Salary Range:
$32,000 (average)

Opportunity Outlook:
14-24% growth

Environmental Conditions:
Inside

Physical Demands:
Light—lifting of no more than 20 pounds
Reaching, handling, fingering, and feeling required
Talking or hearing required
Seeing required

Temperaments:
Dealing with people beyond giving and receiving information
Influencing the actions and beliefs of others

Vocational Preparation:
4-10 years

Art Therapist

DOT = 076.127-010   GOE = 10.02.02

Plans and conducts art therapy programs, using such activities as painting, drawing, and sculpture, in public and private health institutions to rehabilitate mentally ill and physically disabled patients.

Aptitudes:
Intelligence	High
Verbal	High
Numerical	Moderate
Spatial	High
Form Perception	High
Clerical Perception	Moderate
Motor Coordination	Low
Finger Dexterity	Moderate
Manual Dexterity	Moderate
Eye-Hand-Foot Coordination	Low
Color Discrimination	Moderate

Data = High   People = High   Things = Low

Salary Range:
$15,000–$30,500

Opportunity Outlook:
25–34% growth

Environmental Conditions:
Inside

Physical Demands:
Light—lifting of no more than 20 pounds
Reaching, handling, fingering, and feeling required
Talking or hearing required
Seeing required

Temperaments:
Directing, controlling, or planning the work of others
Making decisions based upon senses and feelings
Performing a variety of tasks

Vocational Preparation:
4–10 years

Artists' Model

DOT = 961.667-010   GOE = 01.08.01

Poses as a subject for paintings, sculptures, photographs, or other types of art for a professional artist.

Aptitudes:
Intelligence	Moderate
Verbal	Low
Numerical	Low
Spatial	Low
Form Perception	Low
Clerical Perception	Low
Motor Coordination	Low
Finger Dexterity	Low
Manual Dexterity	Low
Eye-Hand-Foot Coordination	Low
Color Discrimination	Low

Data = Low   People = Low   Things = Low

Salary Range:
Varies

Opportunity Outlook:
14–24% growth

Environmental Conditions:
Inside

Physical Demands:
Light—lifting of no more than 20 pounds

Temperaments:
Interpreting the feelings and ideas of others

Vocational Preparation:
1–3 months

Association Executive

DOT = 189.117-010   GOE = 11.05.01

Directs and coordinates the activities of a professional or trade association in accordance with established policies to further advance the goals, objectives, and standards of the association and members who belong to the association.

Aptitudes:
Intelligence	High
Verbal	High
Numerical	High
Spatial	Low
Form Perception	Low
Clerical Perception	Moderate
Motor Coordination	Low
Finger Dexterity	Low
Manual Dexterity	Low
Eye-Hand-Foot Coordination	Low
Color Discrimination	Low

Data = High   People = High   Things = Low

Salary Range:
$30,000–$100,000

Opportunity Outlook:
14–24% growth

Environmental Conditions:
Inside

Physical Demands:
Sedentary—little or no lifting
Talking or hearing required

Temperaments:
Performing a variety of tasks
Directing, controlling, or planning the work of others
Influencing the actions and beliefs of others
Dealing with people beyond giving and receiving information
Performing under stressful, pressure-packed, or emergency conditions

Vocational Preparation:
4–10 years

Astronomer

DOT = 021.067-010   GOE = 02.01.01

Observes and studies stars, planets, and other celestial objects and attempts to interpret findings for a clearer and deeper understanding and practical use of the universe.

Aptitudes:
Intelligence	High
Verbal	High
Numerical	High
Spatial	High
Form Perception	Moderate
Clerical Perception	High
Motor Coordination	Moderate
Finger Dexterity	Moderate
Manual Dexterity	Low
Eye-Hand-Foot Coordination	Low
Color Discrimination	Moderate

Data = High   People = Low   Things = Low

Salary Range:
$29,200–$60,300

Opportunity Outlook:
5–13% growth

Environmental Conditions:
Inside

Physical Demands:
Light—lifting of no more than 20 pounds
Seeing required

Temperaments:
Making decisions based upon senses and feelings
Making decisions based upon facts
Attempting to attain set limits

Vocational Preparation:
4–10 years

Athletic Director

DOT = 090.117-022   GOE = 11.07.06

Plans, administers, and directs the intercollegiate athletic activities for a college or university.

Aptitudes:
Intelligence	High
Verbal	High
Numerical	Moderate
Spatial	Low
Form Perception	Moderate
Clerical Perception	Moderate
Motor Coordination	Low
Finger Dexterity	Low
Manual Dexterity	Low
Eye-Hand-Foot Coordination	Low
Color Discrimination	Low

Data = High   People = High   Things = Low

Salary Range:
$35,000–$80,000

Opportunity Outlook:
14–24% growth

Environmental Conditions:
Inside

Physical Demands:
Sedentary—little or no lifting
Talking or hearing required

Temperaments:
Performing a variety of tasks
Directing, controlling, or planning the work of others
Dealing with people beyond giving and receiving information
Making decisions based upon facts

Vocational Preparation:
4–10 years

Athletic Manager

DOT = 153.117-014   GOE = 11.12.03

Manages the business affairs of professional athletes by negotiating with promoters or others to settle contracts and business matters; may also be involved in the training of athletes.

Aptitudes:
Intelligence	High
Verbal	High
Numerical	High
Spatial	Low
Form Perception	Low
Clerical Perception	Moderate
Motor Coordination	Low
Finger Dexterity	Low
Manual Dexterity	Low
Eye-Hand-Foot Coordination	Low
Color Discrimination	Low

Data = High   People = High   Things = Low

Salary Range:
Varies

Opportunity Outlook:
25–34% growth

Environmental Conditions:
Inside and outside

Physical Demands:
Light—lifting of no more than 20 pounds
Talking or hearing required

Temperaments:
Performing a variety of tasks
Directing, controlling, or planning the work of others
Dealing with people beyond giving and receiving information
Influencing the actions and beliefs of others
Making decisions based upon senses and feelings

Vocational Preparation:
2–4 years

Auctioneer

DOT = 294.257-010 GOE = 08.02.03

Sells articles and objects at an auction to highest bidders, appraises merchandise before sale, and attempts to obtain the highest price for each item.

Aptitudes:
Intelligence	Moderate
Verbal	High
Numerical	Low
Spatial	Low
Form Perception	Moderate
Clerical Perception	Moderate
Motor Coordination	Low
Finger Dexterity	Low
Manual Dexterity	Low
Eye-Hand-Foot Coordination	Low
Color Discrimination	Low

Data = High   People = Mod   Things = Low

Salary Range:
Varies

Opportunity Outlook:
14-24% growth

Environmental Conditions:
Inside and outside

Physical Demands:
Light—lifting of no more than 20 pounds
Reaching, handling, fingering, and feeling required
Talking or hearing required
Seeing required

Temperaments:
Influencing the actions and beliefs of others
Making decisions based upon senses and feelings
Dealing with people beyond giving and receiving information
Interpreting the feelings and ideas of others

Vocational Preparation:
1-2 years

Audiometrist

DOT = 078.362-010 GOE = 10.03.01

Under the supervision of a doctor, an audiometrist will administer tests to individuals to check their hearing; will also fit individuals with hearing-aid devices and instruct them in their proper use and function.

Aptitudes:
Intelligence	High
Verbal	Moderate
Numerical	Moderate
Spatial	Low
Form Perception	Moderate
Clerical Perception	High
Motor Coordination	Moderate
Finger Dexterity	Moderate
Manual Dexterity	Moderate
Eye-Hand-Foot Coordination	Low
Color Discrimination	Low

Data = Mod   People = Mod   Things = High

Salary Range:
$25,000 (average)

Opportunity Outlook:
14-24% growth

Environmental Conditions:
Inside

Physical Demands:
Light—lifting of no more than 20 pounds
Reaching, handling, fingering, and feeling required
Talking or hearing required
Seeing required

Temperaments:
Dealing with people beyond giving and receiving information
Making decisions based upon facts

Vocational Preparation:
1-2 years

Audiovisual Technician

DOT = 960.382-010   GOE = 05.10.05

Operates audiovisual or sound equipment to provide or complement educational or public service programs conducted by institutions, such as museums, zoos, or libraries.

Aptitudes:
Intelligence	Moderate
Verbal	Moderate
Numerical	Low
Spatial	Moderate
Form Perception	Moderate
Clerical Perception	Low
Motor Coordination	Moderate
Finger Dexterity	Moderate
Manual Dexterity	Moderate
Eye-Hand-Foot Coordination	Low
Color Discrimination	Low

Data = Mod   People = Low   Things = Mod

Salary Range:
$15,000–$37,000

Opportunity Outlook:
25–34% growth

Environmental Conditions:
Inside

Physical Demands:
Moderate—lifting of no more than 50 pounds
Reaching, handling, fingering, and feeling required
Talking or hearing required
Seeing required

Temperaments:
Making decisions based upon senses and feelings
Attempting to attain set limits

Vocational Preparation:
1–3 months

Auditor

DOT = 160.162.014   GOE = 11.06.01

Examines and analyzes accounting records of a business and prepares detailed reports concerning its overall financial status and financial operating procedures.

Aptitudes:
Intelligence	High
Verbal	High
Numerical	High
Spatial	Low
Form Perception	Low
Clerical Perception	High
Motor Coordination	Low
Finger Dexterity	Low
Manual Dexterity	Low
Eye-Hand-Foot Coordination	Low
Color Discrimination	Low

Data = High   People = Low   Things = Mod

Salary Range:
$17,000–$80,000

Opportunity Outlook:
25–34% growth

Environmental Conditions:
Inside

Physical Demands:
Sedentary—little or no lifting
Talking or hearing required
Seeing required

Temperaments:
Directing, controlling, or planning the work of others
Making decisions based upon facts
Attempting to attain set limits
Performing a variety of tasks

Vocational Preparation:
4–10 years

Auto Club Travel Counselor

DOT = 238.167-014   GOE = 07.05.01

Plans trips for members of an automobile club. Prepares maps, marks routes, indicates points of interests, and may reserve hotel, motel, or resort accommodations for members.

Aptitudes:
Intelligence	Moderate
Verbal	Moderate
Numerical	Moderate
Spatial	Low
Form Perception	Low
Clerical Perception	High
Motor Coordination	Low
Finger Dexterity	Low
Manual Dexterity	Low
Eye-Hand-Foot Coordination	Low
Color Discrimination	Low

Data = High   People = Low   Things = Low

Salary Range:
$12,000–$22,000

Opportunity Outlook:
14–24% growth

Environmental Conditions:
Inside

Physical Demands:
Sedentary—little or no lifting
Reaching, handling, fingering, and feeling required
Talking or hearing required

Temperaments:
Performing a variety of tasks

Vocational Preparation:
1/2–1 year

Automobile Body Repairer

DOT = 807.381-010   GOE = 05.05.06

Repairs damaged bodies and body parts of automotive vehicles, such as cars, buses, and trucks, according to repair manuals, using hand and power tools.

Aptitudes:
Intelligence	Moderate
Verbal	Moderate
Numerical	Moderate
Spatial	High
Form Perception	High
Clerical Perception	Low
Motor Coordination	Moderate
Finger Dexterity	Moderate
Manual Dexterity	Moderate
Eye-Hand-Foot Coordination	Low
Color Discrimination	Low

Data = Mod   People = Low   Things = High

Salary Range:
$16,500–$36,500

Opportunity Outlook:
14–24% growth

Environmental Conditions:
Inside
Presence of loud noises and vibrations

Physical Demands:
Moderate—lifting of no more than 50 pounds
Stooping, kneeling, crouching, or crawling required
Reaching, handling, fingering, and feeling required
Seeing required

Temperaments:
Performing a variety of tasks
Making decisions based upon facts
Attempting to attain set limits

Vocational Preparation:
2–4 years

Automobile-Laboratory Technician

DOT = 019.381-010   GOE = 02.04.01

Using various high-tech equipment, tests soundproofing materials for possible use in automobiles to reduce the noise level inside the vehicle.

Aptitudes:
Intelligence	Moderate
Verbal	Moderate
Numerical	Moderate
Spatial	Moderate
Form Perception	Low
Clerical Perception	Moderate
Motor Coordination	Moderate
Finger Dexterity	Low
Manual Dexterity	Moderate
Eye-Hand-Foot Coordination	Low
Color Discrimination	Low

Data = Mod   People = Low   Things = High

Salary Range:
$16,000–$50,000

Opportunity Outlook:
5–13% growth

Environmental Conditions:
Inside

Physical Demands:
Light—lifting of no more than 20 pounds
Reaching, handling, fingering, and feeling required
Talking or hearing required
Seeing required

Temperaments:
Making decisions based upon facts

Vocational Preparation:
1/2–1 year

Automobile Racer

DOT = 153.243-010   GOE = 12.01.03

Drives specially adapted and equipped automobile in competitive road races.

Aptitudes:
Intelligence	Moderate
Verbal	Moderate
Numerical	Low
Spatial	High
Form Perception	High
Clerical Perception	Low
Motor Coordination	High
Finger Dexterity	High
Manual Dexterity	High
Eye-Hand-Foot Coordination	High
Color Discrimination	Low

Data = Mod   People = Mod   Things = Mod

Salary Range:
Varies

Opportunity Outlook:
Not available

Environmental Conditions:
Outside
Extremely hot work environment
Presence of loud noises and vibrations
Presence of physical hazards

Physical Demands:
Moderate—lifting of no more than 50 pounds
Reaching, handling, fingering, and feeling required
Seeing required

Temperaments:
Performing under stressful, pressure-packed, or emergency conditions
Making decisions based upon senses and feelings
Attempting to attain set limits

Vocational Preparation:
1–2 years

Automobile Rental Clerk

DOT = 295.477-010   GOE = 09.04.02

Rents automobiles to customers at airports, hotels, marinas, and other locations.

Aptitudes:
Intelligence	Moderate
Verbal	Moderate
Numerical	Moderate
Spatial	Low
Form Perception	Low
Clerical Perception	Moderate
Motor Coordination	Low
Finger Dexterity	Low
Manual Dexterity	Low
Eye-Hand-Foot Coordination	Low
Color Discrimination	Low

Data = Mod   People = Low   Things = Low

Salary Range:
$8,000–$25,100

Opportunity Outlook:
25–34% growth

Environmental Conditions:
Inside

Physical Demands:
Light—lifting of no more than 20 pounds
Reaching, handling, fingering, and feeling required
Talking or hearing required

Temperaments:
Making decisions based upon facts

Vocational Preparation:
3–6 months

Automobile Repair Service Estimator

DOT = 620.261-018   GOE = 05.07.02

Inspects and tests automobiles and trucks to determine what needs to be repaired and the cost of the repairs.

Aptitudes:
Intelligence	Moderate
Verbal	Moderate
Numerical	Moderate
Spatial	Moderate
Form Perception	Low
Clerical Perception	Moderate
Motor Coordination	Low
Finger Dexterity	Low
Manual Dexterity	Moderate
Eye-Hand-Foot Coordination	Low
Color Discrimination	Low

Data = Mod   People = Low   Things = High

Salary Range:
$19,800–$39,800

Opportunity Outlook:
14–24% growth

Environmental Conditions:
Inside

Physical Demands:
Light—lifting of no more than 20 pounds
Reaching, handling, fingering, and feeling required
Talking or hearing required
Seeing required

Temperaments:
Performing a variety of tasks
Making decisions based upon senses and feelings
Making decisions based upon proven facts

Vocational Preparation:
2–4 years

Ballistics Expert

DOT = 199.267-010   GOE = 02.04.01

Examines and tests firearms, spent bullets, and related evidence in criminal cases to develop facts useful in the apprehension and prosecution of suspects.

Aptitudes:
Intelligence	High
Verbal	High
Numerical	High
Spatial	High
Form Perception	High
Clerical Perception	Moderate
Motor Coordination	Moderate
Finger Dexterity	Moderate
Manual Dexterity	Moderate
Eye-Hand-Foot Coordination	Low
Color Discrimination	Moderate

Data = High   People = Low   Things = Mod

Salary Range:
$16,000–$55,000

Opportunity Outlook:
25–34% growth

Environmental Conditions:
Inside
Presence of loud noises and vibrations

Physical Demands:
Light—lifting of no more than 20 pounds
Reaching, handling, fingering, and feeling required
Talking or hearing required
Seeing required

Temperaments:
Making decisions based upon senses and feelings
Making decisions based upon facts
Performing a variety of tasks

Vocational Preparation:
2–4 years

Bank Collection Clerk

DOT = 216.362-014   GOE = 07.02.02

Receives and processes collection items (negotiable instruments), such as checks, bank drafts, and coupons, presented to a bank by a customer or corresponding bank.

Aptitudes:
Intelligence	Moderate
Verbal	Moderate
Numerical	Moderate
Spatial	Low
Form Perception	Moderate
Clerical Perception	High
Motor Coordination	Moderate
Finger Dexterity	Moderate
Manual Dexterity	Low
Eye-Hand-Foot Coordination	Low
Color Discrimination	Low

Data = Mod   People = Low   Things = Mod

Salary Range:
$11,300–$31,000

Opportunity Outlook:
14–24% growth

Environmental Conditions:
Inside

Physical Demands:
Sedentary—little or no lifting
Reaching, handling, fingering, and feeling required
Seeing required

Temperaments:
Performing repetitive tasks
Attempting to attain set limits

Vocational Preparation:
1/2–1 year

Bank Loan Counselor

DOT = 186.267-014   GOE = 07.01.01

Analyzes bank loan contracts and attempts to obtain payment of overdue installments from customers.

Aptitudes:
Intelligence	High
Verbal	High
Numerical	Moderate
Spatial	Low
Form Perception	Low
Clerical Perception	Moderate
Motor Coordination	Low
Finger Dexterity	Low
Manual Dexterity	Low
Eye-Hand-Foot Coordination	Low
Color Discrimination	Low

Data = High   People = Low   Things = Low

Salary Range:
$16,000–$50,000+

Opportunity Outlook:
25–34% growth

Environmental Conditions:
Inside

Physical Demands:
Sedentary—little or no lifting
Talking or hearing required

Temperaments:
Influencing the actions and beliefs of others
Making decisions based upon senses and feelings
Making decisions based upon facts

Vocational Preparation:
2–4 years

Bank President

DOT = 186.117-054   GOE = 11.05.01

Plans and directs the policies and practices of a bank, savings and loan institution, trust company, or mortgage company to insure that the financial objectives, goals, and growth are met in accordance with the corporate charter and governmental regulations.

Aptitudes:
Intelligence	High
Verbal	High
Numerical	Moderate
Spatial	Low
Form Perception	Low
Clerical Perception	Moderate
Motor Coordination	Low
Finger Dexterity	Low
Manual Dexterity	Low
Eye-Hand-Foot Coordination	Low
Color Discrimination	Low

Data = High   People = High   Things = Low

Salary Range:
$30,000–$100,000

Opportunity Outlook:
5–13% growth

Environmental Conditions:
Inside

Physical Demands:
Sedentary—little or no lifting
Talking or hearing required

Temperaments:
Directing, controlling, or planning the work of others
Making decisions based upon senses and feelings
Making decisions based upon facts
Dealing with people beyond giving and receiving information

Vocational Preparation:
Over 10 years

Bank Proof Machine Operator

DOT = 217.382-010   GOE = 07.06.02

Operates machines to sort, record, and prove records of bank transactions, such as checks, deposit slips, and withdrawal slips.

Aptitudes:
Intelligence	Moderate
Verbal	Moderate
Numerical	Moderate
Spatial	Low
Form Perception	Moderate
Clerical Perception	High
Motor Coordination	Moderate
Finger Dexterity	High
Manual Dexterity	Moderate
Eye-Hand-Foot Coordination	Low
Color Discrimination	Low

Data = Mod   People = Low   Things = Mod

Salary Range:
$10,000–$16,000

Opportunity Outlook:
14–24% growth

Environmental Conditions:
Inside
Presence of loud noises and vibrations

Physical Demands:
Sedentary—little or no lifting
Reaching, handling, fingering, and feeling required
Seeing required

Temperaments:
Performing repetitive tasks
Attempting to attain set limits

Vocational Preparation:
3–6 months

Bank Teller

DOT = 211.362-018   GOE = 07.06.01

Receives and pays out money to bank customers, and keeps records of money and negotiable instruments necessary to conduct various banking and financial transactions.

Aptitudes:
Intelligence	Moderate
Verbal	Moderate
Numerical	Moderate
Spatial	Low
Form Perception	Moderate
Clerical Perception	High
Motor Coordination	Moderate
Finger Dexterity	Moderate
Manual Dexterity	Moderate
Eye-Hand-Foot Coordination	Low
Color Discrimination	Low

Data = Mod   People = Low   Things = Mod

Salary Range:
$10,000–$21,500

Opportunity Outlook:
5% decline or more

Environmental Conditions:
Inside

Physical Demands:
Light—lifting of no more than 20 pounds
Reaching, handling, fingering, and feeling required
Talking or hearing required
Seeing required

Temperaments:
Performing repetitive tasks
Attempting to attain set limits

Vocational Preparation:
1/2–1 year

Barber

DOT = 330.371-010   GOE = 09.02.02

Cuts, blows-dries, trims, and tapers hair, using clippers, comb, hair-dryer, and scissors, as well as various hair care products.

Aptitudes:
Intelligence	Moderate
Verbal	Moderate
Numerical	Low
Spatial	Moderate
Form Perception	High
Clerical Perception	Low
Motor Coordination	High
Finger Dexterity	Moderate
Manual Dexterity	Moderate
Eye-Hand-Foot Coordination	Low
Color Discrimination	Low

Data = Mod   People = Low   Things = High

Salary Range:
$14,000–$30,000

Opportunity Outlook:
14–24% growth

Environmental Conditions:
Inside

Physical Demands:
Light—lifting of no more than 20 pounds
Reaching, handling, fingering, and feeling required
Talking or hearing required
Seeing required

Temperaments:
Making decisions based upon senses and feelings
Attempting to attain set limits

Vocational Preparation:
1–2 years

Bartender

DOT = 312.474-010   GOE = 09.04.01

Mixes and serves alcoholic and nonalcoholic drinks to patrons in a bar or restaurant.

Aptitudes:
Intelligence	Moderate
Verbal	Moderate
Numerical	Low
Spatial	Low
Form Perception	Low
Clerical Perception	Low
Motor Coordination	Low
Finger Dexterity	Low
Manual Dexterity	Moderate
Eye-Hand-Foot Coordination	Low
Color Discrimination	Low

Data = Mod   People = Mod   Things = Mod

Salary Range:
$9,500–$22,300

Opportunity Outlook:
25–34% growth

Environmental Conditions:
Inside

Physical Demands:
Light—lifting of no more than 20 pounds
Reaching, handling, fingering, and feeling required
Talking or hearing required
Seeing required

Temperaments:
Making decisions based upon facts

Vocational Preparation:
1–3 months

Bell Captain

DOT = 324.137-014   GOE = 09.05.03

Supervises bellhops who are engaged in such duties as paging guests, running errands, carrying luggage, and escorting guests to their rooms in a hotel.

Aptitudes:
Intelligence	Moderate
Verbal	Moderate
Numerical	Low
Spatial	Low
Form Perception	Low
Clerical Perception	Low
Motor Coordination	Low
Finger Dexterity	Low
Manual Dexterity	Low
Eye-Hand-Foot Coordination	Low
Color Discrimination	Low

Data = Mod   People = Mod   Things = Low

Salary Range:
$16,000–$25,000

Opportunity Outlook:
25–34% growth

Environmental Conditions:
Inside

Physical Demands:
Moderate—lifting of no more than 50 pounds
Reaching, handling, fingering, and feeling required
Talking or hearing required

Temperaments:
Performing a variety of tasks
Directing, controlling, or planning the work of others
Dealing with people beyond giving and receiving information

Vocational Preparation:
1–2 years

Bibliographer

DOT = 100.367-010   GOE = 11.02.04

Compiles lists of books, periodical articles, and audiovisual materials on specialized subjects for publishing companies, libraries, or individuals involved in a research project.

Aptitudes:
Intelligence	High
Verbal	High
Numerical	Moderate
Spatial	Low
Form Perception	Low
Clerical Perception	High
Motor Coordination	Low
Finger Dexterity	Low
Manual Dexterity	Low
Eye-Hand-Foot Coordination	Low
Color Discrimination	Low

Data = Mod   People = Low   Things = Low

Salary Range:
$23,400–$41,200

Opportunity Outlook:
5–13% growth

Environmental Conditions:
Inside

Physical Demands:
Sedentary—little or no lifting
Reaching, handling, fingering, and feeling required
Seeing required

Temperaments:
Making decisions based upon senses and feelings
Making decisions based upon facts
Attempting to attain set limits

Vocational Preparation:
2–4 years

Bill Collector

DOT = 241.367-010   GOE = 07.06.01

Locates customers to collect payments on overdue accounts, damage claims, or on nonpayable checks. May phone or visit customer in an attempt to collect the money due.

Aptitudes:
Intelligence	Moderate
Verbal	Moderate
Numerical	Moderate
Spatial	Low
Form Perception	Low
Clerical Perception	Moderate
Motor Coordination	Low
Finger Dexterity	Low
Manual Dexterity	Low
Eye-Hand-Foot Coordination	Low
Color Discrimination	Low

Data = Mod   People = Low   Things = Low

Salary Range:
$11,300–$31,000

Opportunity Outlook:
14–24% growth

Environmental Conditions:
Inside and outside

Physical Demands:
Light—lifting of no more than 20 pounds
Talking or hearing required

Temperaments:
Influencing the actions and beliefs of others

Vocational Preparation:
3–6 months

Billing Clerk

DOT = 214.362-042   GOE = 07.02.04

Operates calculator, typewriter, word processing machine, or computer to compile and prepare customer charges (bills) to be sent to customers for payment and collection.

Aptitudes:
Intelligence	Moderate
Verbal	Moderate
Numerical	Moderate
Spatial	Low
Form Perception	Low
Clerical Perception	High
Motor Coordination	Moderate
Finger Dexterity	Moderate
Manual Dexterity	Moderate
Eye-Hand-Foot Coordination	Low
Color Discrimination	Low

Data = Mod   People = Low   Things = High

Salary Range:
$16,700 (average)

Opportunity Outlook:
0–4% growth or decline

Environmental Conditions:
Inside

Physical Demands:
Sedentary—little or no lifting
Reaching, handling, fingering, and feeling required
Seeing required

Temperaments:
Performing repetitive tasks
Attempting to attain set limits

Vocational Preparation:
3–6 months

Biochemist

DOT = 041.061-026   GOE = 02.02.03

Studies the chemical processes of living organisms; conducts research to determine the effect of certain foods, drugs, serums, hormones, and other substances on tissues and vital processes of living organisms.

Aptitudes:
Intelligence	High
Verbal	High
Numerical	High
Spatial	High
Form Perception	High
Clerical Perception	High
Motor Coordination	Moderate
Finger Dexterity	Moderate
Manual Dexterity	Moderate
Eye-Hand-Foot Coordination	Low
Color Discrimination	Moderate

Data = High   People = Low   Things = High

Salary Range:
$13,100–$55,600

Opportunity Outlook:
25–34% growth

Environmental Conditions:
Inside

Physical Demands:
Light—lifting of no more than 20 pounds
Reaching, handling, fingering, and feeling required
Seeing required

Temperaments:
Making decisions based upon facts
Attempting to attain set limits

Vocational Preparation:
4–10 years

Biographer

DOT = 052.067-010   GOE = 01.01.02

Researches the life history of individuals and reconstructs their lives, usually in writing a book for publication.

Aptitudes:
Intelligence	High
Verbal	High
Numerical	Moderate
Spatial	Low
Form Perception	Low
Clerical Perception	High
Motor Coordination	Low
Finger Dexterity	Low
Manual Dexterity	Low
Eye-Hand-Foot Coordination	Low
Color Discrimination	Low

Data = High   People = Low   Things = Low

Salary Range:
Varies

Opportunity Outlook:
Not available

Environmental Conditions:
Inside

Physical Demands:
Sedentary—little or no lifting
Talking or hearing required

Temperaments:
Making decisions based upon senses and feelings
Making decisions based upon facts

Vocational Preparation:
2–4 years

Biologist

DOT = 041.061.030   GOE = 02.02.03

Studies the origin, relationship of one species to another, natural development, anatomy, functions, and other basic principles of plant and animal life.

Aptitudes:
Intelligence	High
Verbal	High
Numerical	Moderate
Spatial	High
Form Perception	High
Clerical Perception	Moderate
Motor Coordination	Moderate
Finger Dexterity	Moderate
Manual Dexterity	Moderate
Eye-Hand-Foot Coordination	Low
Color Discrimination	Moderate

Data = High   People = Low   Things = High

Salary Range:
$13,100–$55,600

Opportunity Outlook:
25–34% growth

Environmental Conditions:
Inside and outside

Physical Demands:
Light—lifting of no more than 20 pounds
Reaching, handling, fingering, and feeling required
Seeing required

Temperaments:
Making decisions based upon facts

Vocational Preparation:
4–10 years

Biomedical Equipment Technician

DOT = 019.261-010   GOE = 02.04.02

Repairs, calibrates, and maintains medical equipment and instruments used in a health-care facility, such as a hospital or nursing home, or a laboratory.

Aptitudes:
Intelligence	Moderate
Verbal	Moderate
Numerical	Moderate
Spatial	High
Form Perception	High
Clerical Perception	Moderate
Motor Coordination	Moderate
Finger Dexterity	Moderate
Manual Dexterity	Moderate
Eye-Hand-Foot Coordination	Low
Color Discrimination	Moderate

Data = High   People = Low   Things = High

Salary Range:
$16,000–$45,000

Opportunity Outlook:
35% growth or more

Environmental Conditions:
Inside

Physical Demands:
Light—lifting of no more than 20 pounds
Reaching, handling, fingering, and feeling required
Seeing required

Temperaments:
Making decisions based upon facts
Attempting to attain set limits

Vocational Preparation:
1–2 years

Blaster

DOT = 931.261-010   GOE = 05.10.06

Determines strength and pattern of explosive blast desired, and then detonates explosives in a mine, pit, or quarry to fracture and separate stone.

Aptitudes:
Intelligence	Moderate
Verbal	Low
Numerical	Low
Spatial	Moderate
Form Perception	Low
Clerical Perception	Low
Motor Coordination	Moderate
Finger Dexterity	Moderate
Manual Dexterity	Moderate
Eye-Hand-Foot Coordination	Low
Color Discrimination	Low

Data = Mod   People = Low   Things = High

Salary Range:
Not available

Opportunity Outlook:
Not available

Environmental Conditions:
Inside and outside
Presence of loud noises and vibrations
Presence of physical hazards
Presence of atmospheric dangers

Physical Demands:
Moderate—lifting of no more than 50 pounds
Climbing or balancing required
Stooping, kneeling, crouching, or crawling required
Reaching, handling, fingering, and feeling required
Seeing required

Temperaments:
Making decisions based upon facts
Performing under stressful, pressure-packed, or emergency conditions

Vocational Preparation:
2-4 years

Blood Laboratory Assistant

DOT = 078.687-010   GOE = 02.04.02

Performs routine laboratory tasks related to the processing of whole blood and blood components, tests blood samples for disease, and prepares the blood for storage and use at a later time.

Aptitudes:
Intelligence	Moderate
Verbal	Moderate
Numerical	Moderate
Spatial	Low
Form Perception	Low
Clerical Perception	Moderate
Motor Coordination	Moderate
Finger Dexterity	Moderate
Manual Dexterity	Moderate
Eye-Hand-Foot Coordination	Low
Color Discrimination	Moderate

Data = Mod   People = Low   Things = Mod

Salary Range:
$23,500–$42,000

Opportunity Outlook:
25–34% growth

Environmental Conditions:
Inside

Physical Demands:
Light—lifting of no more than 20 pounds
Reaching, handling, fingering, and feeling required
Seeing required

Temperaments:
Making decisions based upon facts
Making decisions based upon senses and feelings
Performing repetitive tasks
Attempting to attain set limits

Vocational Preparation:
1-2 years

Bodyguard

DOT = 372.667-014   GOE = 04.02.02

Escorts individuals when they travel to protect them from bodily injury, kidnapping, or invasion of their privacy.

Aptitudes:
Intelligence	Moderate
Verbal	Moderate
Numerical	Low
Spatial	Low
Form Perception	Low
Clerical Perception	Low
Motor Coordination	Moderate
Finger Dexterity	Low
Manual Dexterity	Moderate
Eye-Hand-Foot Coordination	Low
Color Discrimination	Low

Data = Low   People = Low   Things = Low

Salary Range:
Varies

Opportunity Outlook:
Not available

Environmental Conditions:
Inside and outside
Presence of physical hazards

Physical Demands:
Light—lifting of no more than 20 pounds
Reaching, handling, fingering, and feeling required
Talking or hearing required
Seeing required

Temperaments:
Dealing with people beyond giving and receiving information
Performing under stressful, pressure-packed, or emergency conditions
Making decisions based upon senses and feelings

Vocational Preparation:
1–3 months

Boiler Operator

DOT = 950.382-010   GOE = 05.06.02

Operates automatically fired boilers to generate steam that supplies heat or power for buildings or industrial plants.

Aptitudes:
Intelligence	Moderate
Verbal	Moderate
Numerical	Moderate
Spatial	Moderate
Form Perception	Low
Clerical Perception	Moderate
Motor Coordination	Moderate
Finger Dexterity	Moderate
Manual Dexterity	Moderate
Eye-Hand-Foot Coordination	Low
Color Discrimination	Low

Data = Mod   People = Low   Things = Mod

Salary Range:
$22,000 (average)

Opportunity Outlook:
0–4% growth or decline

Environmental Conditions:
Inside
Extremely hot work environment
Presence of loud noises and vibrations
Presence of physical hazards

Physical Demands:
Moderate—lifting of no more than 50 pounds
Reaching, handling, fingering, and feeling required
Seeing required

Temperaments:
Making decisions based upon facts
Attempting to attain set limits

Vocational Preparation:
2–4 years

Bookkeeper

DOT = 210.382-018   GOE = 07.02.01

Keeps and maintains a set of financial records for a company, association, or organization to help accountants understand the financial condition of the institution. Records daily financial transactions.

Aptitudes:
Intelligence	Moderate
Verbal	Moderate
Numerical	High
Spatial	Low
Form Perception	Moderate
Clerical Perception	High
Motor Coordination	Moderate
Finger Dexterity	Moderate
Manual Dexterity	Moderate
Eye-Hand-Foot Coordination	Low
Color Discrimination	Low

Data = Mod   People = Low   Things = Mod

Salary Range:
$16,500 (average)

Opportunity Outlook:
5% decline or more

Environmental Conditions:
Inside

Physical Demands:
Sedentary—little or no lifting
Reaching, handling, fingering, and feeling required
Seeing required

Temperaments:
Attempting to attain set limits

Vocational Preparation:
3–6 months

Botanist

DOT = 041.061-038   GOE = 02.02.02

Studies the development and life processes, physiology, heredity, environment, anatomy, morphology, and economic value of plants for use in such fields as agronomy, forestry, horticulture, and pharmacology.

Aptitudes:
Intelligence	High
Verbal	High
Numerical	Moderate
Spatial	High
Form Perception	High
Clerical Perception	Moderate
Motor Coordination	Moderate
Finger Dexterity	Moderate
Manual Dexterity	Low
Eye-Hand-Foot Coordination	Low
Color Discrimination	Moderate

Data = High   People = Low   Things = High

Salary Range:
$13,100–$55,600

Opportunity Outlook:
25–34% growth

Environmental Conditions:
Inside and outside

Physical Demands:
Light—lifting of no more than 20 pounds
Stooping, kneeling, crouching, or crawling required
Reaching, handling, fingering, and feeling required
Seeing required

Temperaments:
Making decisions based upon facts
Making decisions based upon senses and feelings

Vocational Preparation:
4–10 years

Bricklayer

DOT = 861.381-018   GOE = 05.05.01

Lays building materials, such as brick, structural tile, concrete cinder, glass, gypsum, or terra cotta blocks to construct or repair walls, partitions, arches, sewers, and other structures.

Aptitudes:
Intelligence	Moderate
Verbal	Moderate
Numerical	Moderate
Spatial	Moderate
Form Perception	Moderate
Clerical Perception	Low
Motor Coordination	Moderate
Finger Dexterity	Moderate
Manual Dexterity	Moderate
Eye-Hand-Foot Coordination	Moderate
Color Discrimination	Low

Data = Mod   People = Low   Things = High

Salary Range:
$14,500–$43,500

Opportunity Outlook:
14–24% growth

Environmental Conditions:
Inside and outside
Presence of physical hazards

Physical Demands:
Moderate—lifting of no more than 50 pounds
Climbing or balancing required
Stooping, kneeling, crouching, or crawling required
Reaching, handling, fingering, and feeling required
Seeing required

Temperaments:
Making decisions based upon facts
Attempting to attain set limits

Vocational Preparation:
1/2–1 year

Bridge Inspector

DOT = 869.287-010   GOE = 05.07.01

Inspects railroad bridges, trestles, culverts, and waterways to detect damage or wear and to ensure that structures conform to safety regulations, building codes, and engineering specifications.

Aptitudes:
Intelligence	High
Verbal	Moderate
Numerical	Moderate
Spatial	High
Form Perception	High
Clerical Perception	Moderate
Motor Coordination	Low
Finger Dexterity	Low
Manual Dexterity	Low
Eye-Hand-Foot Coordination	Low
Color Discrimination	Low

Data = Mod   People = Low   Things = Low

Salary Range:
$19,000–$46,000

Opportunity Outlook:
14–24% growth

Environmental Conditions:
Outside

Physical Demands:
Moderate—lifting of no more than 50 pounds
Climbing or balancing required
Stooping, kneeling, crouching, or crawling required
Reaching, handling, fingering, and feeling required
Seeing required

Temperaments:
Performing a variety of tasks
Making decisions based upon senses and feelings
Making decisions based upon facts
Attempting to attain set limits

Vocational Preparation:
2–4 years

Budget Analyst

DOT = 161.267-030   GOE = 11.06.05

Analyzes current and past financial budgets, prepares and justifies budget requests, and allocates funds according to the spending priorities determined by the management team of a business, organization, or institution.

Aptitudes:
Intelligence	High
Verbal	High
Numerical	High
Spatial	Low
Form Perception	Low
Clerical Perception	High
Motor Coordination	Low
Finger Dexterity	Low
Manual Dexterity	Low
Eye-Hand-Foot Coordination	Low
Color Discrimination	Low

Data = High   People = Low   Things = Low

Salary Range:
$16,900–$40,500

Opportunity Outlook:
14–24% growth

Environmental Conditions:
Inside

Physical Demands:
Sedentary—little or no lifting
Reaching, handling, fingering, and feeling required
Seeing required

Temperaments:
Directing, controlling, or planning the work of others
Making decisions based upon senses and feelings
Attempting to attain set limits

Vocational Preparation:
2–4 years

Building Inspector

DOT = 168.167-030   GOE = 05.03.06

Inspects new and existing buildings and structures to enforce conformance to building, grading, and zoning laws and approved plans, specifications, and standards.

Aptitudes:
Intelligence	High
Verbal	Moderate
Numerical	Moderate
Spatial	High
Form Perception	Moderate
Clerical Perception	Moderate
Motor Coordination	Low
Finger Dexterity	Low
Manual Dexterity	Low
Eye-Hand-Foot Coordination	Moderate
Color Discrimination	Low

Data = Mod   People = Low   Things = Low

Salary Range:
$19,700–$46,000

Opportunity Outlook:
14–24% growth

Environmental Conditions:
Inside and outside

Physical Demands:
Light—lifting of no more than 20 pounds required
Climbing or balancing required
Stooping, kneeling, crouching, or crawling required
Talking or hearing required
Seeing required

Temperaments:
Dealing with people beyond giving and receiving information
Making decisions based upon senses and feelings
Making decisions based upon facts
Attempting to attain set limits

Vocational Preparation:
2–4 years

Bulldozer Operator

DOT = 850.683-010   GOE = 05.11.01

Operates a tractor equipped with a blade to gouge, level, or distribute earth or to push trees and rocks from land to build roads or buildings or to plant crops, or in mining, quarrying, and lumbering operations.

Aptitudes:
Intelligence	Moderate
Verbal	Low
Numerical	Low
Spatial	Moderate
Form Perception	Moderate
Clerical Perception	Low
Motor Coordination	Moderate
Finger Dexterity	Moderate
Manual Dexterity	Moderate
Eye-Hand-Foot Coordination	Moderate
Color Discrimination	Low

Data = Low   People = Low   Things = Mod

Salary Range:
$13,000–$38,000

Opportunity Outlook:
25–34% growth

Environmental Conditions:
Outside
Presence of physical hazards
Presence of atmospheric dangers

Physical Demands:
Heavy—lifting of no more than 100 pounds required
Climbing or balancing required
Stooping, kneeling, crouching, or crawling required
Reaching, handling, fingering, or feeling required
Talking or hearing required
Seeing required

Temperaments:
Making decisions based upon senses and feelings
Attempting to attain set limits

Vocational Preparation:
1/2–1 year

Bus Driver

DOT = 913.463-010   GOE = 09.03.01

Drives a bus to transport passengers over a specified route to a local or distant location according to a predetermined schedule.

Aptitudes:
Intelligence	Moderate
Verbal	Moderate
Numerical	Low
Spatial	Moderate
Form Perception	Low
Clerical Perception	Low
Motor Coordination	Moderate
Finger Dexterity	Low
Manual Dexterity	Moderate
Eye-Hand-Foot Coordination	Moderate
Color Discrimination	Low

Data = Mod   People = Low   Things = Mod

Salary Range:
$10,400–$31,700

Opportunity Outlook:
25–34% growth

Environmental Conditions:
Inside
Presence of loud noises and vibrations

Physical Demands:
Moderate—lifting of no more than 50 pounds required
Reaching, handling, fingering, or feeling required
Talking or hearing required
Seeing required

Temperaments:
Making decisions based upon facts
Making decisions based upon senses and feelings

Vocational Preparation:
1/2–1 year

Business Manager (College/University)

DOT = 186.117-010   GOE = 11.05.02

Manages the business affairs of a college or university; prepares operating budget for approval by President or Board of Trustees; responsible for collection, custody, investment, disbursement, accounting, and auditing of all monies.

Aptitudes:
Intelligence	High
Verbal	High
Numerical	High
Spatial	Low
Form Perception	Low
Clerical Perception	High
Motor Coordination	Low
Finger Dexterity	Low
Manual Dexterity	Low
Eye-Hand-Foot Coordination	Low
Color Discrimination	Low

Data = High   People = High   Things = Low

Salary Range:
Not available

Opportunity Outlook:
Not available

Environmental Conditions:
Inside

Physical Demands:
Sedentary—little or no lifting
Talking or hearing required

Temperaments:
Directing, controlling, or planning the work of others
Dealing with people beyond giving and receiving information
Making decisions based upon senses and feelings
Making decisions based upon facts

Vocational Preparation:
4–10 years

Buyer

DOT = 162.157-018   GOE = 08.01.03

Purchases merchandise or commodities for resale. May inspect, grade, or appraise the merchandise to ensure it meets the specifications as determined by the company or individual wishing to buy the merchandise.

Aptitudes:
Intelligence	High
Verbal	High
Numerical	High
Spatial	Low
Form Perception	Moderate
Clerical Perception	Moderate
Motor Coordination	Low
Finger Dexterity	Low
Manual Dexterity	Low
Eye-Hand-Foot Coordination	Low
Color Discrimination	Low

Data = High   People = Mod   Things = Low

Salary Range:
$13,500–$46,700

Opportunity Outlook:
14–24% growth

Environmental Conditions:
Inside

Physical Demands:
Light lifting required
Reaching, handling, fingering, or feeling required
Talking or hearing required

Temperaments:
Influencing the actions and beliefs of others
Making decisions based upon senses and feelings
Dealing with people beyond giving and receiving information
Performing a variety of tasks

Vocational Preparation:
1–2 years

Cable Maintainer (Light/Heat/Power)

DOT = 952.464-010   GOE = 05.06.01

Maintains pressure in oil-filled and gas-filled cable used to transmit high-voltage electricity. Inspects and repairs damaged cables when necessary.

Aptitudes:
Intelligence	Moderate
Verbal	Moderate
Numerical	Moderate
Spatial	Moderate
Form Perception	Low
Clerical Perception	Low
Motor Coordination	Low
Finger Dexterity	Moderate
Manual Dexterity	Moderate
Eye-Hand-Foot Coordination	Low
Color Discrimination	Low

Data = Mod   People = Low   Things = Mod

Salary Range:
$24,000 (average)

Opportunity Outlook:
25–34% growth

Environmental Conditions:
Outside
Wet and humid work environment
Presence of physical hazards

Physical Demands:
Light—lifting of no more than 20 rounds required
Climbing or balancing required
Stooping, kneeling, crouching, or crawling required
Reaching, handling, fingering, or feeling required

Temperaments:
Making decisions based upon facts
Attempting to attain set limits

Vocational Preparation:
1/2–1 year

Cafeteria Attendant

DOT = 311.677-010   GOE = 09.05.02

Carries trays from food counters to tables for cafeteria patrons, as well as dirty dishes to the kitchen; may set tables with clean linen, silverware, and other items to prepare table for use by patrons.

Aptitudes:
Intelligence	Low
Verbal	Low
Numerical	Low
Spatial	Low
Form Perception	Low
Clerical Perception	Low
Motor Coordination	Low
Finger Dexterity	Low
Manual Dexterity	Moderate
Eye-Hand-Foot Coordination	Low
Color Discrimination	Low

Data = Low   People = Low   Things = Low

Salary Range:
$8,000–$10,400

Opportunity Outlook:
25–34% growth

Environmental Conditions:
Inside

Physical Demands:
Light—lifting of no more than 20 pounds required
Reaching, handling, fingering, or feeling required

Temperaments:
Performing repetitive tasks

Vocational Preparation:
1–30 days

Car Rental Vehicle Deliverer

DOT = 919.663-010   GOE = 05.08.03

Delivers rental cars to customers, servicing them prior to delivery; may clean interior, wash windows, inflate tires, check fluids, or add gas and oil to ensure vehicle is in proper working condition.

Aptitudes:
Intelligence	Low
Verbal	Low
Numerical	Low
Spatial	Moderate
Form Perception	Low
Clerical Perception	Low
Motor Coordination	Moderate
Finger Dexterity	Low
Manual Dexterity	Moderate
Eye-Hand-Foot Coordination	Moderate
Color Discrimination	Low

Data = Low   People = Low   Things = Mod

Salary Range:
Varies

Opportunity Outlook:
Not available

Environmental Conditions:
Inside and outside

Physical Demands:
Light—lifting of no more than 20 pounds required
Reaching, handling, fingering, or feeling required
Talking or hearing required
Seeing required

Temperaments:
Performing repetitive tasks

Vocational Preparation:
1–3 months

Cardiopulmonary Technologist

DOT = 078.362-030   GOE = 10.03.01

Performs diagnostic tests of heart and lung systems of hospital patients, using a variety of laboratory equipment and devices to help physicians diagnose and treat these kinds of health problems.

Aptitudes:
Intelligence	High
Verbal	High
Numerical	High
Spatial	Moderate
Form Perception	High
Clerical Perception	High
Motor Coordination	High
Finger Dexterity	Moderate
Manual Dexterity	Moderate
Eye-Hand-Foot Coordination	Low
Color Discrimination	Moderate

Data = Mod   People = Low   Things = Mod

Salary Range:
$14,000–$28,000

Opportunity Outlook:
14–24% growth

Environmental Conditions:
Inside

Physical Demands:
Light—lifting of no more than 20 pounds required
Reaching, handling, fingering, or feeling required
Talking or hearing required
Seeing required

Temperaments:
Attempting to attain set limits
Making decisions based upon facts

Vocational Preparation:
2–4 years

Cargo Agent

DOT = 248.367-018   GOE = 05.09.01

Plans the route inbound and outbound air freight should take to get to its desired destination; may make arrangements with customers as to where freight may be dropped off or picked up by customers.

Aptitudes:

Intelligence	Moderate
Verbal	Moderate
Numerical	Moderate
Spatial	Moderate
Form Perception	Low
Clerical Perception	Moderate
Motor Coordination	Moderate
Finger Dexterity	Moderate
Manual Dexterity	Moderate
Eye-Hand-Foot Coordination	Low
Color Discrimination	Low

Data = Mod   People = Low   Things = Low

Salary Range:
$14,000–$20,000

Opportunity Outlook:
14–24% growth

Environmental Conditions:
Inside

Physical Demands:
Moderate—lifting of no more than 50 pounds required
Reaching, handling, fingering, or feeling required
Talking or hearing required

Temperaments:
Making decisions based upon facts
Performing a variety of tasks

Vocational Preparation:
1/2–1 year

Carpenter

DOT = 860.381-022   GOE = 05.05.02

Constructs, erects, installs, and repairs structures and fixtures of wood, plywood, or wallboard, using carpenter's handtools and various power tools according to predetermined plans or building codes; usually involved in building homes, office buildings, and other similar structures.

Aptitudes:

Intelligence	Moderate
Verbal	Moderate
Numerical	Moderate
Spatial	Moderate
Form Perception	Moderate
Clerical Perception	Low
Motor Coordination	Moderate
Finger Dexterity	Moderate
Manual Dexterity	Moderate
Eye-Hand-Foot Coordination	Moderate
Color Discrimination	Low

Data = Mod   People = Low   Things = High

Salary Range:
$12,400–$38,500

Opportunity Outlook:
14–24% growth

Environmental Conditions:
Inside and outside
Presence of loud noises and vibrations
Presence of physical hazards

Physical Demands:
Moderate—lifting of no more than 50 pounds
Climbing or balancing required
Stooping, kneeling, crouching, or crawling required
Reaching, handling, fingering, or feeling required
Seeing required

Temperaments:
Performing a variety of tasks
Making decisions based upon facts
Attempting to attain set limits

Vocational Preparation:
2–4 years

Carpet & Rug Weaver

DOT = 683.682-034   GOE = 06.02.06

Operates power looms equipped with rollers and shuttles to weave twisted yarns and other similar materials to produce carpets and rugs.

Aptitudes:
Intelligence	Moderate
Verbal	Low
Numerical	Low
Spatial	Moderate
Form Perception	Moderate
Clerical Perception	Low
Motor Coordination	Moderate
Finger Dexterity	Moderate
Manual Dexterity	Moderate
Eye-Hand-Foot Coordination	Moderate
Color Discrimination	Moderate

Data = Low   People = Low   Things = Mod

Salary Range:
$14,000–$18,000

Opportunity Outlook:
0–4% growth or decline

Environmental Conditions:
Inside
Presence of loud noises and vibrations

Physical Demands:
Moderate—lifting of no more than 50 pounds required
Climbing or balancing required
Stooping, kneeling, crouching, or crawling required
Reaching, handling, fingering, or feeling required
Seeing required

Temperaments:
Performing repetitive tasks
Attempting to attain set limits

Vocational Preparation:
1/2–1 year

Cashier (Gambling Casino)

DOT = 211.462-022   GOE = 07.03.01

Accepts and pays off bets placed by patrons of cardrooms, bookmaking, or other gambling establishments.

Aptitudes:
Intelligence	Moderate
Verbal	Moderate
Numerical	Moderate
Spatial	Low
Form Perception	Low
Clerical Perception	Moderate
Motor Coordination	Moderate
Finger Dexterity	Moderate
Manual Dexterity	Low
Eye-Hand-Foot Coordination	Low
Color Discrimination	Moderate

Data = Mod   People = Low   Things = Mod

Salary Range:
$7,400–$20,600

Opportunity Outlook:
25–34% growth

Environmental Conditions:
Inside

Physical Demands:
Sedentary—little or no lifting
Reaching, handling, fingering, or feeling required
Talking or hearing required
Seeing required

Temperaments:
Performing repetitive tasks
Attempting to attain set limits

Vocational Preparation:
3–6 months

Casting Director

DOT = 159.267-010   GOE = 01.03.01

Auditions and interviews performers for specific parts in a play or movie, considering such factors as physical size and appearance, quality of voice, expressiveness, and experience.

Aptitudes:
Intelligence	High
Verbal	High
Numerical	Moderate
Spatial	Low
Form Perception	Low
Clerical Perception	Moderate
Motor Coordination	Low
Finger Dexterity	Low
Manual Dexterity	Low
Eye-Hand-Foot Coordination	Low
Color Discrimination	Moderate

Data = High   People = Mod   Things = Low

Salary Range:
Not available

Opportunity Outlook:
Not available

Environmental Conditions:
Inside

Physical Demands:
Sedentary—little or no lifting
Talking or hearing required
Seeing required

Temperaments:
Performing a variety of tasks
Dealing with people beyond giving and receiving information
Making decisions based upon senses and feelings

Vocational Preparation:
2-4 years

Cemetery Supervisor

DOT = 406.134-010   GOE = 03.02.03

Supervises and coordinates activities of workers engaged in preparing grave sites, maintaining cemetery grounds, and in keeping the cemetery property in proper order.

Aptitudes:
Intelligence	Moderate
Verbal	Moderate
Numerical	Low
Spatial	Moderate
Form Perception	Low
Clerical Perception	Low
Motor Coordination	Low
Finger Dexterity	Low
Manual Dexterity	Moderate
Eye-Hand-Foot Coordination	Low
Color Discrimination	Low

Data = Mod   People = Mod   Things = Mod

Salary Range:
$12,500-$28,000

Opportunity Outlook:
35% growth or more

Environmental Conditions:
Outside
Presence of loud noises and vibrations

Physical Demands:
Moderate—lifting of no more than 50 pounds required
Reaching, handling, fingering, or feeling required
Talking or hearing required
Seeing required

Temperaments:
Directing, controlling, or planning the work of others
Making decisions based upon senses and feelings
Making decisions based upon facts
Dealing with people beyond giving and receiving information

Vocational Preparation: 1-2 years

Chauffeur

DOT = 913.663-010   GOE = 09.03.02

Drives automobile or limousine to transport individuals from one location to another; may work for a private individual, company, or limo service.

Aptitudes:
Intelligence	Moderate
Verbal	Low
Numerical	Low
Spatial	Moderate
Form Perception	Low
Clerical Perception	Low
Motor Coordination	Moderate
Finger Dexterity	Low
Manual Dexterity	Moderate
Eye-Hand-Foot Coordination	Moderate
Color Discrimination	Low

Data = Low   People = Low   Things = Mod

Salary Range:
$15,000–$30,000

Opportunity Outlook:
25–34% growth

Environmental Conditions:
Inside and outside

Physical Demands:
Light—lifting of no more than 20 pounds required
Reaching, handling, fingering, and feeling required
Seeing required

Temperaments:
Making decisions based upon facts
Making decisions based upon senses and feelings

Vocational Preparation:
1–3 months

Check Cashier

DOT = 211.462.026   GOE = 07.03.01

Cashes checks, prepares money orders, receives payment for utility bills, and collects and records fees charged for check-cashing service.

Aptitudes:
Intelligence	Moderate
Verbal	Moderate
Numerical	Moderate
Spatial	Low
Form Perception	Low
Clerical Perception	Moderate
Motor Coordination	Low
Finger Dexterity	Low
Manual Dexterity	Low
Eye-Hand-Foot Coordination	Low
Color Discrimination	Low

Data = Mod   People = Low   Things = Mod

Salary Range:
$7,400–$20,000

Opportunity Outlook:
25–34% growth

Environmental Conditions:
Inside

Physical Demands:
Sedentary—little or no lifting
Reaching, handling, fingering, or feeling required
Talking or hearing required

Temperaments:
Performing repetitive tasks
Attempting to attain set limits

Vocational Preparation:
1–3 months

Chemical-Laboratory Technician

DOT = 022.261-010   GOE = 02.04.01

Conducts chemical and physical laboratory tests and analyzes materials, liquids, and gases for research, development of new materials, processing and production methods, quality control, criminology, environmental, and other applications.

Aptitudes:
Intelligence	High
Verbal	High
Numerical	Moderate
Spatial	Moderate
Form Perception	High
Clerical Perception	Moderate
Motor Coordination	Moderate
Finger Dexterity	Moderate
Manual Dexterity	Moderate
Eye-Hand-Foot Coordination	Low
Color Discrimination	Low

Data = High   People = Low   Things = High

Salary Range:
$13,700–$42,600

Opportunity Outlook:
14–24% growth

Environmental Conditions:
Inside
Presence of atmospheric dangers

Physical Demands:
Light—lifting of no more than 20 pounds required
Reaching, handling, fingering, or feeling required
Seeing required

Temperaments:
Making decisions based upon facts
Attempting to attain set limits

Vocational Preparation:
2–4 years

Chemical Processing Supervisor

DOT = 559.130-010   GOE = 06.01.01

Supervises and coordinates activities of workers engaged in processing organic chemicals, plant and animal tissue, and solvents for use in manufacturing medications.

Aptitudes:
Intelligence	Moderate
Verbal	Moderate
Numerical	Moderate
Spatial	Moderate
Form Perception	Moderate
Clerical Perception	Moderate
Motor Coordination	Moderate
Finger Dexterity	Low
Manual Dexterity	Moderate
Eye-Hand-Foot Coordination	Low
Color Discrimination	Low

Data = High   People = Mod   Things = Mod

Salary Range:
$22,000–$29,000

Opportunity Outlook:
14–24% growth

Environmental Conditions:
Inside
Presence of loud noises and vibrations
Presence of atmospheric dangers such as fumes

Physical Demands:
Moderate—lifting of no more than 50 pounds
Reaching, handling, fingering, or feeling required

Temperaments:
Directing, controlling, or planning the work of others
Dealing with people beyond giving and receiving information
Making decisions based upon facts
Attempting to attain set limits

Vocational Preparation:
4–10 years

Chemical Test Engineer

DOT = 008.061-026   GOE = 05.01.04

Conducts tests on chemicals, fuels, and processes used to manufacturer chemicals and fuels.

Aptitudes:
Intelligence	High
Verbal	High
Numerical	High
Spatial	High
Form Perception	Moderate
Clerical Perception	Moderate
Motor Coordination	Moderate
Finger Dexterity	Moderate
Manual Dexterity	Moderate
Eye-Hand-Foot Coordination	Low
Color Discrimination	Moderate

Data = High   People = Low   Things = High

Salary Range:
$28,000–$36,000

Opportunity Outlook:
5–13% growth

Environmental Conditions:
Inside
Presence of atmospheric dangers such as fumes, odors, etc.

Physical Demands:
Light—lifting of no more than 20 pounds required
Reaching, handling, fingering, or feeling required
Seeing required

Temperaments:
Performing a variety of tasks
Making decisions based upon facts
Attempting to attain set limits

Vocational Preparation:
4–10 years

Chemist

DOT = 022.061-010   GOE = 02.01.01

Conducts research, analysis, and experimentation on chemicals, liquids, solids, and gaseous materials, substances, and compounds to develop new products and processes, improve quality control, analyze the quantity and quality of various substances, and find new uses for various products.

Aptitudes:
Intelligence	High
Verbal	High
Numerical	High
Spatial	High
Form Perception	High
Clerical Perception	High
Motor Coordination	Moderate
Finger Dexterity	Moderate
Manual Dexterity	Moderate
Eye-Hand-Foot Coordination	Low
Color Discrimination	Moderate

Data = High   People = Low   Things = High

Salary Range:
$23,000–$55,000

Opportunity Outlook:
14–24% growth

Environmental Conditions:
Inside
Presence of atmospheric dangers such as fumes, odors, etc.

Physical Demands:
Light—lifting of no more than 20 pounds required
Reaching, handling, fingering, or feeling required
Seeing required

Temperaments:
Directing, controlling, or planning the work of others
Making decisions based upon facts
Attempting to attain set limits
Performing a variety of tasks

Vocational Preparation:
4–10 years

Chief Bank Examiner

DOT = 160.167-046   GOE = 11.10.01

Directs the investigation of banking practices within a particular state to enforce laws governing banking procedures and to ensure the financial solvency of all financial institutions.

Aptitudes:
Intelligence	High
Verbal	High
Numerical	High
Spatial	Low
Form Perception	Low
Clerical Perception	High
Motor Coordination	Low
Finger Dexterity	Low
Manual Dexterity	Low
Eye-Hand-Foot Coordination	Low
Color Discrimination	Low

Data = High   People = Mod   Things = Low

Salary Range:
$28,000–$60,000

Opportunity Outlook:
25–34% growth

Environmental Conditions:
Inside

Physical Demands:
Sedentary—little or no lifting
Talking or hearing required

Temperaments:
Performing a variety of tasks
Directing, controlling, or planning the work of others
Dealing with people beyond giving and receiving information
Making decisions based upon senses and feelings
Making decisions based upon facts

Vocational Preparation:
4–10 years

Chief Deputy Sheriff

DOT = 377.167-010   GOE = 04.01.01

Directs and coordinates the activities of a county sheriff's office, supervising all criminal investigations, managing personnel policies, and handling other management-related activities.

Aptitudes:
Intelligence	High
Verbal	High
Numerical	Moderate
Spatial	Low
Form Perception	Moderate
Clerical Perception	Moderate
Motor Coordination	Moderate
Finger Dexterity	Low
Manual Dexterity	Low
Eye-Hand-Foot Coordination	Low
Color Discrimination	Low

Data = High   People = Mod   Things = Low

Salary Range:
$22,000–$65,000

Opportunity Outlook:
14–24% growth

Environmental Conditions:
Inside and outside
Presence of physical hazards

Physical Demands:
Sedentary—little or no lifting
Talking or hearing required

Temperaments:
Directing, controlling, or planning the work of others
Dealing with people beyond giving and receiving information
Performing under stress or in emergencies
Making decisions based upon senses and feelings

Vocational Preparation:
4–10 years

Children's Librarian

DOT = 100.167-018 GOE = 11.02.04

Manages a special collection of books and other materials within a library especially for children; selects books and other materials for purchase, plans and conducts programs for children, and prepares materials for use by teachers and other professionals working with children.

Aptitudes:
Intelligence	High
Verbal	High
Numerical	Moderate
Spatial	Low
Form Perception	Low
Clerical Perception	Moderate
Motor Coordination	Low
Finger Dexterity	Low
Manual Dexterity	Low
Eye-Hand-Foot Coordination	Low
Color Discrimination	Low

Data = High   People = Low   Things = Low

Salary Range:
$23,400–$31,100

Opportunity Outlook:
5–13% growth

Environmental Conditions:
Inside

Physical Demands:
Light—lifting of no more than 20 pounds required
Talking or hearing required
Reaching, handling, fingering, and feeling required

Temperaments:
Performing a variety of tasks
Making decisions based upon senses and feelings

Vocational Preparation:
2–4 years

Chiropractor

DOT = 079.101-010 GOE = 02.03.04

Adjusts the spinal column and other skeletal parts of the human body to correct abnormalities that cause discomfort and pain.

Aptitudes:
Intelligence	High
Verbal	High
Numerical	Moderate
Spatial	High
Form Perception	High
Clerical Perception	Low
Motor Coordination	High
Finger Dexterity	High
Manual Dexterity	High
Eye-Hand-Foot Coordination	Low
Color Discrimination	Low

Data = High   People = High   Things = High

Salary Range:
$24,000–$180,000

Opportunity Outlook:
25–34% growth

Environmental Conditions:
Inside

Physical Demands:
Moderate—lifting of no more than 50 pounds required
Reaching, handling, fingering, or feeling required
Talking or hearing required

Temperaments:
Directing, controlling, or planning the work of others
Dealing with people beyond giving and receiving information
Making decisions based upon senses and feelings
Making decisions based upon facts

Vocational Preparation:
2–4 years

Choral Director

DOT = 152.047-010   GOE = 01.04.01

Conducts vocal music groups, such as choirs and glee clubs, auditions and selects members, selects music to suit performance and expertise of members, and directs the group during rehearsals and actual performance.

Aptitudes:
Intelligence	High
Verbal	High
Numerical	Moderate
Spatial	Moderate
Form Perception	High
Clerical Perception	Moderate
Motor Coordination	High
Finger Dexterity	Moderate
Manual Dexterity	Moderate
Eye-Hand-Foot Coordination	Low
Color Discrimination	Low

Data = High   People = Mod   Things = Low

Salary Range:
Varies

Opportunity Outlook:
14–24% growth

Environmental Conditions:
Inside

Physical Demands:
Light—lifting of no more than 20 pounds required
Reaching, handling, fingering, or feeling required
Talking or hearing required
Seeing required

Temperaments:
Directing, controlling, or planning the work of others
Dealing with people beyond giving and receiving information
Making decisions based upon senses and feelings
Interpreting the feelings and ideas of others

Vocational Preparation:
4–10 years

Choreographer

DOT = 151.027-010   GOE = 01.05.01

Creates and teaches original dance routines for ballets, musicals, or revues to be performed on stage or for television, motion pictures, or nightclub production.

Aptitudes:
Intelligence	High
Verbal	High
Numerical	Moderate
Spatial	Moderate
Form Perception	Moderate
Clerical Perception	Low
Motor Coordination	Low
Finger Dexterity	Low
Manual Dexterity	Moderate
Eye-Hand-Foot Coordination	High
Color Discrimination	Moderate

Data = High   People = High   Things = Low

Salary Range:
Varies

Opportunity Outlook:
35% growth or more

Environmental Conditions:
Inside

Physical Demands:
Light—lifting of no more than 20 pounds required
Talking or hearing required
Seeing required

Temperaments:
Directing, controlling, or planning the work of others
Interpreting the feelings and ideas of others
Making decisions based upon senses and feelings
Dealing with people beyond giving and receiving information
Performing a variety of tasks

Vocational Preparation:
4–10 years

City Manager

DOT = 188.117-114   GOE = 11.05.03

Directs and coordinates the administrative functions of a city or county government in accordance with the policies determined by the city council or other authorized elected officials.

Aptitudes:
Intelligence	High
Verbal	High
Numerical	Moderate
Spatial	Low
Form Perception	Low
Clerical Perception	Low
Motor Coordination	Low
Finger Dexterity	Low
Manual Dexterity	Low
Eye-Hand-Foot Coordination	Low
Color Discrimination	Low

Data = High   People = High   Things = Low

Salary Range:
$33,000–$125,000

Opportunity Outlook:
0–4% growth or decline

Environmental Conditions:
Inside

Physical Demands:
Sedentary—little or no lifting
Talking or hearing required

Temperaments:
Directing, controlling, or planning the work of others
Making decisions based upon senses and feelings
Dealing with people beyond giving and receiving information
Performing a variety of tasks

Vocational Preparation:
4–10 years

Civil Engineer

DOT = 005.061-014   GOE = 05.01.07

Plans, designs, and directs the construction and maintenance of such structures and facilities as roads, railroads, airports, bridges, harbors, channels, dams, irrigation projects, water and sewage systems, and waste disposal units.

Aptitudes:
Intelligence	High
Verbal	High
Numerical	High
Spatial	High
Form Perception	High
Clerical Perception	High
Motor Coordination	Moderate
Finger Dexterity	Moderate
Manual Dexterity	Moderate
Eye-Hand-Foot Coordination	Low
Color Discrimination	Moderate

Data = High   People = Mod   Things = High

Salary Range:
$24,000–$58,000

Opportunity Outlook:
25–34% growth

Environmental Conditions
Inside and outside

Physical Demands:
Light—lifting of no more than 20 pounds required
Reaching, handling, fingering, or feeling required
Seeing required

Temperaments:
Performing a variety of tasks
Making decisions based upon facts
Directing, controlling, or planning the work of others
Attempting to attain set limits

Vocational Preparation:
4–10 years

Claim Examiner

DOT = 241.267-018   GOE = 11.12.01

Analyzes insurance claims to determine extent of insurance company's liability and then attempts to settle claims with individuals who have filed a claim for compensation in accordance with the policy provisions as stated in the insurance contract.

Aptitudes:

Intelligence	High
Verbal	High
Numerical	Moderate
Spatial	Low
Form Perception	Low
Clerical Perception	High
Motor Coordination	Low
Finger Dexterity	Low
Manual Dexterity	Low
Eye-Hand-Foot Coordination	Low
Color Discrimination	Low

Data = High   People = Mod   Things = Low

Salary Range:
$30,000 (average)

Opportunity Outlook:
14–24% growth

Environmental Conditions:
Inside

Physical Demands:
Sedentary—little or no lifting
Reaching, handling, fingering, or feeling required
Talking or hearing required

Temperaments:
Making decisions based upon facts
Dealing with people beyond giving and receiving information

Vocational Preparation:
2–4 years

Classified Ad Clerk

DOT = 247.387-022   GOE = 07.05.02

Records information from individuals wishing to place a classified ad in a newspaper; examines and marks ad according to copy sheet specifications to assist composing room typesetter in preparing ad for printing in newspaper.

Aptitudes:

Intelligence	Moderate
Verbal	Moderate
Numerical	Moderate
Spatial	Low
Form Perception	Low
Clerical Perception	High
Motor Coordination	Low
Finger Dexterity	Low
Manual Dexterity	Low
Eye-Hand-Foot Coordination	Low
Color Discrimination	Low

Data = Mod   People = Low   Things = Low

Salary Range:
$8,000–$14,000

Opportunity Outlook:
14–24% growth

Environmental Conditions:
Inside

Physical Demands:
Sedentary—little or no lifting
Reaching, handling, fingering, or feeling required
Talking or hearing required
Seeing required

Temperaments:
Performing repetitive tasks
Attempting to attain set limits

Vocational Preparation:
1/2–1 year

Clergy Member

DOT = 120.007-010 GOE = 10.01.01

Leads others in conducting religious worship services and performs other spiritual functions associated with the beliefs and practices of a particular religious faith or denomination.

Aptitudes:
Intelligence	High
Verbal	High
Numerical	Moderate
Spatial	Low
Form Perception	Low
Clerical Perception	Moderate
Motor Coordination	Low
Finger Dexterity	Low
Manual Dexterity	Low
Eye-Hand-Foot Coordination	Low
Color Discrimination	Low

Data = High   People = High   Things = Low

Salary Range:
Varies

Opportunity Outlook:
14–24% growth

Environmental Conditions:
Inside

Physical Demands:
Light—lifting of no more than 20 pounds required
Talking or hearing required

Temperaments:
Interpreting the feelings and ideas of others
Influencing the actions and beliefs of others
Making decisions based upon senses and feelings
Dealing with people beyond giving and receiving information
Performing a variety of tasks

Vocational Preparation:
4–10 years

Clerk-Typist

DOT = 203.362-010 GOE = 07.06.02

Compiles data and operates a typewriter or word processor in order to carry out clerical duties, and to maintain business records and reports; may type reports, letters, forms, shipping records, or other similar documents.

Aptitudes:
Intelligence	Moderate
Verbal	Moderate
Numerical	Moderate
Spatial	Low
Form Perception	Moderate
Clerical Perception	High
Motor Coordination	Moderate
Finger Dexterity	Moderate
Manual Dexterity	Moderate
Eye-Hand-Foot Coordination	Low
Color Discrimination	Low

Data = Mod   People = Low   Things = High

Salary Range:
$12,400–$18,800

Opportunity Outlook:
0–4% growth or decline

Environmental Conditions:
Inside

Physical Demands:
Sedentary—little or no lifting
Reaching, handling, fingering, or feeling required
Talking or hearing required
Seeing required

Temperaments:
Attempting to attain set limits

Vocational Preparation:
3–6 months

Clinical Psychologist

DOT = 045.107-022   GOE = 10.01.02

Interviews and examines patients, using counseling and testing techniques, to diagnose and evaluate mental and emotional disorders, and then administers a program of treatment for the disorder.

Aptitudes:
Intelligence	High
Verbal	High
Numerical	Moderate
Spatial	Low
Form Perception	Moderate
Clerical Perception	Low
Motor Coordination	Low
Finger Dexterity	Moderate
Manual Dexterity	Moderate
Eye-Hand-Foot Coordination	Low
Color Discrimination	Low

Data = High   People = High   Things = Low

Salary Range:
$17,000–$67,000

Opportunity Outlook:
35% growth or more

Environmental Conditions:
Inside

Physical Demands:
Sedentary—little or no lifting
Talking or hearing required
Seeing required

Temperaments:
Performing a variety of tasks
Dealing with people beyond giving and receiving information
Making decisions based upon senses and feelings
Making decisions based upon facts

Vocational Preparation:
4–10 years

Clothes Designer

DOT = 142.061-018   GOE = 01.02.03

Designs men's, women's, and children's garments, shoes, handbags, and related items.

Aptitudes:
Intelligence	High
Verbal	High
Numerical	Moderate
Spatial	High
Form Perception	High
Clerical Perception	Moderate
Motor Coordination	Moderate
Finger Dexterity	High
Manual Dexterity	Moderate
Eye-Hand-Foot Coordination	Low
Color Discrimination	High

Data = High   People = Low   Things = High

Salary Range:
$11,800–$50,000

Opportunity Outlook:
25–34% growth

Environmental Conditions:
Inside

Physical Demands:
Light—lifting of no more than 20 pounds required
Reaching, handling, fingering, or feeling required
Talking or hearing required
Seeing required

Temperaments:
Performing a variety of tasks
Making decisions based upon senses and feelings
Attempting to attain set limits
Interpreting the feelings and ideas of others

Vocational Preparation:
2–4 years

Clothes Model

DOT = 297.667-014 GOE = 01.08.01

Models clothing, such as dresses, coats, underclothing, swimwear, and business suits for garment and clothing designers and manufacturers. May also model clothing for public viewing.

Aptitudes:
Intelligence	Moderate
Verbal	Moderate
Numerical	Low
Spatial	Low
Form Perception	Low
Clerical Perception	Low
Motor Coordination	Low
Finger Dexterity	Low
Manual Dexterity	Low
Eye-Hand-Foot Coordination	Low
Color Discrimination	Moderate

Data = Low   People = Low   Things = Low

Salary Range:
Varies

Opportunity Outlook:
14–24% growth

Environmental Conditions:
Inside

Physical Demands:
Light—lifting of no more than 20 pounds required
Reaching, handling, fingering, or feeling required
Talking or hearing required

Temperaments:
Performing repetitive tasks

Vocational Preparation:
1–3 months

Coin-Machine Collector

DOT = 292.687-010 GOE = 07.07.03

Collects coins or coin boxes from parking meters or telephone pay stations and returns coins or boxes to central station for processing. May also record amount of money collected, report defective equipment to repair service, or adjust or repair equipment.

Aptitudes:
Intelligence	Moderate
Verbal	Low
Numerical	Low
Spatial	Low
Form Perception	Low
Clerical Perception	Low
Motor Coordination	Moderate
Finger Dexterity	Moderate
Manual Dexterity	Moderate
Eye-Hand-Foot Coordination	Moderate
Color Discrimination	Low

Data = Low   People = Low   Things = Low

Salary Range:
$10,000–$14,000

Opportunity Outlook:
14–24% growth

Environmental Conditions:
Outside

Physical Demands:
Light—lifting of no more than 20 pounds required
Reaching, handling, fingering, or feeling required
Seeing required

Temperaments
Performing repetitive tasks

Vocational Preparation:
1–30 days

Comedian

DOT = 159.047-014   GOE = 01.03.02

Attempts to make an audience laugh by telling jokes, delivering comic lines, singing a humorous song, performing a comedy dance or walk, wearing a funny costume, or some other similar device.

Aptitudes:
Intelligence	High
Verbal	High
Numerical	Low
Spatial	Moderate
Form Perception	Low
Clerical Perception	Low
Motor Coordination	Moderate
Finger Dexterity	Low
Manual Dexterity	Low
Eye-Hand-Foot Coordination	Moderate
Color Discrimination	Low

Data = High   People = Mod   Things = Low

Salary Range:
Varies

Opportunity Outlook:
25-34% growth

Environmental Conditions:
Inside

Physical Demands:
Light—lifting of no more than 20 pounds required
Talking or hearing required

Temperaments:
Performing a variety of tasks
Dealing with people beyond giving and receiving information
Interpreting the feelings and ideas of others

Vocational Preparation:
1/2–1 year

Commercial Airplane Pilot

DOT = 196.263-014   GOE = 05.04.01

Pilots airplane to transport passengers and freight from one location to another; inspects and records condition of aircraft and reports maintenance requirements; monitors operational systems and conditions, such as fuel supply, weather conditions, and flight route.

Aptitudes:
Intelligence	High
Verbal	High
Numerical	High
Spatial	High
Form Perception	High
Clerical Perception	Moderate
Motor Coordination	High
Finger Dexterity	Moderate
Manual Dexterity	Moderate
Eye-Hand-Foot Coordination	Moderate
Color Discrimination	Moderate

Data = High   People = Low   Things = High

Salary Range:
$80,000 (average)

Opportunity Outlook:
25-34% growth

Environmental Conditions:
Presence of loud noises and vibrations
Presence of physical hazards

Physical Demands:
Light—lifting of no more than 20 pounds required
Reaching, handling, fingering, or feeling required
Talking or hearing required
Seeing required

Temperaments:
Performing a variety of tasks
Making decisions based upon senses and feelings
Making decisions based upon facts
Performing under stress or in emergencies

Vocational Preparation:
4-10 years

Composer

DOT = 152.067-014 GOE = 01.04.02

Writes musical compositions by creating musical ideas, using knowledge of harmonic, rhythmic, melodic, and tonal structures and other elements of music theory, including instrumental and vocal capabilities; may create a song, sonata, symphony, opera, or any other work involving music.

Aptitudes:

Intelligence	High
Verbal	High
Numerical	Moderate
Spatial	Low
Form Perception	Moderate
Clerical Perception	High
Motor Coordination	Low
Finger Dexterity	Low
Manual Dexterity	Low
Eye-Hand-Foot Coordination	Low
Color Discrimination	Low

Data = High   People = Low   Things = Low

Salary Range:
Varies

Opportunity Outlook:
5–13% growth

Environmental Conditions:
Inside

Physical Demands:
Sedentary—little or no lifting
Reaching, handling, fingering, or feeling required

Temperaments:
Making decisions based upon senses and feelings
Interpreting the feelings and ideas of others

Vocational Preparation:
More than 10 years

Computer Operator

DOT = 213.362-010 GOE = 07.06.01

Monitors and controls electronic computer equipment to process business, scientific, engineering, or other data, according to operating instructions.

Aptitudes:

Intelligence	Moderate
Verbal	Moderate
Numerical	Moderate
Spatial	Moderate
Form Perception	Moderate
Clerical Perception	High
Motor Coordination	Moderate
Finger Dexterity	Moderate
Manual Dexterity	Low
Eye-Hand-Foot Coordination	Low
Color Discrimination	Low

Data = Mod   People = Low   Things = Mod

Salary Range:
$12,300–$33,900

Opportunity Outlook:
0–4% growth or decline

Environmental Conditions:
Inside

Physical Demands:
Light—lifting of no more than 20 pounds required
Reaching, handling, fingering, or feeling required
Talking or hearing required
Seeing required

Temperaments:
Performing a variety of tasks
Attempting to attain set limits

Vocational Preparation:
1–2 years

Computer Software Technician

DOT = 020.262-010   GOE = 11.01.01

Analyzes problems, plans and develops software programs, transfers programs to memory chips, installs chips on printed circuit boards, and tests and corrects operation of chips and boards, using various computer equipment.

Aptitudes:
Intelligence	High
Verbal	High
Numerical	High
Spatial	Low
Form Perception	High
Clerical Perception	High
Motor Coordination	Low
Finger Dexterity	Moderate
Manual Dexterity	Moderate
Eye-Hand-Foot Coordination	Low
Color Discrimination	Low

Data = High   People = Mod   Things = Mod

Salary Range:
$14,000–$30,000

Opportunity Outlook:
25–34% growth

Environmental Conditions:
Inside

Physical Demands:
Light—lifting of no more than 20 pounds required
Reaching, handling, fingering, or feeling required
Talking or hearing required
Seeing required

Temperaments
Making decisions based upon senses and feelings
Attempting to attain set limits

Vocational Preparation:
2–4 years

Computer Subassembly Supervisor

DOT = 726.131-010   GOE = 06.01.01

Supervises and coordinates activities of workers engaged in assembly and testing of electronic computer equipment.

Aptitudes:
Intelligence	High
Verbal	Moderate
Numerical	Low
Spatial	Moderate
Form Perception	Moderate
Clerical Perception	Moderate
Motor Coordination	Moderate
Finger Dexterity	Moderate
Manual Dexterity	Moderate
Eye-Hand-Foot Coordination	Low
Color Discrimination	Low

Data = High   People = Mod   Things = Mod

Salary Range:
$20,000–$26,000

Opportunity Outlook:
14–24% growth

Environmental Conditions:
Inside

Physical Demands:
Light—lifting of no more than 20 pounds required
Reaching, handling, fingering, or feeling required
Talking or hearing required
Seeing required

Temperaments:
Directing, controlling, or planning the work of others
Dealing with people beyond giving and receiving information

Vocational Preparation:
2–4 years

Concrete-Mixing Truck Driver

DOT = 900.683-010   GOE = 05.08.03

Drives truck equipped with auxiliary concrete mixer to deliver concrete to construction job sites.

Aptitudes:
Intelligence	Moderate
Verbal	Low
Numerical	Low
Spatial	Moderate
Form Perception	Low
Clerical Perception	Low
Motor Coordination	Moderate
Finger Dexterity	Low
Manual Dexterity	Moderate
Eye-Hand-Foot Coordination	Moderate
Color Discrimination	Low

Data = Low   People = Low   Things = Mod

Salary Range:
$19,000–$29,000

Opportunity Outlook:
14–24% growth

Environmental Conditions:
Inside and outside
Presence of loud noises and vibrations

Physical Demands:
Moderate—lifting of no more than 50 pounds required
Reaching, handling, fingering, or feeling required

Temperaments:
Performing repetitive tasks

Vocational Preparation:
1–3 months

Concrete-Paving Machine Operator

DOT = 853.663-014   GOE = 05.11.01

Operates concrete paving machine to spread and smooth freshly poured concrete surfaces for concrete roads and landing fields.

Aptitudes:
Intelligence	Moderate
Verbal	Low
Numerical	Low
Spatial	Moderate
Form Perception	Moderate
Clerical Perception	Low
Motor Coordination	Moderate
Finger Dexterity	Low
Manual Dexterity	Moderate
Eye-Hand-Foot Coordination	Moderate
Color Discrimination	Low

Data = Low   People = Low   Things = Mod

Salary Range:
$19,000 (average)

Opportunity Outlook:
25–34% growth

Environmental Conditions:
Outside
Wet and humid work environment
Presence of loud noises and vibrations

Physical Demands:
Moderate—lifting of no more than 50 pounds required
Reaching, handling, fingering, or feeling required
Seeing required

Temperaments:
Performing repetitive tasks
Attempting to attain set limits

Vocational Preparation:
1–3 months

Construction Drill Operator

DOT = 930.382-010   GOE = 05.11.02

Sets up and operates self-propelled or truck-mounted drilling machine to bore blasting holes in the earth at strip mine, open pit, quarry, or construction sites.

Aptitudes:
Intelligence	Moderate
Verbal	Low
Numerical	Low
Spatial	Moderate
Form Perception	Low
Clerical Perception	Low
Motor Coordination	Moderate
Finger Dexterity	Low
Manual Dexterity	Moderate
Eye-Hand-Foot Coordination	Low
Color Discrimination	Low

Data = Mod   People = Low   Things = Mod

Salary Range:
$13,000–$38,000

Opportunity Outlook:
5–13% growth

Environmental Conditions:
Outside
Presence of loud noises and vibrations
Presence of physical hazards
Presence of atmospheric dangers

Physical Demands:
Heavy—lifting of no more than 100 pounds required
Reaching, handling, fingering, or feeling required
Seeing required

Temperaments:
Performing repetitive tasks
Making decisions based upon facts

Vocational Preparation:
1/2–1 year

Construction-Maintenance Inspector

DOT = 914.362-014   GOE = 05.07.01

Inspects petroleum-dispensing equipment and machinery for signs of defective equipment at wholesale distributing plants or refineries.

Aptitudes:
Intelligence	Moderate
Verbal	Moderate
Numerical	Low
Spatial	Low
Form Perception	Low
Clerical Perception	Moderate
Motor Coordination	Low
Finger Dexterity	Low
Manual Dexterity	Moderate
Eye-Hand-Foot Coordination	Low
Color Discrimination	Low

Data = Mod   People = Low   Things = Mod

Salary Range:
$19,000–$46,000

Opportunity Outlook:
14–24% growth

Environmental Conditions:
Outside

Physical Demands:
Light—lifting of no more than 20 pounds required
Reaching, handling, fingering, or feeling required
Seeing required

Temperaments:
Making decisions based upon facts
Attempting to attain set limits

Vocational Preparation:
1/2–1 year

Construction Worker

DOT = 869.687-026   GOE = 05.12.03

Performs a variety of tasks on a construction site, such as measuring distances, driving wooden stakes into the ground, bolting or nailing wooden concrete forms together, shoveling dirt, or mixing and pouring concrete.

Aptitudes:
Intelligence	Low
Verbal	Low
Numerical	Low
Spatial	Low
Form Perception	Low
Clerical Perception	Low
Motor Coordination	Low
Finger Dexterity	Low
Manual Dexterity	Moderate
Eye-Hand-Foot Coordination	Low
Color Discrimination	Low

Data = Low   People = Low   Things = Mod

Salary Range:
$9,400–$28,600

Opportunity Outlook:
5–13% growth

Environmental Conditions:
Inside and outside
Presence of loud noises and vibrations
Presence of physical hazards
Presence of atmospheric dangers

Physical Demands:
Very heavy—lifting of more than 100 pounds
Climbing or balancing required
Stooping, kneeling, crouching, or crawling required
Reaching, handling, fingering, or feeling required
Seeing required

Temperaments:
Performing repetitive tasks

Vocational Preparation:
3–6 months

Consumer Affairs Director

DOT = 188.117-050   GOE = 11.10.02

Administers consumer affairs program, including development of operational policies; conducts investigations of consumer products and services to ensure consumer protection laws are not violated; forwards information on unsafe and illegal products and services to legal authorities for prosecution.

Aptitudes:
Intelligence	High
Verbal	High
Numerical	Moderate
Spatial	Low
Form Perception	Low
Clerical Perception	Moderate
Motor Coordination	Low
Finger Dexterity	Low
Manual Dexterity	Low
Eye-Hand-Foot Coordination	Low
Color Discrimination	Low

Data = High   People = Mod   Things = Low

Salary Range:
$17,700–$49,500

Opportunity Outlook:
25–34% growth

Environmental Conditions:
Inside

Physical Demands:
Light—lifting of no more than 20 pounds required
Reaching, handling, fingering, or feeling required
Talking or hearing required
Seeing required

Temperaments:
Directing, controlling, or planning the work of others
Dealing with people beyond giving and receiving information
Performing a variety of tasks

Vocational Preparation:
4–10 years

Contract Administrator

DOT = 162.117-014   GOE = 11.12.04

Directs activities concerned with contracts for the purchase or sale of equipment, materials, products, or services; may examine cost estimates, actual merchandise, delivery schedules, and negotiate actual sales contract.

Aptitudes:
Intelligence	High
Verbal	High
Numerical	Moderate
Spatial	Low
Form Perception	Low
Clerical Perception	High
Motor Coordination	Low
Finger Dexterity	Low
Manual Dexterity	Low
Eye-Hand-Foot Coordination	Low
Color Discrimination	Low

Data = High   People = Mod   Things = Low

Salary Range:
$16,100–$51,900

Opportunity Outlook:
14–24% growth

Environmental Conditions:
Inside

Physical Demands:
Sedentary—little or no lifting
Talking or hearing required

Temperaments:
Directing, controlling, or planning the work of others
Influencing the actions and beliefs of others
Making decisions based upon facts
Dealing with people beyond giving and receiving information
Performing a variety of tasks

Vocational Preparation:
4–10 years

Contractor (Construction)

DOT = 182.167-010   GOE = 11.12.04

Contracts with various companies and/or individuals to provide services (electrical, plumbing, carpentry, structural, etc.) necessary to complete construction of a building or project; may estimate costs of materials, labor, equipment, and negotiate terms of each contract.

Aptitudes:
Intelligence	Moderate
Verbal	Moderate
Numerical	High
Spatial	High
Form Perception	High
Clerical Perception	Moderate
Motor Coordination	Moderate
Finger Dexterity	Moderate
Manual Dexterity	Moderate
Eye-Hand-Foot Coordination	Moderate
Color Discrimination	Moderate

Data = High   People = Mod   Things = Low

Salary Range:
$28,000–$100,000

Opportunity Outlook:
25–34% growth

Environmental Conditions:
Inside and outside
Presence of loud noises and vibrations

Physical Demands:
Light—lifting of no more than 20 pounds required
Talking or hearing required
Seeing required

Temperaments:
Performing a variety of tasks
Directing, controlling, or planning the work of others
Dealing with people beyond giving and receiving information
Making decisions based upon facts

Vocational Preparation:
2–4 years

Cook

DOT = 313.361-014   GOE = 05.05.17

Prepares, seasons, and cooks soups, meats, vegetables, desserts, and other foodstuffs for consumption in hotels and restaurants; may specialize in a particular kind of food, and may adapt cooking to meet the special needs of patrons.

Aptitudes:

Intelligence	Moderate
Verbal	Moderate
Numerical	Moderate
Spatial	Low
Form Perception	Moderate
Clerical Perception	Moderate
Motor Coordination	Low
Finger Dexterity	Low
Manual Dexterity	Moderate
Eye-Hand-Foot Coordination	Low
Color Discrimination	Low

Data = Mod   People = Low   Things = High

Salary Range:
$8,000–$50,000

Opportunity Outlook:
25–34% growth

Environmental Conditions:
Inside

Physical Demands:
Moderate—lifting of no more than 50 pounds required
Reaching, handling, fingering, or feeling required
Seeing required

Temperaments:
Making decisions based upon senses and feelings
Attempting to attain set limits
Performing a variety of tasks

Vocational Preparation:
2–4 years

Copy Writer

DOT = 131.067-014   GOE = 01.01.02

Writes advertising copy for use by publication or broadcast media to promote the sale of a product or service.

Aptitudes:

Intelligence	High
Verbal	High
Numerical	Moderate
Spatial	Low
Form Perception	Moderate
Clerical Perception	Moderate
Motor Coordination	Moderate
Finger Dexterity	Moderate
Manual Dexterity	Low
Eye-Hand-Foot Coordination	Low
Color Discrimination	Low

Data = High   People = Mod   Things = Low

Salary Range:
$20,000–$45,000

Opportunity Outlook:
25–34% growth

Environmental Conditions:
Inside

Physical Demands:
Sedentary—little or no lifting
Reaching, handling, fingering, or feeling required
Talking or hearing required
Seeing required

Temperaments:
Influencing the actions and beliefs of others
Making decisions based upon senses and feelings
Interpreting the feelings and ideas of others
Making decisions based upon facts
Dealing with people beyond giving and receiving information

Vocational Preparation:
2–4 years

Correctional Officer

DOT = 372.667-018   GOE = 04.02.01

Guards inmates in prison in accordance with established policies and procedures; observes conduct and behavior of inmates to prevent disturbances and escapes.

Aptitudes:
Intelligence	Moderate
Verbal	Moderate
Numerical	Low
Spatial	Low
Form Perception	Moderate
Clerical Perception	Low
Motor Coordination	Moderate
Finger Dexterity	Low
Manual Dexterity	Moderate
Eye-Hand-Foot Coordination	Low
Color Discrimination	Low

Data = Low   People = Mod   Things = Low

Salary Range:
$12,400–$37,400

Opportunity Outlook:
35% growth

Environmental Conditions:
Inside
Presence of physical hazards

Physical Demands:
Light—lifting of no more than 20 pounds required
Reaching, handling, fingering, or feeling required
Talking or hearing required
Seeing required

Temperaments:
Dealing with people beyond giving and receiving information
Making decisions based upon senses and feelings
Performing under stress or in emergencies

Vocational Preparation:
3–6 months

Corrosion Prevention Metal Sprayer

DOT = 843.482-010   GOE = 05.12.14

Controls and operates portable equipment to spray corrosion-resistant coatings on various objects as they are being manufactured in a factory.

Aptitudes:
Intelligence	Moderate
Verbal	Low
Numerical	Moderate
Spatial	Low
Form Perception	Moderate
Clerical Perception	Low
Motor Coordination	Moderate
Finger Dexterity	Low
Manual Dexterity	Moderate
Eye-Hand-Foot Coordination	Low
Color Discrimination	Low

Data = Mod   People = Low   Things = Mod

Salary Range:
$14,600–$34,100

Opportunity Outlook:
0–4% growth or decline

Environmental Conditions:
Inside
Presence of loud noises and vibrations
Presence of physical hazards
Presence of atmospheric dangers

Physical Demands:
Moderate—lifting of no more than 50 pounds required
Stooping, kneeling, crouching, or crawling required
Reaching, handling, fingering, or feeling required
Seeing required

Temperaments:
Making decisions based upon facts
Attempting to attain set limits

Vocational Preparation:
1/2–1 year

Cosmetologist

DOT = 332.271-010 GOE = 09.02.01

Provides beauty services to customers, such as analyzing hair to determine condition, applying bleach or dyes to color hair, shampooing hair, cutting and trimming hair, applying cosmetics, or coloring fingernails and toenails.

Aptitudes:
Intelligence	Moderate
Verbal	Moderate
Numerical	Low
Spatial	Moderate
Form Perception	High
Clerical Perception	Low
Motor Coordination	High
Finger Dexterity	High
Manual Dexterity	Moderate
Eye-Hand-Foot Coordination	Low
Color Discrimination	High

Data = Mod   People = Low   Things = High

Salary Range:
$14,500–$32,000

Opportunity Outlook:
14–24% growth

Environmental Conditions:
Inside

Physical Demands:
Light—lifting of no more than 20 pounds required
Reaching, handling, fingering, or feeling required
Talking or hearing required
Seeing required

Temperaments:
Performing a variety of tasks
Making decisions based upon senses and feelings

Vocational Preparation:
1–2 years

Counselor (Professional)

DOT = 045.107-010 GOE = 10.01.02

Counsels individuals or groups in various matters, such as educational and career planning, finding and securing financial aid, personal and social development, drug and alcohol treatment, and sexual relationships.

Aptitudes:
Intelligence	High
Verbal	High
Numerical	Moderate
Spatial	Low
Form Perception	Low
Clerical Perception	Low
Motor Coordination	Low
Finger Dexterity	Low
Manual Dexterity	Low
Eye-Hand-Foot Coordination	Low
Color Discrimination	Low

Data = High   People = High   Things = Low

Salary Range:
$17,700–$49,300

Opportunity Outlook:
25–34% growth

Environmental Conditions:
Inside

Physical Demands:
Light—lifting of no more than 20 pounds required
Reaching, handling, fingering, or feeling required
Talking or hearing required
Seeing required

Temperaments:
Making decisions based upon senses and feelings
Making decisions based upon facts
Dealing with people beyond giving and receiving information
Performing a variety of tasks

Vocational Preparation:
4–10 years

County Agricultural Agent

DOT = 096.127-010   GOE = 11.02.03

Organizes and conducts cooperative extension programs to advise and instruct farmers and others in various agricultural findings that can result in improved farming procedures.

Aptitudes:
Intelligence	High
Verbal	High
Numerical	Moderate
Spatial	Low
Form Perception	Low
Clerical Perception	Moderate
Motor Coordination	Low
Finger Dexterity	Low
Manual Dexterity	Low
Eye-Hand-Foot Coordination	Low
Color Discrimination	Moderate

Data = High   People = Mod   Things = Low

Salary Range:
$26,000 (average)

Opportunity Outlook:
14–24% growth

Environmental Conditions:
Inside and outside

Physical Demands:
Light—lifting of no more than 20 pounds required
Talking or hearing required

Temperaments:
Performing a variety of tasks
Directing, controlling, or planning the work of others
Dealing with people beyond giving and receiving information
Influencing the actions and beliefs of others
Making decisions based upon senses and feelings

Vocational Preparation:
2–4 years

Credit Analyst

DOT = 241.267-022   GOE = 07.01.04

Analyzes bill-paying habits of customers who are delinquent in payment of their bills and recommends corrective action; may recommend closing of certain accounts, bill-paying schedule and amounts, credit limits, and may negotiate with creditors on behalf of customers to resolve payment disputes.

Aptitudes:
Intelligence	Moderate
Verbal	Moderate
Numerical	Moderate
Spatial	Low
Form Perception	Low
Clerical Perception	Moderate
Motor Coordination	Low
Finger Dexterity	Low
Manual Dexterity	Low
Eye-Hand-Foot Coordination	Low
Color Discrimination	Low

Data = High   People = Mod   Things = Low

Salary Range:
$20,000–$34,500

Opportunity Outlook:
25–34% growth

Environmental Conditions:
Inside

Physical Demands:
Sedentary—little or no lifting
Talking or hearing required

Temperaments:
Making decisions based upon facts
Dealing with people beyond giving and receiving information

Vocational Preparation:
2–4 years

Criminalist

DOT = 029.281-010   GOE = 02.04.01

Using scientific principles of analysis, identification, and classification, and armed with various equipment and resources, examines evidence taken from a crime scene to determine the exact nature of the crime and the identity of the person(s) responsible.

Aptitudes:

Intelligence	High
Verbal	High
Numerical	High
Spatial	High
Form Perception	High
Clerical Perception	High
Motor Coordination	Moderate
Finger Dexterity	Moderate
Manual Dexterity	Moderate
Eye-Hand-Foot Coordination	Low
Color Discrimination	High

Data = High   People = Low   Things = High

Salary Range:
  $16,000–$50,000+

Opportunity Outlook:
  25–34% growth

Environmental Conditions:
  Inside and outside

Physical Demands:
  Light—lifting of no more than 20 pounds required
  Stooping, kneeling, crouching, or crawling required
  Reaching, handling, fingering, or feeling required
  Talking or hearing required
  Seeing required

Temperaments:
  Making decisions based upon facts
  Attempting to attain set limits
  Performing a variety of tasks

Vocational Preparation:
  2–4 years

Critic

DOT = 131.067-018   GOE = 01.01.03

Reviews literary, musical, theatrical, or artistic works and performances for broadcast and publication.

Aptitudes:

Intelligence	High
Verbal	High
Numerical	Low
Spatial	Moderate
Form Perception	Moderate
Clerical Perception	Low
Motor Coordination	Low
Finger Dexterity	Low
Manual Dexterity	Low
Eye-Hand-Foot Coordination	Low
Color Discrimination	Moderate

Data = High   People = Low   Things = Low

Salary Range:
  $15,000–$60,000

Opportunity Outlook:
  14–24% growth

Environmental Conditions:
  Inside

Physical Demands:
  Sedentary—little or no lifting
  Talking or hearing required
  Seeing required

Temperaments
  Performing a variety of tasks
  Making decisions based upon senses and feelings
  Interpreting the feelings and ideas of others
  Influencing the actions and beliefs of others

Vocational Preparation:
  4–10 years

Customs Inspector

DOT = 168.267-022   GOE = 11.10.04

Inspects cargo, baggage, articles worn or carried by persons, and vessels, vehicles, or aircraft entering or leaving the United States to enforce customs and related laws dealing with the illegal transport of various items, including drugs and weapons.

Aptitudes:
Intelligence	Moderate
Verbal	Moderate
Numerical	Moderate
Spatial	Moderate
Form Perception	Moderate
Clerical Perception	High
Motor Coordination	Moderate
Finger Dexterity	Moderate
Manual Dexterity	Moderate
Eye-Hand-Foot Coordination	Moderate
Color Discrimination	Moderate

Data = Mod   People = Low   Things = Low

Salary Range:
$25,000–$45,000

Opportunity Outlook:
25–34% growth

Environmental Conditions:
Inside

Physical Demands:
Light—lifting of no more than 20 pounds required
Climbing or balancing required
Stooping, kneeling, crouching, or crawling required
Reaching, handling, fingering, or feeling required
Talking or hearing required
Seeing required

Temperaments
Making decisions based upon senses and feelings
Making decisions based upon facts

Vocational Preparation:
1–2 years

Customs Patrol Officer

DOT = 168.167-010   GOE = 04.01.02

Patrols United States borders by foot, vehicle, boat or aircraft to keep smuggled merchandise, contraband, or illegal aliens out of the country.

Aptitudes:
Intelligence	Moderate
Verbal	Moderate
Numerical	Moderate
Spatial	Moderate
Form Perception	Moderate
Clerical Perception	Moderate
Motor Coordination	High
Finger Dexterity	Low
Manual Dexterity	High
Eye-Hand-Foot Coordination	Moderate
Color Discrimination	Low

Data = Mod   People = Mod   Things = Low

Salary Range:
$19,000–$42,000

Opportunity Outlook:
25–34% growth

Environmental Conditions:
Inside and outside
Presence of physical hazards

Physical Demands:
Light—lifting of no more than 20 pounds required
Climbing or balancing required
Stooping, kneeling, crouching, or crawling required
Reaching, handling, fingering, or feeling required
Talking or hearing required
Seeing required

Temperaments:
Dealing with people . . .
Performing under stress or in emergencies
Performing a variety of tasks
Making decisions based upon senses and feelings
Making decisions based upon facts

Vocational Preparation: 4–10 years

Dairy Farm Supervisor

DOT = 410.131-018   GOE = 03.02.01

Supervises and coordinates activities of workers engaged in milking, breeding, and caring for cows on a dairy farm.

Aptitudes:
Intelligence	Moderate
Verbal	Moderate
Numerical	Low
Spatial	Moderate
Form Perception	Moderate
Clerical Perception	Low
Motor Coordination	Moderate
Finger Dexterity	Moderate
Manual Dexterity	Moderate
Eye-Hand-Foot Coordination	Moderate
Color Discrimination	Low

Data = Mod   People = Mod   Things = Mod

Salary Range:
$15,000–$32,000

Opportunity Outlook:
14–24% growth

Environmental Conditions:
Inside and outside
Presence of physical hazards
Presence of atmospheric dangers

Physical Demands:
Moderate—lifting of no more than 50 pounds required
Stooping, kneeling, crouching, or crawling required
Reaching, handling, fingering, or feeling required
Talking or hearing required
Seeing required

Temperaments:
Directing, controlling, or planning the work of others
Making decisions based upon senses and feelings
Performing a variety of tasks

Vocational Preparation: 2–4 years

Dance Studio Manager

DOT = 187.167-086   GOE = 01.05.01

Performs administrative duties necessary to operate a dance studio in accordance with established policies and procedures; may teach dance routines to customers, sell dance instructional services, keep records, train staff, and coordinate sales efforts.

Aptitudes:
Intelligence	Moderate
Verbal	Moderate
Numerical	Low
Spatial	Moderate
Form Perception	Low
Clerical Perception	Moderate
Motor Coordination	High
Finger Dexterity	Low
Manual Dexterity	Moderate
Eye-Hand-Foot Coordination	High
Color Discrimination	Low

Data = High   People = Mod   Things = Low

Salary Range:
Not available

Opportunity Outlook:
Not available

Environmental Conditions:
Inside

Physical Demands:
Light—lifting of no more than 20 pounds required
Talking or hearing required

Temperaments:
Directing, controlling, or planning the work of others
Influencing the actions and beliefs of others
Making decisions based upon senses and feelings
Attempting to attain set limits

Vocational Preparation:
1–2 years

Dancer

DOT = 151.047-010   GOE = 01.05.02

Dances alone, with a partner, or in a group to entertain an audience; may perform classical, modern, or acrobatic dance routines, coordinating body movements to musical accompaniment.

Aptitudes:
Intelligence	High
Verbal	Moderate
Numerical	Moderate
Spatial	High
Form Perception	Moderate
Clerical Perception	Low
Motor Coordination	High
Finger Dexterity	Moderate
Manual Dexterity	Moderate
Eye-Hand-Foot Coordination	High
Color Discrimination	Low

Data = High   People = Mod   Things = Low

Salary Range:
Varies

Opportunity Outlook:
14–24% growth

Environmental Conditions:
Inside

Physical Demands:
Heavy—lifting of no more than 100 pounds required
Climbing or balancing required
Stooping, kneeling, crouching, or crawling required
Reaching, handling, fingering, or feeling required
Seeing required

Temperaments:
Interpreting the feelings and ideas of others
Making decisions based upon senses and feelings
Attempting to attain set limits

Vocational Preparation:
2–4 years

Dancing Instructor

DOT = 151.027-014   GOE = 01.05.01

Instructs students in ballet, ballroom, tap, or other forms of dance; explains and demonstrates dance routines; evaluates performance of students and suggests ways of improving performance.

Aptitudes:
Intelligence	High
Verbal	Moderate
Numerical	Low
Spatial	High
Form Perception	Low
Clerical Perception	Low
Motor Coordination	High
Finger Dexterity	Moderate
Manual Dexterity	Moderate
Eye-Hand-Foot Coordination	High
Color Discrimination	Low

Data = High   People = Mod   Things = Low

Salary Range:
Varies

Opportunity Outlook:
Not available

Environmental Conditions:
Inside

Physical Demands:
Heavy—lifting of no more than 100 pounds required
Climbing or balancing required
Reaching, handling, fingering, or feeling required
Talking or hearing required
Seeing required

Temperaments:
Directing, controlling, or planning the work of others
Dealing with people beyond giving and receiving information
Interpreting the feelings and ideas of others
Attempting to attain set limits

Vocational Preparation:
2–4 years

Deaf Interpreter

DOT = 137.267-014   GOE = 01.03.02

Helps individuals who are deaf communicate with hearing individuals by translating spoken language into sign language and vice versa.

Aptitudes:
Intelligence	Moderate
Verbal	High
Numerical	Low
Spatial	Low
Form Perception	Moderate
Clerical Perception	Moderate
Motor Coordination	High
Finger Dexterity	Moderate
Manual Dexterity	Moderate
Eye-Hand-Foot Coordination	Low
Color Discrimination	Low

Data = High   People = Mod   Things = Low

Salary Range:
$12,600–$22,000

Opportunity Outlook:
14–24% growth

Environmental Conditions:
Inside

Physical Demands:
Sedentary—little or no lifting
Talking or hearing required
Seeing required

Temperaments:
Making decisions based upon senses and feelings
Dealing with people beyond giving and receiving information

Vocational Preparation:
1/2–1 year

Dealer (Gambling Establishment)

DOT = 343.467-018   GOE = 09.04.02

Operates a gambling table for dice, roulette, or cards in a gambling casino.

Aptitudes:
Intelligence	Moderate
Verbal	Moderate
Numerical	Moderate
Spatial	Low
Form Perception	Moderate
Clerical Perception	Moderate
Motor Coordination	Moderate
Finger Dexterity	Moderate
Manual Dexterity	Moderate
Eye-Hand-Foot Coordination	Low
Color Discrimination	Low

Data = Mod   People = Low   Things = Low

Salary Range:
$15,500–$20,000

Opportunity Outlook:
14–24% growth

Environmental Conditions:
Inside

Physical Demands:
Sedentary—little or no lifting
Reaching, handling, fingering, or feeling required
Talking or hearing required
Seeing required

Temperaments:
Performing repetitive tasks
Making decisions based upon senses and feelings

Vocational Preparation:
1–3 months

Dean of Students (College)

DOT = 090.117-018 GOE = 10.01.02

Directs and coordinates all the student services (counseling, financial, social, cultural, recreational) of a college or university; works with other administrators to set policies and procedures; may counsel students who are experiencing academic, financial, or personal and social problems.

Aptitudes:
Intelligence	High
Verbal	High
Numerical	Moderate
Spatial	Low
Form Perception	Moderate
Clerical Perception	High
Motor Coordination	Low
Finger Dexterity	Low
Manual Dexterity	Low
Eye-Hand-Foot Coordination	Low
Color Discrimination	Low

Data = High People = High Things = Low

Salary Range:
$30,000–$60,000+

Opportunity Outlook:
14–24% growth

Environmental Conditions:
Inside

Physical Demands:
Sedentary—little or no lifting
Talking or hearing required

Temperaments:
Directing, controlling, or planning the work of others
Dealing with people beyond giving and receiving information
Influencing the actions and beliefs of others

Vocational Preparation:
4–10 years

Delivery Person (In-Town)

DOT = 230.667-010 GOE = 07.07.02

Delivers messages, telegrams, documents, packages, and other items to business establishments and private homes, traveling on foot or by bicycle, motorcycle, automobile, or public transportation.

Aptitudes:
Intelligence	Low
Verbal	Low
Numerical	Low
Spatial	Low
Form Perception	Low
Clerical Perception	Low
Motor Coordination	Low
Finger Dexterity	Low
Manual Dexterity	Low
Eye-Hand-Foot Coordination	Low
Color Discrimination	Low

Data = Low People = Low Things = Low

Salary Range:
$8,500–$12,700

Opportunity Outlook:
25–34% growth

Environmental Conditions:
Inside and outside

Physical Demands:
Light—lifting of no more than 20 pounds required
Reaching, handling, fingering, or feeling required

Temperaments:
Performing repetitive tasks

Vocational Preparation:
1–30 days

Demonstrator

DOT = 297.354-010   GOE = 08.02.05

Demonstrates merchandise and products to customers to promote sales; displays merchandise and products and explains features to customers; may take orders or sell items at the time of the demonstration.

Aptitudes:
Intelligence	Moderate
Verbal	Moderate
Numerical	Moderate
Spatial	Low
Form Perception	Low
Clerical Perception	Low
Motor Coordination	Moderate
Finger Dexterity	Moderate
Manual Dexterity	Moderate
Eye-Hand-Foot Coordination	Low
Color Discrimination	Low

Data = Mod   People = Mod   Things = Mod

Salary Range:
$8,800–$12,000

Opportunity Outlook:
14–24% growth

Environmental Conditions:
Inside

Physical Demands:
Light—lifting of no more than 20 pounds required
Reaching, handling, fingering, or feeling required
Talking or hearing required

Temperaments:
Dealing with people beyond giving and receiving of information
Influencing the actions and beliefs of others
Making decisions based upon senses and feelings

Vocational Preparation:
1–3 months

Dental Assistant

DOT = 079.371-010   GOE = 10.03.02

Assists a dentist in a variety of tasks, such as diagnosing dental problems, surgical procedures to repair dental disease or damage, examining and treatment of patients, recording dental information, sterilizing instruments, and advising patients in proper dental hygiene.

Aptitudes:
Intelligence	Moderate
Verbal	Moderate
Numerical	Moderate
Spatial	Low
Form Perception	Moderate
Clerical Perception	Moderate
Motor Coordination	Low
Finger Dexterity	Moderate
Manual Dexterity	Moderate
Eye-Hand-Foot Coordination	Low
Color Discrimination	Low

Data = Mod   People = Low   Things = High

Salary Range:
$14,300–$18,500

Opportunity Outlook:
25–34% growth

Environmental Conditions:
Inside

Physical Demands:
Light—lifting of no more than 20 pounds required
Reaching, handling, fingering, or feeling required
Seeing required

Temperaments:
Attempting to attain set limits

Vocational Preparation:
1–2 years

Dental Hygienist

DOT = 078.36-010   GOE = 10.02.02

Cleans teeth of harmful plaque and other deposits, using special cleaning instruments and compounds; may take x-ray images of teeth to look for evidence of tooth decay or damage; keeps exact records of the condition of each patient's teeth for examination by dentist.

Aptitudes:
Intelligence	High
Verbal	High
Numerical	High
Spatial	High
Form Perception	Moderate
Clerical Perception	Moderate
Motor Coordination	High
Finger Dexterity	High
Manual Dexterity	High
Eye-Hand-Foot Coordination	Low
Color Discrimination	Moderate

Data = Mod   People = Mod   Things = High

Salary Range:
$20,000–$32,000

Opportunity Outlook:
25–34% growth

Environmental Conditions:
Inside

Physical Demands:
Light—lifting of no more than 20 pounds required
Reaching, handling, fingering, or feeling required
Talking or hearing required
Seeing required

Temperaments:
Dealing with people beyond giving and receiving information
Attempting to attain set limits

Vocational Preparation:
1–2 years

Dentist

DOT = 072.101-010   GOE = 02.03.02

Diagnoses and treats diseases, injuries, and malformations of teeth and gums and related oral structures. Examines patients, using x-ray machine and other devices, to determine condition of teeth and oral cavity to determine proper corrective therapy.

Aptitudes:
Intelligence	High
Verbal	High
Numerical	High
Spatial	High
Form Perception	High
Clerical Perception	Moderate
Motor Coordination	Low
Finger Dexterity	High
Manual Dexterity	High
Eye-Hand-Foot Coordination	Low
Color Discrimination	Low

Data = High   People = High   Things = High

Salary Range:
$31,000–$100,000+

Opportunity Outlook:
25–34% growth

Environmental Conditions:
Inside

Physical Demands:
Light—lifting of no more than 20 pounds required
Reaching, handling, fingering, or feeling required
Talking or hearing required
Seeing required

Temperaments:
Performing a variety of tasks
Dealing with people beyond giving and receiving information
Making decisions based upon facts

Vocational Preparation:
4–10 years

Department Manager

DOT = 189.167-022   GOE = 11.05.02

Directs and coordinates, through subordinate personnel, all departmental activities and functions within a commercial, industrial, or service establishment, following policies and procedures as established by higher-ranking administrative officers.

Aptitudes:
Intelligence	Moderate
Verbal	Moderate
Numerical	Moderate
Spatial	Moderate
Form Perception	Moderate
Clerical Perception	Moderate
Motor Coordination	Low
Finger Dexterity	Low
Manual Dexterity	Low
Eye-Hand-Foot Coordination	Low
Color Discrimination	Low

Data = High   People = Mod   Things = Low

Salary Range:
$22,000–$30,500

Opportunity Outlook:
14–24% growth

Environmental Conditions:
Inside

Physical Demands:
Sedentary—little or no lifting
Talking or hearing required

Temperaments:
Directing, controlling, or planning the work of others
Dealing with people beyond giving and receiving information

Vocational Preparation:
2–4 years

Detective

DOT = 375.267-010   GOE = 04.01.02

Carries out investigations to prevent crimes or solve criminal cases; investigates known or suspected criminals or facts, interrogates individuals, examines crime scenes, and may arrest individuals suspected of committing crimes.

Aptitudes:
Intelligence	High
Verbal	High
Numerical	Low
Spatial	Low
Form Perception	Moderate
Clerical Perception	Moderate
Motor Coordination	Moderate
Finger Dexterity	Low
Manual Dexterity	Moderate
Eye-Hand-Foot Coordination	Low
Color Discrimination	Low

Data = High   People = Mod   Things = Low

Salary Range:
$21,000–$36,000

Opportunity Outlook:
25–34% growth

Environmental Conditions:
Inside and outside
Presence of physical hazards

Physical Demands:
Light—lifting of no more than 20 pounds required
Talking or hearing required
Seeing required

Temperaments:
Performing a variety of tasks
Dealing with people beyond giving and receiving information
Performing under stress or in emergencies
Making decisions based upon senses and feelings
Making decisions based upon facts

Vocational Preparation:
2–4 years

Dialysis Technician

DOT = 078.362-014   GOE = 10.02.02

Sets up and operates artificial kidney machine to provide dialysis treatment for patients with kidney disorders or failure; attaches machine to patients, advises patients in the proper use of the machine, and monitors patients during treatment.

Aptitudes:
Intelligence	Moderate
Verbal	Moderate
Numerical	Moderate
Spatial	Moderate
Form Perception	Moderate
Clerical Perception	Moderate
Motor Coordination	High
Finger Dexterity	High
Manual Dexterity	Moderate
Eye-Hand-Foot Coordination	Low
Color Discrimination	Low

Data = Mod   People = Low   Things = Mod

Salary Range:
$12,000–$28,500

Opportunity Outlook:
25–34% growth

Environmental Conditions:
Inside

Physical Demands:
Light—lifting of no more than 20 pounds required
Reaching, handling, fingering, or feeling required
Seeing required

Temperaments:
Attempting to attain set limits

Vocational Preparation:
1–2 years

Director of Admissions

DOT = 090.167-014   GOE = 11.07.03

Directs and coordinates admission program of a public or private college or university, according to policies and procedures developed by governing board of the institution; creates or applies policies and procedures to determine which student applicants are accepted for admission.

Aptitudes:
Intelligence	High
Verbal	High
Numerical	Moderate
Spatial	Low
Form Perception	Moderate
Clerical Perception	High
Motor Coordination	Low
Finger Dexterity	Low
Manual Dexterity	Low
Eye-Hand-Foot Coordination	Low
Color Discrimination	Low

Data = High   People = Mod   Things = Low

Salary Range:
$21,000–$75,000

Opportunity Outlook:
5–13% growth

Environmental Conditions:
Inside

Physical Demands:
Sedentary—little or no lifting
Talking or hearing required

Temperaments:
Directing, controlling, or planning the work of others
Dealing with people beyond giving and receiving information

Vocational Preparation:
4–10 years

Director of Placement (College)

DOT = 166.167-014   GOE = 10.01.02

Coordinates activities of job placement office for college students and graduates; develops placement policies and procedures; counsels students to help determine their aptitudes and career options; advises students on seeking employment after graduation.

Aptitudes:
Intelligence	High
Verbal	High
Numerical	High
Spatial	Low
Form Perception	Low
Clerical Perception	Moderate
Motor Coordination	Low
Finger Dexterity	Low
Manual Dexterity	Low
Eye-Hand-Foot Coordination	Low
Color Discrimination	Low

Data = High   People = Mod   Things = Low

Salary Range:
$22,100–$35,000

Opportunity Outlook:
14–24% growth

Environmental Conditions:
Inside

Physical Demands:
Sedentary—little or no lifting
Reaching, handling, fingering, or feeling required
Talking or hearing required

Temperaments:
Performing a variety of tasks
Directing, controlling, or planning the work of others
Dealing with people beyond giving and receiving information
Influencing the actions and beliefs of others
Making decisions based upon senses and feelings

Vocational Preparation:
4–10 years

Disc Jockey

DOT = 159.147-014   GOE = 01.03.03

Announces radio program of musical selections; selects music to be played based on program specialty and knowledge of audience taste; may specialize in classical, folk, country, blues, jazz, rock and roll, or some other music style.

Aptitudes:
Intelligence	Moderate
Verbal	High
Numerical	Moderate
Spatial	Low
Form Perception	Low
Clerical Perception	Moderate
Motor Coordination	Low
Finger Dexterity	Low
Manual Dexterity	Low
Eye-Hand-Foot Coordination	Low
Color Discrimination	Low

Data = Mod   People = Low   Things = Mod

Salary Range:
$15,000–$60,000+

Opportunity Outlook:
5–13% growth

Environmental Conditions:
Inside

Physical Demands:
Moderate—lifting of no more than 50 pounds required
Talking or hearing required

Temperaments:
Performing a variety of tasks

Vocational Preparation:
1/2–1 year

District Attorney

DOT = 110.117-010 GOE = 11.04.02

Conducts prosecution of accused individuals in a court of law on behalf of a city, county, state, or (as U.S. Attorney) the federal government; gathers and analyzes evidence in a case, and then presents the evidence to a jury in an effort to solicit a guilty verdict of the accused.

Aptitudes:
Intelligence	High
Verbal	High
Numerical	Moderate
Spatial	Moderate
Form Perception	Low
Clerical Perception	Moderate
Motor Coordination	Low
Finger Dexterity	Low
Manual Dexterity	Low
Eye-Hand-Foot Coordination	Low
Color Discrimination	Low

Data = High   People = High   Things = Low

Salary Range:
Varies

Opportunity Outlook:
Not available

Environmental Conditions:
Inside

Physical Demands:
Sedentary—little or no lifting
Talking or hearing required

Temperaments:
Dealing with people beyond giving and receiving information
Influencing the actions and beliefs of others
Making decisions based upon senses and feelings
Making decisions based upon facts

Vocational Preparation:
4–10 years

Diver (Amusement)

DOT = 349.247-010 GOE = 01.07.02

Feeds, describes, and identifies fish enclosed in an aquarium or community fish tank for public amusement; may use diving suit and helmet to enter the tank to feed the fish and other marine life.

Aptitudes:
Intelligence	Moderate
Verbal	Moderate
Numerical	Low
Spatial	Moderate
Form Perception	Low
Clerical Perception	Low
Motor Coordination	Moderate
Finger Dexterity	Low
Manual Dexterity	Moderate
Eye-Hand-Foot Coordination	Low
Color Discrimination	Low

Data = Mod   People = Low   Things = Low

Salary Range:
Varies

Opportunity Outlook:
Not available

Environmental Conditions:
Inside and outside
Wet and humid work environment
Presence of physical hazards

Physical Demands:
Moderate—lifting of no more than 50 pounds
Climbing or balancing required
Reaching, handling, fingering, or feeling required
Talking or hearing required
Seeing required

Temperaments:
Performing a variety of tasks
Performing under stress or in emergencies

Vocational Preparation:
3–6 months

Dog Groomer

DOT = 418.674-010   GOE = 03.03.02

Combs, clips, trims, and shapes dogs' coats to improve their appearance, using knowledge of canine characteristics and grooming techniques and styles.

Aptitudes:

Intelligence	Moderate
Verbal	Low
Numerical	Low
Spatial	Moderate
Form Perception	Moderate
Clerical Perception	Low
Motor Coordination	Moderate
Finger Dexterity	Moderate
Manual Dexterity	Moderate
Eye-Hand-Foot Coordination	Low
Color Discrimination	Low

Data = Low   People = Low   Things = Mod

Salary Range:
$10,000–$16,000

Opportunity Outlook:
35% growth

Environmental Conditions:
Inside
Presence of physical hazards

Physical Demands:
Moderate—lifting of no more than 50 pounds required
Reaching, handling, fingering, or feeling required
Seeing required

Temperaments:
Making decisions based upon senses and feelings

Vocational Preparation:
3–6 months

Double (Film/TV)

DOT = 961.364-010   GOE = 01.08.01

Stands in for a movie or television actor during shooting of a film or program to enable camera operators to set and adjust filming equipment.

Aptitudes:

Intelligence	Moderate
Verbal	Moderate
Numerical	Low
Spatial	Moderate
Form Perception	Low
Clerical Perception	Low
Motor Coordination	Moderate
Finger Dexterity	Low
Manual Dexterity	Low
Eye-Hand-Foot Coordination	Low
Color Discrimination	Low

Data = Mod   People = Low   Things = Low

Salary Range:
Not available

Opportunity Outlook:
35% growth

Environmental Conditions:
Inside and outside

Physical Demands:
Light—lifting required
Climbing or balancing required
Stooping, kneeling, crouching, or crawling required

Temperaments:
Interpreting the feelings and ideas of others

Vocational Preparation:
1–3 months

Dramatic Coach

DOT = 150.027-010   GOE = 01.03.01

Coaches actors in acting techniques; conducts readings to evaluate actors' abilities, and then instructs actors in how to improve their performances in such areas as stage presence, voice projection, or character interpretation.

Aptitudes:
Intelligence	High
Verbal	High
Numerical	Moderate
Spatial	Moderate
Form Perception	Low
Clerical Perception	Moderate
Motor Coordination	Low
Finger Dexterity	Low
Manual Dexterity	Low
Eye-Hand-Foot Coordination	Low
Color Discrimination	Low

Data = High   People = High   Things = Low

Salary Range:
Not available

Opportunity Outlook:
35% growth or more

Environmental Conditions:
Inside

Physical Demands:
Light—lifting of no more than 20 pounds required
Talking or hearing required

Temperaments:
Directing, controlling, or planning the work of others
Dealing with people beyond giving and receiving information
Making decisions based upon senses and feelings
Interpreting the feelings and ideas of others

Vocational Preparation:
2-4 years

Drill Press Operator

DOT = 606.682-014   GOE = 06.02.02

Operates a drilling machine, such as a single- or multiple-spindle drill press, to drill, ream, countersink, spot face, or tap holes in metal or nonmetal materials according to set specifications.

Aptitudes:
Intelligence	Low
Verbal	Low
Numerical	Low
Spatial	Low
Form Perception	Low
Clerical Perception	Low
Motor Coordination	Moderate
Finger Dexterity	Moderate
Manual Dexterity	Moderate
Eye-Hand-Foot Coordination	Low
Color Discrimination	Low

Data = Low   People = Low   Things = Mod

Salary Range:
$15,000-$22,000

Opportunity Outlook:
14-24% growth

Environmental Conditions:
Inside
Presence of loud noises and vibrations

Physical Demands:
Moderate—lifting of no more than 50 pounds required
Reaching, handling, fingering, or feeling required
Seeing required

Temperaments:
Performing repetitive tasks
Attempting to attain set limits

Vocational Preparation:
1-3 months

Driving Instructor

DOT = 099.223-010 GOE = 09.03.03

Instructs individuals or groups in how to safely operate a motor vehicle, including proper driving techniques, mechanical operation of various systems, and how to handle a vehicle in an emergency.

Aptitudes:
Intelligence	Moderate
Verbal	Moderate
Numerical	Low
Spatial	Moderate
Form Perception	Moderate
Clerical Perception	Moderate
Motor Coordination	High
Finger Dexterity	Moderate
Manual Dexterity	Moderate
Eye-Hand-Foot Coordination	High
Color Discrimination	Low

Data = Mod   People = Mod   Things = Mod

Salary Range:
$16,000–$20,000

Opportunity Outlook:
14–24% growth

Environmental Conditions:
Inside and outside
Presence of physical hazards

Physical Demands:
Light—lifting of no more than 20 pounds required
Reaching, handling, fingering, or feeling required
Talking or hearing required
Seeing required

Temperaments:
Influencing the actions and beliefs of others
Making decisions based upon senses and feelings
Performing under stress or in emergencies

Vocational Preparation:
3–6 months

Dust Sampler (Mining)

DOT = 939.585-010 GOE = 05.07.04

Uses special equipment to measure the amount of coal dust suspended in the air in underground coal mines; informs mine safety personnel when the level of dust is unsafe for miners.

Aptitudes:
Intelligence	Low
Verbal	Low
Numerical	Low
Spatial	Moderate
Form Perception	Low
Clerical Perception	Low
Motor Coordination	Moderate
Finger Dexterity	Low
Manual Dexterity	Low
Eye-Hand-Foot Coordination	Low
Color Discrimination	Low

Data = Low   People = Low   Things = Low

Salary Range:
Not available

Opportunity Outlook:
Not available

Environmental Conditions:
Inside
Presence of atmospheric dangers

Physical Demands:
Light—lifting of no more than 20 pounds required
Reaching, handling, fingering, or feeling required

Temperaments:
Making decisions based upon facts
Attempting to attain set limits

Vocational Preparation:
1–3 months

Economist

DOT = 050.067-010   GOE = 11.03.05

Plans, directs, and conducts research to understand the economic relationships that exists within the economy, and possible solutions to problems that arise from the production and distribution of goods and services.

Aptitudes:
   Intelligence   High
   Verbal   High
   Numerical   High
   Spatial   Low
   Form Perception   Low
   Clerical Perception   High
   Motor Coordination   Low
   Finger Dexterity   Low
   Manual Dexterity   Low
   Eye-Hand-Foot Coordination   Low
   Color Discrimination   Low

Data = High   People = Low   Things = Low

Salary Range:
   $14,000–$67,800

Opportunity Outlook:
   14–24% growth

Environmental Conditions:
   Inside

Physical Demands:
   Sedentary—little or no lifting
   Seeing required

Temperaments:
   Making decisions based upon senses and feelings
   Making decisions based upon facts
   Attempting to attain set limits

Vocational Preparation:
   4–10 years

Editor, Dictionary

DOT = 132.067-018   GOE = 11.08.01

Researches information about words that make up a language (such as English) and writes or reviews a definition for each word for publication in a dictionary.

Aptitudes:
   Intelligence   High
   Verbal   High
   Numerical   Low
   Spatial   Low
   Form Perception   Low
   Clerical Perception   High
   Motor Coordination   Low
   Finger Dexterity   Low
   Manual Dexterity   Low
   Eye-Hand-Foot Coordination   Low
   Color Discrimination   Low

Data = High   People = Low   Things = Low

Salary Range:
   $9,700–$18,000

Opportunity Outlook:
   82–53% growth

Environmental Conditions:
   Inside

Physical Demands:
   Sedentary—little or no lifting
   Seeing required

Temperaments:
   Making decisions based upon facts
   Attempting to attain set limits

Vocational Preparation:
   4–10 years

Editor, News

DOT = 132.067-026   GOE = 11.08.01

Plans layout of a newspaper; reviews news copy and photographs, and then makes up a dummy page layout marked to indicate text columns, photo placements, and advertising space; may edit copy and/or confer with news reporters to prepare final edition.

Aptitudes:

Intelligence	High
Verbal	High
Numerical	Moderate
Spatial	Moderate
Form Perception	Moderate
Clerical Perception	Moderate
Motor Coordination	Moderate
Finger Dexterity	Moderate
Manual Dexterity	Low
Eye-Hand-Foot Coordination	Low
Color Discrimination	Low

Data = High   People = Low   Things = Low

Salary Range:
$20,000–$60,000

Opportunity Outlook:
25–34% growth

Environmental Conditions:
Inside

Physical Demands:
Sedentary—little or no lifting
Talking or hearing required
Seeing required

Temperaments:
Directing, controlling, or planning the work of others
Making decisions based upon senses and feelings
Making decisions based upon facts
Interpreting the feelings and ideas of others

Vocational Preparation:
4–10 years

Editor, Film

DOT = 962.264-010   GOE = 01.01.01

Edits motion picture film, television video tape, and/or sound tracks to produce the desired story or sound track as determined by the director or creator of the film or sound track; uses mechanical and electronic devices to splice film or edit sound tracks.

Aptitudes:

Intelligence	High
Verbal	High
Numerical	Moderate
Spatial	Moderate
Form Perception	High
Clerical Perception	Low
Motor Coordination	Low
Finger Dexterity	Moderate
Manual Dexterity	Moderate
Eye-Hand-Foot Coordination	Low
Color Discrimination	Moderate

Data = High   People = Low   Things = Mod

Salary Range:
$30,000 (average)

Opportunity Outlook:
5–13% growth

Environmental Conditions:
Inside

Physical Demands:
Sedentary—little or no lifting
Reaching, handling, fingering, or feeling required
Seeing required

Temperaments:
Interpreting the feelings and ideas of others
Making decisions based upon senses and feelings

Vocational Preparation:
4–10 years

Editor, Publications

DOT = 132.037-022   GOE = 01.01.01

Reads and evaluates materials submitted for publication; edits those materials accepted for publication to improve writing style, grammar, punctuation, and overall presentation; confers with authors in preparation of manuscript; may also formulate policy and procedures regarding material submissions and acceptance.

Aptitudes:
Intelligence	High
Verbal	High
Numerical	Moderate
Spatial	Moderate
Form Perception	Moderate
Clerical Perception	Moderate
Motor Coordination	Moderate
Finger Dexterity	Moderate
Manual Dexterity	Low
Eye-Hand-Foot Coordination	Low
Color Discrimination	Low

Data = High   People = Mod   Things = Low

Salary Range:
$18,700–$60,000

Opportunity Outlook:
25–34% growth

Environmental Conditions:
Inside

Physical Demands:
Sedentary—little or no lifting
Talking or hearing required
Seeing required

Temperaments:
Directing, controlling, or planning the work of others
Dealing with people beyond giving and receiving information
Making decisions based upon senses and feelings
Interpreting the feelings and ideas of others
Influencing the actions and beliefs of others

Vocational Preparation:
4–10 years

Editorial Assistant

DOT = 132.267-014   GOE = 11.08.01

Prepares written materials for publication; reads copy to detect errors in spelling, punctuation, and syntax; verifies facts, dates, and statistics, using standard reference sources; prepares final copy for typesetting.

Aptitudes:
Intelligence	High
Verbal	High
Numerical	Moderate
Spatial	Moderate
Form Perception	Moderate
Clerical Perception	High
Motor Coordination	Low
Finger Dexterity	Low
Manual Dexterity	Low
Eye-Hand-Foot Coordination	Low
Color Discrimination	Low

Data = High   People = Low   Things = Low

Salary Range:
$14,500–$21,000

Opportunity Outlook:
25–34% growth

Environmental Conditions:
Inside

Physical Demands:
Sedentary—little or no lifting
Reaching, handling, fingering, or feeling required
Seeing required

Temperaments:
Making decisions based upon senses and feelings
Making decisions based upon facts
Attempting to attain set limits

Vocational Preparation:
2–4 years

Electrical Appliance Repairer

DOT = 723.381-010   GOE = 05.10.03

Repairs electrical household appliances, such as toasters, mixers, and irons, using hand tools and electrical testing instruments.

Aptitudes:
Intelligence	Moderate
Verbal	Low
Numerical	Low
Spatial	Moderate
Form Perception	Moderate
Clerical Perception	Low
Motor Coordination	Moderate
Finger Dexterity	Moderate
Manual Dexterity	Moderate
Eye-Hand-Foot Coordination	Low
Color Discrimination	Low

Data = Mod   People = Low   Things = High

Salary Range:
$16,600–$29,100

Opportunity Outlook:
0–4% growth or decline

Environmental Conditions:
Inside

Physical Demands:
Light—lifting of no more than 20 pounds required
Reaching, handling, fingering, or feeling required

Temperaments:
Making decisions based upon facts
Attempting to attain set limits

Vocational Preparation:
1–2 years

Electrical Equipment Tester

DOT = 729.381-010   GOE = 06.01.05

Tests and adjusts electrical equipment and accessories as they are being installed in aircraft to insure they conform to established specifications.

Aptitudes:
Intelligence	Moderate
Verbal	Moderate
Numerical	Moderate
Spatial	Low
Form Perception	Moderate
Clerical Perception	Moderate
Motor Coordination	Low
Finger Dexterity	Moderate
Manual Dexterity	Moderate
Eye-Hand-Foot Coordination	Low
Color Discrimination	Low

Data = Mod   People = Low   Things = High

Salary Range:
$10,000–$16,000

Opportunity Outlook:
25–34% growth

Environmental Conditions:
Inside

Physical Demands:
Light—lifting of no more than 20 pounds required
Reaching, handling, fingering, or feeling required
Seeing required

Temperaments:
Making decisions based upon facts
Attempting to attain set limits

Vocational Preparation:
1–2 years

Electrician

DOT = 824.261-010   GOE = 05.05.05

Plans layout, installs, and repairs electrical wiring, fixtures, apparatus, and control equipment in homes, office buildings, and other structures.

Aptitudes:
Intelligence	High
Verbal	Moderate
Numerical	High
Spatial	High
Form Perception	High
Clerical Perception	Moderate
Motor Coordination	Moderate
Finger Dexterity	Moderate
Manual Dexterity	Moderate
Eye-Hand-Foot Coordination	Low
Color Discrimination	Low

Data = High   People = Low   Things = High

Salary Range:
$15,400–$43,600

Opportunity Outlook:
25–34% growth

Environmental Conditions:
Inside and outside
Presence of physical hazards

Physical Demands:
Moderate—lifting of no more than 50 pounds required
Climbing or balancing required
Stooping, kneeling, crouching, or crawling required
Reaching, handling, fingering, or feeling required
Seeing required

Temperaments:
Performing a variety of tasks
Making decisions based upon senses and feelings
Making decisions based upon facts
Attempting to attain set limits

Vocational Preparation: 2–4 years

Electrologist

DOT = 339.371-010   GOE = 09.05.01

Uses special electrical equipment to remove unwanted hair from the face, arms, legs, back, or other body parts of customers who wish to improve their appearance.

Aptitudes:
Intelligence	Moderate
Verbal	Moderate
Numerical	Low
Spatial	Low
Form Perception	High
Clerical Perception	Low
Motor Coordination	Moderate
Finger Dexterity	High
Manual Dexterity	Moderate
Eye-Hand-Foot Coordination	Low
Color Discrimination	Low

Data = Mod   People = Low   Things = High

Salary Range:
Varies

Opportunity Outlook:
14–24% growth

Environmental Conditions:
Inside

Physical Demands:
Light—lifting of no more than 20 pounds required
Reaching, handling, fingering, or feeling required
Seeing required

Temperaments:
Making decisions based upon facts

Vocational Preparation:
1/2–1 year

Electronic Typeset Machine Operator

DOT = 203.582-074 GOE = 07.06.02

Prepares written and graphic materials for printing by operating the terminal keyboard of an electronic typesetting machine to create the desired design layout and content.

Aptitudes:
Intelligence	Moderate
Verbal	Moderate
Numerical	Low
Spatial	Low
Form Perception	Moderate
Clerical Perception	High
Motor Coordination	Moderate
Finger Dexterity	Moderate
Manual Dexterity	Moderate
Eye-Hand-Foot Coordination	Low
Color Discrimination	Low

Data = Mod   People = Low   Things = Mod

Salary Range:
$18,700–$22,600

Opportunity Outlook:
14–24% growth

Environmental Conditions:
Inside

Physical Demands:
Sedentary—little or no lifting
Reaching, handling, fingering, or feeling required
Seeing required

Temperaments:
Attempting to attain set limits

Vocational Preparation:
1–2 years

Electronics Research Engineer

DOT = 003.061-038 GOE = 05.01.01

Conducts research into new and existing electronic devices and equipment to find new and better ways of using electronics to solve human needs and problems.

Aptitudes:
Intelligence	High
Verbal	High
Numerical	High
Spatial	High
Form Perception	High
Clerical Perception	Moderate
Motor Coordination	Moderate
Finger Dexterity	Moderate
Manual Dexterity	Moderate
Eye-Hand-Foot Coordination	Low
Color Discrimination	Moderate

Data = High   People = Low   Things = High

Salary Range:
$23,600–$50,000

Opportunity Outlook:
35% growth or more

Environmental Conditions:
Inside

Physical Demands:
Light—lifting of no more than 20 pounds required
Reaching, handling, fingering, or feeling required
Talking or hearing required
Seeing required

Temperaments:
Performing a variety of tasks
Making decisions based upon senses and feelings
Making decisions based upon facts
Attempting to attain set limits

Vocational Preparation:
4–10 years

Elevator Operator

DOT = 388.663-010   GOE = 09.05.09

Operates elevator to transport people between floors of an office building, apartment house, department store, or hotel.

Aptitudes:
Intelligence	Low
Verbal	Moderate
Numerical	Low
Spatial	Low
Form Perception	Low
Clerical Perception	Low
Motor Coordination	Moderate
Finger Dexterity	Low
Manual Dexterity	Moderate
Eye-Hand-Foot Coordination	Low
Color Discrimination	Low

Data = Low   People = Low   Things = Mod

Salary Range:
$8,000–$11,000

Opportunity Outlook:
14–24% growth

Environmental Conditions:
Inside

Physical Demands:
Light—lifting of no more than 20 pounds required
Reaching, handling, fingering, or feeling required
Talking or hearing required

Temperaments:
Performing repetitive tasks

Vocational Preparation:
1–30 days

Emergency Medical Technician

DOT = 079.374-010   GOE = 10.03.02

Administers first-aid treatment to sick or injured people at the scene of an accident, in their homes or offices, or elsewhere in the community, and transports them to a medical facility for further care.

Aptitudes:
Intelligence	Moderate
Verbal	Moderate
Numerical	Moderate
Spatial	Moderate
Form Perception	High
Clerical Perception	Moderate
Motor Coordination	High
Finger Dexterity	High
Manual Dexterity	High
Eye-Hand-Foot Coordination	Moderate
Color Discrimination	Moderate

Data = Mod   People = Low   Things = Mod

Salary Range:
$16,400–$33,100

Opportunity Outlook:
14–24% growth

Environmental Conditions:
Inside and outside

Physical Demands:
Heavy—lifting of over 50 pounds required
Climbing or balancing required
Stooping, kneeling, crouching, or crawling required
Reaching, handling, fingering, or feeling required
Talking or hearing required
Seeing required

Temperaments:
Making decisions based upon senses and feelings
Making decisions based upon facts
Performing under stress or in emergencies

Vocational Preparation:
1/2–1 year

Engineering Analyst

DOT = 020.067-010   GOE = 11.01.01

Conducts logical analyses of scientific, engineering, and other technical problems and then formulates a mathematical model of each problem. Enters models into a computer and uses analytical power of the computer to find possible solutions to the problems.

Aptitudes:
Intelligence	High
Verbal	High
Numerical	High
Spatial	High
Form Perception	High
Clerical Perception	High
Motor Coordination	Low
Finger Dexterity	Low
Manual Dexterity	Low
Eye-Hand-Foot Coordination	Low
Color Discrimination	Low

Data = High   People = Low   Things = Mod

Salary Range:
$23,500–$36,800

Opportunity Outlook:
25–34% growth

Environmental Conditions:
Inside

Physical Demands:
Sedentary—little or no lifting
Talking or hearing required
Seeing required

Temperaments:
Performing a variety of tasks
Making decisions based upon senses and feelings
Making decisions based upon facts

Vocational Preparation:
4–10 years

Environmental Analyst

DOT = 029.081-010   GOE = 02.01.02

Conducts research studies to develop theories and methods of abating or controlling sources of environmental pollution, utilizing knowledge of the principles and concepts of various scientific and engineering disciplines.

Aptitudes:
Intelligence	High
Verbal	High
Numerical	High
Spatial	High
Form Perception	High
Clerical Perception	Moderate
Motor Coordination	Moderate
Finger Dexterity	Moderate
Manual Dexterity	Moderate
Eye-Hand-Foot Coordination	Low
Color Discrimination	Low

Data = High   People = Low   Things = High

Salary Range:
$24,000–$39,000

Opportunity Outlook:
35% growth or more

Environmental Conditions:
Inside and outside

Physical Demands:
Light—lifting of no more than 20 pounds required
Reaching, handling, fingering, or feeling required

Temperaments:
Directing, controlling, or planning the work of others
Making decisions based upon facts
Attempting to attain set limits

Vocational Preparation:
4–10 years

Equal Opportunity Representative

DOT = 168.167-014   GOE = 11.10.02

Organizes and implements federally funded programs related to equal employment opportunity by providing consultation to public and private employers, encouraging good will between employers and minority communities, and evaluating employment practices.

Aptitudes:
Intelligence	High
Verbal	Moderate
Numerical	Moderate
Spatial	Low
Form Perception	Low
Clerical Perception	Moderate
Motor Coordination	Low
Finger Dexterity	Low
Manual Dexterity	Low
Eye-Hand-Foot Coordination	Low
Color Discrimination	Low

Data = High   People = Mod   Things = Low

Salary Range:
$17,700–$49,400

Opportunity Outlook:
25–34% growth

Environmental Conditions:
Inside

Physical Demands:
Sedentary—little or no lifting
Talking or hearing required

Temperaments:
Directing, controlling, or planning the work of others
Influencing the actions and beliefs of others
Making decisions based upon senses and feelings
Making decisions based upon facts
Dealing with people beyond giving and receiving information

Vocational Preparation:
4–10 years

Equestrian

DOT = 159.344-010   GOE = 12.02.01

Rides horses at circus, carnival, exhibition, or horse show, performing acrobatic stunts on saddled or saddleless horse or feats of equestrian skill and daring to entertain audience.

Aptitudes:
Intelligence	Moderate
Verbal	Moderate
Numerical	Low
Spatial	Moderate
Form Perception	Low
Clerical Perception	Low
Motor Coordination	Moderate
Finger Dexterity	Moderate
Manual Dexterity	High
Eye-Hand-Foot Coordination	High
Color Discrimination	Low

Data = Mod   People = Low   Things = Low

Salary Range:
Varies

Opportunity Outlook:
Not available

Environmental Conditions:
Inside and outside
Presence of physical hazards

Physical Demands:
Moderate—lifting of no more than 50 pounds
Climbing or balancing required
Reaching, handling, fingering, or feeling required
Talking or hearing required
Seeing required

Temperaments:
Performing a variety of tasks
Making decisions based upon senses and feelings

Vocational Preparation:
1–2 years

Exhaust Emissions Inspector

DOT = 806.364-010   GOE = 06.03.01

Inspects and tests automobile emission control systems, using handtools and testing equipment, to determine if systems meet established standards; may repair systems to bring them up to established standards, or refer vehicle to repair service.

Aptitudes:
Intelligence	Moderate
Verbal	Moderate
Numerical	Moderate
Spatial	Moderate
Form Perception	Moderate
Clerical Perception	Moderate
Motor Coordination	Moderate
Finger Dexterity	Moderate
Manual Dexterity	Moderate
Eye-Hand-Foot Coordination	Low
Color Discrimination	Low

Data = Mod   People = Low   Things = Mod

Salary Range:
$10,900–$35,300

Opportunity Outlook:
0–4% growth or decline

Environmental Conditions:
Inside and outside

Physical Demands:
Light—lifting of no more than 20 pounds required
Reaching, handling, fingering, or feeling required
Seeing required

Temperaments:
Making decisions based upon facts
Attempting to attain set limits

Vocational Preparation:
1/2–1 year

Exhibit Artist (Museum)

DOT = 49.261-010   GOE = 01.02.03

Creates artwork for use in permanent or temporary museum exhibit, zoo, or similar establishment; may paint indoor or outdoor scenes on canvas, build sculptures, create human or animal figures, build scenes to represent a house or building, or create other kinds of exhibit displays.

Aptitudes:
Intelligence	High
Verbal	Moderate
Numerical	Moderate
Spatial	High
Form Perception	High
Clerical Perception	Low
Motor Coordination	High
Finger Dexterity	High
Manual Dexterity	High
Eye-Hand-Foot Coordination	Low
Color Discrimination	High

Data = High   People = Low   Things = High

Salary Range:
Varies

Opportunity Outlook:
14–24% growth

Environmental Conditions:
Inside

Physical Demands:
Light—lifting of no more than 20 pounds required
Reaching, handling, fingering, or feeling required
Seeing required

Temperaments:
Interpreting the feelings and ideas of others
Making decisions based upon senses and feelings
Performing a variety of tasks

Vocational Preparation:
4–10 years

Exhibit Builder (Museum)

DOT = 739.261-010   GOE = 01.06.02

Constructs and installs museum exhibit structures, electrical wiring, and fixtures from materials, such as wood, plywood, and fiberglass using hand and power tools following the design created by a museum artist.

Aptitudes:
Intelligence	Moderate
Verbal	Moderate
Numerical	Moderate
Spatial	High
Form Perception	High
Clerical Perception	Low
Motor Coordination	Moderate
Finger Dexterity	Moderate
Manual Dexterity	High
Eye-Hand-Foot Coordination	Low
Color Discrimination	Low

Data = Mod   People = Low   Things = High

Salary Range:
Varies

Opportunity Outlook:
14–24% growth

Environmental Conditions:
Inside

Physical Demands:
Moderate—lifting of no more than 50 pounds required
Reaching, handling, fingering, or feeling required
Seeing required

Temperaments:
Making decisions based upon senses and feelings
Attempting to attain set limits
Performing a variety of tasks

Vocational Preparation:
2–4 years

Extra (Film/Stage/TV)

DOT = 159.647-014   GOE = 01.08.01

Performs a nonspeaking role in a scene or scenes for a stage production, motion picture film, or television program.

Aptitudes:
Intelligence	Moderate
Verbal	Moderate
Numerical	Low
Spatial	Low
Form Perception	Low
Clerical Perception	Low
Motor Coordination	Low
Finger Dexterity	Low
Manual Dexterity	Low
Eye-Hand-Foot Coordination	Low
Color Discrimination	Low

Data = Low   People = Low   Things = Low

Salary Range:
Varies

Opportunity Outlook:
14–24% growth

Environmental Conditions:
Inside and outside

Physical Demands:
Light—lifting of no more than 20 pounds required
Reaching, handling, fingering, or feeling required

Temperaments:
Performing repetitive tasks

Vocational Preparation:
1–30 days

Faculty Member (College/University)

DOT = 090.227-010   GOE = 11.02.01

Teaches college students on the undergraduate or graduate level; may conduct research in a particular subject area, perform certain administrative duties, teach a laboratory section, or train graduate students.

Aptitudes:
Intelligence	High
Verbal	High
Numerical	High
Spatial	Moderate
Form Perception	Moderate
Clerical Perception	High
Motor Coordination	Low
Finger Dexterity	Low
Manual Dexterity	Low
Eye-Hand-Foot Coordination	Low
Color Discrimination	Low

Data = High   People = High   Things = Low

Salary Range:
$26,100–$75,000

Opportunity Outlook:
14–24% growth

Environmental Conditions:
Inside

Physical Demands:
Light—lifting of no more than 20 pounds required
Talking or hearing required

Temperaments:
Directing, controlling, or planning the work of others
Dealing with people beyond giving and receiving information
Influencing the actions and beliefs of others
Making decisions based upon senses and feelings
Making decisions based upon facts

Vocational Preparation:
4–10 years

Farm Machine Operator

DOT = 409.683-010   GOE = 03.04.01

Drives and operates one or more farm machines, such as a tractor, truck, or harvester to raise animals for food or plant or harvest farm produce.

Aptitudes:
Intelligence	Moderate
Verbal	Low
Numerical	Low
Spatial	Moderate
Form Perception	Moderate
Clerical Perception	Low
Motor Coordination	Moderate
Finger Dexterity	Low
Manual Dexterity	Moderate
Eye-Hand-Foot Coordination	Moderate
Color Discrimination	Low

Data = Low   People = Low   Things = Mod

Salary Range:
$8,200–$15,500

Opportunity Outlook:
5% decline or more

Environmental Conditions:
Outside
Presence of loud noises and vibrations
Presence of physical hazards
Presence of atmospheric dangers

Physical Demands:
Heavy—lifting of no more than 100 pounds required
Climbing or balancing required
Reaching, handling, fingering, or feeling required
Seeing required

Temperaments:
Making decisions based upon senses and feelings
Attempting to attain set limits
Performing a variety of tasks

Vocational Preparation:
1–3 months

Farmer

DOT = 421.161-010   GOE = 03.01.01

Raises farm crops and/or livestock to sell to food distribution outlets or directly to consumers; may also manage farm.

Aptitudes:
Intelligence	Moderate
Verbal	Moderate
Numerical	Moderate
Spatial	High
Form Perception	Moderate
Clerical Perception	Moderate
Motor Coordination	Moderate
Finger Dexterity	Low
Manual Dexterity	Moderate
Eye-Hand-Foot Coordination	Low
Color Discrimination	Low

Data = Mod   People = Low   Things = High

Salary Range:
$15,000–$100,000

Opportunity Outlook:
5% decline or more

Environmental Conditions:
Inside and outside
Presence of physical hazards
Presence of atmospheric dangers

Physical Demands:
Very heavy—lifting of more than 100 pounds
Climbing or balancing required
Stooping, kneeling, crouching, or crawling required
Reaching, handling, fingering, or feeling required
Seeing required

Temperaments:
Performing a variety of tasks
Making decisions based upon senses and feelings
Making decisions based upon facts

Vocational Preparation: 2–4 years

Fashion Coordinator

DOT = 185.157-010   GOE = 11.09.01

Promotes new fashions by coordinating promotional activities, such as fashion shows, to induce consumer acceptance; may travel to garment centers or talk to fashion designers and retailers to learn which fashions are most likely to be desired by consumers.

Aptitudes:
Intelligence	Moderate
Verbal	High
Numerical	Moderate
Spatial	Low
Form Perception	Moderate
Clerical Perception	Moderate
Motor Coordination	Low
Finger Dexterity	Low
Manual Dexterity	Low
Eye-Hand-Foot Coordination	Low
Color Discrimination	High

Data = High   People = Mod   Things = Low

Salary Range:
$19,000–$21,000

Opportunity Outlook:
35% growth or more

Environmental Conditions:
Inside

Physical Demands:
Light—lifting of no more than 20 pounds required
Reaching, handling, fingering, or feeling required
Talking or hearing required
Seeing required

Temperaments:
Influencing the actions and beliefs of others
Making decisions based upon senses and feelings
Dealing with people beyond giving and receiving information

Vocational Preparation:
2–4 years

Fast-Foods Worker

DOT = 311.472-010   GOE = 09.04.01

Serves food to customers in a fast food restaurant; requests customer's order and records selections using an electronic cash register; assembles order on serving tray; may also stock food items on shelves, clean machinery and counter tops, and prepare foodstuffs, such as drinks, dessert items, hot beverages, etc.

Aptitudes:
Intelligence	Low
Verbal	Low
Numerical	Low
Spatial	Low
Form Perception	Low
Clerical Perception	Moderate
Motor Coordination	Moderate
Finger Dexterity	Moderate
Manual Dexterity	Moderate
Eye-Hand-Foot Coordination	Low
Color Discrimination	Low

Data = Low   People = Low   Things = Mod

Salary Range:
$7,500–$15,400

Opportunity Outlook:
25–34% growth

Environmental Conditions:
Inside

Physical Demands:
Light—lifting of no more than 20 pounds required
Reaching, handling, fingering, or feeling required
Talking or hearing required
Seeing required

Temperaments:
Performing a variety of tasks

Vocational Preparation:
1–30 days

Ferryboat Captain

DOT = 197.163-010   GOE = 05.04.02

Commands and operates a ferryboat to transport passengers, vehicles, or freight across lakes, bays, sounds, or rivers.

Aptitudes:
Intelligence	High
Verbal	Moderate
Numerical	Moderate
Spatial	High
Form Perception	High
Clerical Perception	Moderate
Motor Coordination	Moderate
Finger Dexterity	Low
Manual Dexterity	Moderate
Eye-Hand-Foot Coordination	Low
Color Discrimination	High

Data = High   People = Mod   Things = Mod

Salary Range:
$17,000–$40,000

Opportunity Outlook:
5% decline or more

Environmental Conditions:
Inside and outside

Physical Demands:
Light—lifting of no more than 20 pounds required
Talking or hearing required
Seeing required

Temperaments:
Directing, controlling, or planning the work of others
Making decisions based upon senses and feelings
Dealing with people beyond giving and receiving information
Making decisions based upon facts
Attempting to attain set limits

Vocational Preparation:
2–4 years

Final Inspector, Musical Instruments

DOT = 730.367-010 GOE = 06.03.01

Inspects finished musical instruments to ascertain conformance to standards for fit, finish, and tone; plays instrument to ensure that it operates and sounds properly.

Aptitudes:
Intelligence	Moderate
Verbal	Low
Numerical	Low
Spatial	Moderate
Form Perception	Moderate
Clerical Perception	Low
Motor Coordination	Moderate
Finger Dexterity	Moderate
Manual Dexterity	Moderate
Eye-Hand-Foot Coordination	Low
Color Discrimination	Moderate

Data = Mod   People = Low   Things = Mod

Salary Range:
$10,900–$35,300

Opportunity Outlook:
0–4% growth or decline

Environmental Conditions:
Inside

Physical Demands:
Light—lifting of no more than 20 pounds required
Reaching, handling, fingering, or feeling required
Talking or hearing required
Seeing required

Temperaments:
Making decisions based upon facts
Attempting to attain set limits

Vocational Preparation:
1/2–1 year

Financial Aid Officer

DOT = 090.117-030 GOE = 11.07.06

Directs a scholarship, grant, and loan program that provides financial aid to college or vocational students in need of assistance.

Aptitudes:
Intelligence	High
Verbal	High
Numerical	High
Spatial	Low
Form Perception	Low
Clerical Perception	High
Motor Coordination	Low
Finger Dexterity	Low
Manual Dexterity	Low
Eye-Hand-Foot Coordination	Low
Color Discrimination	Low

Data = High   People = High   Things = Low

Salary Range:
$38,000 (average)

Opportunity Outlook:
14–24% growth

Environmental Conditions:
Inside

Physical Demands:
Sedentary—little or no lifting
Talking or hearing required

Temperaments:
Directing, controlling, or planning the work of others
Dealing with people beyond giving and receiving information

Vocational Preparation:
4–10 years

Financial Analyst

DOT = 020.167-014 GOE = 11.01.02

Conducts research and statistical analysis of various financial investment programs for use by banks, insurance companies, and brokerage and investment houses.

Aptitudes:
Intelligence	High
Verbal	High
Numerical	High
Spatial	Low
Form Perception	Low
Clerical Perception	High
Motor Coordination	Low
Finger Dexterity	Low
Manual Dexterity	Low
Eye-Hand-Foot Coordination	Low
Color Discrimination	Low

Data = High   People = Low   Things = Low

Salary Range:
$28,400–$56,000

Opportunity Outlook:
25–34% growth

Environmental Conditions:
Inside

Physical Demands:
Sedentary—little or no lifting
Reaching, handling, fingering, or feeling required
Seeing required

Temperaments:
Making decisions based upon senses and feelings
Making decisions based upon facts
Attempting to attain set limits

Vocational Preparation:
4–10 years

Finished Carpet Inspector

DOT = 689.564-010 GOE = 06.03.02

Examines finished carpeting for weaving or tufting defects, variations in color and finish, soil, or uneven shearing prior to carpet's leaving manufacturer.

Aptitudes:
Intelligence	Moderate
Verbal	Low
Numerical	Low
Spatial	Moderate
Form Perception	Moderate
Clerical Perception	Low
Motor Coordination	Low
Finger Dexterity	Moderate
Manual Dexterity	Moderate
Eye-Hand-Foot Coordination	Low
Color Discrimination	Moderate

Data = Low   People = Low   Things = Mod

Salary Range:
$10,900–$35,300

Opportunity Outlook:
0–4% growth or decline

Environmental Conditions:
Inside

Physical Demands:
Light—lifting of no more than 20 pounds required
Stooping, kneeling, crouching, or crawling required
Reaching, handling, fingering, or feeling required
Talking or hearing required
Seeing required

Temperaments:
Performing repetitive tasks
Making decisions based upon facts
Attempting to attain set limits

Vocational Preparation:
3–6 months

Finishing Machine Operator

DOT = 690.685-170 GOE = 06.04.02

Operates a sanding and buffing machine to smooth and polish the surface of various kinds of plastic sheets according to specified finish standards.

Aptitudes:
Intelligence	Low
Verbal	Low
Numerical	Low
Spatial	Low
Form Perception	Moderate
Clerical Perception	Low
Motor Coordination	Moderate
Finger Dexterity	Low
Manual Dexterity	Moderate
Eye-Hand-Foot Coordination	Low
Color Discrimination	Low

Data = Low   People = Low   Things = Mod

Salary Range:
$14,700–$38,800

Opportunity Outlook:
5–13% growth

Environmental Conditions:
Inside

Physical Demands:
Moderate—lifting of no more than 50 pounds required
Reaching, handling, fingering, or feeling required

Temperaments:
Performing repetitive tasks
Attempting to attain set limits

Vocational Preparation:
1–30 days

Fire Fighter

DOT = 373.364-010 GOE = 04.02.04

Attempts to protect human life and property by controlling and extinguishing fires in buildings, homes, or outdoors; may administer first aid to injured or burned victims, clean and repair fire-fighting equipment, or teach others about fire safety.

Aptitudes:
Intelligence	Moderate
Verbal	Moderate
Numerical	Low
Spatial	Moderate
Form Perception	Moderate
Clerical Perception	Low
Motor Coordination	Moderate
Finger Dexterity	Low
Manual Dexterity	High
Eye-Hand-Foot Coordination	High
Color Discrimination	Moderate

Data = Mod   People = Low   Things = Mod

Salary Range:
$19,700–$31,400

Opportunity Outlook:
14–24% growth

Environmental Conditions:
Inside and outside
Extremely hot work environment
Wet and humid work environment
Presence of loud noises and vibrations
Presence of physical hazards

Physical Demands:
Very heavy—lifting of more than 100 pounds
Climbing or balancing required
Stooping, kneeling, crouching, or crawling required
Reaching, handling, fingering, or feeling required
Seeing required

Temperaments:
Performing under stress or in emergencies
Making decisions based upon senses and feelings

Vocational Preparation: 1–2 years

Fire Marshall

DOT = 373.167-018   GOE = 04.01.01

Supervises and coordinates the activities of firefighting personnel and facility; may also inspect fire-fighting equipment and fire safety procedures of commercial establishments or factories to insure they comply with the law; may investigate causes of fires.

Aptitudes:
Intelligence	Moderate
Verbal	Moderate
Numerical	Moderate
Spatial	High
Form Perception	Low
Clerical Perception	Moderate
Motor Coordination	Low
Finger Dexterity	Low
Manual Dexterity	High
Eye-Hand-Foot Coordination	Moderate
Color Discrimination	Low

Data = High   People = Mod   Things = Low

Salary Range:
$23,600–$40,000

Opportunity Outlook:
14–24% growth

Environmental Conditions:
Inside and outside
Presence of physical hazards
Presence of atmospheric dangers

Physical Demands:
Moderate—lifting of no more than 50 pounds
Talking or hearing required
Seeing required

Temperaments:
Directing, controlling, or planning the work of others
Making decisions based upon senses and feelings
Making decisions based upon facts
Performing under stress or in emergencies

Vocational Preparation:
2–4 years

Fish Farmer

DOT = 446.161-010   GOE = 03.01.02

Spawns and raises fish for commercial sale.

Aptitudes:
Intelligence	Moderate
Verbal	Moderate
Numerical	Low
Spatial	Low
Form Perception	Moderate
Clerical Perception	Low
Motor Coordination	Low
Finger Dexterity	Moderate
Manual Dexterity	Moderate
Eye-Hand-Foot Coordination	Low
Color Discrimination	Low

Data = Mod   People = Low   Things = High

Salary Range:
$16,000–$36,000

Opportunity Outlook:
25–34% growth

Environmental Conditions:
Outside
Wet and humid work environment

Physical Demands:
Moderate—lifting of no more than 50 pounds required
Climbing or balancing required
Stooping, kneeling, crouching, or crawling required
Reaching, handling, fingering, or feeling required
Seeing required

Temperaments:
Directing, controlling, or planning the work of others
Making decisions based upon facts

Vocational Preparation:
1–2 years

Fishing Vessel Captain

DOT = 197.133-010   GOE = 05.04.02

Commands the operation of a fishing vessel crew engaged in catching fish and other marine life.

Aptitudes:
Intelligence	Moderate
Verbal	Moderate
Numerical	Moderate
Spatial	High
Form Perception	High
Clerical Perception	Moderate
Motor Coordination	Moderate
Finger Dexterity	Low
Manual Dexterity	Moderate
Eye-Hand-Foot Coordination	Moderate
Color Discrimination	Low

Data = Mod   People = Mod   Things = Mod

Salary Range:
$25,000–$90,000

Opportunity Outlook:
14–24% growth

Environmental Conditions:
Inside and outside
Wet and humid work environment
Presence of physical hazards

Physical Demands:
Light—lifting of no more than 20 pounds required
Climbing or balancing required
Reaching, handling, fingering, or feeling required
Talking or hearing required
Seeing required

Temperaments:
Directing, controlling, or planning the work of others
Performing under stress or in emergencies
Making decisions based upon facts
Attempting to attain set limits

Vocational Preparation:
2–4 years

Floral Designer

DOT = 142.081-010   GOE = 01.02.03

Designs and fashions live, cut, dried, or artificial flowers and floral arrangements for various events, such as birthdays, weddings, anniversaries, or funerals.

Aptitudes:
Intelligence	Moderate
Verbal	Moderate
Numerical	Moderate
Spatial	Moderate
Form Perception	High
Clerical Perception	Moderate
Motor Coordination	Moderate
Finger Dexterity	High
Manual Dexterity	High
Eye-Hand-Foot Coordination	Low
Color Discrimination	High

Data = Mod   People = Low   Things = High

Salary Range:
$10,500–$15,000

Opportunity Outlook:
25–34% growth

Environmental Conditions:
Inside
Extremely cold work environment
Wet and humid work environment

Physical Demands:
Light—lifting of no more than 20 pounds required
Reaching, handling, fingering, or feeling required
Seeing required

Temperaments:
Interpreting the feelings and ideas of others
Making decisions based upon senses and feelings

Vocational Preparation:
1–2 years

Flying Instructor

DOT = 196.223-010   GOE = 05.04.01

Instructs student pilots in flight procedures and techniques; may accompany students on training flights to demonstrate techniques for controlling aircraft during takeoff, landing, spins, stalls, and turns.

Aptitudes:
Intelligence	High
Verbal	High
Numerical	High
Spatial	High
Form Perception	High
Clerical Perception	High
Motor Coordination	Moderate
Finger Dexterity	Low
Manual Dexterity	Moderate
Eye-Hand-Foot Coordination	High
Color Discrimination	Low

Data = High   People = Mod   Things = Mod

Salary Range:
$21,000–$31,000

Opportunity Outlook:
14–24% growth

Environmental Conditions:
Inside and outside
Presence of loud noises and vibrations
Presence of physical hazards

Physical Demands:
Light—lifting of no more than 20 pounds required
Reaching, handling, fingering, or feeling required
Talking or hearing required
Seeing required

Temperaments:
Dealing with people beyond giving and receiving information
Performing under stress or in emergencies
Making decisions based upon senses and feelings

Vocational Preparation:
2–4 years

Food & Drug Inspector

DOT = 168.267-042   GOE = 11.10.03

Inspects establishments where foods, drugs, cosmetics, and similar consumer items are manufactured, handled, stored, or sold to enforce laws regarding sanitation, purity, and grading.

Aptitudes:
Intelligence	Moderate
Verbal	High
Numerical	Moderate
Spatial	Moderate
Form Perception	Low
Clerical Perception	Low
Motor Coordination	Low
Finger Dexterity	Low
Manual Dexterity	Low
Eye-Hand-Foot Coordination	Low
Color Discrimination	Moderate

Data = Mod   People = Low   Things = Low

Salary Range:
$17,700–$49,400

Opportunity Outlook:
25–34% growth

Environmental Conditions:
Inside

Physical Demands:
Light—lifting of no more than 20 pounds required
Reaching, handling, fingering, or feeling required
Talking or hearing required
Seeing required

Temperaments:
Making decisions based upon facts
Attempting to attain set limits

Vocational Preparation:
1–2 years

Food Technologist

DOT = 041.081-010   GOE = 02.02.04

Applies scientific and engineering knowledge and principles to improve the research, development, production, quality control, packaging, processing, and utilization of foods.

Aptitudes:
Intelligence	High
Verbal	High
Numerical	High
Spatial	High
Form Perception	High
Clerical Perception	High
Motor Coordination	Moderate
Finger Dexterity	High
Manual Dexterity	Moderate
Eye-Hand-Foot Coordination	Low
Color Discrimination	Moderate

Data = High   People = Low   Things = High

Salary Range:
$21,000–$40,500

Opportunity Outlook:
25–34% growth

Environmental Conditions:
Inside

Physical Demands:
Light—lifting of no more than 20 pounds required
Reaching, handling, fingering, or feeling required
Seeing required

Temperaments:
Making decisions based upon facts
Attempting to attain set limits
Performing a variety of tasks

Vocational Preparation:
4–10 years

Foreign Service Officer

DOT = 188.117-106   GOE = 11.09.03

Represents the interests of the United States government and nationals by conducting relations with foreign nations and international organizations; attempts to protect and advance U.S. political, economic, and commercial interests overseas.

Aptitudes:
Intelligence	High
Verbal	High
Numerical	Moderate
Spatial	Moderate
Form Perception	Moderate
Clerical Perception	Moderate
Motor Coordination	Low
Finger Dexterity	Low
Manual Dexterity	Low
Eye-Hand-Foot Coordination	Low
Color Discrimination	Low

Data = High   People = High   Things = Low

Salary Range:
$18,000–$69,000

Opportunity Outlook:
14–24% growth

Environmental Conditions:
Inside

Physical Demands:
Sedentary—little or no lifting
Talking or hearing required

Temperaments:
Interpreting the feelings and ideas of others
Influencing the actions and beliefs of others
Making decisions based upon senses and feelings
Dealing with people beyond giving and receiving information
Performing a variety of tasks

Vocational Preparation:
4–10 years

Forest Fire Fighter

DOT = 452.687-014 GOE = 03.04.02

Attempts to extinguish forest fires, working alone or as a member of a fire-fighting crew; may cut down trees, cut and clear brush, and dig trenches in an attempt to contain and extinguish fire; may parachute to fire scene.

Aptitudes:

Intelligence	Moderate
Verbal	Moderate
Numerical	Low
Spatial	Moderate
Form Perception	Moderate
Clerical Perception	Low
Motor Coordination	Moderate
Finger Dexterity	Low
Manual Dexterity	High
Eye-Hand-Foot Coordination	High
Color Discrimination	Moderate

Data = Low   People = Low   Things = Mod

Salary Range:
$12,000–$20,000

Opportunity Outlook:
14–24% growth

Environmental Conditions:
Outside
Extremely hot work environment
Wet and humid work environment
Presence of loud noises and vibrations
Presence of physical hazards
Presence of atmospheric dangers

Physical Demands:
Very heavy—lifting of more than 100 pounds
Climbing or balancing required
Stooping, kneeling, crouching, or crawling required
Reaching, handling, fingering, or feeling required

Temperaments:
Performing repetitive tasks
Performing under stress or in emergencies

Vocational Preparation: 1/2–1 year

Forest Fire Ranger

DOT = 452.367-014 GOE = 04.02.02

Patrols assigned area of forest to locate and report fires and hazardous conditions and to ensure that travelers and campers comply with fire regulations and laws.

Aptitudes:

Intelligence	Moderate
Verbal	Moderate
Numerical	Low
Spatial	Moderate
Form Perception	Low
Clerical Perception	Low
Motor Coordination	Moderate
Finger Dexterity	Low
Manual Dexterity	Moderate
Eye-Hand-Foot Coordination	Moderate
Color Discrimination	Low

Data = Mod   People = Low   Things = Mod

Salary Range:
$14,000–$19,000

Opportunity Outlook:
14–24% growth

Environmental Conditions:
Outside

Physical Demands:
Moderate—lifting of no more than 50 pounds required
Climbing or balancing required
Stooping, kneeling, crouching, or crawling required
Reaching, handling, fingering, or feeling required
Talking or hearing required
Seeing required

Temperaments:
Performing a variety of tasks
Performing under stress or in emergencies
Making decisions based upon senses and feelings

Vocational Preparation:
3–6 months

Forest Nursery Supervisor

DOT = 451.137-010 GOE = 03.02.02

Supervises and coordinates the activities of workers engaged in planting, cultivating, harvesting, and shipping seedling forest trees.

Aptitudes:
Intelligence	Moderate
Verbal	Moderate
Numerical	Moderate
Spatial	Moderate
Form Perception	Moderate
Clerical Perception	Low
Motor Coordination	Low
Finger Dexterity	Low
Manual Dexterity	Low
Eye-Hand-Foot Coordination	Low
Color Discrimination	Low

Data = High   People = Mod   Things = Low

Salary Range:
$16,000–$19,000

Opportunity Outlook:
5–13% growth

Environmental Conditions:
Inside and outside

Physical Demands:
Light—lifting of no more than 20 pounds required
Reaching, handling, fingering, or feeling required
Talking or hearing required

Temperaments:
Directing, controlling, or planning the work of others
Making decisions based upon facts
Dealing with people beyond giving and receiving information

Vocational Preparation:
1–2 years

Forester

DOT = 040.061-034 GOE = 03.01.04

Manages and develops forest lands and their resources for economic and recreational use; plans and directs how trees will be cut and replanted and estimates amount of timber available in certain areas; may be involved in firefighting and planning of recreational areas and facilities.

Aptitudes:
Intelligence	High
Verbal	High
Numerical	Moderate
Spatial	Moderate
Form Perception	Moderate
Clerical Perception	Moderate
Motor Coordination	Low
Finger Dexterity	Low
Manual Dexterity	Low
Eye-Hand-Foot Coordination	Low
Color Discrimination	Low

Data = High   People = Low   Things = Mod

Salary Range:
$15,000–$75,000

Opportunity Outlook:
25–34% growth

Environmental Conditions:
Inside and outside

Physical Demands:
Light—lifting of no more than 20 pounds required
Talking or hearing required
Seeing required

Temperaments:
Directing, controlling, or planning the work of others
Dealing with people beyond giving and receiving information
Performing a variety of tasks

Vocational Preparation:
4–10 years

Forester Aide

DOT = 452.364-010   GOE = 03.02.02

Compiles data pertaining to size, content, condition, and other characteristics of forest tracts of land, and assists other professionals in planting forest trees, fighting fires, and caring for facilities used by foresters.

Aptitudes:
Intelligence	Moderate
Verbal	Moderate
Numerical	Low
Spatial	Moderate
Form Perception	Moderate
Clerical Perception	Low
Motor Coordination	Moderate
Finger Dexterity	Low
Manual Dexterity	High
Eye-Hand-Foot Coordination	High
Color Discrimination	Moderate

Data = Mod   People = Low   Things = Low

Salary Range:
$12,000–$28,000

Opportunity Outlook:
14–24% growth

Environmental Conditions:
Outside
Extremely hot work environment
Wet and humid work environment
Presence of physical hazards
Presence of atmospheric dangers . . .

Physical Demands:
Very heavy—lifting of more than 50 pounds
Climbing or balancing required
Stooping, kneeling, crouching, or crawling required
Reaching, handling, fingering, or feeling required
Seeing required

Temperaments:
Performing a variety of tasks
Performing under stressful . . . conditions

Vocational Preparation: 1–30 days

Front-End Loader Operator

DOT = 921.683-042   GOE = 05.11.04

Operates a tractor-like vehicle equipped with a front-mounted hydraulically powered bucket or scoop to lift and transport heavy or bulky materials from one location to another.

Aptitudes:
Intelligence	Moderate
Verbal	Low
Numerical	Low
Spatial	Moderate
Form Perception	Low
Clerical Perception	Low
Motor Coordination	Moderate
Finger Dexterity	Moderate
Manual Dexterity	Moderate
Eye-Hand-Foot Coordination	Moderate
Color Discrimination	Low

Data = Low   People = Low   Things = Mod

Salary Range:
$13,000–$38,000

Opportunity Outlook:
25–34% growth

Environmental Conditions:
Inside and outside
Presence of loud noises and vibrations
Presence of atmospheric dangers

Physical Demands:
Moderate—lifting of no more than 50 pounds required
Reaching, handling, fingering, or feeling required
Seeing required

Temperaments:
Performing repetitive tasks
Attempting to attain set limits

Vocational Preparation:
1–3 months

Fund Raiser

DOT = 293.357-014 GOE = 08.02.08

Contacts individuals and firms by telephone, in person, or by mail to solicit funds for a charity or other cause.

Aptitudes:
Intelligence	Moderate
Verbal	Moderate
Numerical	Moderate
Spatial	Low
Form Perception	Low
Clerical Perception	Moderate
Motor Coordination	Low
Finger Dexterity	Low
Manual Dexterity	Low
Eye-Hand-Foot Coordination	Low
Color Discrimination	Low

Data = Mod   People = Mod   Things = Low

Salary Range:
$15,000–$100,000+

Opportunity Outlook:
35% growth or more

Environmental Conditions:
Inside and outside

Physical Demands:
Light—lifting of no more than 20 pounds required
Talking or hearing required

Temperaments:
Influencing the actions and beliefs of others
Dealing with people beyond giving and receiving information

Vocational Preparation:
1–30 days

Funeral Attendant

DOT = 359.677-014 GOE = 09.01.04

Performs a variety of tasks during a funeral, such as placing the casket in a parlor or chapel, arranging floral offerings, controlling lighting, and greeting mourners.

Aptitudes:
Intelligence	Low
Verbal	Low
Numerical	Low
Spatial	Low
Form Perception	Low
Clerical Perception	Low
Motor Coordination	Low
Finger Dexterity	Low
Manual Dexterity	Low
Eye-Hand-Foot Coordination	Low
Color Discrimination	Low

Data = Low   People = Low   Things = Low

Salary Range:
$10,000–$15,000

Opportunity Outlook:
14–24% growth

Environmental Conditions:
Inside

Physical Demands:
Heavy—lifting of no more than 100 pounds required
Reaching, handling, fingering, or feeling required
Talking or hearing required

Temperaments:
Performing under stressful, pressure-packed, or emergency conditions

Vocational Preparation:
1–3 months

Funeral Director

DOT = 187.167-030 GOE = 11.11.04

Arranges and directs all aspects of a funeral service in accordance with the wishes of the family of the deceased.

Aptitudes:
Intelligence	High
Verbal	High
Numerical	Moderate
Spatial	Moderate
Form Perception	Moderate
Clerical Perception	Moderate
Motor Coordination	Low
Finger Dexterity	Low
Manual Dexterity	Low
Eye-Hand-Foot Coordination	Low
Color Discrimination	Low

Data = Mod   People = Mod   Things = Low

Salary Range:
$16,000–$60,000+

Opportunity Outlook:
25–34% growth

Environmental Conditions:
Inside and outside

Physical Demands:
Moderate light—lifting of no more than 50 pounds
Reaching, handling, fingering, or feeling required
Talking or hearing required
Seeing required

Temperaments:
Performing a variety of tasks
Directing, controlling, or planning the work of others
Dealing with people beyond giving and receiving information
Making decisions based upon senses and feelings
Making decisions based upon facts

Vocational Preparation: 2–4 years

Gas Dispatcher (Light/Heat/Power)

DOT = 953.167-010 GOE = 05.06.03

Manages and coordinates the flow of natural gas throughout a public utility distribution system to insure that volume and pressure of gas are properly maintained to meet the needs of customers.

Aptitudes:
Intelligence	High
Verbal	High
Numerical	Moderate
Spatial	Moderate
Form Perception	Moderate
Clerical Perception	Moderate
Motor Coordination	Low
Finger Dexterity	Low
Manual Dexterity	Low
Eye-Hand-Foot Coordination	Low
Color Discrimination	Low

Data = Mod   People = Mod   Things = Low

Salary Range:
$16,000–$22,300

Opportunity Outlook:
14–24% growth

Environmental Conditions:
Inside and outside

Physical Demands:
Sedentary—little or no lifting
Reaching, handling, fingering, or feeling required
Talking or hearing required

Temperaments:
Performing a variety of tasks
Directing, controlling, or planning the work of others
Making decisions based upon facts
Attempting to attain set limits

Vocational Preparation:
4–10 years

Geographer

DOT =029.067-010   GOE = 02.01.01

Studies the nature and uses of various areas of the earth's surface in an attempt to understand the interaction of physical and cultural phenomena; conducts research on physical and climatic aspects, landforms, soils, plants, animals, and human activity.

Aptitudes:
Intelligence	High
Verbal	High
Numerical	High
Spatial	Moderate
Form Perception	Moderate
Clerical Perception	Low
Motor Coordination	Low
Finger Dexterity	Low
Manual Dexterity	Low
Eye-Hand-Foot Coordination	Low
Color Discrimination	Low

Data = High   People = Low   Things = Low

Salary Range:
$16,000–$67,800

Opportunity Outlook:
5–13% growth

Environmental Conditions:
Inside and outside
Extremely cold work environment
Extremely hot work environment
Wet and humid work environment
Presence of atmospheric dangers

Physical Demands:
Light—lifting of no more than 20 pounds required
Reaching, handling, fingering, or feeling required
Seeing required

Temperaments:
Performing a variety of tasks
Directing, controlling, or planning the work of others
Making decisions based upon senses and feelings
Making decisions based upon facts

Vocational Preparation: 4–10 years

Geologist (Petroleum)

DOT = 024.061-022   GOE = 02.01.02

Explores and charts the stratigraphic arrangement and structure of the earth to locate gas and oil deposits for commercial use.

Aptitudes:
Intelligence	High
Verbal	High
Numerical	High
Spatial	High
Form Perception	High
Clerical Perception	Moderate
Motor Coordination	Low
Finger Dexterity	Moderate
Manual Dexterity	Low
Eye-Hand-Foot Coordination	Low
Color Discrimination	Low

Data = High   People = Low   Things = High

Salary Range:
$23,400–$48,000

Opportunity Outlook:
14–24% growth

Environmental Conditions:
Inside and outside
Extremely cold work environment
Extremely hot work environment
Wet and humid work environment
Presence of atmospheric dangers

Physical Demands:
Light—lifting of no more than 20 pounds required
Climbing or balancing required
Stooping, kneeling, crouching, or crawling required
Reaching, handling, fingering, or feeling required

Temperaments:
Making decisions based upon senses and feelings
Making decisions based upon facts
Attempting to attain set limits

Vocational Preparation: 4–10 years

Glass Inspector

DOT = 579.687-022   GOE = 06.03.02

Visually inspects plate glass or glass products for defects, such as scratches, cracks, chips, holes, or bubbles, before they are shipped to retail outlets.

Aptitudes:
Intelligence	Low
Verbal	Low
Numerical	Low
Spatial	Low
Form Perception	Moderate
Clerical Perception	Low
Motor Coordination	Low
Finger Dexterity	Low
Manual Dexterity	Moderate
Eye-Hand-Foot Coordination	Low
Color Discrimination	Low

Data = Low   People = Low   Things = Low

Salary Range:
$10,800–$35,300

Opportunity Outlook:
14–24% growth

Environmental Conditions:
Inside

Physical Demands:
Light—lifting of no more than 20 pounds required
Reaching, handling, fingering, or feeling required
Seeing required

Temperaments:
Performing repetitive tasks
Attempting to attain set limits

Vocational Preparation:
1–3 months

Golf Club Manager

DOT = 187.167-114   GOE = 11.11.02

Manages public or private golf club; may oversee operation of club restaurant, grounds and grounds keeping crew, equipment, pro shop, and personnel.

Aptitudes:
Intelligence	High
Verbal	High
Numerical	High
Spatial	Low
Form Perception	Low
Clerical Perception	High
Motor Coordination	Low
Finger Dexterity	Low
Manual Dexterity	Low
Eye-Hand-Foot Coordination	Low
Color Discrimination	Low

Data = High   People = Mod   Things = Low

Salary Range:
$22,000–$95,000

Opportunity Outlook:
14–24% growth

Environmental Conditions:
Inside

Physical Demands:
Sedentary—little or no lifting
Talking or hearing required

Temperaments:
Performing a variety of tasks
Directing, controlling, or planning the work of others
Making decisions based upon senses and feelings
Dealing with people beyond giving and receiving information

Vocational Preparation:
1–2 years

Graphologist

DOT = 159.247-018   GOE = 01.07.01

Analyses handwriting samples to determine the personality characteristics and traits of the person who created the sample.

Aptitudes:
Intelligence	Moderate
Verbal	Moderate
Numerical	Low
Spatial	Low
Form Perception	High
Clerical Perception	Low
Motor Coordination	Low
Finger Dexterity	Low
Manual Dexterity	Low
Eye-Hand-Foot Coordination	Low
Color Discrimination	Low

Data = Mod   People = Low   Things = Low

Salary Range:
Varies

Opportunity Outlook:
Not available

Environmental Conditions:
Inside

Physical Demands:
Sedentary—little or no lifting
Talking or hearing required
Seeing required

Temperaments:
Interpreting the feelings and ideas of others
Making decisions based upon senses and feelings

Vocational Preparation:
3–6 months

Grip (Film/TV)

DOT = 962.687-022   GOE = 05.12.04

Operates a variety of control levers and wheels to guide cranes, booms, and dollies to move cameras and other equipment on the set of a movie or television production.

Aptitudes:
Intelligence	Moderate
Verbal	Moderate
Numerical	Low
Spatial	Moderate
Form Perception	Moderate
Clerical Perception	Low
Motor Coordination	Moderate
Finger Dexterity	Moderate
Manual Dexterity	Moderate
Eye-Hand-Foot Coordination	Moderate
Color Discrimination	Low

Data = Low   People = Low   Things = Mod

Salary Range:
$12,000–$18,000

Opportunity Outlook:
5–13% growth

Environmental Conditions:
Inside
Presence of physical hazards

Physical Demands:
Heavy—lifting of no more than 100 pounds required
Climbing or balancing required
Stooping, kneeling, crouching, or crawling required
Reaching, handling, fingering, or feeling required
Seeing required

Temperaments:
Performing a variety of tasks

Vocational Preparation:
1/2–1 year

Hair Stylist

DOT = 332.271-018   GOE = 09.02.01

Specializes in creating hair styles that meet the needs or preferences of patrons; may specialize in modern, contemporary styles, period styles, or character portrayals; shapes, trims, and colors hair to create the desired look.

Aptitudes:
Intelligence	Moderate
Verbal	Moderate
Numerical	Low
Spatial	Moderate
Form Perception	Moderate
Clerical Perception	Low
Motor Coordination	High
Finger Dexterity	Moderate
Manual Dexterity	Moderate
Eye-Hand-Foot Coordination	Low
Color Discrimination	Moderate

Data = Mod   People = Low   Things = High

Salary Range:
$14,500–$29,000+

Opportunity Outlook:
14–24% growth

Environmental Conditions:
Inside

Physical Demands:
Light—lifting of no more than 20 pounds required
Reaching, handling, fingering, or feeling required
Talking or hearing required
Seeing required

Temperaments:
Making decisions based upon senses and feelings
Performing a variety of tasks

Vocational Preparation:
1–2 years

Hand Engraver

DOT = 704.381-030   GOE = 01.06.01

Engraves lettering and ornamental designs on soft metal articles, such as silverware, trophies, aluminum or plastic eyeglass frames, and jewelry items.

Aptitudes:
Intelligence	Moderate
Verbal	Moderate
Numerical	Low
Spatial	High
Form Perception	High
Clerical Perception	Low
Motor Coordination	Moderate
Finger Dexterity	High
Manual Dexterity	High
Eye-Hand-Foot Coordination	Low
Color Discrimination	Low

Data = Mod   People = Low   Things = High

Salary Range:
$14,000–$30,000

Opportunity Outlook:
14–24% growth

Environmental Conditions:
Inside

Physical Demands:
Sedentary—little or no lifting
Reaching, handling, fingering, or feeling required
Seeing required

Temperaments:
Making decisions based upon facts
Attempting to attain set limits

Vocational Preparation:
2–4 years

Helicopter Pilot

DOT = 196.263-038   GOE = 05.04.01

Pilots a helicopter to transport people, cargo, mail, fight fires, or to spread seeds for reforestation or pesticides.

Aptitudes:
Intelligence	High
Verbal	High
Numerical	Moderate
Spatial	High
Form Perception	Moderate
Clerical Perception	Moderate
Motor Coordination	High
Finger Dexterity	Moderate
Manual Dexterity	Moderate
Eye-Hand-Foot Coordination	Moderate
Color Discrimination	Low

Data = High   People = Low   Things = Mod

Salary Range:
$43,000–$74,000

Opportunity Outlook:
25–34% growth

Environmental Conditions:
Inside and outside
Presence of loud noises and vibrations
Presence of physical hazards

Physical Demands:
Light—lifting of no more than 20 pounds required
Reaching, handling, fingering, or feeling required
Seeing required

Temperaments:
Making decisions based upon senses and feelings
Making decisions based upon facts
Performing under stress or in emergencies
Attempting to attain set limits

Vocational Preparation: 2–4 years

Highway Maintenance Worker

DOT = 899.684-014   GOE = 05.12.12

Maintains highways, municipal and rural roads, and rights-of-way to keep them in safe condition; may erect guard rails, signs and markers, and snow fences, as well as patch holes, plow snow, or cut grass adjacent to roadway.

Aptitudes:
Intelligence	Moderate
Verbal	Low
Numerical	Low
Spatial	Low
Form Perception	Low
Clerical Perception	Low
Motor Coordination	Moderate
Finger Dexterity	Low
Manual Dexterity	Moderate
Eye-Hand-Foot Coordination	Low
Color Discrimination	Low

Data = Low   People = Low   Things = Mod

Salary Range:
$20,000–$30,000

Opportunity Outlook:
25–34% growth

Environmental Conditions:
Inside and outside
Presence of physical hazards

Physical Demands:
Very heavy—lifting of more than 100 pounds required
Stooping, kneeling, crouching, or crawling required
Reaching, handling, fingering, or feeling required
Seeing required

Temperaments:
Performing repetitive tasks
Attempting to attain set limits

Vocational Preparation:
1–3 months

Historian

DOT = 052.067-022   GOE = 11.03.03

Conducts scholarly research to understand the history of mankind, especially individual behavior, social, political, and cultural events; may write about findings or teach courses in history.

Aptitudes:
Intelligence	High
Verbal	High
Numerical	Moderate
Spatial	Low
Form Perception	Low
Clerical Perception	High
Motor Coordination	Low
Finger Dexterity	Low
Manual Dexterity	Low
Eye-Hand-Foot Coordination	Low
Color Discrimination	Low

Data = High   People = Mod   Things = Low

Salary Range:
$16,200–$67,800

Opportunity Outlook:
25–34% growth

Environmental Conditions:
Inside

Physical Demands:
Sedentary—little or no lifting
Reaching, handling, fingering, or feeling required
Talking or hearing required

Temperaments:
Directing, controlling, or planning the work of others
Making decisions based upon senses and feelings
Making decisions based upon facts

Vocational Preparation:
4–10 years

Home Economist

DOT = 096.121-014   GOE = 11.02.03

Organizes and conducts consumer education or research programs to better understand how to effectively use various household equipment, food, textiles, or utility services; may advise homeowners in the proper use of such materials and equipment, and may also teach courses in home economics.

Aptitudes:
Intelligence	High
Verbal	High
Numerical	Moderate
Spatial	Moderate
Form Perception	Moderate
Clerical Perception	High
Motor Coordination	Moderate
Finger Dexterity	Moderate
Manual Dexterity	Moderate
Eye-Hand-Foot Coordination	Low
Color Discrimination	Moderate

Data = High   People = Mod   Things = High

Salary Range:
$12,000–$42,000

Opportunity Outlook:
25–34% growth

Environmental Conditions:
Inside

Physical Demands:
Light—lifting of no more than 20 pounds required
Reaching, handling, fingering, or feeling required
Talking or hearing required
Seeing required

Temperaments:
Performing a variety of tasks
Dealing with people beyond giving and receiving information
Making decisions based upon senses and feelings
Influencing the actions and beliefs of others

Vocational Preparation:
2–4 years

Home Housekeeper

DOT = 301.137-010   GOE = 05.12.01

Supervises and coordinates the activities of household employees in a private residence; may also perform some or many of the daily household chores.

Aptitudes:
Intelligence	Moderate
Verbal	Moderate
Numerical	Moderate
Spatial	Low
Form Perception	Moderate
Clerical Perception	Low
Motor Coordination	Moderate
Finger Dexterity	Low
Manual Dexterity	Moderate
Eye-Hand-Foot Coordination	Low
Color Discrimination	Low

Data = Low   People = Mod   Things = Low

Salary Range:
$8,900–$15,000

Opportunity Outlook:
5% decline or more

Environmental Conditions:
Inside

Physical Demands:
Light—lifting of no more than 20 pounds required
Reaching, handling, fingering, or feeling required
Stooping, kneeling, crouching, or crawling required

Temperaments:
Performing a variety of tasks
Directing, controlling, or planning the work of others
Dealing with people beyond giving and receiving information

Vocational Preparation:
1–2 years

Horse Trainer

DOT = 419.224-010   GOE = 03.03.01

Trains horses for riding, racing, or harness; may feed, exercise, and groom horses, and work with them until they are familiar with and comfortable around people.

Aptitudes:
Intelligence	Moderate
Verbal	Low
Numerical	Low
Spatial	Moderate
Form Perception	Moderate
Clerical Perception	Moderate
Motor Coordination	Moderate
Finger Dexterity	Moderate
Manual Dexterity	Moderate
Eye-Hand-Foot Coordination	Moderate
Color Discrimination	Moderate

Data = Mod   People = Mod   Things = Low

Salary Range:
Varies

Opportunity Outlook:
Not available

Environmental Conditions:
Inside and outside

Physical Demands:
Moderate—lifting of no more than 50 pounds
Climbing or balancing required
Stooping, kneeling, crouching, or crawling required
Reaching, handling, fingering, or feeling required
Talking or hearing required
Seeing required

Temperaments:
Making decisions based upon senses and feelings
Dealing with people beyond giving and receiving information
Performing a variety of tasks

Vocational Preparation: 2–4 years

Hospital Administrator

DOT = 187.117-010   GOE = 11.07.02

Directs the administration of a hospital according to rules and regulations established by a board of directors; may establish policies and procedures for dealing with finances, personnel, patient admissions, scientific research, community services, medical and vocational rehabilitation services, and other activities.

Aptitudes:
Intelligence	High
Verbal	High
Numerical	Moderate
Spatial	Low
Form Perception	Low
Clerical Perception	Moderate
Motor Coordination	Low
Finger Dexterity	Low
Manual Dexterity	Low
Eye-Hand-Foot Coordination	Low
Color Discrimination	Low

Data = High   People = High   Things = Low

Salary Range:
$71,000–$203,400

Opportunity Outlook:
35% growth or more

Environmental Conditions:
Inside

Physical Demands:
Light—lifting of no more than 20 pounds required
Talking or hearing required

Temperaments:
Performing a variety of tasks
Directing, controlling, or planning the work of others
Making decisions based upon senses and feelings
Dealing with people beyond giving and receiving information

Vocational Preparation:
4–10 years

Hospital Admitting Clerk

DOT = 205.362-018   GOE = 07.04.01

Interviews incoming hospital patients (or their representatives) to record information required for admission and then assists patients to their room.

Aptitudes:
Intelligence	Moderate
Verbal	Moderate
Numerical	Moderate
Spatial	Low
Form Perception	Low
Clerical Perception	Moderate
Motor Coordination	Moderate
Finger Dexterity	Moderate
Manual Dexterity	Low
Eye-Hand-Foot Coordination	Low
Color Discrimination	Low

Data = Mod   People = Low   Things = Low

Salary Range:
$15,000–$18,000

Opportunity Outlook:
25–34% growth

Environmental Conditions:
Inside

Physical Demands:
Sedentary—little or no lifting
Talking or hearing required
Seeing required

Temperaments:
Performing a variety of tasks

Vocational Preparation:
1–2 years

Hospital Orderly

DOT = 355.674-018   GOE = 10.03.02

May perform any of the following duties in a hospital as directed by a nurse or medical staff member: bathe patients, clean and shave hair from a patient's body prior to operation, measure and record intake and output of liquids, record temperatures, pulse, and respiration rates, and other activities.

Aptitudes:
Intelligence	Moderate
Verbal	Moderate
Numerical	Low
Spatial	Low
Form Perception	Low
Clerical Perception	Low
Motor Coordination	Moderate
Finger Dexterity	Low
Manual Dexterity	Moderate
Eye-Hand-Foot Coordination	Low
Color Discrimination	Low

Data = Low   People = Low   Things = Mod

Salary Range:
$12,000–$16,000

Opportunity Outlook:
35% growth or more

Environmental Conditions:
Inside
Presence of physical hazards

Physical Demands:
Moderate—lifting of no more than 20 pounds required
Stooping, kneeling, crouching, or crawling required
Reaching, handling, fingering, or feeling required
Talking or hearing required
Seeing required

Temperaments:
Performing a variety of tasks
Performing under stress or in emergencies

Vocational Preparation: 3–6 months

Host

DOT = 352.667-010   GOE = 09.01.01

Greets guests arriving at a country club, catered social function, restaurant, or other public or private gathering, and then may direct guests to various activities or to their seats in preparation for dinner or some other function.

Aptitudes:
Intelligence	Moderate
Verbal	Moderate
Numerical	Low
Spatial	Low
Form Perception	Low
Clerical Perception	Low
Motor Coordination	Low
Finger Dexterity	Low
Manual Dexterity	Low
Eye-Hand-Foot Coordination	Low
Color Discrimination	Low

Data = Low   People = Mod   Things = Low

Salary Range:
$8,000–$18,300

Opportunity Outlook:
25–34% growth

Environmental Conditions:
Inside

Physical Demands:
Light—lifting of no more than 20 pounds required
Talking or hearing required
Seeing required

Temperaments:
Performing a variety of tasks

Vocational Preparation:
1–3 months

Hotel Clerk

DOT = 238.362-010   GOE = 07.04.03

Greets guests arriving at a hotel or motel, and assists them in registering for a room and various service accommodations.

Aptitudes:
Intelligence	Moderate
Verbal	Moderate
Numerical	Moderate
Spatial	Low
Form Perception	Low
Clerical Perception	Moderate
Motor Coordination	Low
Finger Dexterity	Moderate
Manual Dexterity	Low
Eye-Hand-Foot Coordination	Low
Color Discrimination	Low

Data = Mod   People = Low   Things = Mod

Salary Range:
$12,000 (average)

Opportunity Outlook:
25-34% growth

Environmental Conditions:
Inside

Physical Demands:
Light—lifting of no more than 20 pounds required
Talking or hearing required

Temperaments:
Performing a variety of tasks

Vocational Preparation:
3-6 months

Hotel/Motel Manager

DOT = 187.117-038   GOE = 11.11.01

Manages hotel or motel to insure efficient and profitable operation; may oversee personnel, financial, advertising and marketing, housekeeping, restaurant and bar operations, and other functions.

Aptitudes:
Intelligence	High
Verbal	High
Numerical	High
Spatial	Moderate
Form Perception	Moderate
Clerical Perception	Moderate
Motor Coordination	Low
Finger Dexterity	Low
Manual Dexterity	Low
Eye-Hand-Foot Coordination	Low
Color Discrimination	Low

Data = High   People = High   Things = Low

Salary Range:
$42,300-$81,800

Opportunity Outlook:
35% growth or more

Environmental Conditions:
Inside

Physical Demands:
Sedentary—little or no lifting
Talking or hearing required

Temperaments:
Performing a variety of tasks
Dealing with people beyond giving and receiving information
Directing, controlling, or planning the work of others
Making decisions based upon senses and feelings

Vocational Preparation:
4-10 years

Hunting & Fishing Guide

DOT = 353.161-010   GOE = 09.01.01

Plans, organizes, and conducts hunting and fishing trips for individuals and groups; plans route, determines supplies and equipment, selects appropriate transportation, and instructs individuals in hunting and fishing techniques.

Aptitudes:
Intelligence	Moderate
Verbal	Moderate
Numerical	Low
Spatial	Moderate
Form Perception	Low
Clerical Perception	Low
Motor Coordination	Moderate
Finger Dexterity	Moderate
Manual Dexterity	High
Eye-Hand-Foot Coordination	Moderate
Color Discrimination	Low

Data = Mod   People = Mod   Things = Mod

Salary Range:
Varies

Opportunity Outlook:
14-24% growth

Environmental Conditions:
Outside

Physical Demands:
Heavy—lifting of no more than 100 pounds required
Stooping, kneeling, crouching, or crawling required
Reaching, handling, fingering, or feeling required
Talking or hearing required
Seeing required

Temperaments:
Directing, controlling, or planning the work of others
Making decisions based upon senses and feelings
Dealing with people beyond giving and receiving information
Performing a variety of tasks

Vocational Preparation: 2-4 years

Hydroelectric Station Operator

DOT = 952.362-018   GOE = 05.06.01

Controls and operates hydraulic and electrical equipment and machinery at a hydroelectric plant to generate electricity.

Aptitudes:
Intelligence	Moderate
Verbal	Moderate
Numerical	Moderate
Spatial	Low
Form Perception	Low
Clerical Perception	Moderate
Motor Coordination	Moderate
Finger Dexterity	Moderate
Manual Dexterity	Moderate
Eye-Hand-Foot Coordination	Low
Color Discrimination	Low

Data = Mod   People = Low   Things = Mod

Salary Range:
$21,500-$31,000

Opportunity Outlook:
14-24% growth

Environmental Conditions:
Inside
Presence of loud noises and vibrations
Presence of physical hazards

Physical Demands:
Light—lifting of no more than 20 pounds required
Reaching, handling, fingering, or feeling required
Seeing required

Temperaments:
Making decisions based upon facts
Performing repetitive tasks
Attempting to attain set limits

Vocational Preparation:
2-4 years

Illustrator (Commercial)

DOT = 141.061-022   GOE = 01.02.03

Draws or paints illustrations for use by various media, such as television stations, newspapers, and magazines, to explain or adorn printed or spoken words.

Aptitudes:
Intelligence	High
Verbal	High
Numerical	Moderate
Spatial	High
Form Perception	High
Clerical Perception	Moderate
Motor Coordination	High
Finger Dexterity	High
Manual Dexterity	High
Eye-Hand-Foot Coordination	Low
Color Discrimination	High

Data = High   People = Low   Things = High

Salary Range:
$12,500–$36,600

Opportunity Outlook:
25–34% growth

Environmental Conditions:
Inside

Physical Demands:
Sedentary—little or no lifting
Reaching, handling, fingering, or feeling required
Seeing required

Temperaments:
Interpreting the feelings and ideas of others
Making decisions based upon senses and feelings

Vocational Preparation:
2–4 years

Incinerator Plant Supervisor

DOT = 184.167-046   GOE = 05.06.04

Supervises and coordinates the activities of workers engaged in operating blast furnaces to incinerate garbage and trash.

Aptitudes:
Intelligence	High
Verbal	Moderate
Numerical	Moderate
Spatial	Low
Form Perception	Moderate
Clerical Perception	Moderate
Motor Coordination	Low
Finger Dexterity	Low
Manual Dexterity	Low
Eye-Hand-Foot Coordination	Low
Color Discrimination	Low

Data = Mod   People = Low   Things = Low

Salary Range:
$16,000–$28,000

Opportunity Outlook:
5–13% growth

Environmental Conditions:
Inside

Physical Demands:
Sedentary—little or no lifting
Talking or hearing required

Temperaments:
Directing, controlling, or planning the work of others
Making decisions based upon facts
Performing a variety of tasks

Vocational Preparation:
1–2 years

Industrial Engineer

DOT = 012.167-030   GOE = 05.01.06

Develops plans to improve the utilization of production facilities and personnel in an effort to improve the overall efficiency of an industrial manufacturing plant.

Aptitudes:
Intelligence	High
Verbal	High
Numerical	High
Spatial	High
Form Perception	Moderate
Clerical Perception	Moderate
Motor Coordination	Moderate
Finger Dexterity	Moderate
Manual Dexterity	Moderate
Eye-Hand-Foot Coordination	Low
Color Discrimination	Moderate

Data = High   People = Low   Things = Low

Salary Range:
$30,500–$93,500

Opportunity Outlook:
14–24% growth

Environmental Conditions:
Inside

Physical Demands:
Sedentary—little or no lifting
Talking or hearing required
Seeing required

Temperaments:
Making decisions based upon facts
Attempting to attain set limits
Performing a variety of tasks

Vocational Preparation:
4–10 years

Information Scientist

DOT = 109.067-010   GOE = 11.01.01

Designs computer-based information systems to provide management personnel or business clients with specific data (usually from computer processed information) to aid them in their business management decisions and plans.

Aptitudes:
Intelligence	High
Verbal	High
Numerical	High
Spatial	High
Form Perception	Low
Clerical Perception	Moderate
Motor Coordination	Low
Finger Dexterity	Low
Manual Dexterity	Low
Eye-Hand-Foot Coordination	Low
Color Discrimination	Low

Data = High   People = Low   Things = Low

Salary Range:
$20,000–$36,000

Opportunity Outlook:
35% growth

Environmental Conditions:
Inside

Physical Demands:
Sedentary—little or no lifting
Seeing required

Temperaments:
Making decisions based upon facts
Attempting to attain set limits

Vocational Preparation:
4–10 years

Injection-Molding Machine Offbearer

DOT = 690.686-042   GOE = 06.04.02

Removes musical instruments or parts from the discharge outlet end of an injection-molding machine to inspect for defects in manufacturing.

Aptitudes:
Intelligence	Low
Verbal	Low
Numerical	Low
Spatial	Low
Form Perception	Low
Clerical Perception	Low
Motor Coordination	Low
Finger Dexterity	Low
Manual Dexterity	Low
Eye-Hand-Foot Coordination	Low
Color Discrimination	Low

Data = Low   People = Low   Things = Low

Salary Range:
$28,000–$41,200

Opportunity Outlook:
25–34% growth

Environmental Conditions:
Inside
Wet and humid work environment
Presence of physical hazards

Physical Demands:
Moderate—lifting of no more than 50 pounds required
Reaching, handling, fingering, or feeling required

Temperaments:
Performing repetitive tasks

Vocational Preparation:
1–30 days

Insect/Disease Inspection Supervisor

DOT = 408.137-010   GOE = 03.02.04

Supervises and coordinates the activities of workers engaged in detecting the presence of noxious insects and plant disease in agricultural field crops to study the impact of these factors on the food supply.

Aptitudes:
Intelligence	High
Verbal	Moderate
Numerical	Moderate
Spatial	Low
Form Perception	Moderate
Clerical Perception	Moderate
Motor Coordination	Low
Finger Dexterity	Low
Manual Dexterity	Moderate
Eye-Hand-Foot Coordination	Low
Color Discrimination	Moderate

Data = High   People = Mod   Things = Low

Salary Range:
Not available

Opportunity Outlook:
Not available

Environmental Conditions:
Inside and outside

Physical Demands:
Light—lifting of no more than 20 pounds required
Reaching, handling, fingering, or feeling required
Talking or hearing required
Seeing required

Temperaments:
Directing, controlling, or planning the work of others
Making decisions based upon facts
Dealing with people beyond giving and receiving information

Vocational Preparation:
2–4 years

Insurance Claim Examiner (Clerk)

DOT = 168.267-014   GOE = 07.02.03

Reviews settled insurance claims to determine that payments and settlements have been made in accordance with company practices and regulations.

Aptitudes:
Intelligence	Moderate
Verbal	Moderate
Numerical	Moderate
Spatial	Low
Form Perception	Low
Clerical Perception	Moderate
Motor Coordination	Low
Finger Dexterity	Low
Manual Dexterity	Low
Eye-Hand-Foot Coordination	Low
Color Discrimination	Low

Data = High   People = Low   Things = Low

Salary Range:
$15,800 (average)

Opportunity Outlook:
14-24% growth

Environmental Conditions:
Inside

Physical Demands:
Sedentary—little or no lifting
Reaching, handling, fingering, or feeling required
Seeing required

Temperaments:
Making decisions based upon facts
Performing a variety of tasks

Vocational Preparation:
2-4 years

Insurance Estate Planner

DOT = 186.167-010   GOE = 08.01.02

Reviews the assets and liabilities of a person's estate to determine if the insurance coverage is adequate to protect the person from financial harm; may recommend additional insurance coverage to satisfy the financial needs and desires of the estate owner.

Aptitudes:
Intelligence	High
Verbal	High
Numerical	High
Spatial	Low
Form Perception	Low
Clerical Perception	Moderate
Motor Coordination	Low
Finger Dexterity	Low
Manual Dexterity	Low
Eye-Hand-Foot Coordination	Low
Color Discrimination	Low

Data = High   People = Mod   Things = Low

Salary Range:
$20,000-$80,000

Opportunity Outlook:
25-34% growth

Environmental Conditions:
Inside

Physical Demands:
Sedentary—little or no lifting
Talking or hearing required

Temperaments:
Making decisions based upon senses and feelings
Making decisions based upon facts
Dealing with people beyond giving and receiving information

Vocational Preparation:
4-10 years

Insurance Sales Agent

DOT = 250.257-010   GOE = 08.01.02

Sells life, health, medical, and other forms of insurance to individuals to help them protect themselves financially.

Aptitudes:

Intelligence	High
Verbal	High
Numerical	High
Spatial	Low
Form Perception	Low
Clerical Perception	High
Motor Coordination	Moderate
Finger Dexterity	Moderate
Manual Dexterity	Low
Eye-Hand-Foot Coordination	Low
Color Discrimination	Low

Data = High   People = Low   Things = Low

Salary Range:
$18,000–$50,300

Opportunity Outlook:
14–24% growth

Environmental Conditions:
Inside

Physical Demands:
Sedentary—little or no lifting required
Talking or hearing required

Temperaments:
Influencing the actions and beliefs of others
Making decisions based upon senses and feelings
Making decisions based upon facts
Dealing with people beyond giving and receiving information

Vocational Preparation:
2–4 years

Insurance Underwriter

DOT = 169.167-058   GOE = 11.06.03

Reviews individual applications for various kinds of insurance to evaluate the degree of risk involved, and then develops an insurance policy in accordance with the policy rules and regulations adopted by the insurance company.

Aptitudes:

Intelligence	High
Verbal	High
Numerical	High
Spatial	Low
Form Perception	Low
Clerical Perception	High
Motor Coordination	Low
Finger Dexterity	Low
Manual Dexterity	Low
Eye-Hand-Foot Coordination	Low
Color Discrimination	Low

Data = High   People = Low   Things = Low

Salary Range:
$23,900–$37,200

Opportunity Outlook:
14–24% growth

Environmental Conditions:
Inside

Physical Demands:
Sedentary—little or no lifting
Reaching, handling, fingering, or feeling required
Talking or hearing required
Seeing required

Temperaments:
Directing, controlling, or planning the work of others
Making decisions based upon senses and feelings
Making decisions based upon facts
Attempting to attain set limits

Vocational Preparation:
4–10 years

Intelligence Specialist

DOT = 059.267-010   GOE = 11.03.02

Evaluates data concerning subversive activities, enemy propaganda, and military or political conditions in foreign countries, and then prepares recommended countermeasures to be undertaken by various agents of the United States.

Aptitudes:
Intelligence	High
Verbal	High
Numerical	Moderate
Spatial	Moderate
Form Perception	Moderate
Clerical Perception	Moderate
Motor Coordination	Low
Finger Dexterity	Low
Manual Dexterity	Low
Eye-Hand-Foot Coordination	Low
Color Discrimination	Low

Data = High   People = Low   Things = Low

Salary Range:
$19,000–$80,000

Opportunity Outlook:
14–24% growth

Environmental Conditions:
Inside

Physical Demands:
Sedentary—little or no lifting
Talking or hearing required

Temperaments:
Interpreting the feelings and ideas of others
Making decisions based upon senses and feelings
Performing a variety of tasks

Vocational Preparation:
4–10 years

Interior Designer

DOT = 142.051-014   GOE = 01.02.03

Plans, designs, and furnishes interiors of residential, commercial, and industrial buildings, based upon the specific needs and preferences of the owners.

Aptitudes:
Intelligence	High
Verbal	High
Numerical	Moderate
Spatial	High
Form Perception	High
Clerical Perception	Moderate
Motor Coordination	Moderate
Finger Dexterity	High
Manual Dexterity	Moderate
Eye-Hand-Foot Coordination	Low
Color Discrimination	High

Data = High   People = Mod   Things = High

Salary Range:
$11,800–$50,000

Opportunity Outlook:
25–34% growth

Environmental Conditions:
Inside

Physical Demands:
Light—lifting of no more than 20 pounds required
Reaching, handling, fingering, or feeling required
Talking or hearing required
Seeing required

Temperaments:
Directing, controlling, or planning the work of others
Influencing the actions and beliefs of others
Dealing with people beyond giving and receiving information
Interpreting the feelings and ideas of others
Making decisions based upon senses and feelings

Vocational Preparation: 2–4 years

Interpreter

DOT = 137.267-010   GOE = 11.08.04

Translates spoken passages or converts written information from one language into another.

Aptitudes:
Intelligence	High
Verbal	High
Numerical	Low
Spatial	Low
Form Perception	Low
Clerical Perception	Moderate
Motor Coordination	Low
Finger Dexterity	Low
Manual Dexterity	Low
Eye-Hand-Foot Coordination	Low
Color Discrimination	Low

Data = High   People = Low   Things = Low

Salary Range:
$20,000–$55,000

Opportunity Outlook:
5–13% growth

Environmental Conditions:
Inside

Physical Demands:
Sedentary—little or no lifting
Reaching, handling, fingering, or feeling required
Talking or hearing required

Temperaments:
Making decisions based upon facts

Vocational Preparation:
1–2 years

Inventory Clerk

DOT = 222.387-026   GOE = 05.09.01

Compiles records of amount, kind, and value of merchandise, material, or stock on hand in a store, factory, warehouse, or similar facility.

Aptitudes:
Intelligence	Moderate
Verbal	Moderate
Numerical	Moderate
Spatial	Low
Form Perception	Low
Clerical Perception	High
Motor Coordination	Low
Finger Dexterity	Low
Manual Dexterity	Low
Eye-Hand-Foot Coordination	Low
Color Discrimination	Low

Data = Mod   People = Low   Things = Low

Salary Range:
$16,000 (average)

Opportunity Outlook:
5–13% growth

Environmental Conditions:
Inside

Physical Demands:
Light—lifting of no more than 20 pounds required
Reaching, handling, fingering, or feeling required
Seeing required

Temperaments:
Making decisions based upon facts
Performing repetitive tasks

Vocational Preparation:
3–6 months

Investigator (Utility Bill Complaints)

DOT = 241.267-034   GOE = 07.05.02

Investigates customers' complaints regarding their gas or electric bills; may examine weather reports during billing period to determine use of service; may also recommend that the customer's equipment be checked for defects; advises customers regarding findings and correct service charge.

Aptitudes:
Intelligence	Moderate
Verbal	Moderate
Numerical	Moderate
Spatial	Low
Form Perception	Low
Clerical Perception	High
Motor Coordination	Low
Finger Dexterity	Low
Manual Dexterity	Low
Eye-Hand-Foot Coordination	Low
Color Discrimination	Low

Data = High   People = Low   Things = Low

Salary Range:
$12,500–$18,000

Opportunity Outlook:
14–24% growth

Environmental Conditions:
Inside

Physical Demands:
Light—lifting of no more than 20 pounds required
Talking or hearing required
Seeing required

Temperaments:
Making decisions based upon facts

Vocational Preparation:
1–2 years

Investigator

DOT = 168.267-062   GOE = 11.10.01

Investigates regulated business activities to assure compliance with federal, state, or municipal laws; may locate and interview plaintiffs or witnesses in alleged business abuse cases, view actual conditions in question, and prepare reports on findings for use by legal authorities.

Aptitudes:
Intelligence	High
Verbal	High
Numerical	Moderate
Spatial	Moderate
Form Perception	Moderate
Clerical Perception	Moderate
Motor Coordination	Low
Finger Dexterity	Low
Manual Dexterity	Low
Eye-Hand-Foot Coordination	Low
Color Discrimination	Low

Data = Mod   People = Low   Things = Low

Salary Range:
$24,000 (average)

Opportunity Outlook:
14–24% growth

Environmental Conditions:
Inside and outside

Physical Demands:
Light—lifting of no more than 20 pounds required
Talking or hearing required
Seeing required

Temperaments:
Making decisions based upon senses and feelings
Making decisions based upon facts

Vocational Preparation:
1–2 years

Ironworker Machine Operator

DOT = 615.482-018   GOE = 06.02.02

Sets up and operates machinery that cuts, punches, and trims iron sections for use in constructing homes, offices, and other structures.

Aptitudes:
Intelligence	Moderate
Verbal	Low
Numerical	Low
Spatial	Moderate
Form Perception	Low
Clerical Perception	Low
Motor Coordination	Moderate
Finger Dexterity	Low
Manual Dexterity	Moderate
Eye-Hand-Foot Coordination	Moderate
Color Discrimination	Low

Data = Mod   People = Low   Things = High

Salary Range:
$11,800–$32,300

Opportunity Outlook:
5% decline or more

Environmental Conditions:
Inside
Presence of loud noises and vibrations
Presence of physical hazards

Physical Demands:
Heavy—lifting of no more than 100 pounds required
Stooping, kneeling, crouching, or crawling required
Reaching, handling, fingering, or feeling required
Seeing required

Temperaments:
Performing repetitive tasks
Attempting to attain set limits

Vocational Preparation:
3–6 months

Janitor

DOT = 382.664-010   GOE = 05.12.18

Keeps hotel, office building, apartment house, factory, school, or other building clean and in orderly condition; may also adjust and repair equipment, such as air conditioners, boilers, and hot water tanks to maintain the building in operational order.

Aptitudes:
Intelligence	Moderate
Verbal	Low
Numerical	Moderate
Spatial	Moderate
Form Perception	Low
Clerical Perception	Low
Motor Coordination	Moderate
Finger Dexterity	Low
Manual Dexterity	Moderate
Eye-Hand-Foot Coordination	Low
Color Discrimination	Low

Data = Low   People = Low   Things = Mod

Salary Range:
$8,800–$24,400

Opportunity Outlook:
14–24% growth

Environmental Conditions:
Inside and outside

Physical Demands:
Moderate—lifting of no more than 50 pounds required
Reaching, handling, fingering, or feeling required
Talking or hearing required
Seeing required

Temperaments:
Attempting to attain set limits
Performing a variety of tasks

Vocational Preparation:
1–3 months

Jeweler

DOT = 700.281-010   GOE = 01.06.02

Makes jewelry items, such as rings, brooches, pendants, bracelets, and lockets, out of metal and gemstones; may also repair and clean jewelry.

Aptitudes:
Intelligence	Moderate
Verbal	Moderate
Numerical	Moderate
Spatial	High
Form Perception	High
Clerical Perception	Low
Motor Coordination	Moderate
Finger Dexterity	High
Manual Dexterity	Moderate
Eye-Hand-Foot Coordination	Low
Color Discrimination	Moderate

Data = Mod   People = Low   Things = High

Salary Range:
$20,000–$30,000

Opportunity Outlook:
14–24% growth

Environmental Conditions:
Inside

Physical Demands:
Sedentary—little or no lifting
Reaching, handling, fingering, or feeling required
Seeing required

Temperaments:
Making decisions based upon senses and feelings
Attempting to attain set limits
Performing a variety of tasks

Vocational Preparation:
2–4 years

Job Analyst

DOT = 166.267-018   GOE = 11.03.04

Collects, analyzes, and prepares occupational information to help personnel, administration, and management define the nature of each occupational position required to operate the business.

Aptitudes:
Intelligence	High
Verbal	High
Numerical	High
Spatial	Moderate
Form Perception	Moderate
Clerical Perception	Moderate
Motor Coordination	Low
Finger Dexterity	Low
Manual Dexterity	Low
Eye-Hand-Foot Coordination	Low
Color Discrimination	Low

Data = High   People = Mod   Things = Low

Salary Range:
$17,000–$41,000

Opportunity Outlook:
25–34% growth

Environmental Conditions:
Inside

Physical Demands:
Light—lifting of no more than 20 pounds required
Talking or hearing required
Seeing required

Temperaments:
Directing, controlling, or planning the work of others
Making decisions based upon senses and feelings
Making decisions based upon facts
Dealing with people beyond giving and receiving information

Vocational Preparation:
2–4 years

Jockey

DOT = 153.244-010   GOE = 12.01.03

Rides racehorses at a racetrack; using knowledge of riding, capabilities of the horse, and track and weather conditions, determines how best to win the horse race.

Aptitudes:
Intelligence	Moderate
Verbal	Moderate
Numerical	Low
Spatial	High
Form Perception	High
Clerical Perception	Low
Motor Coordination	Moderate
Finger Dexterity	Moderate
Manual Dexterity	Moderate
Eye-Hand-Foot Coordination	Moderate
Color Discrimination	Low

Data = Mod   People = Low   Things = Low

Salary Range:
Varies

Opportunity Outlook:
14–24% growth

Environmental Conditions:
Outside
Presence of physical hazards

Physical Demands:
Moderate—lifting of no more than 50 pounds
Climbing or balancing required
Stooping, kneeling, crouching, or crawling required
Reaching, handling, fingering, or feeling required
Talking or hearing required
Seeing required

Temperaments:
Making decisions based upon senses and feelings
Performing under stress or in emergencies

Vocational Preparation: 1–2 years

Judge

DOT = 111.107-010   GOE = 11.04.01

Presides over the activities of a trial or hearing in a court of law; advises counsel about legally acceptable behavior and procedures; advises jury members and litigants regarding their rights and obligations; may advise and instruct court personnel to ensure proper conduct during proceedings.

Aptitudes:
Intelligence	High
Verbal	High
Numerical	High
Spatial	Low
Form Perception	Low
Clerical Perception	Low
Motor Coordination	Low
Finger Dexterity	Low
Manual Dexterity	Low
Eye-Hand-Foot Coordination	Low
Color Discrimination	Low

Data = High   People = High   Things = Low

Salary Range:
$55,200–$132,700

Opportunity Outlook:
14–24% growth

Environmental Conditions:
Inside

Physical Demands:
Sedentary—little or no lifting
Talking or hearing required

Temperaments:
Directing, controlling, or planning the work of others
Influencing the actions and beliefs of others
Making decisions based upon senses and feelings
Dealing with people beyond giving and receiving information
Making decisions based upon facts

Vocational Preparation:
More than 10 years

Laboratory Assistant (Zoo)

DOT = 073.361-014   GOE = 02.04.02

Assists professional veterinary workers in the examination and treatment of animals that may be sick or injured; may also assist veterinary workers who are engaged in research work with animals.

Aptitudes:
Intelligence	Moderate
Verbal	Moderate
Numerical	Moderate
Spatial	Moderate
Form Perception	Moderate
Clerical Perception	High
Motor Coordination	High
Finger Dexterity	Moderate
Manual Dexterity	Moderate
Eye-Hand-Foot Coordination	Low
Color Discrimination	Moderate

Data = Mod   People = Low   Things = High

Salary Range:
$11,900–$20,700

Opportunity Outlook:
35% growth or more

Environmental Conditions:
Inside and outside
Presence of physical hazards

Physical Demands:
Moderate—lifting of no more than 50 pounds required
Reaching, handling, fingering, or feeling required
Seeing required

Temperaments:
Performing under stress or in emergencies
Attempting to attain set limits

Vocational Preparation:
1/2–1 year

Landscape Gardener

DOT = 408.161-010   GOE = 03.01.03

Cares for and maintains lawns, shrubs, trees, and gardens owned by private individuals, companies, or other organizations.

Aptitudes:
Intelligence	Moderate
Verbal	Moderate
Numerical	Low
Spatial	Moderate
Form Perception	Moderate
Clerical Perception	Low
Motor Coordination	Moderate
Finger Dexterity	Moderate
Manual Dexterity	Moderate
Eye-Hand-Foot Coordination	Low
Color Discrimination	Moderate

Data = Low   People = Low   Things = High

Salary Range:
$8,800–$23,400

Opportunity Outlook:
35% growth or more

Environmental Conditions:
Outside
Presence of loud noises and vibrations
Presence of physical hazards

Physical Demands:
Heavy—lifting of no more than 100 pounds required
Stooping, kneeling, crouching, or crawling required
Reaching, handling, fingering, or feeling required
Seeing required

Temperaments:
Making decisions based upon senses and feelings
Making decisions based upon facts
Performing a variety of tasks

Vocational Preparation: 1–2 years

Landscape Laborer

DOT = 408.687-014   GOE = 03.04.04

Moves soil, equipment, and materials, digs holes, and performs related tasks to assist landscape gardeners in caring for public or private lawns, trees, shrubs, and gardens.

Aptitudes:
Intelligence	Low
Verbal	Low
Numerical	Low
Spatial	Low
Form Perception	Low
Clerical Perception	Low
Motor Coordination	Low
Finger Dexterity	Low
Manual Dexterity	Moderate
Eye-Hand-Foot Coordination	Low
Color Discrimination	Low

Data = Low   People = Low   Things = Low

Salary Range:
$12,700–$15,200

Opportunity Outlook:
35% growth or more

Environmental Conditions:
Outside
Presence of loud noises and vibrations
Presence of physical hazards

Physical Demands:
Heavy—lifting of no more than 100 pounds required
Stooping, kneeling, crouching, or crawling required
Reaching, handling, fingering, or feeling required

Temperaments:
Attempting to attain set limits
Performing a variety of tasks

Vocational Preparation:
1–30 days

Lawn Service Worker

DOT = 408.684-010   GOE = 03.04.04

Cares for lawns using power mowers and thatchers, and waters and uses various chemicals to fertilize lawns to promote growth.

Aptitudes:
Intelligence	Moderate
Verbal	Low
Numerical	Low
Spatial	Moderate
Form Perception	Low
Clerical Perception	Low
Motor Coordination	Moderate
Finger Dexterity	Low
Manual Dexterity	Moderate
Eye-Hand-Foot Coordination	Low
Color Discrimination	Low

Data = Low   People = Low   Things = Mod

Salary Range:
$15,000–$17,700

Opportunity Outlook:
35% growth or more

Environmental Conditions:
Outside
Presence of loud noises and vibrations
Presence of physical hazards
Presence of atmospheric dangers such as fumes, odors, etc.

Physical Demands:
Heavy—lifting of no more than 100 pounds required
Reaching, handling, fingering, or feeling required
Seeing required

Temperaments:
Attempting to attain set limits

Vocational Preparation:
3–6 months

Lawn/Tree Spray Service Supervisor

DOT = 408.131-010   GOE = 03.02.03

Supervises and coordinates the activities of workers engaged in pruning trees and shrubs, cultivating lawns, and applying pesticides and fertilizers to promote the growth of lawns.

Aptitudes:
Intelligence	Moderate
Verbal	Moderate
Numerical	Moderate
Spatial	Moderate
Form Perception	Low
Clerical Perception	Moderate
Motor Coordination	Low
Finger Dexterity	Low
Manual Dexterity	Low
Eye-Hand-Foot Coordination	Low
Color Discrimination	Low

Data = Mod   People = Mod   Things = Mod

Salary Range:
$19,500 (average)

Opportunity Outlook:
35% growth or more

Environmental Conditions:
Inside and outside
Presence of atmospheric dangers such as fumes

Physical Demands:
Light—lifting of no more than 20 pounds required
Reaching, handling, fingering, or feeling required
Seeing required

Temperaments:
Directing, controlling, or planning the work of others
Making decisions based upon facts
Dealing with people beyond giving and receiving information
Performing a variety of tasks

Vocational Preparation: 1–2 years

Lawyer

DOT = 110.107-010   GOE = 11.04.02

Conducts criminal and/or civil lawsuits in a court of law to defend the rights of a client; draws up legal documents, advises clients as to their legal rights, conducts research to prepare a client's case, and may also argue a client's case in a court of law before a judge or jury.

Aptitudes:
Intelligence	High
Verbal	High
Numerical	High
Spatial	Low
Form Perception	Low
Clerical Perception	Moderate
Motor Coordination	Low
Finger Dexterity	Low
Manual Dexterity	Low
Eye-Hand-Foot Coordination	Low
Color Discrimination	Low

Data = High   People = High   Things = Low

Salary Range:
$25,000–$1,000,000

Opportunity Outlook:
25–34% growth

Environmental Conditions:
Inside

Physical Demands:
Sedentary—little or no lifting
Talking or hearing required

Temperaments:
Influencing the actions and beliefs of others
Making decisions based upon senses and feelings
Dealing with people beyond giving and receiving information
Performing a variety of tasks
Making decisions based upon facts

Vocational Preparation:
4–10 years

Librarian

DOT = 100.127-014   GOE = 11.02.04

Maintains the collection of books, publications, documents, audiovisual resources, and other materials found in a public or private library; may purchase new materials, teach people how to use library, shelve materials, and manage the overall facility operation.

Aptitudes:
Intelligence	High
Verbal	High
Numerical	Moderate
Spatial	Low
Form Perception	Low
Clerical Perception	High
Motor Coordination	Low
Finger Dexterity	Low
Manual Dexterity	Low
Eye-Hand-Foot Coordination	Low
Color Discrimination	Low

Data = High   People = Mod   Things = Low

Salary Range:
$23,400–$41,200

Opportunity Outlook:
5–13% growth

Environmental Conditions:
Inside

Physical Demands:
Light—lifting of no more than 20 pounds required
Reaching, handling, fingering, or feeling required
Talking or hearing required

Temperaments:
Making decisions based upon senses and feelings
Dealing with people beyond giving and receiving information
Performing a variety of tasks

Vocational Preparation:
4–10 years

Library Technical Assistant

DOT = 100.367-018   GOE = 11.02.04

Assists librarians in maintaining the collection of materials (books, publications, audiovisual resources, etc.) found in a public or private library; shelves materials, assists individuals in finding desired information, orders new materials, and carries out basic operational activities.

Aptitudes:
Intelligence	Moderate
Verbal	Moderate
Numerical	Moderate
Spatial	Low
Form Perception	Moderate
Clerical Perception	High
Motor Coordination	Low
Finger Dexterity	Low
Manual Dexterity	Low
Eye-Hand-Foot Coordination	Low
Color Discrimination	Low

Data = Mod   People = Low   Things = Low

Salary Range:
$21,000 (average)

Opportunity Outlook:
5–13% growth

Environmental Conditions:
Inside

Physical Demands:
Light—lifting of no more than 20 pounds required
Reaching, handling, fingering, or feeling required
Seeing required

Temperaments:
Performing a variety of tasks

Vocational Preparation:
1–2 years

Lifeguard

DOT = 379.667-014   GOE = 04.02.03

Monitors the activities of swimmers at a beach or in a pool to prevent accidents and drowning; may swim or boat out to reach swimmers in distress; may apply lifesaving techniques to such swimmers.

Aptitudes:
Intelligence	Moderate
Verbal	Moderate
Numerical	Low
Spatial	Moderate
Form Perception	Low
Clerical Perception	Low
Motor Coordination	High
Finger Dexterity	Low
Manual Dexterity	High
Eye-Hand-Foot Coordination	Moderate
Color Discrimination	Low

Data = Low   People = Low   Things = Low

Salary Range:
Varies

Opportunity Outlook:
25–34% growth

Environmental Conditions:
Outside

Physical Demands:
Very heavy—lifting of more than 100 pounds required
Reaching, handling, fingering, or feeling required
Talking or hearing required
Seeing required

Temperaments:
Making decisions based upon senses and feelings
Performing under stress or in emergencies

Vocational Preparation:
3–6 months

Literary Agent

DOT = 191.117-034   GOE = 11.12.03

Attempts to market the writings of clients to publishers of literary works, such as newspapers, magazines, and book publishers; reads and advises clients how best to prepare or revise manuscripts.

Aptitudes:
Intelligence	High
Verbal	High
Numerical	Moderate
Spatial	Moderate
Form Perception	Moderate
Clerical Perception	Moderate
Motor Coordination	Low
Finger Dexterity	Low
Manual Dexterity	Low
Eye-Hand-Foot Coordination	Low
Color Discrimination	Low

Data = High   People = High   Things = Low

Salary Range:
$20,000–$60,000+

Opportunity Outlook:
14–24% growth

Environmental Conditions:
Inside

Physical Demands:
Sedentary—little or no lifting
Talking or hearing required

Temperaments:
Influencing the actions and beliefs of others
Dealing with people beyond giving and receiving information

Vocational Preparation:
2–4 years

Livestock Farm Worker

DOT = 410.664-010   GOE = 03.04.01

Assists livestock ranchers in caring for and raising farm livestock, such as cattle, sheep, pigs, and goats.

Aptitudes:
Intelligence	Low
Verbal	Low
Numerical	Low
Spatial	Low
Form Perception	Low
Clerical Perception	Low
Motor Coordination	Moderate
Finger Dexterity	Low
Manual Dexterity	Moderate
Eye-Hand-Foot Coordination	Low
Color Discrimination	Low

Data = Low   People = Low   Things = Mod

Salary Range:
$8,500–$16,000

Opportunity Outlook:
5% decline or more

Environmental Conditions:
Inside and outside
Presence of physical hazards
Presence of atmospheric dangers

Physical Demands:
Heavy—lifting of no more than 100 pounds required
Stooping, kneeling, crouching, or crawling required
Reaching, handling, fingering, or feeling required

Temperaments:
Performing a variety of tasks

Vocational Preparation:
3–6 months

Livestock Rancher

DOT = 410.161-018   GOE = 03.01.01

Breeds and raises livestock, such as beef and dairy cattle, goats, pigs, horses, sheep, reindeer, for such purposes as sale of meat, riding, or working stock.

Aptitudes:
Intelligence	Moderate
Verbal	Moderate
Numerical	Moderate
Spatial	Low
Form Perception	Low
Clerical Perception	Low
Motor Coordination	Moderate
Finger Dexterity	Low
Manual Dexterity	Moderate
Eye-Hand-Foot Coordination	Low
Color Discrimination	Low

Data = Mod   People = Low   Things = High

Salary Range:
$15,000–$75,000+

Opportunity Outlook:
5–13% growth

Environmental Conditions:
Inside and outside
Presence of physical hazards
Presence of atmospheric dangers

Physical Demands:
Very heavy—lifting of more than 100 pounds required
Stooping, kneeling, crouching, or crawling required
Reaching, handling, fingering, or feeling required
Seeing required

Temperaments:
Making decisions based upon senses and feelings
Performing a variety of tasks

Vocational Preparation:
2–4 years

Lobbyist

DOT = 165.017-010   GOE = 11.09.03

Contacts and confers with members of Congress or other legislative bodies or other public office holders to persuade them to support legislation favorable to the interests of the clients who have hired the lobbyist.

Aptitudes:
Intelligence	High
Verbal	High
Numerical	High
Spatial	Low
Form Perception	Low
Clerical Perception	Moderate
Motor Coordination	Low
Finger Dexterity	Low
Manual Dexterity	Low
Eye-Hand-Foot Coordination	Low
Color Discrimination	Low

Data = High   People = High   Things = Low

Salary Range:
$20,000–$100,000+

Opportunity Outlook:
25–34% growth

Environmental Conditions:
Inside

Physical Demands:
Sedentary—little or no lifting
Talking or hearing required

Temperaments:
Directing, controlling, or planning the work of others
Influencing the actions and beliefs of others
Making decisions based upon senses and feelings
Dealing with people beyond giving and receiving information

Vocational Preparation:
2–4 years

Locomotive Engineer

DOT = 910.363-014   GOE = 05.08.02

Drives electric, diesel-electric, or gas-turbine-electric locomotive trains carrying passengers and freight from one location to another.

Aptitudes:
Intelligence	Moderate
Verbal	Moderate
Numerical	Low
Spatial	Moderate
Form Perception	Moderate
Clerical Perception	Moderate
Motor Coordination	Moderate
Finger Dexterity	Low
Manual Dexterity	Moderate
Eye-Hand-Foot Coordination	Moderate
Color Discrimination	Low

Data = Mod   People = Low   Things = Mod

Salary Range:
$55,000 (average)

Opportunity Outlook:
5% decline or more

Environmental Conditions:
Inside
Presence of loud noises and vibrations

Physical Demands:
Light—lifting of no more than 20 pounds required
Reaching, handling, fingering, or feeling required
Talking or hearing required
Seeing required

Temperaments:
Making decisions based upon senses and feelings
Making decisions based upon facts
Performing a variety of tasks

Vocational Preparation:
2–4 years

Log Loader

DOT = 921.683-058   GOE = 05.11.04

Operates a hydraulic or pneumatic lifting device in a sawmill yard to load cut logs onto a flatbed truck for shipment to lumber yards.

Aptitudes:
Intelligence	Moderate
Verbal	Low
Numerical	Low
Spatial	Moderate
Form Perception	Low
Clerical Perception	Low
Motor Coordination	Moderate
Finger Dexterity	Low
Manual Dexterity	Moderate
Eye-Hand-Foot Coordination	Moderate
Color Discrimination	Low

Data = Low   People = Low   Things = Mod

Salary Range:
$15,900 (average)

Opportunity Outlook:
0–4% growth or decline

Environmental Conditions:
Outside
Presence of loud noises and vibrations

Physical Demands:
Light—lifting of no more than 20 pounds required
Seeing required
Reaching, handling, fingering, and feeling required

Temperaments:
Performing repetitive tasks
Attempting to attain set limits

Vocational Preparation:
3–6 months

Logging Operations Inspector

DOT = 168.267-070   GOE = 03.01.04

Inspects lumber logging operations to ensure that they adhere to the contract provisions created by the logging developers and buyers; also, inspects safety procedures to ensure that they comply with state and federal laws and regulations.

Aptitudes:
Intelligence	High
Verbal	High
Numerical	Moderate
Spatial	Moderate
Form Perception	Low
Clerical Perception	Moderate
Motor Coordination	Low
Finger Dexterity	Low
Manual Dexterity	Low
Eye-Hand-Foot Coordination	Low
Color Discrimination	Low

Data = Mod   People = Low   Things = Low

Salary Range:
$16,000–$18,500

Opportunity Outlook:
5–13% growth

Environmental Conditions:
Inside

Physical Demands:
Light—lifting of no more than 20 pounds required
Talking or hearing required
Seeing required

Temperaments:
Making decisions based upon senses and feelings
Making decisions based upon facts

Vocational Preparation:
2–4 years

Machine Operator

DOT = 616.360-018   GOE = 06.01.03

Sets up and operates metal fabricating machines to cut, bend, straighten, or form metal sheets into various objects.

Aptitudes:
Intelligence	Moderate
Verbal	Low
Numerical	Moderate
Spatial	Moderate
Form Perception	Moderate
Clerical Perception	Low
Motor Coordination	Moderate
Finger Dexterity	Moderate
Manual Dexterity	Moderate
Eye-Hand-Foot Coordination	Moderate
Color Discrimination	Low

Data = Mod   People = Low   Things = High

Salary Range:
$12,500–$28,000

Opportunity Outlook:
14–24% growth

Environmental Conditions:
Inside
Presence of loud noises and vibrations
Presence of physical hazards
Presence of atmospheric dangers

Physical Demands:
Moderate—lifting of no more than 50 pounds required
Stooping, kneeling, crouching, or crawling required
Reaching, handling, fingering, or feeling required
Seeing required

Temperaments:
Making decisions based upon facts
Attempting to attain set limits

Vocational Preparation: 1–2 years

Machine Setup Worker

DOT = 600.380-018   GOE = 06.01.03

Sets up and operates different types of machines, such as lathes, milling machines, boring machines, and grinders, to make objects from metal or wood.

Aptitudes:
Intelligence	Moderate
Verbal	Moderate
Numerical	Moderate
Spatial	Moderate
Form Perception	Moderate
Clerical Perception	Low
Motor Coordination	Moderate
Finger Dexterity	Moderate
Manual Dexterity	Moderate
Eye-Hand-Foot Coordination	Low
Color Discrimination	Low

Data = Mod   People = Low   Things = High

Salary Range:
$11,700–$32,300

Opportunity Outlook:
5% decline or more

Environmental Conditions:
Inside
Presence of loud noises and vibrations

Physical Demands:
Moderate—lifting of no more than 50 pounds required
Reaching, handling, fingering, or feeling required
Seeing required

Temperaments:
Making decisions based upon facts
Attempting to attain set limits
Performing a variety of tasks

Vocational Preparation:
1–2 years

Machinist

DOT = 600.280-022   GOE = 05.05.07

Sets up and operates machinery and tools that in turn are used to make metal parts for other machines and tools.

Aptitudes:
Intelligence	Moderate
Verbal	Moderate
Numerical	Moderate
Spatial	High
Form Perception	High
Clerical Perception	Low
Motor Coordination	Moderate
Finger Dexterity	High
Manual Dexterity	High
Eye-Hand-Foot Coordination	Low
Color Discrimination	Low

Data = Mod   People = Low   Things = High

Salary Range:
$14,700–$38,800

Opportunity Outlook:
5–13% decline

Environmental Conditions:
Inside
Presence of loud noises and vibrations

Physical Demands:
Moderate—lifting of no more than 50 pounds required
Stooping, kneeling, crouching, or crawling required
Reaching, handling, fingering, or feeling required
Seeing required

Temperaments:
Making decisions based upon facts
Attempting to attain set limits
Performing a variety of tasks

Vocational Preparation: 2–4 years

Magician

DOT = 159.041-010   GOE = 01.03.02

Performs original and stock tricks of illusion and sleight of hand to entertain and mystify an audience.

Aptitudes:
Intelligence	Moderate
Verbal	Moderate
Numerical	Low
Spatial	Moderate
Form Perception	Moderate
Clerical Perception	Low
Motor Coordination	High
Finger Dexterity	High
Manual Dexterity	High
Eye-Hand-Foot Coordination	Low
Color Discrimination	Low

Data = Mod   People = Low   Things = Mod

Salary Range:
Varies

Opportunity Outlook:
Not available

Environmental Conditions:
Inside

Physical Demands:
Light—lifting of no more than 20 pounds required
Reaching, handling, fingering, or feeling required
Talking or hearing required
Seeing required

Temperaments:
Interpreting the feelings and ideas of others
Making decisions based upon senses and feelings

Vocational Preparation:
1–2 years

Mail Carrier

DOT = 230.367-010   GOE = 07.05.04

Sorts mail for delivery and then delivers mail to individual homes and businesses following a predetermined route; may deliver mail on foot or from a vehicle.

Aptitudes:
Intelligence	Moderate
Verbal	Moderate
Numerical	Low
Spatial	Low
Form Perception	Low
Clerical Perception	Moderate
Motor Coordination	Moderate
Finger Dexterity	Low
Manual Dexterity	Moderate
Eye-Hand-Foot Coordination	Low
Color Discrimination	Low

Data = Mod   People = Low   Things = Low

Salary Range:
$23,600–$29,100

Opportunity Outlook:
5–13% growth

Environmental Conditions:
Inside and outside

Physical Demands:
Light—lifting of no more than 20 pounds required
Reaching, handling, fingering, or feeling required
Seeing required

Temperaments:
Performing repetitive tasks

Vocational Preparation:
3–6 months

Mailroom Supervisor

DOT = 222.137-022   GOE = 07.07.02

Supervises and coordinates the activities of workers engaged in wrapping and addressing printed materials, such as periodicals, books, and newspapers, for mailing and dispatching.

Aptitudes:
Intelligence	Moderate
Verbal	Moderate
Numerical	Moderate
Spatial	Low
Form Perception	Moderate
Clerical Perception	Moderate
Motor Coordination	Low
Finger Dexterity	Low
Manual Dexterity	Low
Eye-Hand-Foot Coordination	Low
Color Discrimination	Low

Data = Mod   People = Mod   Things = Low

Salary Range:
$12,000–$26,000

Opportunity Outlook:
14–24% growth

Environmental Conditions:
Inside

Physical Demands:
Light—lifting of no more than 20 pounds required
Seeing required

Temperaments:
Directing, controlling, or planning the work of others
Making decisions based upon facts
Dealing with people beyond giving and receiving information
Performing a variety of tasks

Vocational Preparation:
2–4 years

Maintenance Superintendent

DOT = 189.167-046   GOE = 05.02.02

Directs and coordinates, through subordinate personnel, the activities of workers engaged in the repair, maintenance, and installation of machines, tools, and equipment in a mill, industrial plant, or similar type of facility.

Aptitudes:
Intelligence	High
Verbal	High
Numerical	Moderate
Spatial	Moderate
Form Perception	Low
Clerical Perception	Moderate
Motor Coordination	Low
Finger Dexterity	Low
Manual Dexterity	Low
Eye-Hand-Foot Coordination	Low
Color Discrimination	Low

Data = High   People = Mod   Things = Low

Salary Range:
$16,000 (average)

Opportunity Outlook:
14–24% growth

Environmental Conditions:
Inside

Physical Demands:
Light—lifting of no more than 20 pounds required
Talking or hearing required

Temperaments:
Directing, controlling, or planning the work of others
Making decisions based upon facts
Dealing with people beyond giving and receiving information

Vocational Preparation:
2–4 years

Make-Up Artist (Film/TV)

DOT = 333.071-010   GOE = 01.06.02

Studies film and TV production requirements, such as character, period, setting, and situation, and applies make-up to actors to alter their appearance to match with their roles.

Aptitudes:
Intelligence	Moderate
Verbal	Moderate
Numerical	Low
Spatial	Moderate
Form Perception	High
Clerical Perception	Low
Motor Coordination	Moderate
Finger Dexterity	Moderate
Manual Dexterity	Moderate
Eye-Hand-Foot Coordination	Low
Color Discrimination	High

Data = Mod   People = Low   Things = Mod

Salary Range:
$14,500–$29,100

Opportunity Outlook:
14–24% growth

Environmental Conditions:
Inside

Physical Demands:
Light—lifting of no more than 20 pounds required
Reaching, handling, fingering, or feeling required
Talking or hearing required
Seeing required

Temperaments:
Interpreting the feelings and ideas of others
Making decisions based upon senses and feelings
Performing a variety of tasks

Vocational Preparation:
1–2 years

Manicurist

DOT = 331.674-010   GOE = 09.05.01

Cleans, shapes, and polishes customers' fingernails and toenails.

Aptitudes:
Intelligence	Low
Verbal	Low
Numerical	Low
Spatial	Low
Form Perception	Moderate
Clerical Perception	Low
Motor Coordination	Moderate
Finger Dexterity	Moderate
Manual Dexterity	Moderate
Eye-Hand-Foot Coordination	Low
Color Discrimination	Moderate

Data = Low   People = Low   Things = Mod

Salary Range:
$14,500–$29,100

Opportunity Outlook:
14–24% growth

Environmental Conditions:
Inside

Physical Demands:
Sedentary—little or no lifting
Reaching, handling, fingering, or feeling required
Seeing required

Temperaments:
Making decisions based upon senses and feelings

Vocational Preparation:
1–3 months

Manufacturers' Representative

DOT = 279.157-010   GOE = 08.02.01

Sells merchandise produced by a company to wholesale distributors, outlets, and stores.

Aptitudes:
Intelligence	High
Verbal	High
Numerical	Moderate
Spatial	Low
Form Perception	Moderate
Clerical Perception	Moderate
Motor Coordination	Low
Finger Dexterity	Low
Manual Dexterity	Low
Eye-Hand-Foot Coordination	Low
Color Discrimination	Low

Data = High   People = Mod   Things = Low

Salary Range:
$15,500–$59,000

Opportunity Outlook:
14–24% growth

Environmental Conditions:
Inside

Physical Demands:
Light—lifting of no more than 20 pounds required
Reaching, handling, fingering, or feeling required
Talking or hearing required

Temperaments:
Influencing the actions and beliefs of others
Making decisions based upon senses and feelings
Dealing with people beyond giving and receiving information

Vocational Preparation:
1–2 years

Masseur

DOT = 334.374-010   GOE = 09.05.01

Massages customers' back, neck, arms, and legs and administers various body conditioning treatments to relieve muscle strain and tension.

Aptitudes:
Intelligence	Moderate
Verbal	Moderate
Numerical	Low
Spatial	Moderate
Form Perception	Moderate
Clerical Perception	Low
Motor Coordination	Moderate
Finger Dexterity	Moderate
Manual Dexterity	High
Eye-Hand-Foot Coordination	Low
Color Discrimination	Low

Data = Mod   People = Low   Things = Mod

Salary Range:
Varies

Opportunity Outlook:
25-34% growth

Environmental Conditions:
Inside

Physical Demands:
Moderate—lifting of no more than 50 pounds required
Reaching, handling, fingering, or feeling required

Temperaments:
Making decisions based upon senses and feelings
Performing a variety of tasks

Vocational Preparation:
3-6 months

Material Coordinator

DOT = 221.167-014   GOE = 05.09.02

Coordinates and expedites the flow of materials, parts, and assembled goods within or between various departments of a large organization in accordance with the production and shipping schedules of each department.

Aptitudes:
Intelligence	Moderate
Verbal	Moderate
Numerical	Moderate
Spatial	Low
Form Perception	Moderate
Clerical Perception	Moderate
Motor Coordination	Low
Finger Dexterity	Low
Manual Dexterity	Low
Eye-Hand-Foot Coordination	Low
Color Discrimination	Low

Data = Mod   People = Low   Things = Low

Salary Range:
$16,500 (average)

Opportunity Outlook:
14-24% growth

Environmental Conditions:
Inside

Physical Demands:
Light—lifting of no more than 20 pounds required
Reaching, handling, fingering, or feeling required
Talking or hearing required
Seeing required

Temperaments:
Making decisions based upon facts
Attempting to attain set limits
Performing a variety of tasks

Vocational Preparation:
1-2 years

Mathematician

DOT = 020.067-014   GOE = 02.01.01

Conducts research into fundamental mathematics and in the application of mathematical techniques to solve problems in engineering, science, business, medicine, and other fields.

Aptitudes:
Intelligence	High
Verbal	High
Numerical	High
Spatial	High
Form Perception	Low
Clerical Perception	Low
Motor Coordination	Low
Finger Dexterity	Low
Manual Dexterity	Low
Eye-Hand-Foot Coordination	Low
Color Discrimination	Low

Data = High   People = Low   Things = Low

Salary Range:
$27,000–$49,500

Opportunity Outlook:
5–13% growth

Environmental Conditions:
Inside

Physical Demands:
Sedentary—little or no lifting
Reaching, handling, fingering, or feeling required
Seeing required

Temperaments:
Making decisions based upon senses and feelings
Making decisions based upon facts

Vocational Preparation:
4–10 years

Mechanical Shovel Operator

DOT = 932.683-018   GOE = 05.11.02

Operates a power shovel that loads coal or rock into mine cars or onto conveyor belts in underground mines.

Aptitudes:
Intelligence	Moderate
Verbal	Low
Numerical	Low
Spatial	Moderate
Form Perception	Low
Clerical Perception	Low
Motor Coordination	Moderate
Finger Dexterity	Low
Manual Dexterity	Moderate
Eye-Hand-Foot Coordination	Moderate
Color Discrimination	Low

Data = Low   People = Low   Things = Mod

Salary Range:
$16,000–$38,000

Opportunity Outlook:
25–34% growth

Environmental Conditions:
Inside and outside
Presence of loud noises and vibrations
Presence of atmospheric dangers

Physical Demands:
Moderate—lifting of no more than 50 pounds required
Reaching, handling, fingering, or feeling required
Seeing required

Temperaments:
Performing repetitive tasks

Vocational Preparation:
1/2–1 year

Media Director

DOT = 164.117-018   GOE = 11.09.01

Plans and coordinates all the media programs, such as television and newspaper advertising, for a corporation or organization.

Aptitudes:
Intelligence	High
Verbal	High
Numerical	Moderate
Spatial	Moderate
Form Perception	Moderate
Clerical Perception	Moderate
Motor Coordination	Low
Finger Dexterity	Low
Manual Dexterity	Low
Eye-Hand-Foot Coordination	Low
Color Discrimination	Moderate

Data = High   People = High   Things = Low

Salary Range:
$26,500–$40,000+

Opportunity Outlook:
35% growth or more

Environmental Conditions:
Inside

Physical Demands:
Sedentary—little or no lifting
Reaching, handling, fingering, or feeling required
Talking or hearing required
Seeing required

Temperaments:
Directing, controlling, or planning the work of others
Making decisions based upon senses and feelings
Dealing with people beyond giving and receiving information

Vocational Preparation:
4–10 years

Medical Equipment Repairer

DOT = 639.281-022   GOE = 05.10.02

Using various hand and power tools, repairs medical equipment, such as manual or powered wheelchairs, hospital beds, and surgical equipment.

Aptitudes:
Intelligence	Moderate
Verbal	Low
Numerical	Low
Spatial	Moderate
Form Perception	Low
Clerical Perception	Low
Motor Coordination	Low
Finger Dexterity	Moderate
Manual Dexterity	Moderate
Eye-Hand-Foot Coordination	Low
Color Discrimination	Low

Data = Mod   People = Low   Things = High

Salary Range:
$14,000–$40,000

Opportunity Outlook:
35% growth or more

Environmental Conditions:
Inside

Physical Demands:
Heavy—lifting of no more than 100 pounds required
Stooping, kneeling, crouching, or crawling required
Reaching, handling, fingering, or feeling required
Seeing required

Temperaments:
Making decisions based upon senses and feelings
Attempting to attain set limits

Vocational Preparation:
1/2–1 year

Membership Director

DOT = 189.167-026   GOE = 11.09.02

Manages the division of a fraternal, charitable, or similar kind of organization responsible for soliciting new members as well as for providing membership services to existing members.

Aptitudes:
Intelligence	High
Verbal	High
Numerical	Moderate
Spatial	Low
Form Perception	Low
Clerical Perception	Moderate
Motor Coordination	Low
Finger Dexterity	Low
Manual Dexterity	Low
Eye-Hand-Foot Coordination	Low
Color Discrimination	Low

Data = High   People = Mod   Things = Low

Salary Range:
$20,000–$30,000

Opportunity Outlook:
5–13% growth

Environmental Conditions:
Inside

Physical Demands:
Light—lifting of no more than 20 pounds required
Reaching, handling, fingering, or feeling required
Talking or hearing required
Seeing required

Temperaments:
Directing, controlling, or planning the work of others
Influencing the actions and beliefs of others
Dealing with people beyond giving and receiving information
Performing a variety of tasks

Vocational Preparation: 2–4 years

Membership Solicitor

DOT = 293.357-022   GOE = 08.02.08

Solicits new members for a club, trade association, fraternal, or social organization; may speak directly to potential members, or conduct media campaigns to recruit new members.

Aptitudes:
Intelligence	Moderate
Verbal	Moderate
Numerical	Low
Spatial	Low
Form Perception	Low
Clerical Perception	Moderate
Motor Coordination	Low
Finger Dexterity	Low
Manual Dexterity	Low
Eye-Hand-Foot Coordination	Low
Color Discrimination	Low

Data = Mod   People = Mod   Things = Low

Salary Range:
$14,000–$18,000

Opportunity Outlook:
25–34% growth

Environmental Conditions:
Inside

Physical Demands:
Light—lifting of no more than 20 pounds required
Talking or hearing required

Temperaments:
Influencing the actions and beliefs of others
Dealing with people beyond giving and receiving information

Vocational Preparation:
3–6 months

Mental Retardation Aide

DOT = 355.377-018   GOE = 10.03.02

Assists professional counselors and therapists in helping individuals who are mentally retarded care for themselves, in such ways as learning how to bathe, eat, and dress.

Aptitudes:
Intelligence	Moderate
Verbal	Moderate
Numerical	Low
Spatial	Low
Form Perception	Low
Clerical Perception	Low
Motor Coordination	Moderate
Finger Dexterity	Low
Manual Dexterity	Moderate
Eye-Hand-Foot Coordination	Low
Color Discrimination	Low

Data = Mod   People = Mod   Things = Low

Salary Range:
$8,100–$22,400

Opportunity Outlook:
25–34% growth

Environmental Conditions:
Inside

Physical Demands:
Very heavy—lifting of more than 100 pounds required
Reaching, handling, fingering, or feeling required
Talking or hearing required
Seeing required

Temperaments:
Making decisions based upon senses and feelings
Performing a variety of tasks

Vocational Preparation:
1–2 years

Meteorologist

DOT = 025.062-010   GOE = 02.01.01

Analyzes and interprets data about the weather gathered by surface and upper-air stations, satellites, and radar to prepare reports and forecasts for public and private users.

Aptitudes:
Intelligence	High
Verbal	High
Numerical	High
Spatial	High
Form Perception	High
Clerical Perception	High
Motor Coordination	Low
Finger Dexterity	Low
Manual Dexterity	Moderate
Eye-Hand-Foot Coordination	Low
Color Discrimination	Low

Data = High   People = Low   Things = Mod

Salary Range:
$17,000–$44,700

Opportunity Outlook:
25–34% growth

Environmental Conditions:
Inside

Physical Demands:
Light—lifting of no more than 20 pounds required
Seeing required

Temperaments:
Making decisions based upon senses and feelings
Making decisions based upon facts

Vocational Preparation:
4–10 years

Microfilm Document Preparer

DOT = 249.587-018   GOE = 07.05.03

Prepares documents, such as books, legal documents, bank statements, brochures, pamphlets, and catalogs for microfilming; arranges documents on special camera stand for photographing and conversion to microfilm.

Aptitudes:
Intelligence	Moderate
Verbal	Low
Numerical	Low
Spatial	Moderate
Form Perception	Low
Clerical Perception	Moderate
Motor Coordination	Low
Finger Dexterity	Low
Manual Dexterity	Low
Eye-Hand-Foot Coordination	Low
Color Discrimination	Low

Data = Low   People = Low   Things = Low

Salary Range:
$8,300–$13,500

Opportunity Outlook:
25–34% growth

Environmental Conditions:
Inside

Physical Demands:
Light—lifting of no more than 20 pounds required
Reaching, handling, fingering, or feeling required
Seeing required

Temperaments:
Attempting to attain set limits
Performing a variety of tasks

Vocational Preparation:
1–30 days

Mine Superintendent

DOT = 181.117-014   GOE = 05.02.05

Plans and coordinates the activities of workers engaged in mining coal, ore, or rock at one or more underground or surface mines, pits, or quarries.

Aptitudes:
Intelligence	High
Verbal	High
Numerical	High
Spatial	High
Form Perception	Moderate
Clerical Perception	Moderate
Motor Coordination	Low
Finger Dexterity	Low
Manual Dexterity	Low
Eye-Hand-Foot Coordination	Low
Color Discrimination	Low

Data = High   People = High   Things = Low

Salary Range:
Not available

Opportunity Outlook:
Not available

Environmental Conditions:
Inside and outside

Physical Demands:
Light—lifting of no more than 20 pounds required
Talking or hearing required

Temperaments:
Directing, controlling, or planning the work of others
Dealing with people beyond giving and receiving information
Performing a variety of tasks

Vocational Preparation:
4–10 years

Modeling Instructor

DOT = 099.277-026   GOE = 01.08.01

Instructs individuals and groups in the techniques and methods of self-improvement, utilizing the principles of modeling, such as poise, wardrobe coordination, and cosmetic application.

Aptitudes:
Intelligence	Moderate
Verbal	Moderate
Numerical	Low
Spatial	Low
Form Perception	Low
Clerical Perception	Low
Motor Coordination	Moderate
Finger Dexterity	Low
Manual Dexterity	Moderate
Eye-Hand-Foot Coordination	Low
Color Discrimination	Moderate

Data = Mod   People = Mod   Things = Low

Salary Range:
Varies

Opportunity Outlook:
25-34% growth

Environmental Conditions:
Inside

Physical Demands:
Light—lifting of no more than 20 pounds required
Reaching, handling, fingering, or feeling required
Talking or hearing required
Seeing required

Temperaments:
Interpreting the feelings and ideas of others
Making decisions based upon senses and feelings
Dealing with people beyond giving and receiving information

Vocational Preparation:
3-6 months

Mortgage Accounting Clerk

DOT = 216.362-026   GOE = 07.02.02

Keeps records of mortgage loans at a mortgage loan establishment; compiles information such as names and addresses of lenders, selling prices of properties, taxes on mortgaged properties, etc.

Aptitudes:
Intelligence	Moderate
Verbal	Moderate
Numerical	Moderate
Spatial	Low
Form Perception	Moderate
Clerical Perception	High
Motor Coordination	Low
Finger Dexterity	Moderate
Manual Dexterity	Moderate
Eye-Hand-Foot Coordination	Low
Color Discrimination	Low

Data = Mod   People = Low   Things = Mod

Salary Range:
$9,500-$17,900

Opportunity Outlook:
14-24% growth

Environmental Conditions:
Inside

Physical Demands:
Sedentary—little or no lifting
Reaching, handling, fingering, or feeling required
Seeing required

Temperaments:
Performing repetitive tasks

Vocational Preparation:
1-3 months

Motorboat Operator

DOT = 911.663-010   GOE = 05.08.04

Operates a motor-driven boat to ferry passengers or freight from one location to another, or to guide other boats, rafts, and barges in dangerous waters.

Aptitudes:
Intelligence	Moderate
Verbal	Low
Numerical	Low
Spatial	Moderate
Form Perception	Moderate
Clerical Perception	Low
Motor Coordination	Moderate
Finger Dexterity	Low
Manual Dexterity	Moderate
Eye-Hand-Foot Coordination	Moderate
Color Discrimination	Low

Data = Low   People = Low   Things = Mod

Salary Range:
$14,000 (average)

Opportunity Outlook:
5–13% growth

Environmental Conditions:
Inside and outside

Physical Demands:
Moderate—lifting of no more than 50 pounds required
Reaching, handling, fingering, or feeling required
Seeing required

Temperaments:
Making decisions based upon facts
Performing a variety of tasks

Vocational Preparation:
1/2–1 year

Museum Curator

DOT = 102.017-010   GOE = 11.07.04

Directs and coordinates the activities of workers engaged in operating a museum, botanical garden, arboretum, art gallery, herbarium, or zoo.

Aptitudes:
Intelligence	High
Verbal	High
Numerical	Moderate
Spatial	Moderate
Form Perception	Moderate
Clerical Perception	Moderate
Motor Coordination	Low
Finger Dexterity	Low
Manual Dexterity	Low
Eye-Hand-Foot Coordination	Low
Color Discrimination	Moderate

Data = High   People = High   Things = Low

Salary Range:
$17,000–$44,800

Opportunity Outlook:
14–24% growth

Environmental Conditions:
Inside and outside

Physical Demands:
Light—lifting of no more than 20 pounds required
Reaching, handling, fingering, or feeling required

Temperaments:
Directing, controlling, or planning the work of others
Making decisions based upon senses and feelings
Making decisions based upon facts
Dealing with people beyond giving and receiving information
Performing a variety of tasks

Vocational Preparation:
More than 10 years

Music Director (Film/Radio/TV)

DOT = 152.047-018   GOE = 01.04.01

Plans and directs the activities of workers in a studio music department and conducts studio orchestra; selects vocal, instrumental, and recorded music suitable to type of program or motion picture and to the entertainers who will perform the selections.

Aptitudes:
Intelligence	High
Verbal	High
Numerical	Moderate
Spatial	Moderate
Form Perception	High
Clerical Perception	Moderate
Motor Coordination	High
Finger Dexterity	High
Manual Dexterity	Moderate
Eye-Hand-Foot Coordination	Low
Color Discrimination	Low

Data = High   People = Mod   Things = Low

Salary Range:
Varies

Opportunity Outlook:
14–24% growth

Environmental Conditions:
Inside

Physical Demands:
Light—lifting of no more than 20 pounds required
Reaching, handling, fingering, or feeling required
Talking or hearing required

Temperaments:
Directing, controlling, or planning the work of others
Interpreting the feelings and ideas of others
Making decisions based upon senses and feelings
Dealing with people beyond giving and receiving information
Performing a variety of tasks

Vocational Preparation: More than 10 years

Music Teacher

DOT = 152.021-010   GOE = 01.04.01

Teaches individuals and groups instrumental or vocal music privately or in a public or private school or college.

Aptitudes:
Intelligence	High
Verbal	High
Numerical	Moderate
Spatial	Low
Form Perception	Moderate
Clerical Perception	Moderate
Motor Coordination	Moderate
Finger Dexterity	High
Manual Dexterity	High
Eye-Hand-Foot Coordination	Moderate
Color Discrimination	Low

Data = High   People = High   Things = High

Salary Range:
$26,000 (average)

Opportunity Outlook:
14–24% growth

Environmental Conditions:
Inside

Physical Demands:
Light—lifting of no more than 20 pounds required
Reaching, handling, fingering, or feeling required
Talking or hearing required
Seeing required

Temperaments:
Directing, controlling, or planning the work of others
Interpreting the feelings and ideas of others
Making decisions based upon senses and feelings
Dealing with people beyond giving and receiving information

Vocational Preparation: 4–10 years

Musician

DOT = 152.041-010 GOE = 01.04.04

Plays a musical instrument as a soloist or as a member of a musical group, such as an orchestra or band, to entertain an audience.

Aptitudes:
Intelligence	High
Verbal	High
Numerical	Moderate
Spatial	Low
Form Perception	Moderate
Clerical Perception	High
Motor Coordination	High
Finger Dexterity	High
Manual Dexterity	High
Eye-Hand-Foot Coordination	Moderate
Color Discrimination	Low

Data = High   People = Low   Things = High

Salary Range:
$2,000–$59,200

Opportunity Outlook:
5–13% growth

Environmental Conditions:
Inside and outside
Presence of loud noises and vibrations

Physical Demands:
Light—lifting of no more than 20 pounds required
Reaching, handling, fingering, or feeling required
Talking or hearing required

Temperaments:
Interpreting the feelings and ideas of others
Making decisions based upon senses and feelings

Vocational Preparation:
4–10 years

Narrator

DOT = 150.147-010 GOE = 01.03.03

Makes explanatory comments to accompany a television program or motion picture; reads from a script into a microphone as program or film is projected, timing comments to fit the action or sequence of events; may write the script.

Aptitudes:
Intelligence	High
Verbal	High
Numerical	Moderate
Spatial	Low
Form Perception	Low
Clerical Perception	Low
Motor Coordination	Low
Finger Dexterity	Low
Manual Dexterity	Low
Eye-Hand-Foot Coordination	Low
Color Discrimination	Low

Data = High   People = Low   Things = Low

Salary Range:
Varies

Opportunity Outlook:
25–34% growth

Environmental Conditions:
Inside

Physical Demands:
Sedentary—little or no lifting required
Talking or hearing required
Seeing required

Temperaments:
Interpreting the feelings and ideas of others
Making decisions based upon senses and feelings

Vocational Preparation:
1/2–1 year

Navigator

DOT = 196.167-014   GOE = 05.03.01

Locates position and directs course of airplane while in flight, using navigational aids such as charts, maps, sextants, and various electronic equipment.

Aptitudes:
Intelligence	High
Verbal	Moderate
Numerical	High
Spatial	High
Form Perception	High
Clerical Perception	High
Motor Coordination	Moderate
Finger Dexterity	Low
Manual Dexterity	Moderate
Eye-Hand-Foot Coordination	Low
Color Discrimination	Low

Data = High   People = Low   Things = Low

Salary Range:
$24,500–$45,000

Opportunity Outlook:
14–24% growth

Environmental Conditions:
Inside
Presence of loud noises and vibrations

Physical Demands:
Sedentary—little or no lifting
Reaching, handling, fingering, or feeling required
Seeing required

Temperaments:
Making decisions based upon facts
Performing under stress or in emergencies
Attempting to attain set limits
Performing a variety of tasks

Vocational Preparation:
1–2 years

Net Fisher

DOT = 441.684-010   GOE = 03.04.03

Catches finfish, shellfish, and other marine life alone or as a crew member, on shore or aboard a fishing vessel, using various nets and other fishing equipment.

Aptitudes:
Intelligence	Moderate
Verbal	Low
Numerical	Low
Spatial	Low
Form Perception	Low
Clerical Perception	Low
Motor Coordination	Moderate
Finger Dexterity	Low
Manual Dexterity	Moderate
Eye-Hand-Foot Coordination	Moderate
Color Discrimination	Low

Data = Low   People = Low   Things = Mod

Salary Range:
$10,000–$30,000

Opportunity Outlook:
5–13% growth

Environmental Conditions:
Outside
Wet and humid work environment
Presence of physical hazards

Physical Demands:
Heavy—lifting of no more than 100 pounds required
Climbing or balancing required
Stooping, kneeling, crouching, or crawling required
Reaching, handling, fingering, or feeling required
Seeing required

Temperaments:
Performing repetitive tasks

Vocational Preparation:
3–6 months

News Assistant (Radio/TV)

DOT = 209.367-038   GOE = 07.05.03

Compiles, dispenses, and files news stories and related copy to help editorial personnel in a news broadcasting facility prepare the daily news reports and broadcasts.

Aptitudes:
Intelligence	Moderate
Verbal	Moderate
Numerical	Low
Spatial	Low
Form Perception	Low
Clerical Perception	Moderate
Motor Coordination	Low
Finger Dexterity	Low
Manual Dexterity	Low
Eye-Hand-Foot Coordination	Low
Color Discrimination	Low

Data = Mod   People = Low   Things = Low

Salary Range:
$12,000 (average)

Opportunity Outlook:
14–24% growth

Environmental Conditions:
Inside

Physical Demands:
Light—lifting of no more than 20 pounds required
Talking or hearing required

Temperaments:
Making decisions based upon facts

Vocational Preparation:
1–3 months

Newswriter

DOT = 131.267-014   GOE = 11.08.02

Writes news stories for publication or broadcast from written or recorded notes produced by a staff of reporters.

Aptitudes:
Intelligence	High
Verbal	High
Numerical	Moderate
Spatial	Low
Form Perception	Moderate
Clerical Perception	Moderate
Motor Coordination	Moderate
Finger Dexterity	Moderate
Manual Dexterity	Moderate
Eye-Hand-Foot Coordination	Low
Color Discrimination	Low

Data = High   People = Low   Things = Mod

Salary Range:
$20,000–$37,000

Opportunity Outlook:
25–34% growth

Environmental Conditions:
Inside

Physical Demands:
Sedentary—little or no lifting
Talking or hearing required

Temperaments:
Influencing the actions and beliefs of others
Making decisions based upon senses and feelings
Making decisions based upon facts
Performing a variety of tasks

Vocational Preparation:
2–4 years

Nuclear Engineer

DOT = 015.061-014   GOE = 05.01.03

Conducts research into problems of nuclear energy systems; designs and develops nuclear equipment; and monitors testing, operation, and maintenance of nuclear reactors.

Aptitudes:
Intelligence	High
Verbal	High
Numerical	High
Spatial	High
Form Perception	Moderate
Clerical Perception	Moderate
Motor Coordination	Moderate
Finger Dexterity	Moderate
Manual Dexterity	Moderate
Eye-Hand-Foot Coordination	Low
Color Discrimination	Low

Data = High   People = Mod   Things = High

Salary Range:
$31,000–$93,500

Opportunity Outlook:
0–4% growth or decline

Environmental Conditions:
Inside

Physical Demands:
Sedentary—little or no lifting
Reaching, handling, fingering, or feeling required
Seeing required

Temperaments:
Directing, controlling, or planning the work of others
Making decisions based upon facts
Attempting to attain set limits

Vocational Preparation:
4–10 years

Numerical-Control Lathe Operator

DOT = 604.362-010   GOE = 06.01.03

Sets up and operates numerically-controlled horizontal lathe machines to perform various machining operations, such as turning, boring, facing, and threading of parts, castings, forgings, and bar stock.

Aptitudes:
Intelligence	Moderate
Verbal	Moderate
Numerical	Moderate
Spatial	High
Form Perception	High
Clerical Perception	Low
Motor Coordination	Moderate
Finger Dexterity	Moderate
Manual Dexterity	Moderate
Eye-Hand-Foot Coordination	Low
Color Discrimination	Low

Data = Mod   People = Low   Things = High

Salary Range:
$33,000 (average)

Opportunity Outlook:
14–24% growth

Environmental Conditions:
Inside
Presence of loud noises and vibrations

Physical Demands:
Moderate—lifting of no more than 50 pounds required
Reaching, handling, fingering, or feeling required
Seeing required

Temperaments:
Making decisions based upon facts
Attempting to attain set limits

Vocational Preparation:
1–2 years

Nurse (General Duty)

DOT = 075.374-010   GOE = 10.02.01

Provides general nursing care to patients in a hospital, infirmary, sanitarium, or similar type of health-care institution.

Aptitudes:
Intelligence	High
Verbal	High
Numerical	Moderate
Spatial	Moderate
Form Perception	Moderate
Clerical Perception	Moderate
Motor Coordination	Moderate
Finger Dexterity	Moderate
Manual Dexterity	Moderate
Eye-Hand-Foot Coordination	Low
Color Discrimination	Low

Data = Mod   People = Mod   Things = Low

Salary Range:
$31,500–$45,400

Opportunity Outlook:
35% growth or more

Environmental Conditions:
Inside

Physical Demands:
Moderate—lifting of no more than 50 pounds required
Reaching, handling, fingering, or feeling required
Talking or hearing required
Seeing required

Temperaments:
Making decisions based upon facts
Dealing with people beyond giving and receiving information
Performing under stress or in emergencies
Attempting to attain set limits

Vocational Preparation: 2–4 years

Nurse (Licensed Practical)

DOT = 079.374-014   GOE = 10.02.01

Under the supervision of a registered nurse, cares for ill, injured, convalescent, or handicapped individuals in a hospital, clinic, private home, sanitarium, or similar health-care facility.

Aptitudes:
Intelligence	Moderate
Verbal	Moderate
Numerical	Low
Spatial	Moderate
Form Perception	Moderate
Clerical Perception	Moderate
Motor Coordination	Moderate
Finger Dexterity	Moderate
Manual Dexterity	Moderate
Eye-Hand-Foot Coordination	Low
Color Discrimination	Low

Data = Mod   People = Mod   Things = Mod

Salary Range:
$13,900–$28,000

Opportunity Outlook:
35% growth or more

Environmental Conditions:
Inside

Physical Demands:
Moderate—lifting of no more than 50 pounds required
Reaching, handling, fingering, or feeling required
Talking or hearing required
Seeing required

Temperaments:
Dealing with people beyond giving and receiving information
Performing under stress or in emergencies
Attempting to attain set limits
Performing a variety of tasks

Vocational Preparation: 1–2 years

Nurse's Aide

DOT = 355.674-014   GOE = 10.03.02

Assists registered and licensed practical nurses and other health-care workers in caring for people who are sick or injured; performs basic health-care tasks, such as bathing, dressing, and feeding patients.

Aptitudes:
Intelligence	Low
Verbal	Low
Numerical	Low
Spatial	Low
Form Perception	Low
Clerical Perception	Low
Motor Coordination	Moderate
Finger Dexterity	Moderate
Manual Dexterity	Moderate
Eye-Hand-Foot Coordination	Low
Color Discrimination	Low

Data = Low   People = Mod   Things = Low

Salary Range:
$8,000–$22,400

Opportunity Outlook:
35% growth or more

Environmental Conditions:
Inside

Physical Demands:
Moderate—lifting of no more than 50 pounds required
Stooping, kneeling, crouching, or crawling required
Reaching, handling, fingering, or feeling required
Talking or hearing required
Seeing required

Temperaments:
Performing under stress or in emergencies
Performing a variety of tasks

Vocational Preparation:
3–6 months

Nursery School Attendant

DOT = 359.677-018   GOE = 10.03.03

Organizes and leads activities of prekindergarten children in a nursery school or in a playground operated for patrons of a theater, department stores, company, hotel, or similar organization.

Aptitudes:
Intelligence	Moderate
Verbal	Moderate
Numerical	Low
Spatial	Low
Form Perception	Low
Clerical Perception	Low
Motor Coordination	Low
Finger Dexterity	Low
Manual Dexterity	Low
Eye-Hand-Foot Coordination	Low
Color Discrimination	Low

Data = Low   People = Mod   Things = Low

Salary Range:
$8,500–$14,000

Opportunity Outlook:
25–34% growth

Environmental Conditions:
Inside and outside

Physical Demands:
Moderate—lifting of no more than 50 pounds required
Stooping, kneeling, crouching, or crawling required
Reaching, handling, fingering, or feeling required
Talking or hearing required
Seeing required

Temperaments:
Performing a variety of tasks

Vocational Preparation:
3–6 months

Occupational Therapist

DOT = 076.121-010   GOE = 10.02.02

Plans, organizes, and conducts occupational therapy programs in a hospital, clinic, or community facility to help rehabilitate patients with mental, physical, or emotional problems.

Aptitudes:
Intelligence	High
Verbal	High
Numerical	High
Spatial	Moderate
Form Perception	Moderate
Clerical Perception	Low
Motor Coordination	Low
Finger Dexterity	Moderate
Manual Dexterity	Moderate
Eye-Hand-Foot Coordination	Low
Color Discrimination	Low

Data = High   People = High   Things = Mod

Salary Range:
$26,500–$38,500

Opportunity Outlook:
35% growth or more

Environmental Conditions:
Inside

Physical Demands:
Light—lifting of no more than 20 pounds required
Reaching, handling, fingering, or feeling required
Talking or hearing required
Seeing required

Temperaments:
Making decisions based upon senses and feelings
Dealing with people beyond giving and receiving information
Performing a variety of tasks

Vocational Preparation:
2–4 years

Office File Clerk

DOT = 206.367-014   GOE = 07.05.03

Stores, retrieves, and maintains records in a filing system; assists other workers in finding filed information important to their needs; may also perform some basic clerical duties.

Aptitudes:
Intelligence	Moderate
Verbal	Moderate
Numerical	Low
Spatial	Low
Form Perception	Moderate
Clerical Perception	High
Motor Coordination	Low
Finger Dexterity	Moderate
Manual Dexterity	Moderate
Eye-Hand-Foot Coordination	Low
Color Discrimination	Low

Data = Low   People = Low   Things = Low

Salary Range:
$14,700 (average)

Opportunity Outlook:
5–13% growth

Environmental Conditions:
Inside

Physical Demands:
Light—lifting of no more than 20 pounds required
Stooping, kneeling, crouching, or crawling required
Reaching, handling, fingering, or feeling required
Seeing required

Temperaments:
Making decisions based upon facts
Attempting to attain set limits

Vocational Preparation:
1/2–1 year

Office Files Supervisor

DOT = 206.137-010   GOE = 07.07.01

Supervises and coordinates the activities of workers engaged in maintaining central record files in a company or organization; directs and assists workers in filing records, searching for information, and in maintaining the overall filing system.

Aptitudes:
Intelligence	Moderate
Verbal	Moderate
Numerical	Moderate
Spatial	Low
Form Perception	Moderate
Clerical Perception	Moderate
Motor Coordination	Moderate
Finger Dexterity	Low
Manual Dexterity	Low
Eye-Hand-Foot Coordination	Low
Color Discrimination	Low

Data = High   People = Mod   Things = Low

Salary Range:
$15,300–$44,700

Opportunity Outlook:
14–24% growth

Environmental Conditions:
Inside

Physical Demands:
Light—lifting of no more than 20 pounds required
Talking or hearing required
Seeing required

Temperaments:
Directing, controlling, or planning the work of others
Making decisions based upon facts
Dealing with people beyond giving and receiving information
Attempting to attain set limits

Vocational Preparation:
1–2 years

Office Manager

DOT = 169.167-034   GOE = 07.01.02

Manages and coordinates the activities of clerical personnel in a business, office, or similar organization.

Aptitudes:
Intelligence	High
Verbal	High
Numerical	Moderate
Spatial	Low
Form Perception	Low
Clerical Perception	Moderate
Motor Coordination	Low
Finger Dexterity	Low
Manual Dexterity	Low
Eye-Hand-Foot Coordination	Low
Color Discrimination	Low

Data = High   People = Mod   Things = Low

Salary Range:
$15,300–$44,700

Opportunity Outlook:
14–24% growth

Environmental Conditions:
Inside

Physical Demands:
Sedentary—little or no lifting
Talking or hearing required

Temperaments:
Directing, controlling, or planning the work of others
Making decisions based upon senses and feelings
Making decisions based upon facts
Dealing with people beyond giving and receiving information
Performing a variety of tasks

Vocational Preparation:
2–4 years

Offset Press Operator

DOT = 651.482-010 GOE = 05.05.13

Sets up and operates an offset printing press to print single or multicolored copy from lithographic plates; may also clean and repair press when needed.

Aptitudes:
Intelligence	Moderate
Verbal	Moderate
Numerical	Moderate
Spatial	Moderate
Form Perception	High
Clerical Perception	Low
Motor Coordination	Moderate
Finger Dexterity	Moderate
Manual Dexterity	Moderate
Eye-Hand-Foot Coordination	Moderate
Color Discrimination	Moderate

Data = Low   People = Low   Things = High

Salary Range:
$11,900–$36,900

Opportunity Outlook:
14-24% growth

Environmental Conditions:
Inside
Presence of loud noises and vibrations

Physical Demands:
Light—lifting of no more than 20 pounds required
Talking or hearing required
Seeing required

Temperaments:
Making decisions based upon facts
Attempting to attain set limits
Performing a variety of tasks

Vocational Preparation:
2-4 years

Optometric Assistant

DOT = 079.364-014 GOE = 10.03.02

Assists an optometrist in conducting eye examinations; may also obtain the patient's medical records, schedule appointments, record information, and communicate with patients by mail or phone.

Aptitudes:
Intelligence	Moderate
Verbal	Moderate
Numerical	Moderate
Spatial	Moderate
Form Perception	Moderate
Clerical Perception	Moderate
Motor Coordination	Low
Finger Dexterity	Moderate
Manual Dexterity	Moderate
Eye-Hand-Foot Coordination	Moderate
Color Discrimination	Moderate

Data = Mod   People = Mod   Things = Mod

Salary Range:
$39,000–$45,000

Opportunity Outlook:
25-34% growth

Environmental Conditions:
Inside

Physical Demands:
Sedentary—little or no lifting
Reaching, handling, fingering, or feeling required
Talking or hearing required
Seeing required

Temperaments:
Making decisions based upon facts
Dealing with people beyond giving and receiving information

Vocational Preparation:
1-2 years

Orchestra Conductor

DOT = 152.047-014   GOE = 01.04.01

Conducts instrumental music groups, such as orchestras and dance bands; selects music best suited to the skills of the musicians and the theme of the program; may also audition and select members of the group and write or compose the musical scores.

Aptitudes:
Intelligence	High
Verbal	High
Numerical	Moderate
Spatial	Moderate
Form Perception	High
Clerical Perception	High
Motor Coordination	High
Finger Dexterity	Moderate
Manual Dexterity	Moderate
Eye-Hand-Foot Coordination	Low
Color Discrimination	Low

Data = High   People = Mod   Things = Low

Salary Range:
Not available

Opportunity Outlook:
5–13% growth

Environmental Conditions:
Inside

Physical Demands:
Light—lifting of no more than 20 pounds required
Reaching, handling, fingering, or feeling required
Talking or hearing required
Seeing required

Temperaments:
Directing, controlling, or planning the work of others
Interpreting the feelings and ideas of others
Making decisions based upon senses and feelings
Dealing with people beyond giving and receiving information

Vocational Preparation: More than 10 years

Outdoor Advertising Leasing Agent

DOT = 254.357-010   GOE = 11.12.02

Obtains leasing rights for outdoor advertising, such as billboards, for clients who wish to advertise their goods or services.

Aptitudes:
Intelligence	Moderate
Verbal	Moderate
Numerical	Moderate
Spatial	Low
Form Perception	Low
Clerical Perception	Moderate
Motor Coordination	Low
Finger Dexterity	Low
Manual Dexterity	Low
Eye-Hand-Foot Coordination	Low
Color Discrimination	Low

Data = Low   People = Low   Things = Low

Salary Range:
Varies

Opportunity Outlook:
Not available

Environmental Conditions:
Inside and outside

Physical Demands:
Light—lifting of no more than 20 pounds required
Talking or hearing required
Seeing required

Temperaments:
Influencing the actions and beliefs of others
Making decisions based upon senses and feelings
Dealing with people beyond giving and receiving information

Vocational Preparation:
3–6 months

Packing Materials Inspector

DOT = 920.387-010   GOE = 06.03.01

Examines, measures, and tests containers and materials used to package drug and cosmetic products for conformity to specifications.

Aptitudes:
  Intelligence   Moderate
  Verbal   Moderate
  Numerical   Moderate
  Spatial   Moderate
  Form Perception   Moderate
  Clerical Perception   Moderate
  Motor Coordination   Moderate
  Finger Dexterity   Moderate
  Manual Dexterity   Moderate
  Eye-Hand-Foot Coordination   Low
  Color Discrimination   Low

Data = Mod   People = Low   Things = Low

Salary Range:
$10,900–$35,300

Opportunity Outlook:
0–4% growth or decline

Environmental Conditions:
Inside

Physical Demands:
Light—lifting of no more than 20 pounds required
Reaching, handling, fingering, or feeling required
Seeing required

Temperaments:
Making decisions based upon facts
Attempting to attain set limits

Vocational Preparation:
3–6 months

Painter

DOT = 144.061-010   GOE = 01.02.02

Paints a variety of original subject material, such as portraits, landscapes, still lifes, and abstracts, using watercolors, oils, acrylics, tempera, or other paint media.

Aptitudes:
  Intelligence   High
  Verbal   High
  Numerical   Moderate
  Spatial   High
  Form Perception   High
  Clerical Perception   Low
  Motor Coordination   High
  Finger Dexterity   High
  Manual Dexterity   High
  Eye-Hand-Foot Coordination   Low
  Color Discrimination   High

Data = High   People = Low   Things = High

Salary Range:
Varies

Opportunity Outlook:
25–34% growth

Environmental Conditions:
Inside and outside

Physical Demands:
Light—lifting of no more than 20 pounds required
Reaching, handling, fingering, or feeling required
Seeing required

Temperaments:
Interpreting the feelings and ideas of others
Making decisions based upon senses and feelings

Vocational Preparation:
4–10 years

Paperhanger

DOT = 841.381-010   GOE = 05.05.04

Covers interior walls and ceilings of rooms with decorative wallpaper or fabric, using various hand tools and materials.

Aptitudes:
Intelligence	Moderate
Verbal	Moderate
Numerical	Low
Spatial	Moderate
Form Perception	Moderate
Clerical Perception	Low
Motor Coordination	Moderate
Finger Dexterity	Moderate
Manual Dexterity	High
Eye-Hand-Foot Coordination	Low
Color Discrimination	Moderate

Data = Low   People = Low   Things = Mod

Salary Range:
$12,600–$40,500

Opportunity Outlook:
14–24% growth

Environmental Conditions:
Inside

Physical Demands:
Moderate—lifting of no more than 50 pounds required
Climbing or balancing required
Stooping, kneeling, crouching, or crawling required
Reaching, handling, fingering, or feeling required
Seeing required

Temperaments:
Making decisions based upon senses and feelings
Making decisions based upon facts
Attempting to attain set limits

Vocational Preparation:
2–4 years

Paralegal Assistant

DOT = 119.267-026   GOE = 11.04.02

Researches legal cases and the law, investigates facts, interviews individuals, and prepares documents to assist lawyers in carrying out their responsibilities to their clients.

Aptitudes:
Intelligence	High
Verbal	High
Numerical	Moderate
Spatial	Low
Form Perception	Low
Clerical Perception	High
Motor Coordination	Low
Finger Dexterity	Low
Manual Dexterity	Low
Eye-Hand-Foot Coordination	Low
Color Discrimination	Low

Data = High   People = Mod   Things = Low

Salary Range:
$17,000–$32,200

Opportunity Outlook:
35% growth or more

Environmental Conditions:
Inside

Physical Demands:
Sedentary—little or no lifting

Temperaments:
Making decisions based upon facts
Dealing with people beyond giving and receiving information
Attempting to attain set limits
Performing a variety of tasks

Vocational Preparation:
2–4 years

Park Ranger

DOT = 169.167-042 GOE = 04.02.03

Enforces laws, regulations, and policies in state or national parks; may also register vehicles entering the park, collect fees, issue parking and use permits, and provide information and assistance to park visitors.

Aptitudes:
Intelligence	Moderate
Verbal	Moderate
Numerical	Moderate
Spatial	Moderate
Form Perception	Low
Clerical Perception	Low
Motor Coordination	Moderate
Finger Dexterity	Low
Manual Dexterity	Moderate
Eye-Hand-Foot Coordination	Moderate
Color Discrimination	Low

Data = High   People = Low   Things = Low

Salary Range:
$12,000–$20,000

Opportunity Outlook:
5–13% growth

Environmental Conditions:
Inside and outside
Presence of physical hazards

Physical Demands:
Light—lifting of no more than 20 pounds required
Climbing or balancing required
Reaching, handling, fingering, or feeling required
Talking or hearing required
Seeing required

Temperaments:
Making decisions based upon senses and feelings
Making decisions based upon facts
Performing under stress or in emergencies
Performing a variety of tasks

Vocational Preparation: 2–4 years

Park Superintendent

DOT = 188.167-062 GOE = 04.01.01

Coordinates the activities of park rangers and other personnel engaged in the development, protection, and utilization of national, state, or regional parks.

Aptitudes:
Intelligence	High
Verbal	High
Numerical	Moderate
Spatial	Low
Form Perception	Low
Clerical Perception	Moderate
Motor Coordination	Low
Finger Dexterity	Low
Manual Dexterity	Low
Eye-Hand-Foot Coordination	Moderate
Color Discrimination	Low

Data = High   People = Mod   Things = Low

Salary Range:
$25,000–$50,000+

Opportunity Outlook:
5–13% growth

Environmental Conditions:
Inside and outside
Extremely cold work environment
Extremely hot work environment

Physical Demands:
Light—lifting of no more than 20 pounds required
Climbing or balancing required
Reaching, handling, fingering, or feeling required
Talking or hearing required
Seeing required

Temperaments:
Directing, controlling, or planning the work of others
Influencing the actions and beliefs of others
Making decisions based upon senses and feelings
Performing a variety of tasks

Vocational Preparation: 2–4 years

Parking Lot Supervisor

DOT = 915.133-010   GOE = 09.04.02

Supervises and coordinates the activities of workers engaged in parking cars in a parking lot or storage garage.

Aptitudes:
Intelligence	Moderate
Verbal	Low
Numerical	Low
Spatial	Low
Form Perception	Low
Clerical Perception	Moderate
Motor Coordination	Low
Finger Dexterity	Low
Manual Dexterity	Low
Eye-Hand-Foot Coordination	Low
Color Discrimination	Low

Data = Mod   People = Mod   Things = Low

Salary Range:
$11,000 (average)

Opportunity Outlook:
5–13% growth

Environmental Conditions:
Inside and outside

Physical Demands:
Light—lifting of no more than 20 pounds required
Reaching, handling, fingering, or feeling required

Temperaments:
Directing, controlling, or planning the work of others
Dealing with people beyond giving and receiving information

Vocational Preparation:
3–6 months

Parts Manager

DOT = 185.167-038   GOE = 11.11.05

Manages retail or wholesale automotive parts establishment or department of repair shop or service station.

Aptitudes:
Intelligence	High
Verbal	Moderate
Numerical	Moderate
Spatial	Low
Form Perception	Moderate
Clerical Perception	Moderate
Motor Coordination	Low
Finger Dexterity	Low
Manual Dexterity	Low
Eye-Hand-Foot Coordination	Low
Color Discrimination	Low

Data = High   People = Mod   Things = Low

Salary Range:
$12,000–$20,000

Opportunity Outlook:
14–24% growth

Environmental Conditions:
Inside

Physical Demands:
Light—lifting of no more than 20 pounds required
Talking or hearing required
Seeing required

Temperaments:
Directing, controlling, or planning the work of others
Dealing with people beyond giving and receiving information

Vocational Preparation:
2–4 years

Patent Agent

DOT = 119.167-014   GOE = 11.04.04

Prepares and presents patent applications to U.S. Patent Office and before a patent court on behalf of individuals wishing to patent a new product or invention.

Aptitudes:
Intelligence	High
Verbal	High
Numerical	High
Spatial	High
Form Perception	Moderate
Clerical Perception	Moderate
Motor Coordination	Low
Finger Dexterity	Low
Manual Dexterity	Low
Eye-Hand-Foot Coordination	Low
Color Discrimination	Low

Data = High   People = Low   Things = Low

Salary Range:
$23,000 (average)

Opportunity Outlook:
5-13% growth

Environmental Conditions:
Inside

Physical Demands:
Sedentary—little or no lifting
Talking or hearing required
Seeing required

Temperaments:
Interpreting the feelings and ideas of others
Influencing the actions and beliefs of others
Making decisions based upon senses and feelings

Vocational Preparation:
2-4 years

Pawnbroker

DOT = 191.157-010   GOE = 08.01.03

Loans money to individuals based upon the value of items, such as jewelry, cameras, musical instruments, etc., owned by the individuals but left with the pawnbroker until the loan is repaid.

Aptitudes:
Intelligence	Moderate
Verbal	Moderate
Numerical	Moderate
Spatial	Low
Form Perception	Moderate
Clerical Perception	Moderate
Motor Coordination	Low
Finger Dexterity	Low
Manual Dexterity	Low
Eye-Hand-Foot Coordination	Low
Color Discrimination	Moderate

Data = Mod   People = Low   Things = Low

Salary Range:
Varies

Opportunity Outlook:
Not available

Environmental Conditions:
Inside

Physical Demands:
Light—lifting of no more than 20 pounds required
Reaching, handling, fingering, or feeling required
Talking or hearing required
Seeing required

Temperaments:
Making decisions based upon senses and feelings
Making decisions based upon facts
Performing a variety of tasks

Vocational Preparation:
1-2 years

Payroll Clerk

DOT = 215.482-010   GOE = 07.02.05

Examines timesheets and work tickets of employees and computes wages earned; may also record wage data in record books or in a computer software program for later use in preparing paychecks.

Aptitudes:
Intelligence	Moderate
Verbal	Moderate
Numerical	Moderate
Spatial	Low
Form Perception	Low
Clerical Perception	High
Motor Coordination	Low
Finger Dexterity	Moderate
Manual Dexterity	Moderate
Eye-Hand-Foot Coordination	Low
Color Discrimination	Low

Data = Mod   People = Low   Things = Mod

Salary Range:
$19,000 (average)

Opportunity Outlook:
0-4% growth or decline

Environmental Conditions:
Inside

Physical Demands:
Sedentary—little or no lifting
Reaching, handling, fingering, or feeling required
Seeing required

Temperaments:
Performing repetitive tasks
Attempting to attain set limits

Vocational Preparation:
3-6 months

Perfusionist

DOT = 078.362-034   GOE = 10.03.02

Sets up and operates a heart-lung machine in a hospital to take over the functions of a patient's heart and lungs during surgery or respiratory failure.

Aptitudes:
Intelligence	High
Verbal	High
Numerical	Moderate
Spatial	Moderate
Form Perception	Moderate
Clerical Perception	Moderate
Motor Coordination	High
Finger Dexterity	Moderate
Manual Dexterity	Moderate
Eye-Hand-Foot Coordination	Low
Color Discrimination	Low

Data = Mod   People = Low   Things = High

Salary Range:
$22,000-$30,000

Opportunity Outlook:
14-24% growth

Environmental Conditions:
Inside

Physical Demands:
Light—lifting of no more than 20 pounds required
Reaching, handling, fingering, or feeling required
Talking or hearing required
Seeing required

Temperaments:
Performing under stress or in emergencies
Attempting to attain set limits

Vocational Preparation:
2-4 years

Personal Shopper

DOT = 296.357-010   GOE = 09.04.02

Selects and purchases merchandise for department store customers, according to their requests as received by mail or phone.

Aptitudes:
Intelligence	Moderate
Verbal	Moderate
Numerical	Moderate
Spatial	Low
Form Perception	Low
Clerical Perception	Low
Motor Coordination	Low
Finger Dexterity	Low
Manual Dexterity	Low
Eye-Hand-Foot Coordination	Low
Color Discrimination	Moderate

Data = Low   People = Low   Things = Low

Salary Range:
Varies

Opportunity Outlook:
Not available

Environmental Conditions:
Inside

Physical Demands:
Light—lifting of no more than 20 pounds required
Talking or hearing required
Seeing required

Temperaments:
Making decisions based upon facts

Vocational Preparation:
1/2–1 year

Personnel Recruiter

DOT = 166.267-038   GOE = 11.03.04

Seeks out, interviews, screens, and recruits job applicants to fill existing or anticipated job openings; may work with various department personnel to determine qualifications for vacant positions.

Aptitudes:
Intelligence	High
Verbal	High
Numerical	Moderate
Spatial	Low
Form Perception	Low
Clerical Perception	Moderate
Motor Coordination	Low
Finger Dexterity	Low
Manual Dexterity	Low
Eye-Hand-Foot Coordination	Low
Color Discrimination	Low

Data = High   People = Mod   Things = Low

Salary Range:
$23,900–$71,500

Opportunity Outlook:
25–34% growth

Environmental Conditions:
Inside

Physical Demands:
Sedentary—little or no lifting
Talking or hearing required
Seeing required

Temperaments:
Influencing the actions and beliefs of others
Making decisions based upon senses and feelings
Dealing with people beyond giving and receiving information
Performing a variety of tasks

Vocational Preparation:
2–4 years

Petroleum Field Engineer

DOT = 010.261-010   GOE = 05.03.04

Collects fluid samples from oil- or gas-bearing rock formations in the earth, and analyzes samples to determine potential supply of oil or gas.

Aptitudes:
Intelligence	High
Verbal	Moderate
Numerical	High
Spatial	Moderate
Form Perception	High
Clerical Perception	Moderate
Motor Coordination	Low
Finger Dexterity	Moderate
Manual Dexterity	Low
Eye-Hand-Foot Coordination	Low
Color Discrimination	Low

Data = High   People = Low   Things = High

Salary Range:
$31,900–$93,500

Opportunity Outlook:
0–4% growth or decline

Environmental Conditions:
Inside and outside
Presence of physical hazards

Physical Demands:
Light—lifting of no more than 20 pounds required
Reaching, handling, fingering, or feeling required
Talking or hearing required
Seeing required

Temperaments:
Making decisions based upon senses and feelings
Making decisions based upon facts

Vocational Preparation:
2–4 years

Petroleum Inspector

DOT = 222.367-046   GOE = 05.07.05

Inspects the shipments of crude or refined petroleum to certify that shipments conform to the contract specifications as established by the buyer and seller at the time of the sale.

Aptitudes:
Intelligence	Moderate
Verbal	Moderate
Numerical	Low
Spatial	Low
Form Perception	Moderate
Clerical Perception	Moderate
Motor Coordination	Moderate
Finger Dexterity	Low
Manual Dexterity	Low
Eye-Hand-Foot Coordination	Low
Color Discrimination	Low

Data = Mod   People = Low   Things = Low

Salary Range:
$24,000–$36,500

Opportunity Outlook:
25–34% growth

Environmental Conditions:
Outside
Presence of atmospheric dangers

Physical Demands:
Light—lifting of no more than 20 pounds required
Climbing or balancing required
Stooping, kneeling, crouching, or crawling required
Reaching, handling, fingering, or feeling required
Seeing required

Temperaments;
Making decisions based upon senses and feelings
Making decisions based upon facts
Attempting to attain set limits

Vocational Preparation: 1/2–1 year

Photographer

DOT = 143.062-030   GOE = 01.02.03

Photographs people, scenery, still life, or other subjects using camera, color or black-and-white film, and a variety of photographic accessories; may also develop negatives and retouch photographs.

Aptitudes:
Intelligence	High
Verbal	Moderate
Numerical	Moderate
Spatial	High
Form Perception	High
Clerical Perception	Low
Motor Coordination	Moderate
Finger Dexterity	Moderate
Manual Dexterity	Moderate
Eye-Hand-Foot Coordination	Low
Color Discrimination	High

Data = High   People = Low   Things = Mod

Salary Range:
$15,000–$42,200

Opportunity Outlook:
14–24% growth

Environmental Conditions:
Inside and outside

Physical Demands:
Light—lifting of no more than 20 pounds required
Reaching, handling, fingering, or feeling required
Talking or hearing required
Seeing required

Temperaments:
Interpreting the feelings and ideas of others
Making decisions based upon senses and feelings
Attempting to attain set limits

Vocational Preparation:
2–4 years

Photographers' Model

DOT = 961.367-010   GOE = 01.08.01

Poses for pictures taken by a photographer to be used for advertising purposes or artistic displays.

Aptitudes:
Intelligence	Moderate
Verbal	Low
Numerical	Low
Spatial	Low
Form Perception	Low
Clerical Perception	Low
Motor Coordination	Low
Finger Dexterity	Moderate
Manual Dexterity	Moderate
Eye-Hand-Foot Coordination	Low
Color Discrimination	Moderate

Data = Low   People = Low   Things = Low

Salary Range:
Varies

Opportunity Outlook:
25–34% growth

Environmental Conditions:
Inside and outside

Physical Demands:
Light—lifting of no more than 20 pounds required
Reaching, handling, fingering, or feeling required
Talking or hearing required
Seeing required

Temperaments:
Interpreting the feelings and ideas of others

Vocational Preparation:
3–6 months

Physical Education Instructor

DOT = 153.227-014   GOE = 10.02.02

Teaches individuals or groups beginning or advanced calisthenics, gymnastics, reducing exercises, or various athletic or recreational games in a school, private health club, or gymnasium.

Aptitudes:
Intelligence	Moderate
Verbal	Moderate
Numerical	Moderate
Spatial	Low
Form Perception	Low
Clerical Perception	Moderate
Motor Coordination	Moderate
Finger Dexterity	Moderate
Manual Dexterity	Moderate
Eye-Hand-Foot Coordination	High
Color Discrimination	Low

Data = High   People = High   Things = Low

Salary Range:
$30,000 (average)

Opportunity Outlook:
25–34% growth

Environmental Conditions:
Inside and outside

Physical Demands:
Light—lifting of no more than 20 pounds required
Climbing or balancing required
Stooping, kneeling, crouching, or crawling required
Reaching, handling, fingering, or feeling required
Talking or hearing required
Seeing required

Temperaments:
Directing, controlling, or planning the work of others
Dealing with people beyond giving and receiving information

Vocational Preparation: 2–4 years

Physical Therapist

DOT = 076.121-014   GOE = 10.02.02

Plans and administers medically prescribed physical therapy treatment program to help patients regain the use and control of their limbs after surgery, illness, or an accident.

Aptitudes:
Intelligence	High
Verbal	High
Numerical	Moderate
Spatial	High
Form Perception	High
Clerical Perception	Moderate
Motor Coordination	High
Finger Dexterity	High
Manual Dexterity	High
Eye-Hand-Foot Coordination	Low
Color Discrimination	Low

Data = High   People = Mod   Things = Mod

Salary Range:
$30,800–$42,700

Opportunity Outlook:
35% growth or more

Environmental Conditions:
Inside

Physical Demands:
Light—lifting of no more than 20 pounds required
Stooping, kneeling, crouching, or crawling required
Reaching, handling, fingering, or feeling required
Talking or hearing required
Seeing required

Temperaments:
Influencing the actions and beliefs of others
Making decisions based upon senses and feelings
Making decisions based upon facts
Dealing with people . . .

Vocational Preparation: 2–4 years

Physician (General Practitioner)

DOT = 070.101-022   GOE = 02.03.01

Provides direct medical care to patients who are sick or injured; examines patients to determine the cause of their illness or extent of their injuries, and then prescribes appropriate treatment; may refer patients to specialists if special treatment is recommended.

Aptitudes:
Intelligence	High
Verbal	High
Numerical	High
Spatial	High
Form Perception	High
Clerical Perception	High
Motor Coordination	High
Finger Dexterity	High
Manual Dexterity	High
Eye-Hand-Foot Coordination	Low
Color Discrimination	Moderate

Data = High   People = High   Things = High

Salary Range:
$95,900 (average)

Opportunity Outlook:
25-34% growth

Environmental Conditions:
Inside

Physical Demands:
Light—lifting of no more than 20 pounds required
Reaching, handling, fingering, or feeling required
Talking or hearing required
Seeing required

Temperaments:
Directing, controlling, or planning the work of others
Making decisions based upon senses and feelings
Making decisions based upon facts
Dealing with people beyond giving and receiving information

Vocational Preparation: More than 10 years

Physicist

DOT = 023.061-014   GOE = 02.01.01

Conducts research into various types of physical phenomena and attempts to develop theories and laws, on basis of observation and experiments, to explain the phenomena; also attempts to devise methods to apply these laws and theories of physics to industry, medicine, and other fields.

Aptitudes:
Intelligence	High
Verbal	High
Numerical	High
Spatial	High
Form Perception	High
Clerical Perception	Moderate
Motor Coordination	Moderate
Finger Dexterity	Moderate
Manual Dexterity	Moderate
Eye-Hand-Foot Coordination	Low
Color Discrimination	High

Data = High   People = Low   Things = High

Salary Range:
$29,200-$58,000

Opportunity Outlook:
5-13% growth

Environmental Conditions:
Inside

Physical Demands:
Light—lifting of no more than 20 pounds required
Reaching, handling, fingering, or feeling required
Seeing required

Temperaments:
Making decisions based upon senses and feelings
Making decisions based upon facts
Attempting to attain set limits

Vocational Preparation:
4-10 years

Plant Guide

DOT = 353.367-018   GOE = 09.01.02

Escorts individuals or groups of people through industrial establishments, such as plants and factories, and describes features of interests; answers questions and may also demonstrate how various processes work.

Aptitudes:
Intelligence	Moderate
Verbal	Moderate
Numerical	Low
Spatial	Low
Form Perception	Low
Clerical Perception	Low
Motor Coordination	Low
Finger Dexterity	Low
Manual Dexterity	Low
Eye-Hand-Foot Coordination	Low
Color Discrimination	Low

Data = Mod   People = Low   Things = Low

Salary Range:
$9,500–$11,500

Opportunity Outlook:
5–13% growth

Environmental Conditions:
Inside and outside

Physical Demands:
Light—lifting of no more than 20 pounds required
Talking or hearing required
Seeing required

Temperaments:
Performing a variety of tasks

Vocational Preparation:
1–3 months

Playwright

DOT = 131.067-038   GOE = 01.01.02

Writes original plays, such as tragedies, comedies, or dramas, or adapts themes from fictional, historical, or narrative sources, for dramatic presentation.

Aptitudes:
Intelligence	High
Verbal	High
Numerical	Low
Spatial	Low
Form Perception	Low
Clerical Perception	Low
Motor Coordination	Low
Finger Dexterity	Low
Manual Dexterity	Low
Eye-Hand-Foot Coordination	Low
Color Discrimination	Low

Data = High   People = Low   Things = Low

Salary Range:
Varies

Opportunity Outlook:
Not available

Environmental Conditions:
Inside

Physical Demands:
Sedentary—little or no lifting
Talking or hearing required

Temperaments:
Interpreting the feelings and ideas of others
Making decisions based upon senses and feelings

Vocational Preparation:
4–10 years

501 Occupational Profiles 225

Plumber

DOT = 862.381-030   GOE = 05.05.03

Assembles, installs, and repairs pipes, fittings, and fixtures for heating, water, and drainage systems, according to building specifications and plumbing codes.

Aptitudes:
Intelligence	Moderate
Verbal	Moderate
Numerical	Moderate
Spatial	Moderate
Form Perception	Moderate
Clerical Perception	Low
Motor Coordination	Moderate
Finger Dexterity	Moderate
Manual Dexterity	High
Eye-Hand-Foot Coordination	Low
Color Discrimination	Low

Data = Mod   People = Low   Things = High

Salary Range:
$14,600–$34,800

Opportunity Outlook:
14–24% growth

Environmental Conditions:
Inside and outside
Presence of physical hazards

Physical Demands:
Heavy—lifting of no more than 100 pounds required
Climbing or balancing required
Stooping, kneeling, crouching, or crawling required
Reaching, handling, fingering, or feeling required
Seeing required

Temperaments:
Making decisions based upon facts
Attempting to attain set limits
Performing a variety of tasks

Vocational Preparation: 2–4 years

Police Chief

DOT = 375.117-010   GOE = 04.01.01

Directs and coordinates the activities of a municipal police department in accordance with the rules and regulations determined by the governing body.

Aptitudes:
Intelligence	High
Verbal	High
Numerical	Moderate
Spatial	Low
Form Perception	Low
Clerical Perception	Moderate
Motor Coordination	Low
Finger Dexterity	Low
Manual Dexterity	Low
Eye-Hand-Foot Coordination	Low
Color Discrimination	Low

Data = High   People = High   Things = Low

Salary Range:
$22,000–$90,000

Opportunity Outlook:
14–24% growth

Environmental Conditions:
Inside

Physical Demands:
Sedentary—little or no lifting
Talking or hearing required

Temperaments:
Directing, controlling, or planning the work of others
Making decisions based upon senses and feelings
Making decisions based upon facts
Dealing with people beyond giving and receiving information
Performing a variety of tasks

Vocational Preparation:
More than 10 years

Police Officer

DOT = 375.263-014   GOE = 04.01.02

Patrols assigned beat on foot, using a motorcycle or patrol car, or on horseback to control traffic or prevent crimes or disturbances of the peace; investigates crimes and crime scenes; and arrests individuals who break the law.

Aptitudes:
Intelligence	Moderate
Verbal	Moderate
Numerical	Low
Spatial	Moderate
Form Perception	Moderate
Clerical Perception	Moderate
Motor Coordination	Moderate
Finger Dexterity	Low
Manual Dexterity	Moderate
Eye-Hand-Foot Coordination	Moderate
Color Discrimination	Low

Data = Mod   People = Mod   Things = Mod

Salary Range:
$18,900–$37,300

Opportunity Outlook:
14–24% growth

Environmental Conditions:
Inside and outside
Presence of physical hazards

Physical Demands:
Very heavy—lifting of more than 100 pounds
Talking or hearing required
Seeing required

Temperaments:
Making decisions based upon senses and feelings
Dealing with people beyond giving and receiving information
Performing under stressful conditions
Performing a variety of tasks

Vocational Preparation: 1–2 years

Political Scientist

DOT = 051.067-010   GOE = 11.03.02

Studies the phenomena of political behavior, such as the origin, development, and operation of political institutions, to formulate and develop theories concerning political behavior of individuals and groups.

Aptitudes:
Intelligence	High
Verbal	High
Numerical	Moderate
Spatial	Low
Form Perception	Low
Clerical Perception	High
Motor Coordination	Low
Finger Dexterity	Low
Manual Dexterity	Low
Eye-Hand-Foot Coordination	Low
Color Discrimination	Low

Data = High   People = Low   Things = Low

Salary Range:
$17,000–$49,600

Opportunity Outlook:
14–24% growth

Environmental Conditions:
Inside

Physical Demands:
Sedentary—little or no lifting
Talking or hearing required

Temperaments:
Making decisions based upon senses and feelings

Vocational Preparation:
4–10 years

Pollution Control Engineer

DOT = 019.081-018   GOE = 05.01.02

Plans and conducts engineering studies to analyze and evaluate environmental pollution, methods of pollution control, and methods of testing pollution sources to determine the physiochemical nature and concentration of contaminants; also develops procedures for containing and cleaning up existing pollution problems.

Aptitudes:
Intelligence	High
Verbal	High
Numerical	High
Spatial	High
Form Perception	High
Clerical Perception	Moderate
Motor Coordination	Low
Finger Dexterity	Low
Manual Dexterity	High
Eye-Hand-Foot Coordination	Low
Color Discrimination	Low

Data = High   People = Low   Things = High

Salary Range:
$18,000–$60,000+

Opportunity Outlook:
25–34% growth

Environmental Conditions:
Inside and outside
Presence of atmospheric dangers

Physical Demands:
Light—lifting of no more than 20 pounds required
Reaching, handling, fingering, or feeling required
Seeing required

Temperaments:
Making decisions based upon facts
Attempting to attain set limits
Performing a variety of tasks

Vocational Preparation:
4–10 years

Pollution Control Technician

DOT = 029.261-014   GOE = 05.03.08

Conducts tests and field investigations to obtain data for use by environmental, engineering, and scientific personnel in determining sources and methods of controlling environmental pollution.

Aptitudes:
Intelligence	Moderate
Verbal	Moderate
Numerical	Moderate
Spatial	Low
Form Perception	Moderate
Clerical Perception	Moderate
Motor Coordination	Low
Finger Dexterity	Low
Manual Dexterity	Low
Eye-Hand-Foot Coordination	Low
Color Discrimination	Moderate

Data = High   People = Low   Things = High

Salary Range:
$16,000–$37,500

Opportunity Outlook:
25–34% growth

Environmental Conditions:
Inside and outside
Presence of atmospheric dangers such as fumes, odors, etc.

Physical Demands:
Light—lifting of no more than 20 pounds required
Reaching, handling, fingering, or feeling required
Seeing required

Temperaments:
Making decisions based upon facts
Attempting to attain set limits

Vocational Preparation:
1–2 years

Post-Office Clerk

DOT = 243.367-014   GOE = 07.03.01

Performs any combination of the following tasks in a post office: sells stamps, postal cards, and stamped envelopes; issues money orders; registers and insures mail; computes mailing costs; places mail into mail bags and racks; and weighs mail and parcels to determine postage.

Aptitudes:
Intelligence	Moderate
Verbal	Moderate
Numerical	Moderate
Spatial	Low
Form Perception	Moderate
Clerical Perception	High
Motor Coordination	Moderate
Finger Dexterity	Moderate
Manual Dexterity	Moderate
Eye-Hand-Foot Coordination	Low
Color Discrimination	Low

Data = Mod   People = Low   Things = Low

Salary Range:
$23,600–$29,100

Opportunity Outlook:
5–13% growth

Environmental Conditions:
Inside

Physical Demands:
Light—lifting of no more than 20 pounds required
Reaching, handling, fingering, or feeling required
Talking or hearing required
Seeing required

Temperaments:
Performing a variety of tasks

Vocational Preparation:
3–6 months

Poultry Farm Supervisor

DOT = 411.131-010   GOE = 03.02.01

Supervises and coordinates the activities of workers engaged in raising poultry, collecting eggs, crating fryers, and maintaining equipment and machinery on poultry farm.

Aptitudes:
Intelligence	Moderate
Verbal	Moderate
Numerical	Low
Spatial	Low
Form Perception	Low
Clerical Perception	Moderate
Motor Coordination	Low
Finger Dexterity	Low
Manual Dexterity	Moderate
Eye-Hand-Foot Coordination	Low
Color Discrimination	Low

Data = Mod   People = Mod   Things = Low

Salary Range:
$14,500 (average)

Opportunity Outlook:
14–24% growth

Environmental Conditions:
Inside

Physical Demands:
Moderate—lifting of no more than 50 pounds required
Talking or hearing required
Seeing required

Temperaments:
Directing, controlling, or planning the work of others
Making decisions based upon facts
Dealing with people beyond giving and receiving information
Performing a variety of tasks

Vocational Preparation: 2–4 years

Precision Lens Grinder

DOT = 716.382-018   GOE = 06.02.08

Sets up and operates grinding and polishing machines to make lenses, optical flats, and other precision optical elements for various instruments and equipment, such as telescopes, microscopes, aerial cameras, and eyeglasses.

Aptitudes:

Intelligence	Moderate
Verbal	Moderate
Numerical	Moderate
Spatial	High
Form Perception	Moderate
Clerical Perception	Low
Motor Coordination	High
Finger Dexterity	Moderate
Manual Dexterity	Moderate
Eye-Hand-Foot Coordination	Low
Color Discrimination	Low

Data = Mod   People = Low   Things = High

Salary Range:
$22,000 (average)

Opportunity Outlook:
14–24% growth

Environmental Conditions:
Inside

Physical Demands:
Light—lifting of no more than 20 pounds required
Reaching, handling, fingering, or feeling required
Seeing required

Temperaments:
Making decisions based upon facts
Attempting to attain set limits

Vocational Preparation:
2–4 years

Probation & Parole Officer

DOT = 195.107-046   GOE = 10.01.02

Counsels juvenile or adult offenders in how to manage their daily lives in order to satisfy the legal conditions of their probation or parole from prison; often assists offenders in resolving personal, social, financial, and employment problems.

Aptitudes:

Intelligence	High
Verbal	High
Numerical	Moderate
Spatial	Low
Form Perception	Low
Clerical Perception	Moderate
Motor Coordination	Low
Finger Dexterity	Low
Manual Dexterity	Low
Eye-Hand-Foot Coordination	Low
Color Discrimination	Low

Data = High   People = High   Things = Low

Salary Range:
$23,000–$36,000

Opportunity Outlook:
25–34% growth

Environmental Conditions:
Inside

Physical Demands:
Light—lifting of no more than 20 pounds required
Reaching, handling, fingering, or feeling required
Talking or hearing required
Seeing required

Temperaments:
Directing, controlling, or planning the work of others
Making decisions based upon senses and feelings
Dealing with people beyond giving and receiving information
Performing a variety of tasks

Vocational Preparation: 4–10 years

Production Coordinator

DOT = 221.167-018   GOE = 05.09.02

Schedules and coordinates the flow of work within or between departments of a manufacturing plant to improve the efficiency of the production of merchandise and goods.

Aptitudes:
Intelligence	High
Verbal	High
Numerical	Moderate
Spatial	Moderate
Form Perception	Moderate
Clerical Perception	Moderate
Motor Coordination	Low
Finger Dexterity	Low
Manual Dexterity	Low
Eye-Hand-Foot Coordination	Low
Color Discrimination	Low

Data = High   People = Low   Things = Low

Salary Range:
$18,000 (average)

Opportunity Outlook:
14–24% growth

Environmental Conditions:
Inside

Physical Demands:
Light—lifting of no more than 20 pounds required
Presence of loud noises and vibrations

Temperaments:
Directing, controlling, or planning the work of others
Making decisions based upon senses and feelings
Making decisions based upon facts
Attempting to attain set limits

Vocational Preparation:
2–4 years

Production Engine Repairer

DOT = 625.381-010   GOE = 06.01.04

Using various hand and power tools, repairs or replaces defective parts of internal combustion engines that fail various tests during manufacturing.

Aptitudes:
Intelligence	Moderate
Verbal	Moderate
Numerical	Moderate
Spatial	Moderate
Form Perception	Moderate
Clerical Perception	Low
Motor Coordination	Moderate
Finger Dexterity	Moderate
Manual Dexterity	High
Eye-Hand-Foot Coordination	Low
Color Discrimination	Low

Data = Mod   People = Low   Things = High

Salary Range:
$36,000 (average)

Opportunity Outlook:
5–13% growth

Environmental Conditions:
Inside
Presence of loud noises and vibrations

Physical Demands:
Moderate—lifting of no more than 50 pounds required
Reaching, handling, fingering, or feeling required
Seeing required

Temperaments:
Making decisions based upon facts
Attempting to attain set limits

Vocational Preparation:
1–2 years

Production Superintendent

DOT = 183.117-014   GOE = 05.02.03

Directs and coordinates, through subordinate supervisory personnel, the activities or workers engaged in the manufacture or production of merchandise and goods.

Aptitudes:
Intelligence	High
Verbal	High
Numerical	Moderate
Spatial	Moderate
Form Perception	Moderate
Clerical Perception	Moderate
Motor Coordination	Low
Finger Dexterity	Low
Manual Dexterity	Low
Eye-Hand-Foot Coordination	Low
Color Discrimination	Low

Data = High   People = High   Things = Low

Salary Range:
$19,000–$22,500

Opportunity Outlook:
14–24% growth

Environmental Conditions:
Inside

Physical Demands:
Light—lifting of no more than 20 pounds required
Talking or hearing required

Temperaments:
Directing, controlling, or planning the work of others
Making decisions based upon senses and feelings
Dealing with people beyond giving and receiving information
Performing a variety of tasks

Vocational Preparation:
4–10 years

Professional Athlete

DOT = 153.341-010   GOE = 12.01.03

Participates in a professional competitive events, such as football, boxing, hockey, tennis, baseball, or similar sports, to entertain an audience.

Aptitudes:
Intelligence	Moderate
Verbal	Moderate
Numerical	Low
Spatial	High
Form Perception	High
Clerical Perception	Low
Motor Coordination	High
Finger Dexterity	High
Manual Dexterity	High
Eye-Hand-Foot Coordination	High
Color Discrimination	Moderate

Data = Mod   People = Low   Things = High

Salary Range:
Varies

Opportunity Outlook:
14–24% growth

Environmental Conditions:
Inside and outside
Presence of physical hazards

Physical Demands:
Moderate—lifting of no more than 50 pounds required
Climbing or balancing required
Stooping, kneeling, crouching, or crawling required
Reaching, handling, fingering, or feeling required
Talking or hearing required
Seeing required

Temperaments:
Making decisions based upon senses and feelings
Performing under stressful conditions
Attempting to attain set limits

Vocational Preparation: 4–10 years

Professional Athletic Coach

DOT = 153.227-010   GOE = 12.01.01

Analyzes the performance of athletes and instructs them in game strategies and techniques to help them prepare for and improve upon their actual performance during an athletic event.

Aptitudes:
Intelligence	Moderate
Verbal	High
Numerical	Low
Spatial	Moderate
Form Perception	Moderate
Clerical Perception	Low
Motor Coordination	Moderate
Finger Dexterity	Low
Manual Dexterity	Moderate
Eye-Hand-Foot Coordination	High
Color Discrimination	Moderate

Data = High   People = High   Things = Low

Salary Range:
$25,000–$1,000,000+

Opportunity Outlook:
5–13% growth

Environmental Conditions:
Inside and outside

Physical Demands:
Moderate—lifting of no more than 50 pounds
Stooping, kneeling, crouching, or crawling required
Reaching, handling, fingering, or feeling required
Talking or hearing required
Seeing required

Temperaments:
Directing, controlling, or planning the work of others
Making decisions based upon senses and feelings
Dealing with people beyond giving and receiving information

Vocational Preparation: 4–10 years

Professional Sports Scout

DOT = 153.117-018   GOE = 12.01.01

Evaluates the athletic skills of nonprofessional athletes to determine their fitness and potential for participation in a professional sport; may travel extensively to find potential athletes; may also negotiate contracts with athletes on behalf of the club or team that wishes to recruit their services.

Aptitudes:
Intelligence	Moderate
Verbal	High
Numerical	Low
Spatial	Moderate
Form Perception	Moderate
Clerical Perception	Moderate
Motor Coordination	Low
Finger Dexterity	Low
Manual Dexterity	Low
Eye-Hand-Foot Coordination	Low
Color Discrimination	Low

Data = High   People = High   Things = Low

Salary Range:
$16,000–$50,000+

Opportunity Outlook:
14–24% growth

Environmental Conditions:
Inside and outside

Physical Demands:
Sedentary—little or no lifting
Talking or hearing required
Seeing required

Temperaments:
Directing, controlling, or planning the work of others
Influencing the actions and beliefs of others
Making decisions based upon senses and feelings
Dealing with people beyond giving and receiving information
Performing a variety of tasks

Vocational Preparation: 4–10 years

Programmer (Business)

DOT = 020.162-014   GOE = 11.01.01

Using a computer language, such as COBOL, Basic, C, or Pascal, writes the instructional code (software program) that a computer will follow in order to perform a business-related function or functions; may first design software program on paper and arrange informational flow into diagrams.

Aptitudes:
Intelligence	High
Verbal	High
Numerical	High
Spatial	High
Form Perception	Moderate
Clerical Perception	High
Motor Coordination	Low
Finger Dexterity	Moderate
Manual Dexterity	Low
Eye-Hand-Foot Coordination	Moderate
Color Discrimination	Low

Data = High   People = Mod   Things = Mod

Salary Range:
$17,000–$60,000+

Opportunity Outlook:
35% growth or more

Environmental Conditions:
Inside

Physical Demands:
Sedentary—little or no lifting
Talking or hearing required
Seeing required
Reaching, handling, fingering, and feeling required

Temperaments:
Making decisions based upon facts
Attempting to attain set limits

Vocational Preparation:
2–4 years

Programmer (Engineering/Science)

DOT = 020.167-022   GOE = 11.01.01

Using a computer language, such as COBOL, C, or Pascal, writes the instructional code (software program) that a computer will follow in order to solve an engineering- or science-related problem or problems; may first design software program on paper and arrange informational flow into diagrams.

Aptitudes:
Intelligence	High
Verbal	High
Numerical	High
Spatial	High
Form Perception	Moderate
Clerical Perception	High
Motor Coordination	Low
Finger Dexterity	Moderate
Manual Dexterity	Low
Eye-Hand-Foot Coordination	Moderate
Color Discrimination	Low

Data = High   People = Mod   Things = Low

Salary Range:
$17,000–$60,000+

Opportunity Outlook:
35% growth or more

Environmental Conditions:
Inside

Physical Demands:
Sedentary—little or no lifting
Talking or hearing required
Seeing required
Reaching, handling, fingering, and feeling required

Temperaments:
Making decisions based upon senses and feelings
Making decisions based upon facts
Attempting to attain set limits

Vocational Preparation:
2–4 years

Programmer (Information Systems)

DOT = 020.187-010   GOE = 11.01.01

Using a computer language, such as COBOL, Basic, C, or Pascal, writes the instructional code (software program) that a computer will follow to store, retrieve, analyze, and print documents, data, and information for business, and private use; may first design software program on paper and devise flow charts.

Aptitudes:
Intelligence	High
Verbal	High
Numerical	High
Spatial	High
Form Perception	Moderate
Clerical Perception	High
Motor Coordination	Low
Finger Dexterity	Moderate
Manual Dexterity	Low
Eye-Hand-Foot Coordination	Low
Color Discrimination	Low

Data = High   People = Mod   Things = Low

Salary Range:
$19,000–$52,100

Opportunity Outlook:
35% growth or more

Environmental Conditions:
Inside

Physical Demands:
Sedentary—little or no lifting
Talking or hearing required
Seeing required
Reaching, handling, fingering, and feeling required

Temperaments:
Making decisions based upon facts
Attempting to attain set limits

Vocational Preparation:
2–4 years

Promotion Manager

DOT = 163.117-018   GOE = 11.09.01

Plans and administers the sales or public relations policies, programs, and activities of a business or organization to promote the sale of its goods or services.

Aptitudes:
Intelligence	High
Verbal	High
Numerical	Moderate
Spatial	Low
Form Perception	Low
Clerical Perception	Moderate
Motor Coordination	Low
Finger Dexterity	Low
Manual Dexterity	Low
Eye-Hand-Foot Coordination	Low
Color Discrimination	Low

Data = High   People = High   Things = Low

Salary Range:
$28,000 (average)

Opportunity Outlook:
25–34% growth

Environmental Conditions:
Inside

Physical Demands:
Light—lifting of no more than 20 pounds required
Talking or hearing required

Temperaments:
Directing, controlling, or planning the work of others
Making decisions based upon senses and feelings
Dealing with people beyond giving and receiving information
Performing a variety of tasks

Vocational Preparation:
4–10 years

Prop Maker (Film/Stage/TV)

DOT = 962.281-010   GOE = 01.06.02

Makes and assembles props, miniatures, and sets for motion pictures and theatrical productions from a variety of materials, using hand tools and woodworking and metalworking machines, according to the specifications of the production director or script.

Aptitudes:
Intelligence	Moderate
Verbal	Moderate
Numerical	Moderate
Spatial	High
Form Perception	High
Clerical Perception	Low
Motor Coordination	Moderate
Finger Dexterity	High
Manual Dexterity	High
Eye-Hand-Foot Coordination	Low
Color Discrimination	Moderate

Data = Mod   People = Low   Things = High

Salary Range:
$14,000–$18,700

Opportunity Outlook:
14–24% growth

Environmental Conditions:
Inside and outside
Presence of physical hazards

Physical Demands:
Moderate—lifting of no more than 50 pounds required
Reaching, handling, fingering, or feeling required
Seeing required

Temperaments:
Making decisions based upon facts
Performing under stressful conditions
Attempting to attain set limits
Performing a variety of tasks

Vocational Preparation:
2–4 years

Property Manager

DOT = 186.167-046   GOE = 11.11.04

Manages commercial, industrial, or residential real estate properties for clients; may negotiate the terms and conditions of the management service; may also show properties to prospective renters, collect rental fees, and manage the upkeep of each property.

Aptitudes:
Intelligence	High
Verbal	High
Numerical	Moderate
Spatial	Low
Form Perception	Low
Clerical Perception	Moderate
Motor Coordination	Low
Finger Dexterity	Low
Manual Dexterity	Low
Eye-Hand-Foot Coordination	Low
Color Discrimination	Low

Data = Mod   People = Mod   Things = Low

Salary Range:
$10,300–$47,300

Opportunity Outlook:
25–34% growth

Environmental Conditions:
Inside and outside

Physical Demands:
Light—lifting of no more than 20 pounds required
Talking or hearing required

Temperaments:
Directing, controlling, or planning the work of others
Dealing with people beyond giving and receiving information

Vocational Preparation:
4–10 years

Property Utilization Officer

DOT = 188.117-122   GOE = 11.12.02

Coordinates the purchase or rental of property for federal government agencies; reviews bids submitted by various property owners, and selects property most suitable to needs of the agency; may negotiate with property owner the rental or sale fee and terms of the maintenance of the property.

Aptitudes:

Intelligence	High
Verbal	High
Numerical	Moderate
Spatial	Moderate
Form Perception	Moderate
Clerical Perception	Moderate
Motor Coordination	Low
Finger Dexterity	Low
Manual Dexterity	Low
Eye-Hand-Foot Coordination	Low
Color Discrimination	Low

Data = High   People = Mod   Things = Low

Salary Range:
$28,500 (average)

Opportunity Outlook:
5–13% growth

Environmental Conditions:
Inside

Physical Demands:
Light—lifting of no more than 20 pounds required
Talking or hearing required
Seeing required

Temperaments:
Directing, controlling, or planning the work of others
Influencing the actions and beliefs of others
Making decisions based upon senses and feelings
Dealing with people beyond giving and receiving information
Performing a variety of tasks

Vocational Preparation: 4–10 years

Psychiatrist

DOT = 070.107-014   GOE = 02.03.01

Studies, diagnoses, and treats mental, emotional, and behavioral disorders; may prescribe therapy program consisting of counseling and medical treatment.

Aptitudes:

Intelligence	High
Verbal	High
Numerical	High
Spatial	High
Form Perception	High
Clerical Perception	Moderate
Motor Coordination	Low
Finger Dexterity	Low
Manual Dexterity	Low
Eye-Hand-Foot Coordination	Low
Color Discrimination	Low

Data = High   People = High   Things = Low

Salary Range:
$117,700 (average)

Opportunity Outlook:
5–13% growth

Environmental Conditions:
Inside

Physical Demands:
Sedentary—little or no lifting
Reaching, handling, fingering, or feeling required
Talking or hearing required
Seeing required

Temperaments:
Directing, controlling, or planning the work of others
Making decisions based upon senses and feelings
Dealing with people beyond giving and receiving information

Vocational Preparation:
4–10 years

Psychologist (Educational)

DOT = 045.067-010   GOE = 11.03.01

Studies various methods of learning and teaching and develops psychological principles and techniques to be used by educational professionals to foster the intellectual, social, and emotional growth and development of students.

Aptitudes:
Intelligence	High
Verbal	High
Numerical	High
Spatial	Moderate
Form Perception	Moderate
Clerical Perception	Low
Motor Coordination	Low
Finger Dexterity	Low
Manual Dexterity	Low
Eye-Hand-Foot Coordination	Low
Color Discrimination	Low

Data = High   People = Mod   Things = Low

Salary Range:
$41,000 (average)

Opportunity Outlook:
35% growth or more

Environmental Conditions:
Inside

Physical Demands:
Light—lifting of no more than 20 pounds required
Talking or hearing required
Seeing required

Temperaments:
Influencing the actions and beliefs of others
Making decisions based upon senses and feelings
Making decisions based upon facts
Dealing with people beyond giving and receiving information
Performing a variety of tasks

Vocational Preparation: 4–10 years

Psychologist (Industrial)

DOT = 045.107-030   GOE = 11.03.01

Studies human behavior and develops psychological principles and techniques to be used by personnel directors and other business management personnel to promote the growth and development of employees.

Aptitudes:
Intelligence	High
Verbal	High
Numerical	High
Spatial	Moderate
Form Perception	Moderate
Clerical Perception	Low
Motor Coordination	Low
Finger Dexterity	Low
Manual Dexterity	Low
Eye-Hand-Foot Coordination	Low
Color Discrimination	Low

Data = High   People = High   Things = Low

Salary Range:
$67,000 (average)

Opportunity Outlook:
35% growth or more

Environmental Conditions:
Inside

Physical Demands:
Light—lifting of no more than 20 pounds required
Talking or hearing required
Seeing required

Temperaments:
Influencing the actions and beliefs of others
Making decisions based upon senses and feelings
Making decisions based upon facts
Dealing with people beyond giving and receiving information
Performing a variety of tasks

Vocational Preparation: 4–10 years

Public Health Educator

DOT = 079.117-014   GOE = 11.07.02

Plans, organizes, and conducts health education programs for various community groups, agencies, and organizations; conducts research to determine what health problems exist in the community and what steps should be taken to resolve those needs; develops programs to meet those needs.

Aptitudes:
Intelligence	High
Verbal	High
Numerical	Moderate
Spatial	Moderate
Form Perception	Low
Clerical Perception	Moderate
Motor Coordination	Low
Finger Dexterity	Low
Manual Dexterity	Low
Eye-Hand-Foot Coordination	Low
Color Discrimination	Low

Data = High   People = High   Things = Low

Salary Range:
$29,500–$36,000

Opportunity Outlook:
14–24% growth

Environmental Conditions:
Inside and outside

Physical Demands:
Light—lifting of no more than 20 pounds required
Talking or hearing required

Temperaments:
Directing, controlling, or planning the work of others
Influencing the actions and beliefs of others
Making decisions based upon senses and feelings
Dealing with people beyond giving and receiving information

Vocational Preparation:
4–10 years

Public Service Director

DOT = 184.117-010   GOE = 11.09.03

Plans, schedules, and coordinates the broadcasting of public service programs for a radio or television station; creates programs in various fields, such as education, religion, and civic and government affairs, to help educate viewers about problems, needs, and resources.

Aptitudes:
Intelligence	High
Verbal	High
Numerical	Moderate
Spatial	Low
Form Perception	Low
Clerical Perception	Moderate
Motor Coordination	Low
Finger Dexterity	Low
Manual Dexterity	Low
Eye-Hand-Foot Coordination	Low
Color Discrimination	Low

Data = High   People = Mod   Things = Low

Salary Range:
Not available

Opportunity Outlook:
Not available

Environmental Conditions:
Inside

Physical Demands:
Sedentary—little or no lifting
Talking or hearing required

Temperaments:
Directing, controlling, or planning the work of others
Making decisions based upon senses and feelings
Dealing with people beyond giving and receiving information

Vocational Preparation:
4–10 years

Public Works Commissioner

DOT = 188.117-030   GOE = 11.05.03

Directs and coordinates the activities of various city departments that provide services to the community, such as water, sewage, snow removal, and trash collection.

Aptitudes:
Intelligence	High
Verbal	High
Numerical	Moderate
Spatial	Low
Form Perception	Low
Clerical Perception	Low
Motor Coordination	Low
Finger Dexterity	Low
Manual Dexterity	Low
Eye-Hand-Foot Coordination	Low
Color Discrimination	Low

Data = High   People = Mod   Things = Low

Salary Range:
$36,500 (average)

Opportunity Outlook:
14-24% growth

Environmental Conditions:
Inside

Physical Demands:
Sedentary—little or no lifting
Talking or hearing required

Temperaments:
Directing, controlling, or planning the work of others
Making decisions based upon senses and feelings
Dealing with people beyond giving and receiving information
Performing a variety of tasks

Vocational Preparation:
4-10 years

Purchasing Agent

DOT = 162.157-038   GOE = 11.05.04

Purchases raw materials or other unprocessed goods for processing, or machinery, equipment, tools, parts, produce, or other supplies or services necessary for the operation of an organization or company.

Aptitudes:
Intelligence	Moderate
Verbal	Moderate
Numerical	Moderate
Spatial	Low
Form Perception	Low
Clerical Perception	Moderate
Motor Coordination	Low
Finger Dexterity	Low
Manual Dexterity	Low
Eye-Hand-Foot Coordination	Low
Color Discrimination	Low

Data = High   People = Low   Things = Low

Salary Range:
$16,000-$45,300

Opportunity Outlook:
14-24% growth

Environmental Conditions:
Inside

Physical Demands:
Sedentary—little or no lifting
Talking or hearing required

Temperaments:
Making decisions based upon senses and feelings
Making decisions based upon facts
Influencing the actions and beliefs of others

Vocational Preparation:
2-4 years

Quality Control Food Technician

DOT = 529.387-030   GOE = 06.03.01

Inspects raw materials and finished products in a food production facility; tests and adjusts packaging equipment used to process such foods as corn chips, potato chips, and candy bars; determines proper content of such elements as oil, salt, and moisture in foods.

Aptitudes:
Intelligence	Moderate
Verbal	Moderate
Numerical	Low
Spatial	Low
Form Perception	Moderate
Clerical Perception	Moderate
Motor Coordination	Moderate
Finger Dexterity	Moderate
Manual Dexterity	Moderate
Eye-Hand-Foot Coordination	Low
Color Discrimination	Moderate

Data = Mod   People = Low   Things = Low

Salary Range:
$26,228 (average)

Opportunity Outlook:
25–34% growth

Environmental Conditions:
Inside

Physical Demands:
Light—lifting of no more than 20 pounds required
Reaching, handling, fingering, or feeling required
Seeing required

Temperaments:
Making decisions based upon facts
Attempting to attain set limits

Vocational Preparation:
3–6 months

Radial-Arm Saw Operator

DOT = 667.682-054   GOE = 06.02.03

Operates a circular saw mounted on an overhead radial arm to cut boards and other woodstock to specifications for use in building furniture, homes, and other wooden structures and objects.

Aptitudes:
Intelligence	Moderate
Verbal	Low
Numerical	Low
Spatial	Moderate
Form Perception	Moderate
Clerical Perception	Low
Motor Coordination	Moderate
Finger Dexterity	Low
Manual Dexterity	Moderate
Eye-Hand-Foot Coordination	Low
Color Discrimination	Low

Data = Low   People = Low   Things = Mod

Salary Range:
$10,500 (average)

Opportunity Outlook:
5–13% growth

Environmental Conditions:
Inside
Presence of loud noises and vibrations
Presence of physical hazards

Physical Demands:
Moderate—lifting of no more than 50 pounds required
Reaching, handling, fingering, or feeling required
Seeing required

Temperaments:
Performing repetitive tasks
Attempting to attain set limits

Vocational Preparation:
3–6 months

Radiation Therapy Technologist

DOT = 078.361-034   GOE = 02.03.04

Operates radiation therapy equipment in a hospital or medical facility to treat patients with ionizing radiation who suffer from various diseases; positions patient under equipment to expose necessary areas to treatment and adjusts equipment according to system specifications or instructions given by physician.

Aptitudes:
Intelligence	Moderate
Verbal	Moderate
Numerical	Low
Spatial	Moderate
Form Perception	Moderate
Clerical Perception	Moderate
Motor Coordination	Moderate
Finger Dexterity	Low
Manual Dexterity	Moderate
Eye-Hand-Foot Coordination	Moderate
Color Discrimination	Low

Data = Mod   People = Low   Things = High

Salary Range:
$24,600–$35,800

Opportunity Outlook:
35% growth or more

Environmental Conditions:
Inside
Presence of physical hazards

Physical Demands:
Light—lifting of no more than 20 pounds required
Reaching, handling, fingering, or feeling required
Seeing required

Temperaments:
Attempting to attain set limits

Vocational Preparation:
1–2 years

Radio Dispatcher (Fire Service)

DOT = 193.262-014   GOE = 07.04.05

Operates radio and telephone equipment to receive reports and requests from firefighting crews, fire-lookout stations, and mobile units; relays information or orders to officials and support personnel for action.

Aptitudes:
Intelligence	Moderate
Verbal	Moderate
Numerical	Low
Spatial	Low
Form Perception	Low
Clerical Perception	Moderate
Motor Coordination	Low
Finger Dexterity	Low
Manual Dexterity	Moderate
Eye-Hand-Foot Coordination	Low
Color Discrimination	Low

Data = Mod   People = Low   Things = Mod

Salary Range:
$18,000 (average)

Opportunity Outlook:
14–24% growth

Environmental Conditions:
Inside

Physical Demands:
Sedentary—little or no lifting
Reaching, handling, fingering, or feeling required
Seeing required

Temperaments:
Performing a variety of tasks

Vocational Preparation:
1–2 years

Radiographer

DOT = 199.361-010   GOE = 05.03.05

Radiographs metal, plastics, concrete, or other materials for flaws, cracks, or presence of foreign elements to ensure materials are in proper condition for use.

Aptitudes:
Intelligence	Moderate
Verbal	Moderate
Numerical	Moderate
Spatial	Moderate
Form Perception	Moderate
Clerical Perception	Low
Motor Coordination	Moderate
Finger Dexterity	Moderate
Manual Dexterity	Moderate
Eye-Hand-Foot Coordination	Low
Color Discrimination	Moderate

Data = Mod   People = Low   Things = High

Salary Range:
$24,600–$35,800

Opportunity Outlook:
35% growth or more

Environmental Conditions:
Inside
Presence of physical hazards

Physical Demands:
Light—lifting of no more than 20 pounds required
Reaching, handling, fingering, or feeling required
Seeing required

Temperaments:
Making decisions based upon facts
Attempting to attain set limits

Vocational Preparation:
1/2–1 year

Radiologic Technologist

DOT = 078.362-026   GOE = 10.02.02

Operates x-ray equipment in a hospital or medical facility to examine patients who have been injured or are ill; positions patient under equipment to expose necessary areas to x-rays and adjusts equipment according to system specifications or instructions given by physician.

Aptitudes:
Intelligence	High
Verbal	Moderate
Numerical	Moderate
Spatial	Moderate
Form Perception	Moderate
Clerical Perception	Moderate
Motor Coordination	Moderate
Finger Dexterity	Moderate
Manual Dexterity	Moderate
Eye-Hand-Foot Coordination	Low
Color Discrimination	Low

Data = Mod   People = Low   Things = High

Salary Range:
$24,600–$35,800

Opportunity Outlook:
35% growth or more

Environmental Conditions:
Inside
Presence of physical hazards

Physical Demands:
Moderate—lifting of no more than 50 pounds required
Reaching, handling, fingering, or feeling required
Talking or hearing required
Seeing required

Temperaments:
Making decisions based upon facts
Attempting to attain set limits

Vocational Preparation:
1–2 years

Real Estate Sales Agent

DOT = 250.357-018 GOE = 08.02.04

Rents, buys, or sells property for clients on a commission basis; may show property to prospective buyers, negotiate lease or sales agreement, or arrange for maintenance or repairs of property.

Aptitudes:
Intelligence	High
Verbal	High
Numerical	Moderate
Spatial	Moderate
Form Perception	Moderate
Clerical Perception	Moderate
Motor Coordination	Low
Finger Dexterity	Low
Manual Dexterity	Low
Eye-Hand-Foot Coordination	Low
Color Discrimination	Low

Data = Mod   People = Mod   Things = Low

Salary Range:
$19,000–$60,000+

Opportunity Outlook:
14–24% growth

Environmental Conditions:
Inside and outside

Physical Demands:
Light—lifting of no more than 20 pounds required
Talking or hearing required
Seeing required

Temperaments:
Influencing the actions and beliefs of others
Making decisions based upon senses and feelings
Dealing with people beyond giving and receiving information

Vocational Preparation:
1/2–1 year

Receptionist

DOT = 237.367-038 GOE = 07.04.04

Receives callers at a company, organization, or establishment; determines nature of their visit, and directs them to the proper location or person; may record the date, time, and purpose of each visitor.

Aptitudes:
Intelligence	Moderate
Verbal	Moderate
Numerical	Low
Spatial	Low
Form Perception	Low
Clerical Perception	Moderate
Motor Coordination	Low
Finger Dexterity	Low
Manual Dexterity	Low
Eye-Hand-Foot Coordination	Low
Color Discrimination	Low

Data = Mod   People = Mod   Things = Low

Salary Range:
$14,000 (average)

Opportunity Outlook:
35% growth or more

Environmental Conditions:
Inside

Physical Demands:
Sedentary—little or no lifting
Reaching, handling, fingering, or feeling required
Talking or hearing required

Temperaments:
Performing repetitive tasks

Vocational Preparation:
1/2–1 year

Records Analyst Manager

DOT = 161.167-018   GOE = 11.06.02

Directs and coordinates the activities of workers engaged in analyzing various records management systems; determines most effective and efficient method of storing and retrieving records, considering the needs and financial resources of individuals who will use the record keeping system.

Aptitudes:

Intelligence	High
Verbal	High
Numerical	Moderate
Spatial	High
Form Perception	High
Clerical Perception	High
Motor Coordination	Low
Finger Dexterity	Low
Manual Dexterity	Low
Eye-Hand-Foot Coordination	Low
Color Discrimination	Moderate

Data = High   People = Mod   Things = Low

Salary Range:
$26,000–$37,500

Opportunity Outlook:
25–34% growth

Environmental Conditions:
Inside

Physical Demands:
Sedentary—little or no lifting
Talking or hearing required
Seeing required

Temperaments:
Directing, controlling, or planning the work of others
Making decisions based upon facts
Dealing with people beyond giving and receiving information

Vocational Preparation:
4–10 years

Recreational Leader

DOT = 195.227-014   GOE = 09.01.01

Plans and conducts the recreational activities for an assigned group of individuals in a public or private recreational service; determines which activities best meet the needs of the participants, as well as available resources, equipment, and staff.

Aptitudes:

Intelligence	Moderate
Verbal	Moderate
Numerical	Low
Spatial	Moderate
Form Perception	Moderate
Clerical Perception	Low
Motor Coordination	Moderate
Finger Dexterity	Moderate
Manual Dexterity	Moderate
Eye-Hand-Foot Coordination	Moderate
Color Discrimination	Low

Data = Mod   People = Mod   Things = Low

Salary Range:
$11,000–$95,000

Opportunity Outlook:
14–24% growth

Environmental Conditions:
Inside and outside

Physical Demands:
Light—lifting of no more than 20 pounds required
Talking or hearing required

Temperaments:
Directing, controlling, or planning the work of others
Dealing with people beyond giving and receiving information

Vocational Preparation:
2–4 years

Reducing Salon Attendant

DOT = 359.567-010   GOE = 09.05.01

Measures, weighs, and records body statistics of patrons in a public or private weight reduction center; forwards information to weight reduction specialist for use in developing a program of weight control and management for each patron.

Aptitudes:
Intelligence	Low
Verbal	Low
Numerical	Low
Spatial	Low
Form Perception	Low
Clerical Perception	Moderate
Motor Coordination	Moderate
Finger Dexterity	Low
Manual Dexterity	Moderate
Eye-Hand-Foot Coordination	Low
Color Discrimination	Low

Data = Low   People = Low   Things = Low

Salary Range:
$11,600–$15,000

Opportunity Outlook:
25–34% growth

Environmental Conditions:
Inside
Extremely hot work environment
Wet and humid work environment

Physical Demands:
Moderate—lifting of no more than 50 pounds required
Stooping, kneeling, crouching, or crawling required
Reaching, handling, fingering, or feeling required
Talking or hearing required

Temperaments:
Performing repetitive tasks

Vocational Preparation:
1–30 days

Reporter

DOT = 131.267-018   GOE = 11.08.02

Collects and analyzes information about newsworthy events to write news stories for publication or broadcast; may use information gathered by others or collect information directly from individuals involved in the event; verifies information to ensure accuracy; may appear live on radio or television to report findings.

Aptitudes:
Intelligence	High
Verbal	High
Numerical	Moderate
Spatial	Low
Form Perception	Moderate
Clerical Perception	Moderate
Motor Coordination	Moderate
Finger Dexterity	Moderate
Manual Dexterity	Low
Eye-Hand-Foot Coordination	Low
Color Discrimination	Moderate

Data = High   People = Low   Things = Low

Salary Range:
$15,000–$67,000

Opportunity Outlook:
14–24% growth

Environmental Conditions:
Inside and outside

Physical Demands:
Sedentary—little or no lifting
Reaching, handling, fingering, or feeling required
Talking or hearing required
Seeing required

Temperaments:
Influencing the actions and beliefs of others
Making decisions based upon senses and feelings

Vocational Preparation:
2–4 years

Reservations Agent (Airline)

DOT = 238.367-018 GOE = 07.04.03

Makes and confirms reservations for passengers on scheduled airline flights.

Aptitudes:
Intelligence	Moderate
Verbal	Moderate
Numerical	Moderate
Spatial	Low
Form Perception	Low
Clerical Perception	Moderate
Motor Coordination	Moderate
Finger Dexterity	Moderate
Manual Dexterity	Moderate
Eye-Hand-Foot Coordination	Low
Color Discrimination	Low

Data = Mod   People = Mod   Things = Low

Salary Range:
$20,000 (average)

Opportunity Outlook:
25–34% growth

Environmental Conditions:
Inside

Physical Demands:
Sedentary—little or no lifting
Reaching, handling, fingering, or feeling required
Talking or hearing required

Temperaments:
Performing repetitive tasks

Vocational Preparation:
3–6 months

Respiratory Therapist

DOT = 079.361-010 GOE = 10.02.02

Administers respiratory therapy care and life support to patients with deficiencies and abnormalities of the cardiopulmonary system, under the direct care and guidance of a physician or other medical practitioner.

Aptitudes:
Intelligence	Moderate
Verbal	Moderate
Numerical	Moderate
Spatial	Moderate
Form Perception	Moderate
Clerical Perception	Moderate
Motor Coordination	Moderate
Finger Dexterity	Moderate
Manual Dexterity	High
Eye-Hand-Foot Coordination	Low
Color Discrimination	Low

Data = Mod   People = Low   Things = High

Salary Range:
$23,800–$37,400

Opportunity Outlook:
25–34% growth

Environmental Conditions:
Inside
Presence of atmospheric dangers

Physical Demands:
Light—lifting of no more than 20 pounds required
Reaching, handling, fingering, or feeling required
Seeing required

Temperaments:
Making decisions based upon facts
Attempting to attain set limits
Performing a variety of tasks

Vocational Preparation:
1–2 years

Risk & Insurance Manager

DOT = 186.117-066   GOE = 11.06.03

Plans, directs, and coordinates various risk and insurance programs for a company or organization to prevent or control financial loss from accidents or from employees or visitors to the facility or acts of nature.

Aptitudes:
Intelligence	High
Verbal	High
Numerical	High
Spatial	Low
Form Perception	Low
Clerical Perception	Moderate
Motor Coordination	Low
Finger Dexterity	Low
Manual Dexterity	Low
Eye-Hand-Foot Coordination	Low
Color Discrimination	Low

Data = High   People = Mod   Things = Low

Salary Range:
$28,500–$50,000+

Opportunity Outlook:
14–24% growth

Environmental Conditions:
Inside

Physical Demands:
Sedentary—little or no lifting
Talking or hearing required

Temperaments:
Directing, controlling, or planning the work of others
Dealing with people beyond giving and receiving information

Vocational Preparation:
4–10 years

Riveter

DOT = 800.684-010   GOE = 05.10.01

Using power and handtools, joins structural or metal parts together with rivets to assemble aircraft, missiles, space vehicles, railroad cars, or other structural components.

Aptitudes:
Intelligence	Moderate
Verbal	Low
Numerical	Low
Spatial	Moderate
Form Perception	Moderate
Clerical Perception	Low
Motor Coordination	Moderate
Finger Dexterity	Low
Manual Dexterity	Moderate
Eye-Hand-Foot Coordination	Low
Color Discrimination	Low

Data = Low   People = Low   Things = Mod

Salary Range:
$16,000 (average)

Opportunity Outlook:
14–24% growth

Environmental Conditions:
Inside
Presence of loud noises and vibrations
Presence of physical hazards

Physical Demands:
Moderate—lifting of no more than 50 pounds required
Stooping, kneeling, crouching, or crawling required
Reaching, handling, fingering, or feeling required
Seeing required

Temperaments:
Attempting to attain set limits

Vocational Preparation:
3–6 months

Rodeo Performer

DOT = 159.344-014   GOE = 12.02.01

Demonstrates daring and skill by riding wild horses or bulls, calf roping, steer wrestling, or other feats in a rodeo competition to entertain spectators or to compete for a prize.

Aptitudes:
Intelligence	Moderate
Verbal	Moderate
Numerical	Low
Spatial	High
Form Perception	Moderate
Clerical Perception	Low
Motor Coordination	High
Finger Dexterity	Moderate
Manual Dexterity	High
Eye-Hand-Foot Coordination	High
Color Discrimination	Low

Data = Mod   People = Low   Things = Low

Salary Range:
Varies

Opportunity Outlook:
14-24% growth

Environmental Conditions:
Inside and outside
Presence of physical hazards

Physical Demands:
Heavy—lifting of no more than 100 pounds required
Climbing or balancing required
Stooping, kneeling, crouching, or crawling required
Reaching, handling, fingering, or feeling required
Seeing required

Temperaments:
Making decisions based upon senses and feelings
Performing under stressful conditions
Performing a variety of tasks

Vocational Preparation: 1/2-1 year

Rotary Oil Drill Operator

DOT = 930.382-026   GOE = 05.11.03

Operates gasoline, diesel, electric, or steam driven equipment to extract oil or gas from a well driven deep into the ground.

Aptitudes:
Intelligence	Moderate
Verbal	Moderate
Numerical	Moderate
Spatial	Moderate
Form Perception	Moderate
Clerical Perception	Low
Motor Coordination	Moderate
Finger Dexterity	Moderate
Manual Dexterity	Moderate
Eye-Hand-Foot Coordination	Moderate
Color Discrimination	Low

Data = Mod   People = Low   Things = High

Salary Range:
$12,400-$31,000

Opportunity Outlook:
5-13% growth

Environmental Conditions:
Outside
Presence of loud noises and vibrations
Presence of physical hazards

Physical Demands:
Moderate—lifting of no more than 50 pounds
Stooping, kneeling, crouching, or crawling required
Reaching, handling, fingering, or feeling required
Seeing required

Temperaments:
Making decisions based upon facts
Attempting to attain set limits
Performing a variety of tasks

Vocational Preparation: 1-2 years

Safety Coordinator

DOT = 909.127-010   GOE = 11.10.05

Coordinates the traffic safety program for a transportation company; instructs truck and trailer drivers in matters pertaining to proper vehicle operation, traffic and safety regulations, fines and penalties for infraction of the rules, as well as in the care and maintenance of their vehicles.

Aptitudes:
Intelligence	Moderate
Verbal	High
Numerical	Moderate
Spatial	Moderate
Form Perception	Moderate
Clerical Perception	Moderate
Motor Coordination	Low
Finger Dexterity	Low
Manual Dexterity	Moderate
Eye-Hand-Foot Coordination	Moderate
Color Discrimination	Moderate

Data = Mod   People = Mod   Things = Low

Salary Range:
$26,500 (average)

Opportunity Outlook:
14-24% growth

Environmental Conditions:
Inside

Physical Demands:
Light—lifting of no more than 20 pounds required
Reaching, handling, fingering, or feeling required
Talking or hearing required
Seeing required

Temperaments:
Directing, controlling, or planning the work of others
Making decisions based upon facts
Dealing with people beyond giving and receiving information
Performing a variety of tasks

Vocational Preparation: 2-4 years

Sales Agent (Financial Services)

DOT = 251.257-010   GOE = 08.01.02

Calls on industrial, wholesale, and retail establishments, real estate firms, contractors, and individuals to solicit applications for loans and new deposit accounts on behalf of a bank or savings and loan association.

Aptitudes:
Intelligence	High
Verbal	High
Numerical	High
Spatial	Low
Form Perception	Low
Clerical Perception	Moderate
Motor Coordination	Low
Finger Dexterity	Low
Manual Dexterity	Low
Eye-Hand-Foot Coordination	Low
Color Discrimination	Low

Data = Mod   People = Mod   Things = Low

Salary Range:
$19,200-$160,000+

Opportunity Outlook:
35% growth or more

Environmental Conditions:
Inside

Physical Demands:
Light—lifting of no more than 20 pounds required
Reaching, handling, fingering, or feeling required
Talking or hearing required

Temperaments:
Influencing the actions and beliefs of others
Making decisions based upon senses and feelings
Dealing with people beyond giving and receiving information

Vocational Preparation:
1-2 years

Sales Manager

DOT = 163.167-018   GOE = 11.05.04

Plans and directs the sales activities of a company or organization; responsible for such functions as staffing, training, establishment of sales territories, performance evaluation, market analysis, and similar activities.

Aptitudes:
Intelligence	High
Verbal	High
Numerical	High
Spatial	Moderate
Form Perception	Moderate
Clerical Perception	Moderate
Motor Coordination	Low
Finger Dexterity	Low
Manual Dexterity	Low
Eye-Hand-Foot Coordination	Low
Color Discrimination	Low

Data = High   People = Mod   Things = Low

Salary Range:
$20,000–$78,000

Opportunity Outlook:
35% growth or more

Environmental Conditions:
Inside

Physical Demands:
Sedentary—little or no lifting
Talking or hearing required

Temperaments:
Directing, controlling, or planning the work of others
Influencing the actions and beliefs of others
Making decisions based upon senses and feelings
Dealing with people beyond giving and receiving information
Performing a variety of tasks

Vocational Preparation:
4–10 years

Sales Rep (Chemicals & Drugs)

DOT = 262.357-010   GOE = 08.01.01

Sells chemical or pharmaceutical products, such as explosives, acids, industrial or agricultural chemicals, medicines, and drugs to wholesale and commercial establishments.

Aptitudes:
Intelligence	High
Verbal	High
Numerical	Moderate
Spatial	Moderate
Form Perception	Low
Clerical Perception	Moderate
Motor Coordination	Low
Finger Dexterity	Low
Manual Dexterity	Low
Eye-Hand-Foot Coordination	Low
Color Discrimination	Low

Data = Mod   People = Mod   Things = Low

Salary Range:
$15,500–$63,000

Opportunity Outlook:
14–24% growth

Environmental Conditions:
Inside

Physical Demands:
Light—lifting of no more than 20 pounds required
Talking or hearing required

Temperaments:
Influencing the actions and beliefs of others
Making decisions based upon senses and feelings
Dealing with people beyond giving and receiving information

Vocational Preparation:
2–4 years

Sales Rep (Computers)

DOT = 275.257-010   GOE = 08.01.01

Sells computers and electronic data-processing equipment to business and industrial establishments; analyzes customer's needs and resources and suggests appropriate equipment.

Aptitudes:
Intelligence	High
Verbal	High
Numerical	Moderate
Spatial	Moderate
Form Perception	Low
Clerical Perception	Moderate
Motor Coordination	Low
Finger Dexterity	Low
Manual Dexterity	Low
Eye-Hand-Foot Coordination	Low
Color Discrimination	Low

Data = Mod   People = Mod   Things = Low

Salary Range:
$12,000-$40,000+

Opportunity Outlook:
25-34% growth

Environmental Conditions:
Inside

Physical Demands:
Light—lifting of no more than 20 pounds required
Talking or hearing required

Temperaments:
Influencing the actions and beliefs of others
Making decisions based upon senses and feelings
Dealing with people beyond giving and receiving information

Vocational Preparation:
2-4 years

Sales Rep (Data Processing Services)

DOT = 251.157-014   GOE = 08.01.02

Calls upon representatives of government, business, and industrial organizations to sell data processing services, such as inventory control, accounting and payroll, personnel management, and sales analysis.

Aptitudes:
Intelligence	High
Verbal	High
Numerical	Moderate
Spatial	Moderate
Form Perception	Low
Clerical Perception	Moderate
Motor Coordination	Low
Finger Dexterity	Low
Manual Dexterity	Low
Eye-Hand-Foot Coordination	Low
Color Discrimination	Low

Data = Mod   People = Mod   Things = Low

Salary Range:
$24,400-$200,000+

Opportunity Outlook:
35% growth or more

Environmental Conditions:
Inside

Physical Demands:
Light—lifting of no more than 20 pounds required
Talking or hearing required

Temperaments:
Influencing the actions and beliefs of others
Making decisions based upon senses and feelings
Dealing with people beyond giving and receiving information

Vocational Preparation:
2-4 years

Sales Rep (Dental/Medical Supplies)

DOT = 276.257-010   GOE = 08.01.01

Sells medical and dental equipment and supplies, except drugs and medicines, to doctors, dentists, hospitals, medical schools, and retail establishments.

Aptitudes:
Intelligence	High
Verbal	High
Numerical	Moderate
Spatial	Moderate
Form Perception	Low
Clerical Perception	Moderate
Motor Coordination	Low
Finger Dexterity	Low
Manual Dexterity	Low
Eye-Hand-Foot Coordination	Low
Color Discrimination	Low

Data = Mod   People = Mod   Things = Low

Salary Range:
$15,500–$63,000

Opportunity Outlook:
14-24% growth

Environmental Conditions:
Inside

Physical Demands:
Light—lifting of no more than 20 pounds required
Talking or hearing required

Temperaments:
Influencing the actions and beliefs of others
Making decisions based upon senses and feelings
Dealing with people beyond giving and receiving information

Vocational Preparation:
2-4 years

Sales Rep (Livestock)

DOT = 260.257-010   GOE = 08.01.03

Sells cattle, horses, hogs, and other livestock on commission to packing houses, farmers, and other livestock buyers.

Aptitudes:
Intelligence	High
Verbal	High
Numerical	Moderate
Spatial	Moderate
Form Perception	Low
Clerical Perception	Moderate
Motor Coordination	Low
Finger Dexterity	Low
Manual Dexterity	Low
Eye-Hand-Foot Coordination	Low
Color Discrimination	Low

Data = Mod   People = Mod   Things = Low

Salary Range:
$20,000–$36,000+

Opportunity Outlook:
14-24% growth

Environmental Conditions:
Inside

Physical Demands:
Light—lifting of no more than 20 pounds required
Talking or hearing required

Temperaments:
Influencing the actions and beliefs of others
Making decisions based upon senses and feelings
Dealing with people beyond giving and receiving information

Vocational Preparation:
2-4 years

Sales Route Driver

DOT = 292.353-010   GOE = 08.02.07

Drives a truck, car, or van over an established route to deliver and sell merchandise or render a service; collects money from customers and makes appropriate change.

Aptitudes:
Intelligence	Moderate
Verbal	Moderate
Numerical	Moderate
Spatial	Low
Form Perception	Low
Clerical Perception	Moderate
Motor Coordination	Moderate
Finger Dexterity	Low
Manual Dexterity	Low
Eye-Hand-Foot Coordination	Moderate
Color Discrimination	Low

Data = Mod   People = Mod   Things = Mod

Salary Range:
$12,000–$24,500

Opportunity Outlook:
25–34% growth

Environmental Conditions:
Inside

Physical Demands:
Moderate—lifting of no more than 50 pounds required
Reaching, handling, fingering, or feeling required
Talking or hearing required
Seeing required

Temperaments:
Influencing the actions and beliefs of others
Making decisions based upon senses and feelings
Dealing with people beyond giving and receiving information

Vocational Preparation:
1–3 months

Salesperson (General Merchandise)

DOT = 279.357-054   GOE = 08.02.03

Sells various kinds of merchandise in a store or other commercial establishment; collects money from customers and makes change; may also stock inventory.

Aptitudes:
Intelligence	Moderate
Verbal	Moderate
Numerical	Moderate
Spatial	Low
Form Perception	Low
Clerical Perception	Moderate
Motor Coordination	Moderate
Finger Dexterity	Moderate
Manual Dexterity	Moderate
Eye-Hand-Foot Coordination	Low
Color Discrimination	Low

Data = Mod   People = Mod   Things = Low

Salary Range:
$11,300–$34,100

Opportunity Outlook:
25–34% growth

Environmental Conditions:
Inside

Physical Demands:
Light—lifting of no more than 20 pounds required
Reaching, handling, fingering, or feeling required
Talking or hearing required

Temperaments:
Influencing the actions and beliefs of others
Making decisions based upon senses and feelings
Dealing with people beyond giving and receiving information

Vocational Preparation:
3–6 months

Salesperson (Household Appliances)

DOT = 270.357-034   GOE = 08.02.02

Sells stoves, refrigerators, and other household appliances to customers in a retail store.

Aptitudes:
Intelligence	Moderate
Verbal	Moderate
Numerical	Moderate
Spatial	Low
Form Perception	Low
Clerical Perception	Moderate
Motor Coordination	Low
Finger Dexterity	Moderate
Manual Dexterity	Moderate
Eye-Hand-Foot Coordination	Low
Color Discrimination	Low

Data = Mod   People = Mod   Things = Low

Salary Range:
$11,300–$34,100

Opportunity Outlook:
25–34% growth

Environmental Conditions:
Inside

Physical Demands:
Light—lifting of no more than 20 pounds required
Reaching, handling, fingering, or feeling required
Talking or hearing required

Temperaments:
Influencing the actions and beliefs of others
Making decisions based upon senses and feelings
Dealing with people beyond giving and receiving information

Vocational Preparation:
3–6 months

Sanitation Superintendent

DOT = 188.167-098   GOE = 05.02.01

Plans and directs the activities of workers engaged in various sanitation activities, such as collection of garbage, treatment of sewage, recycling of reusable materials, incineration of garbage, or landfill operations.

Aptitudes:
Intelligence	Moderate
Verbal	Moderate
Numerical	Moderate
Spatial	Low
Form Perception	Moderate
Clerical Perception	Moderate
Motor Coordination	Low
Finger Dexterity	Low
Manual Dexterity	Low
Eye-Hand-Foot Coordination	Low
Color Discrimination	Low

Data = Mod   People = Mod   Things = Low

Salary Range:
$42,500 (average)

Opportunity Outlook:
25–34% growth

Environmental Conditions:
Inside

Physical Demands:
Light—lifting of no more than 20 pounds required
Reaching, handling, fingering, or feeling required
Talking or hearing required
Seeing required

Temperaments:
Directing, controlling, or planning the work of others
Making decisions based upon senses and feelings
Making decisions based upon facts
Dealing with people . . .
Performing a variety of tasks

Vocational Preparation: 2–4 years

School Attendance Officer

DOT = 168.367-010   GOE = 07.01.06

Investigates continued absences of pupils from public schools to determine if such absences are lawful and known to parents; reports findings to school officials for corrective action.

Aptitudes:
Intelligence	Moderate
Verbal	Moderate
Numerical	Low
Spatial	Low
Form Perception	Low
Clerical Perception	Moderate
Motor Coordination	Low
Finger Dexterity	Low
Manual Dexterity	Low
Eye-Hand-Foot Coordination	Low
Color Discrimination	Low

Data = Mod   People = Low   Things = Low

Salary Range:
$12,000 (average)

Opportunity Outlook:
25-34% growth

Environmental Conditions:
Inside and outside

Physical Demands:
Light—lifting of no more than 20 pounds required
Reaching, handling, fingering, or feeling required
Talking or hearing required

Temperaments:
Making decisions based upon senses and feelings

Vocational Preparation:
1/2-1 year

School Psychologist

DOT = 045.107-034   GOE = 10.01.02

Evaluates average, gifted, and special needs students in a school, and then plans and administers enrichment programs to help these students attain maximum achievement and adjustment to the educational process.

Aptitudes:
Intelligence	High
Verbal	High
Numerical	Moderate
Spatial	Low
Form Perception	Low
Clerical Perception	Moderate
Motor Coordination	Low
Finger Dexterity	Low
Manual Dexterity	Low
Eye-Hand-Foot Coordination	Low
Color Discrimination	Low

Data = High   People = High   Things = Low

Salary Range:
$25,700-$48,000

Opportunity Outlook:
25-34% growth

Environmental Conditions:
Inside

Physical Demands:
Sedentary—little or no lifting
Reaching, handling, fingering, or feeling required
Talking or hearing required
Seeing required

Temperaments:
Influencing the actions and beliefs of others
Making decisions based upon senses and feelings
Making decisions based upon facts
Dealing with people beyond giving and receiving information

Vocational Preparation: 4-10 years

School Social Worker

DOT = 195.107-038   GOE = 10.01.02

Counsels children who are experiencing social and emotional problems in school; works with students, parents, teachers, and others concerned to identify the problems affecting students, and to find and implement solutions to enable students to succeed in school.

Aptitudes:
Intelligence	High
Verbal	High
Numerical	Moderate
Spatial	Low
Form Perception	Low
Clerical Perception	Low
Motor Coordination	Low
Finger Dexterity	Low
Manual Dexterity	Low
Eye-Hand-Foot Coordination	Low
Color Discrimination	Low

Data = High   People = High   Things = Low

Salary Range:
$23,000–$36,000

Opportunity Outlook:
25–34% growth

Environmental Conditions:
Inside

Physical Demands:
Sedentary—little or no lifting
Reaching, handling, fingering, or feeling required
Talking or hearing required

Temperaments:
Directing, controlling, or planning the work of others
Influencing the actions and beliefs of others
Making decisions based upon senses and feelings
Dealing with people beyond giving and receiving information
Performing a variety of tasks

Vocational Preparation: 2–4 years

Screen Writer

DOT = 131.087-018   GOE = 01.01.02

Writes scripts for motion pictures or television; selects subject and theme for script based on personal interests or experiences, or on the requirements set out by the producer of the film or program.

Aptitudes:
Intelligence	High
Verbal	High
Numerical	Low
Spatial	Low
Form Perception	Low
Clerical Perception	Moderate
Motor Coordination	Low
Finger Dexterity	Low
Manual Dexterity	Low
Eye-Hand-Foot Coordination	Low
Color Discrimination	Low

Data = High   People = Low   Things = Low

Salary Range:
Varies

Opportunity Outlook:
Not available

Environmental Conditions:
Inside

Physical Demands:
Sedentary—little or no lifting
Reaching, handling, fingering, or feeling required

Temperaments:
Interpreting the feelings and ideas of others
Making decisions based upon senses and feelings
Making decisions based upon facts

Vocational Preparation:
2–4 years

Sculptor

DOT = 144.061-018   GOE = 01.02.02

Designs and constructs, using a variety of hand tools, three-dimensional works of art from such materials as stone, metal, concrete, plastic, or wood.

Aptitudes:
Intelligence	Moderate
Verbal	Moderate
Numerical	Moderate
Spatial	High
Form Perception	High
Clerical Perception	Low
Motor Coordination	High
Finger Dexterity	High
Manual Dexterity	High
Eye-Hand-Foot Coordination	Low
Color Discrimination	Moderate

Data = Mod   People = Low   Things = High

Salary Range:
Varies

Opportunity Outlook:
Not available

Environmental Conditions:
Inside

Physical Demands:
Moderate—lifting of no more than 50 pounds required
Reaching, handling, fingering, or feeling required
Seeing required

Temperaments:
Interpreting the feelings and ideas of others
Making decisions based upon senses and feelings
Attempting to attain set limits

Vocational Preparation:
4–10 years

Secretary

DOT = 201.362-030   GOE = 07.01.03

Schedules appointments, gives information to callers, takes dictation, and handles the overall clerical responsibilities in an office setting.

Aptitudes:
Intelligence	Moderate
Verbal	Moderate
Numerical	Moderate
Spatial	Low
Form Perception	High
Clerical Perception	High
Motor Coordination	High
Finger Dexterity	High
Manual Dexterity	Moderate
Eye-Hand-Foot Coordination	Low
Color Discrimination	Moderate

Data = Mod   People = Mod   Things = High

Salary Range:
$20,000–$35,000

Opportunity Outlook:
14–24% growth

Environmental Conditions:
Inside

Physical Demands:
Sedentary—little or no lifting
Reaching, handling, fingering, or feeling required
Talking or hearing required
Seeing required

Temperaments:
Making decisions based upon senses and feelings
Dealing with people beyond giving and receiving information
Attempting to attain set limits
Performing a variety of tasks

Vocational Preparation: 1–2 years

Securities Sales Agent

DOT = 251.157-010 GOE = 11.06.04

Buys and sells stocks and bonds for individuals and organizations as a representative of a stock brokerage firm.

Aptitudes:

Intelligence	High
Verbal	High
Numerical	High
Spatial	Low
Form Perception	Moderate
Clerical Perception	Moderate
Motor Coordination	Low
Finger Dexterity	Low
Manual Dexterity	Low
Eye-Hand-Foot Coordination	Low
Color Discrimination	Low

Data = High   People = Mod   Things = Low

Salary Range:
$19,200–$166,000+

Opportunity Outlook:
35% growth or more

Environmental Conditions:
Inside

Physical Demands:
Sedentary—little or no lifting
Reaching, handling, fingering, or feeling required
Seeing required
Talking or hearing required

Temperaments:
Making decisions based upon senses and feelings
Influencing the actions and beliefs of others
Making decisions based upon facts
Dealing with people beyond giving and receiving information

Vocational Preparation: 2–4 years

Security Guard

DOT = 372.667-034 GOE = 04.02.02

Guards industrial or commercial property against fire, theft, vandalism, and illegal entry; patrols property to observe conditions and situations; may arrest intruders or call for assistance from police and fire departments.

Aptitudes:

Intelligence	Moderate
Verbal	Low
Numerical	Moderate
Spatial	Low
Form Perception	Low
Clerical Perception	Low
Motor Coordination	Low
Finger Dexterity	Low
Manual Dexterity	Low
Eye-Hand-Foot Coordination	Low
Color Discrimination	Low

Data = Low   People = Low   Things = Low

Salary Range:
$8,800–$25,000

Opportunity Outlook:
25–34% growth

Environmental Conditions:
Inside and outside
Presence of physical hazards

Physical Demands:
Moderate—lifting of no more than 50 pounds required
Reaching, handling, fingering, or feeling required
Seeing required

Temperaments:
Performing repetitive tasks
Performing under stressful conditions

Vocational Preparation:
1–3 months

Sewing Machine Operator

DOT = 787.682-046   GOE = 06.02.05

Operates a sewing machine to stitch, join, gather, hem, reinforce, or decorate articles of clothing and other apparel.

Aptitudes:
Intelligence	Low
Verbal	Low
Numerical	Low
Spatial	Moderate
Form Perception	Moderate
Clerical Perception	Low
Motor Coordination	Moderate
Finger Dexterity	Moderate
Manual Dexterity	Moderate
Eye-Hand-Foot Coordination	Low
Color Discrimination	Low

Data = Low   People = Low   Things = High

Salary Range:
$10,100–$23,500

Opportunity Outlook:
5% decline or more

Environmental Conditions:
Inside

Physical Demands:
Light—lifting of no more than 20 pounds required
Reaching, handling, fingering, or feeling required
Seeing required

Temperaments:
Performing repetitive tasks
Attempting to attain set limits

Vocational Preparation:
1/2–1 year

Ship Pilot

DOT = 197.133-026   GOE = 05.04.02

Commands workers on a ship to steer the ship in a certain direction and at a certain speed in order to safely navigate the ship into and out of harbors, estuaries, straits, and sounds, and on rivers, lakes, and bays.

Aptitudes:
Intelligence	High
Verbal	High
Numerical	High
Spatial	High
Form Perception	Low
Clerical Perception	Moderate
Motor Coordination	Moderate
Finger Dexterity	Low
Manual Dexterity	Moderate
Eye-Hand-Foot Coordination	Moderate
Color Discrimination	Low

Data = High   People = Mod   Things = Mod

Salary Range:
$17,400–$64,700

Opportunity Outlook:
5% decline or more

Environmental Conditions:
Inside and outside
Wet and humid work environment

Physical Demands:
Light—lifting of no more than 20 pounds required
Climbing or balancing required
Reaching, handling, fingering, or feeling required
Talking or hearing required
Seeing required

Temperaments:
Directing, controlling, or planning the work of others
Making decisions based upon senses and feelings
Making decisions based upon facts
Dealing with people . . .
Performing under stressful conditions

Vocational Preparation: 4–10 years

Shipping & Receiving Clerk

DOT = 222.387-050   GOE = 05.09.01

Verifies and keeps records of incoming and outgoing shipments and prepares items for shipment at a factory, office, store, or similar establishment.

Aptitudes:
Intelligence	Moderate
Verbal	Moderate
Numerical	Moderate
Spatial	Moderate
Form Perception	Moderate
Clerical Perception	Moderate
Motor Coordination	Low
Finger Dexterity	Low
Manual Dexterity	Moderate
Eye-Hand-Foot Coordination	Low
Color Discrimination	Low

Data = Mod   People = Low   Things = Low

Salary Range:
$16,000–$19,000

Opportunity Outlook:
5–13% growth

Environmental Conditions:
Inside

Physical Demands:
Moderate—lifting of no more than 50 pounds required
Reaching, handling, fingering, or feeling required
Seeing required

Temperaments:
Making decisions based upon facts
Attempting to attain set limits
Performing a variety of tasks

Vocational Preparation:
1/2–1 year

Sightseeing Guide

DOT = 353.363-010   GOE = 09.01.02

Guides individuals on a sightseeing tour of a plant, factory, historical site, art gallery, museum, place of entertainment, or natural site; explains points of interests and responds to questions from sightseers.

Aptitudes:
Intelligence	Moderate
Verbal	Moderate
Numerical	Low
Spatial	Moderate
Form Perception	Low
Clerical Perception	Low
Motor Coordination	Moderate
Finger Dexterity	Low
Manual Dexterity	Moderate
Eye-Hand-Foot Coordination	Moderate
Color Discrimination	Low

Data = Low   People = Mod   Things = Low

Salary Range:
Varies

Opportunity Outlook:
Not available

Environmental Conditions:
Inside and outside

Physical Demands:
Light—lifting of no more than 20 pounds required
Reaching, handling, fingering, or feeling required
Talking or hearing required
Seeing required

Temperaments:
Performing a variety of tasks

Vocational Preparation:
3–6 months

Sign Painter

DOT = 970.381-026   GOE = 01.06.03

Designs, lays out, and paints letters and designs to create signs for business and organizational customers; uses measuring and drawing instruments, brushes, and hand tools to create signs.

Aptitudes:
- Intelligence — Moderate
- Verbal — Moderate
- Numerical — Moderate
- Spatial — Moderate
- Form Perception — High
- Clerical Perception — Low
- Motor Coordination — Moderate
- Finger Dexterity — High
- Manual Dexterity — High
- Eye-Hand-Foot Coordination — Moderate
- Color Discrimination — High

Data = Low   People = Low   Things = High

Salary Range:
$20,000–$31,200

Opportunity Outlook:
25–34% growth

Environmental Conditions:
Inside and outside
Presence of physical hazards

Physical Demands:
Light—lifting of no more than 20 pounds required
Climbing or balancing required
Reaching, handling, fingering, or feeling required
Seeing required

Temperaments:
Making decisions based upon senses and feelings
Making decisions based upon facts
Attempting to attain set limits

Vocational Preparation:
1–2 years

Silversmith

DOT = 700.281-022   GOE = 01.06.02

Makes and repairs items from silver, such as coffee and tea pots, trays, flatware, jewelry, candle holders, and similar items.

Aptitudes:
- Intelligence — Moderate
- Verbal — Low
- Numerical — Low
- Spatial — High
- Form Perception — High
- Clerical Perception — Low
- Motor Coordination — Moderate
- Finger Dexterity — High
- Manual Dexterity — High
- Eye-Hand-Foot Coordination — Low
- Color Discrimination — Low

Data = Mod   People = Low   Things = High

Salary Range:
$20,000–$40,000

Opportunity Outlook:
14–24% growth

Environmental Conditions:
Inside

Physical Demands:
Light—lifting of no more than 20 pounds required
Reaching, handling, fingering, or feeling required
Seeing required

Temperaments:
Making decisions based upon senses and feelings
Attempting to attain set limits
Performing a variety of tasks

Vocational Preparation:
2–4 years

Singer

DOT = 152.047-022   GOE = 01.04.03

Sings songs, ballads, and other musical selections as a soloist or member of a vocal group to entertain an audience; may write songs or sing those written by other individuals.

Aptitudes:

Intelligence	Moderate
Verbal	Moderate
Numerical	Moderate
Spatial	Low
Form Perception	Low
Clerical Perception	Moderate
Motor Coordination	Low
Finger Dexterity	Low
Manual Dexterity	Low
Eye-Hand-Foot Coordination	Low
Color Discrimination	Low

Data = Mod   People = Mod   Things = Low

Salary Range:
Varies

Opportunity Outlook:
Not available

Environmental Conditions:
Inside

Physical Demands:
Light—lifting of no more than 20 pounds required
Talking or hearing required

Temperaments:
Interpreting the feelings and ideas of others
Making decisions based upon senses and feelings
Dealing with people beyond giving and receiving information

Vocational Preparation:
4–10 years

Skip Tracer

DOT = 241.367-026   GOE = 07.04.01

Attempts to locate individuals who have changed residence without notifying creditors to evade payment of bills.

Aptitudes:

Intelligence	Moderate
Verbal	Moderate
Numerical	Low
Spatial	Low
Form Perception	Low
Clerical Perception	Moderate
Motor Coordination	Low
Finger Dexterity	Low
Manual Dexterity	Low
Eye-Hand-Foot Coordination	Low
Color Discrimination	Low

Data = Mod   People = Low   Things = Low

Salary Range:
Varies

Opportunity Outlook:
Not available

Environmental Conditions:
Inside

Physical Demands:
Sedentary—little or no lifting
Talking or hearing required

Temperaments:
Making decisions based upon facts
Making decisions based upon senses and feelings

Vocational Preparation:
3–6 months

Social Director

DOT = 352.167-010   GOE = 09.01.01

Plans and organizes recreational activities and creates a friendly atmosphere for guests at a hotel or resort facility or for passengers on board a cruise ship.

Aptitudes:
Intelligence	Moderate
Verbal	Moderate
Numerical	Moderate
Spatial	Low
Form Perception	Low
Clerical Perception	Moderate
Motor Coordination	Low
Finger Dexterity	Low
Manual Dexterity	Low
Eye-Hand-Foot Coordination	Low
Color Discrimination	Low

Data = Mod   People = Mod   Things = Low

Salary Range:
$20,000–$40,000+

Opportunity Outlook:
14–24% growth

Environmental Conditions:
Inside and outside

Physical Demands:
Light—lifting of no more than 20 pounds required
Talking or hearing required

Temperaments:
Directing, controlling, or planning the work of others
Making decisions based upon senses and feelings
Dealing with people beyond giving and receiving information
Performing a variety of tasks

Vocational Preparation:
1–2 years

Social Service Caseworker

DOT = 195.107-010   GOE = 10.01.02

Counsels and aids individuals and families who request assistance from a social service agency; may counsel individuals and families about social and personal problems, financial matters, employment, health care, nutrition, birth control, and other matters related to their overall well-being.

Aptitudes:
Intelligence	High
Verbal	High
Numerical	Moderate
Spatial	Low
Form Perception	Low
Clerical Perception	Moderate
Motor Coordination	Low
Finger Dexterity	Low
Manual Dexterity	Low
Eye-Hand-Foot Coordination	Low
Color Discrimination	Low

Data = High   People = High   Things = Low

Salary Range:
$23,000–$36,000

Opportunity Outlook:
14–24% growth

Environmental Conditions:
Inside

Physical Demands:
Sedentary—little or no lifting
Talking or hearing required

Temperaments:
Directing, controlling, or planning the work of others
Influencing the actions and beliefs of others
Making decisions based upon senses and feelings
Dealing with people beyond giving and receiving information
Performing a variety of tasks

Vocational Preparation:
2–4 years

Sociologist

DOT = 054.067-014   GOE = 11.03.02

Conducts research into the development, structure, and behavior of groups of people and patterns of culture and social organization that have arisen out of group life.

Aptitudes:

Intelligence	High
Verbal	High
Numerical	Moderate
Spatial	Low
Form Perception	Low
Clerical Perception	Moderate
Motor Coordination	Low
Finger Dexterity	Low
Manual Dexterity	Low
Eye-Hand-Foot Coordination	Low
Color Discrimination	Low

Data = High   People = Mod   Things = Low

Salary Range:
$17,000–$49,600

Opportunity Outlook:
14–24% growth

Environmental Conditions:
Inside

Physical Demands:
Sedentary—little or no lifting
Talking or hearing required

Temperaments:
Directing, controlling, or planning the work of others
Making decisions based upon senses and feelings
Making decisions based upon facts

Vocational Preparation:
2–4 years

Solar-Energy Systems Designer

DOT = 007.161-038   GOE = 05.03.07

Designs solar domestic hot-water and space heating systems for new and existing structures, such as homes, office buildings, and factories.

Aptitudes:

Intelligence	High
Verbal	High
Numerical	High
Spatial	High
Form Perception	High
Clerical Perception	High
Motor Coordination	Moderate
Finger Dexterity	Moderate
Manual Dexterity	Low
Eye-Hand-Foot Coordination	Low
Color Discrimination	Moderate

Data = High   People = Low   Things = High

Salary Range:
$36,000–$46,500

Opportunity Outlook:
25–34% growth

Environmental Conditions:
Inside

Physical Demands:
Light—lifting of no more than 20 pounds required
Talking or hearing required
Seeing required

Temperaments:
Making decisions based upon senses and feelings
Attempting to attain set limits
Performing a variety of tasks

Vocational Preparation:
2–4 years

Solid-Waste Disposal Manager

DOT = 184.167-078   GOE = 05.02.06

Directs and coordinates, through subordinate personnel, the landfill site activities necessary to provide solid-waste disposal services for government agencies and private corporations.

Aptitudes:
Intelligence	Moderate
Verbal	Moderate
Numerical	Moderate
Spatial	Moderate
Form Perception	Moderate
Clerical Perception	Moderate
Motor Coordination	Low
Finger Dexterity	Low
Manual Dexterity	Low
Eye-Hand-Foot Coordination	Low
Color Discrimination	Low

Data = High   People = Mod   Things = Low

Salary Range:
$21,700 (average)

Opportunity Outlook:
5–13% growth

Environmental Conditions:
Inside and outside

Physical Demands:
Light—lifting of no more than 20 pounds required
Talking or hearing required
Seeing required

Temperaments:
Directing, controlling, or planning the work of others
Making decisions based upon senses and feelings
Dealing with people beyond giving and receiving information

Vocational Preparation:
2–4 years

Special Effects Specialist

DOT = 962.281-018   GOE = 01.06.02

Makes, installs, and activates equipment to produce special effects, such as rain, snow, explosions, fire, and other mechanical and electrical effects as required by the script for a television, motion picture, or theatrical production.

Aptitudes:
Intelligence	Moderate
Verbal	Moderate
Numerical	Moderate
Spatial	Moderate
Form Perception	Moderate
Clerical Perception	Low
Motor Coordination	Moderate
Finger Dexterity	Moderate
Manual Dexterity	Moderate
Eye-Hand-Foot Coordination	Moderate
Color Discrimination	Moderate

Data = High   People = Low   Things = High

Salary Range:
Varies

Opportunity Outlook:
25–34% growth

Environmental Conditions:
Inside and outside
Presence of physical hazards
Presence of atmospheric dangers

Physical Demands:
Moderate—lifting of no more than 50 pounds
Climbing or balancing required
Stooping, kneeling, crouching, or crawling required
Reaching, handling, fingering, or feeling required
Seeing required

Temperaments:
Making decisions based upon facts
Attempting to attain set limits
Performing a variety of tasks

Vocational Preparation: 1–2 years

Speech Pathologist

DOT = 076.107-010   GOE = 02.03.04

Specializes in the diagnosis and treatment of speech and language problems; examines patients who suffer from speech problems, determines cause, and prescribes a treatment program to correct the problem.

Aptitudes:
Intelligence	High
Verbal	High
Numerical	Moderate
Spatial	Moderate
Form Perception	High
Clerical Perception	Moderate
Motor Coordination	Moderate
Finger Dexterity	Moderate
Manual Dexterity	Moderate
Eye-Hand-Foot Coordination	Low
Color Discrimination	Low

Data = High   People = High   Things = Low

Salary Range:
$25,000–$38,000

Opportunity Outlook:
25–34% growth

Environmental Conditions:
Inside

Physical Demands:
Light—lifting of no more than 20 pounds required
Reaching, handling, fingering, or feeling required
Talking or hearing required
Seeing required

Temperaments:
Making decisions based upon senses and feelings
Dealing with people beyond giving and receiving information

Vocational Preparation:
4–10 years

Spinning Lathe Operator

DOT = 619.685-082   GOE = 06.04.02

Operates a lathe machine that spins (forms) shaped objects from sheets or plates of metal; controls speed and intensity of machine to create the desired object.

Aptitudes:
Intelligence	Low
Verbal	Low
Numerical	Low
Spatial	Low
Form Perception	Moderate
Clerical Perception	Low
Motor Coordination	Moderate
Finger Dexterity	Moderate
Manual Dexterity	Moderate
Eye-Hand-Foot Coordination	Low
Color Discrimination	Low

Data = Low   People = Low   Things = Mod

Salary Range:
$15,500–$18,700

Opportunity Outlook:
5–13% growth

Environmental Conditions:
Inside
Presence of loud noises and vibrations

Physical Demands:
Light—lifting of no more than 20 pounds required
Reaching, handling, fingering, or feeling required
Seeing required

Temperaments:
Performing repetitive tasks

Vocational Preparation:
1–30 days

Sports Instructor

DOT = 153.227-018   GOE = 12.01.01

Teaches various athletic games and feats to individuals and groups at a private or public recreational facility or school.

Aptitudes:
Intelligence	High
Verbal	High
Numerical	Moderate
Spatial	Low
Form Perception	Moderate
Clerical Perception	Moderate
Motor Coordination	High
Finger Dexterity	High
Manual Dexterity	High
Eye-Hand-Foot Coordination	High
Color Discrimination	Low

Data = High   People = Mod   Things = Low

Salary Range:
$10,000–$100,000+

Opportunity Outlook:
25–34% growth

Environmental Conditions:
Inside and outside

Physical Demands:
Moderate—lifting of no more than 50 pounds
Climbing or balancing required
Stooping, kneeling, crouching, or crawling
Talking or hearing required
Seeing required

Temperaments:
Directing, controlling, or planning the work of others
Making decisions based upon senses and feelings
Making decisions based upon facts
Dealing with people . . .

Vocational Preparation: 4–10 years

Stage Director

DOT = 150.067-010   GOE = 01.03.01

Based upon the contents of a theatrical script, directs technicians to create stage displays that resemble the scenes as depicted in the script or as requested by the director, rehearses actors, approves costumes, and manages sound systems and special effects, along with other theatrical responsibilities.

Aptitudes:
Intelligence	High
Verbal	High
Numerical	Low
Spatial	High
Form Perception	Moderate
Clerical Perception	Moderate
Motor Coordination	Low
Finger Dexterity	Low
Manual Dexterity	Low
Eye-Hand-Foot Coordination	Low
Color Discrimination	Moderate

Data = High   People = Mod   Things = Low

Salary Range:
Varies

Opportunity Outlook:
5–13% growth

Environmental Conditions:
Inside

Physical Demands:
Light—lifting of no more than 20 pounds required
Talking or hearing required
Seeing required

Temperaments:
Directing, controlling, or planning the work of others
Interpreting the feelings and ideas of others
Making decisions based upon senses and feelings
Dealing with people beyond giving and receiving information
Performing a variety of tasks

Vocational Preparation: 4–10 years

Stationary Engineer

DOT = 950.382-026   GOE = 05.06.02

Operates and maintains stationary engines and mechanical equipment, such as steam engines, air compressors, and generators, to produce light, heat, and power for buildings, offices, and industrial facilities.

Aptitudes:
Intelligence	Moderate
Verbal	Moderate
Numerical	Moderate
Spatial	Moderate
Form Perception	Low
Clerical Perception	Moderate
Motor Coordination	Moderate
Finger Dexterity	Moderate
Manual Dexterity	Moderate
Eye-Hand-Foot Coordination	Low
Color Discrimination	Low

Data = Mod   People = Low   Things = High

Salary Range:
$16,400–$48,700

Opportunity Outlook:
0–4% growth or decline

Environmental Conditions:
Inside
Wet, hot, and humid work environment
Presence of loud noises and vibrations
Presence of physical hazards

Physical Demands:
Moderate—lifting of no more than 50 pounds
Climbing or balancing required
Reaching, handling, fingering, or feeling required
Seeing required

Temperaments:
Making decisions based upon facts
Attempting to attain set limits
Performing a variety of tasks

Vocational Preparation: 2–4 years

Statistician

DOT = 020.167-026   GOE = 11.01.02

Plans for and executes the collection of data from experiments, studies, surveys, and other sources, and then analyzes and interprets data; applies various methodologies to interpret data in order to provide scientists, researchers, and business professionals with useful statistical information.

Aptitudes:
Intelligence	High
Verbal	High
Numerical	High
Spatial	Moderate
Form Perception	High
Clerical Perception	High
Motor Coordination	Low
Finger Dexterity	Low
Manual Dexterity	Low
Eye-Hand-Foot Coordination	Low
Color Discrimination	Low

Data = High   People = Low   Things = Low

Salary Range:
$38,600–$54,700

Opportunity Outlook:
5–13% growth

Environmental Conditions:
Inside

Physical Demands:
Sedentary—little or no lifting
Reaching, handling, fingering, or feeling required
Talking or hearing required

Temperaments:
Making decisions based upon senses and feelings
Making decisions based upon facts

Vocational Preparation:
2–4 years

Steam-Cleaning Machine Operator

DOT = 891.685-010   GOE = 05.11.01

Operates and controls portable generators to produce steam for use in steam cleaning exposed building surfaces and structures.

Aptitudes:
Intelligence	Low
Verbal	Low
Numerical	Low
Spatial	Low
Form Perception	Low
Clerical Perception	Low
Motor Coordination	Moderate
Finger Dexterity	Low
Manual Dexterity	Moderate
Eye-Hand-Foot Coordination	Low
Color Discrimination	Low

Data = Low   People = Low   Things = Low

Salary Range:
$12,300 (average)

Opportunity Outlook:
14–24% growth

Environmental Conditions:
Inside and outside

Physical Demands:
Moderate—lifting of no more than 50 pounds required
Reaching, handling, fingering, or feeling required

Temperaments:
Performing repetitive tasks

Vocational Preparation:
3–6 months

Stock Clerk

DOT = 222.387-058   GOE = 05.09.02

Receives, stores, and issues equipment, material, supplies, merchandise, foodstuffs, or tools, and compiles stock records in a stockroom, warehouse, or storage yard.

Aptitudes:
Intelligence	Moderate
Verbal	Moderate
Numerical	Moderate
Spatial	Moderate
Form Perception	Moderate
Clerical Perception	High
Motor Coordination	Low
Finger Dexterity	Low
Manual Dexterity	Moderate
Eye-Hand-Foot Coordination	Low
Color Discrimination	Low

Data = Low   People = Low   Things = Low

Salary Range:
$16,000–$19,000

Opportunity Outlook:
5–13% growth

Environmental Conditions:
Inside

Physical Demands:
Heavy—lifting of no more than 100 pounds required
Stooping, kneeling, crouching, or crawling required
Reaching, handling, fingering, or feeling required

Temperaments:
Making decisions based upon facts
Attempting to attain set limits

Vocational Preparation:
3–6 months

Storage Facility Rental Clerk

DOT = 295.367-026   GOE = 09.04.02

Leases storage space, such as cubicles, storage bins, or garage-like areas, to customers at a rental storage facility.

Aptitudes:
Intelligence	Moderate
Verbal	Moderate
Numerical	Moderate
Spatial	Low
Form Perception	Low
Clerical Perception	Moderate
Motor Coordination	Low
Finger Dexterity	Low
Manual Dexterity	Moderate
Eye-Hand-Foot Coordination	Low
Color Discrimination	Low

Data = Low   People = Low   Things = Low

Salary Range:
$8,000–$26,000

Opportunity Outlook:
25–34% growth

Environmental Conditions:
Inside and outside

Physical Demands:
Light—lifting of no more than 20 pounds required
Reaching, handling, fingering, or feeling required
Seeing required

Temperaments:
Performing a variety of tasks

Vocational Preparation:
1–30 days

Store Cashier Checker

DOT = 211.462-014   GOE = 07.03.01

Operates a cash register to itemize and total a customer's purchase in a store; may also wrap, bag, or box purchased items and may carry items to the customer's car.

Aptitudes:
Intelligence	Moderate
Verbal	Moderate
Numerical	Moderate
Spatial	Low
Form Perception	Moderate
Clerical Perception	Moderate
Motor Coordination	High
Finger Dexterity	High
Manual Dexterity	Moderate
Eye-Hand-Foot Coordination	Low
Color Discrimination	Low

Data = Low   People = Low   Things = Mod

Salary Range:
$7,400–$20,600

Opportunity Outlook:
25–34% growth

Environmental Conditions:
Inside

Physical Demands:
Light—lifting of no more than 20 pounds required
Reaching, handling, fingering, or feeling required
Talking, or hearing required
Seeing required

Temperaments:
Performing repetitive tasks
Attempting to attain set limits

Vocational Preparation:
1–3 months

Story Editor (Film/Radio/TV)

DOT = 132.037-026   GOE = 01.01.01

Selects previously written material, or instructs staff writers in developing written material, for use as the script for a television or radio program or movie film; adapts script to meet the story needs as determined by the director of the program or film.

Aptitudes:
Intelligence	High
Verbal	High
Numerical	Low
Spatial	Moderate
Form Perception	Low
Clerical Perception	Moderate
Motor Coordination	Low
Finger Dexterity	Low
Manual Dexterity	Low
Eye-Hand-Foot Coordination	Low
Color Discrimination	Low

Data = High   People = Mod   Things = Low

Salary Range:
Not available

Opportunity Outlook:
Not available

Environmental Conditions:
Inside

Physical Demands:
Sedentary—little or no lifting
Talking, or hearing required
Seeing required

Temperaments:
Directing, controlling, or planning the work of others
Interpreting the feelings and ideas of others
Making decisions based upon senses and feelings
Dealing with people beyond giving and receiving information

Vocational Preparation:
4–10 years

Streetcar Operator

DOT = 913.463-014   GOE = 09.03.01

Drives electric-powered streetcar to transport passengers from one location to another in a city; collects fares and gives information to passengers concerning arrival and departure schedule and location stops made by the streetcar.

Aptitudes:
Intelligence	Moderate
Verbal	Moderate
Numerical	Moderate
Spatial	Moderate
Form Perception	Low
Clerical Perception	Low
Motor Coordination	Moderate
Finger Dexterity	Low
Manual Dexterity	Moderate
Eye-Hand-Foot Coordination	Moderate
Color Discrimination	Low

Data = Low   People = Low   Things = Mod

Salary Range:
$23,500 (average)

Opportunity Outlook:
14–24% growth

Environmental Conditions:
Inside
Presence of loud noises and vibrations

Physical Demands:
Light—lifting of no more than 20 pounds required
Reaching, handling, fingering, or feeling required
Talking, or hearing required
Seeing required

Temperaments:
Making decisions based upon senses and feelings

Vocational Preparation:
1–3 months

Stunt Performer

DOT = 159.341-014   GOE = 12.02.01

Performs stunts, such as overturning a speeding automobile, falling from a building, or participating in a fight-action scene for a motion picture, television, or stage production.

Aptitudes:
Intelligence	Moderate
Verbal	Moderate
Numerical	Low
Spatial	High
Form Perception	Low
Clerical Perception	Low
Motor Coordination	High
Finger Dexterity	Moderate
Manual Dexterity	High
Eye-Hand-Foot Coordination	High
Color Discrimination	Low

Data = Mod   People = Low   Things = High

Salary Range:
Varies

Opportunity Outlook:
25–34% growth

Environmental Conditions:
Inside and outside
Presence of physical hazards

Physical Demands:
Moderate—lifting of no more than 50 pounds
Climbing, or balancing required
Stooping, kneeling, crouching, or crawling required
Reaching, handling, fingering, or feeling required
Talking, or hearing required
Seeing required

Temperaments:
Making decisions based upon senses and feelings
Performing under stressful conditions
Attempting to attain set limits

Vocational Preparation: 1–2 years

Surgical Dressing Maker

DOT = 689.685-130   GOE = 06.04.05

Operates a machine that automatically cuts and applies gauze backing to absorbent cotton to produce surgical dressings for use in hospitals, medical clinics, and similar facilities.

Aptitudes:
Intelligence	Low
Verbal	Low
Numerical	Low
Spatial	Low
Form Perception	Low
Clerical Perception	Low
Motor Coordination	Low
Finger Dexterity	Moderate
Manual Dexterity	Moderate
Eye-Hand-Foot Coordination	Low
Color Discrimination	Low

Data = Low   People = Low   Things = Mod

Salary Range:
$13,400 (average)

Opportunity Outlook:
14–24% growth

Environmental Conditions:
Inside

Physical Demands:
Light—lifting of no more than 20 pounds required
Reaching, handling, fingering, or feeling required
Seeing required

Temperaments:
Performing repetitive tasks
Attempting to attain set limits

Vocational Preparation:
1–30 days

Tax Attorney

DOT = 110.117-038   GOE = 11.04.02

Advises individuals, businesses, and organizations about income, estate, gift, excise, property, and other federal, state, local, and foreign taxes; may also help individuals prepare and submit appropriate tax records and forms.

Aptitudes:
Intelligence	High
Verbal	High
Numerical	High
Spatial	Low
Form Perception	Low
Clerical Perception	High
Motor Coordination	Low
Finger Dexterity	Low
Manual Dexterity	Low
Eye-Hand-Foot Coordination	Low
Color Discrimination	Low

Data = High   People = High   Things = Low

Salary Range:
$30,000–$100,000+

Opportunity Outlook:
25–34% growth

Environmental Conditions:
Inside

Physical Demands:
Sedentary—little or no lifting
Talking or hearing required
Seeing required

Temperaments:
Making decisions based upon facts
Performing a variety of tasks

Vocational Preparation:
4–10 years

Taxi Driver

DOT = 913.463-018   GOE = 09.03.02

Drives a taxicab to transport passengers and their belongings for a fee from one location to another.

Aptitudes:
Intelligence	Moderate
Verbal	Moderate
Numerical	Moderate
Spatial	Moderate
Form Perception	Low
Clerical Perception	Low
Motor Coordination	Moderate
Finger Dexterity	Low
Manual Dexterity	Moderate
Eye-Hand-Foot Coordination	Moderate
Color Discrimination	Low

Data = Low   People = Low   Things = Mod

Salary Range:
$18,400 (average)

Opportunity Outlook:
25–34% growth

Environmental Conditions:
Inside and outside

Physical Demands:
Moderate—lifting of no more than 50 pounds required
Reaching, handling, fingering, or feeling required
Seeing required

Temperaments:
Making decisions based upon senses and feelings
Making decisions based upon facts

Vocational Preparation:
1–3 months

Taxidermist

DOT = 199.261-010   GOE = 01.06.02

Prepares, stuffs, and mounts skins of birds or animals in a lifelike posture to preserve their appearance for display in a museum, private home, or similar facility.

Aptitudes:
Intelligence	Moderate
Verbal	Moderate
Numerical	Moderate
Spatial	High
Form Perception	High
Clerical Perception	Moderate
Motor Coordination	Moderate
Finger Dexterity	Moderate
Manual Dexterity	Moderate
Eye-Hand-Foot Coordination	Low
Color Discrimination	Moderate

Data = Mod   People = Low   Things = High

Salary Range:
$12,500–$30,000+

Opportunity Outlook:
Not available

Environmental Conditions:
Inside
Presence of atmospheric dangers

Physical Demands:
Moderate—lifting of no more than 50 pounds
Reaching, handling, fingering, or feeling
Seeing required

Temperaments:
Making decisions based upon senses and feelings
Making decisions based upon facts
Attempting to attain set limits
Performing a variety of tasks

Vocational Preparation:
2–4 years

Teacher (Adult Education)

DOT = 099.227-030   GOE = 11.02.01

Teaches out-of-school youths or adults in academic and nonacademic courses in public or private schools or other organizations; may teach courses to help students advance their academic ability and learning, prepare for or advance within a career field, or enjoy a personal interest.

Aptitudes:
Intelligence	High
Verbal	High
Numerical	Moderate
Spatial	Moderate
Form Perception	Moderate
Clerical Perception	High
Motor Coordination	Low
Finger Dexterity	Low
Manual Dexterity	Low
Eye-Hand-Foot Coordination	Low
Color Discrimination	Low

Data = High   People = High   Things = Low

Salary Range:
$12,000–$46,000+

Opportunity Outlook:
25–34% growth

Environmental Conditions:
Inside

Physical Demands:
Light—lifting of no more than 20 pounds required
Reaching, handling, fingering, or feeling required
Talking or hearing required

Temperaments:
Directing, controlling, or planning the work of others
Influencing the actions and beliefs of others
Making decisions based upon senses and feelings
Making decisions based upon facts

Vocational Preparation:
2–4 years

Teacher (Elementary)

DOT = 092.227-010   GOE = 11.02.01

Teaches elementary school students academic, social, and personal development courses; prepares lesson plans, develops and gathers teaching resources and materials, meets with students and parents for private conferences, and may also counsel students about personal and social matters.

Aptitudes:
Intelligence	High
Verbal	High
Numerical	Moderate
Spatial	Low
Form Perception	Moderate
Clerical Perception	High
Motor Coordination	Low
Finger Dexterity	Low
Manual Dexterity	Low
Eye-Hand-Foot Coordination	Low
Color Discrimination	Moderate

Data = High   People = High   Things = Low

Salary Range:
$12,300–$45,600

Opportunity Outlook:
25–34% growth

Environmental Conditions:
Inside

Physical Demands:
Light—lifting of no more than 20 pounds required
Talking or hearing required

Temperaments:
Making decisions based upon senses and feelings
Making decisions based upon facts
Dealing with people beyond giving and receiving information
Performing a variety of tasks

Vocational Preparation:
4–10 years

Teacher (Kindergarten)

DOT = 092.227-014   GOE = 10.02.03

Teaches children between the ages of four and six; helps children develop basic skills and competencies in such areas as numbers and the alphabet to prepare them for higher grades; also helps children develop physical, mental, and social skills.

Aptitudes:
Intelligence	High
Verbal	High
Numerical	Low
Spatial	Low
Form Perception	Moderate
Clerical Perception	Moderate
Motor Coordination	Moderate
Finger Dexterity	Low
Manual Dexterity	Moderate
Eye-Hand-Foot Coordination	Low
Color Discrimination	Moderate

Data = High   People = High   Things = Low

Salary Range:
$32,400 (average)

Opportunity Outlook:
14–24% growth

Environmental Conditions:
Inside

Physical Demands:
Light—lifting of no more than 20 pounds required
Talking or hearing required

Temperaments:
Directing, controlling, or planning the work of others
Dealing with people beyond giving and receiving information
Performing a variety of tasks

Vocational Preparation:
4–10 years

Teacher (Preschool)

DOT = 092.227-018 GOE = 10.02.03

Works with young children between the ages of three and five to develop various social, physical, and emotional skills necessary for success in elementary education.

Aptitudes:

Intelligence	High
Verbal	Moderate
Numerical	High
Spatial	Low
Form Perception	Low
Clerical Perception	Moderate
Motor Coordination	Moderate
Finger Dexterity	Low
Manual Dexterity	Moderate
Eye-Hand-Foot Coordination	Low
Color Discrimination	Moderate

Data = High   People = High   Things = Low

Salary Range:
$32,400 (average)

Opportunity Outlook:
14–24% growth

Environmental Conditions:
Inside

Physical Demands:
Light—lifting of no more than 20 pounds required
Stooping, kneeling, crouching, or crawling required
Reaching, handling, fingering, or feeling required
Talking or hearing required
Seeing required

Temperaments:
Directing, controlling, or planning the work of others
Making decisions based upon senses and feelings
Dealing with people beyond giving and receiving information
Performing a variety of tasks

Vocational Preparation: 2–4 years

Teacher (Secondary)

DOT = 091.227-010 GOE = 11.02.01

Teaches one or more subjects, such as English, math, science, history, or social studies, to students in a public or private high school.

Aptitudes:

Intelligence	High
Verbal	High
Numerical	High
Spatial	Low
Form Perception	Moderate
Clerical Perception	High
Motor Coordination	Low
Finger Dexterity	Low
Manual Dexterity	Low
Eye-Hand-Foot Coordination	Low
Color Discrimination	Moderate

Data = High   People = High   Things = Low

Salary Range:
$33,700 (average)

Opportunity Outlook:
25–34% growth

Environmental Conditions:
Inside

Physical Demands:
Light—lifting of no more than 20 pounds required
Talking or hearing required

Temperaments:
Directing, controlling, or planning the work of others
Influencing the actions and beliefs of others
Making decisions based upon senses and feelings
Dealing with people beyond giving and receiving information
Making decisions based upon facts

Vocational Preparation:
4–10 years

Teacher (Special Needs Students)

DOT = 094.227-018   GOE = 10.02.03

Teaches elementary and secondary students who have special needs, such as students who are physically or mentally challenged.

Aptitudes:
Intelligence	High
Verbal	High
Numerical	Moderate
Spatial	Low
Form Perception	Moderate
Clerical Perception	High
Motor Coordination	Moderate
Finger Dexterity	Low
Manual Dexterity	Low
Eye-Hand-Foot Coordination	Low
Color Discrimination	Low

Data = High   People = High   Things = Low

Salary Range:
$33,700 (average)

Opportunity Outlook:
25-34% growth

Environmental Conditions:
Inside

Physical Demands:
Light—lifting of no more than 20 pounds required
Reaching, handling, fingering, or feeling required
Talking or hearing required

Temperaments:
Directing, controlling, or planning the work of others
Influencing the actions and beliefs of others
Making decisions based upon senses and feelings
Dealing with people beyond giving and receiving information
Making decisions based upon facts

Vocational Preparation:
4-10 years

Technical Director (Radio/TV)

DOT = 962.162-010   GOE = 05.02.04

Coordinates and manages the activities of radio or television studio and control-room personnel to insure the quality of sound or pictures for all programs broadcast from the studio or from a remote site.

Aptitudes:
Intelligence	High
Verbal	High
Numerical	Moderate
Spatial	Moderate
Form Perception	High
Clerical Perception	Moderate
Motor Coordination	Moderate
Finger Dexterity	Moderate
Manual Dexterity	Low
Eye-Hand-Foot Coordination	Low
Color Discrimination	High

Data = High   People = Mod   Things = Mod

Salary Range:
$22,100-$31,200

Opportunity Outlook:
14-24% growth

Environmental Conditions:
Inside

Physical Demands:
Light—lifting of no more than 20 pounds required
Reaching, handling, fingering, or feeling required
Talking or hearing required
Seeing required

Temperaments:
Directing, controlling, or planning the work of others
Making decisions based upon senses and feelings
Attempting to attain set limits
Performing a variety of tasks

Vocational Preparation:
4-10 years

Technical Writer

DOT = 131.267-026   GOE = 11.08.02

Develops, writes, and edits materials that are technical (nonacademic) in nature, such as reports, manuals, briefs, proposals, instruction books, catalogs, guides, and related publications.

Aptitudes:
Intelligence	High
Verbal	High
Numerical	Moderate
Spatial	High
Form Perception	Moderate
Clerical Perception	Moderate
Motor Coordination	Low
Finger Dexterity	Low
Manual Dexterity	Low
Eye-Hand-Foot Coordination	Low
Color Discrimination	Low

Data = High   People = Low   Things = Low

Salary Range:
$24,000–$45,000

Opportunity Outlook:
25–34% growth

Environmental Conditions:
Inside

Physical Demands:
Sedentary—little or no lifting
Reaching, handling, fingering, or feeling required
Talking or hearing required
Seeing required

Temperaments:
Making decisions based upon senses and feelings
Making decisions based upon facts
Performing a variety of tasks

Vocational Preparation:
2–4 years

Telephone Communication Consultant

DOT = 253.157-010   GOE = 08.01.01

Contacts residential, commercial, and industrial telephone company customers who have indicated problems with their telephone service, determines cause of the problems, and then notifies the appropriate personnel to correct the problems.

Aptitudes:
Intelligence	High
Verbal	High
Numerical	Moderate
Spatial	High
Form Perception	High
Clerical Perception	Moderate
Motor Coordination	Low
Finger Dexterity	Low
Manual Dexterity	Low
Eye-Hand-Foot Coordination	Low
Color Discrimination	Low

Data = High   People = Mod   Things = Low

Salary Range:
Varies

Opportunity Outlook:
25–34% growth

Environmental Conditions:
Inside

Physical Demands:
Light—lifting of no more than 20 pounds required
Talking or hearing required
Seeing required

Temperaments:
Influencing the actions and beliefs of others
Making decisions based upon senses and feelings
Making decisions based upon facts
Dealing with people beyond giving and receiving information

Vocational Preparation:
1–2 years

Telephone Operator (Central Office)

DOT = 235.462-010   GOE = 07.04.06

Operates telephone switchboard to assist callers in making local and long-distance phone calls; assists callers in obtaining correct numbers and calling fees.

Aptitudes:
Intelligence	Moderate
Verbal	Moderate
Numerical	Low
Spatial	Low
Form Perception	Low
Clerical Perception	Moderate
Motor Coordination	Moderate
Finger Dexterity	Moderate
Manual Dexterity	Moderate
Eye-Hand-Foot Coordination	Low
Color Discrimination	Low

Data = Low   People = Low   Things = Mod

Salary Range:
$10,100–$26,800

Opportunity Outlook:
5% decline or more

Environmental Conditions:
Inside

Physical Demands:
Light—lifting of no more than 20 pounds required
Reaching, handling, fingering, or feeling required
Talking or hearing required

Temperaments:
Performing repetitive tasks

Vocational Preparation:
1–3 months

Test Pilot

DOT = 196.263-042   GOE = 05.04.01

Pilots new, prototype, experimental, modified, and production aircraft to determine if they are airworthy; puts aircraft through various maneuvers to test all aspects of flight capabilities; reports malfunctions and problems to appropriate engineering personnel.

Aptitudes:
Intelligence	High
Verbal	High
Numerical	High
Spatial	High
Form Perception	Moderate
Clerical Perception	Low
Motor Coordination	Moderate
Finger Dexterity	Low
Manual Dexterity	Moderate
Eye-Hand-Foot Coordination	High
Color Discrimination	Moderate

Data = High   People = Low   Things = High

Salary Range:
$80,000–$150,000+

Opportunity Outlook:
14–24% growth

Environmental Conditions:
Inside and outside
Presence of loud noises and vibrations
Presence of physical hazards

Physical Demands:
Light—lifting of no more than 20 pounds required
Reaching, handling, fingering, or feeling required
Talking or hearing required
Seeing required

Temperaments:
Making decisions based upon senses and feelings
Making decisions based upon facts
Performing under stressful conditions
Attempting to attain set limits

Vocational Preparation: 4–10 years

Theater Manager

DOT = 187.167-154   GOE = 11.11.02

Manages theater for stage productions or motion pictures; coordinates the activities of personnel to insure efficient operation of the theater; responsible for overall maintenance of theater, financial management, sale of tickets, hiring of personnel, and other related functions.

Aptitudes:
Intelligence	High
Verbal	High
Numerical	Moderate
Spatial	Low
Form Perception	Low
Clerical Perception	Moderate
Motor Coordination	Low
Finger Dexterity	Low
Manual Dexterity	Low
Eye-Hand-Foot Coordination	Low
Color Discrimination	Low

Data = High   People = Mod   Things = Low

Salary Range:
$24,000 (average)

Opportunity Outlook:
14–24% growth

Environmental Conditions:
Inside

Physical Demands:
Light—lifting of no more than 20 pounds required
Talking or hearing required

Temperaments:
Directing, controlling, or planning the work of others
Making decisions based upon senses and feelings
Dealing with people beyond giving and receiving information
Making decisions based upon facts

Vocational Preparation:
2–4 years

Threading Machine Operator

DOT = 604.685-038   GOE = 06.04.02

Operates a machine that cuts interior and exterior threads in artillery shells, so that fittings, such as fuse caps, can be attached.

Aptitudes:
Intelligence	Moderate
Verbal	Low
Numerical	Low
Spatial	Moderate
Form Perception	Moderate
Clerical Perception	Low
Motor Coordination	Moderate
Finger Dexterity	Moderate
Manual Dexterity	Moderate
Eye-Hand-Foot Coordination	Low
Color Discrimination	Low

Data = Low   People = Low   Things = Mod

Salary Range:
$16,600 (average)

Opportunity Outlook:
5% decline or more

Environmental Conditions:
Inside
Presence of loud noises and vibrations

Physical Demands:
Light—lifting of no more than 20 pounds required
Reaching, handling, fingering, or feeling required
Seeing required

Temperaments:
Performing repetitive tasks
Attempting to attain set limits

Vocational Preparation:
3–6 months

Ticket Agent

DOT = 238.367-026 GOE = 07.03.01

Sells tickets to customers who wish to travel by airplane, bus, train, streetcar, or by ship; also helps customers plan their route and determine cost of tickets; may check baggage for passengers.

Aptitudes:
Intelligence	Moderate
Verbal	Moderate
Numerical	Moderate
Spatial	Low
Form Perception	Low
Clerical Perception	Moderate
Motor Coordination	Low
Finger Dexterity	Low
Manual Dexterity	Low
Eye-Hand-Foot Coordination	Low
Color Discrimination	Low

Data = Low   People = Mod   Things = Low

Salary Range:
$20,300 (average)

Opportunity Outlook:
25–34% growth

Environmental Conditions:
Inside

Physical Demands:
Light—lifting of no more than 20 pounds required
Reaching, handling, fingering, or feeling required
Talking or hearing required

Temperaments:
Performing repetitive tasks

Vocational Preparation:
1/2–1 year

Title Examiner

DOT = 119.287-010 GOE = 07.01.05

Searches through public records and examines titles of various documents to determine legal owner and condition of specific real estate property.

Aptitudes:
Intelligence	High
Verbal	Moderate
Numerical	Moderate
Spatial	Low
Form Perception	Low
Clerical Perception	High
Motor Coordination	Low
Finger Dexterity	Low
Manual Dexterity	Low
Eye-Hand-Foot Coordination	Low
Color Discrimination	Low

Data = Mod   People = Low   Things = Low

Salary Range:
$21,000–$29,100

Opportunity Outlook:
5–13% growth

Environmental Conditions:
Inside

Physical Demands:
Sedentary—little or no lifting
Reaching, handling, fingering, or feeling required
Talking or hearing required
Seeing required

Temperaments:
Making decisions based upon senses and feelings
Making decisions based upon facts

Vocational Preparation:
2–4 years

Toll Collector

DOT = 211.462-038   GOE = 07.03.01

Collects money for toll charges from car and truck drivers traveling over a toll road, bridge, through a tunnel, or on a ferryboat.

Aptitudes:
Intelligence	Moderate
Verbal	Moderate
Numerical	Moderate
Spatial	Low
Form Perception	Low
Clerical Perception	Moderate
Motor Coordination	Moderate
Finger Dexterity	Moderate
Manual Dexterity	Low
Eye-Hand-Foot Coordination	Low
Color Discrimination	Low

Data = Low   People = Low   Things = Mod

Salary Range:
$12,900 (average)

Opportunity Outlook:
25-34% growth

Environmental Conditions:
Inside and outside

Physical Demands:
Light—lifting of no more than 20 pounds required
Reaching, handling, fingering, or feeling required
Talking or hearing required
Seeing required

Temperaments:
Performing repetitive tasks

Vocational Preparation:
1-30 days

Tool & Equipment Rental Clerk

DOT = 295.357-014   GOE = 09.04.02

Rents tools and equipment to customers in a rental store; records date of rental, equipment rented, charges, and name and address of customer; may also inspect equipment before and after rental and make minor repairs.

Aptitudes:
Intelligence	Moderate
Verbal	Moderate
Numerical	Moderate
Spatial	Low
Form Perception	Moderate
Clerical Perception	Moderate
Motor Coordination	Low
Finger Dexterity	Low
Manual Dexterity	Low
Eye-Hand-Foot Coordination	Low
Color Discrimination	Low

Data = Low   People = Low   Things = Low

Salary Range:
$7,800-$11,400

Opportunity Outlook:
25-34% growth

Environmental Conditions:
Inside

Physical Demands:
Moderate—lifting of no more than 50 pounds required
Reaching, handling, fingering, or feeling required
Seeing required
Talking or hearing required

Temperaments:
Influencing the actions and beliefs of others
Making decisions based upon senses and feelings

Vocational Preparation:
3-6 months

Town Clerk

DOT = 243.367-018   GOE = 07.01.02

Performs a variety of clerical and administrative duties necessary to carry out the municipal functions of a town or community.

Aptitudes:
Intelligence	High
Verbal	High
Numerical	High
Spatial	Low
Form Perception	High
Clerical Perception	High
Motor Coordination	Low
Finger Dexterity	Low
Manual Dexterity	Low
Eye-Hand-Foot Coordination	Low
Color Discrimination	Low

Data = Mod   People = Mod   Things = Mod

Salary Range:
$12,000–$20,000

Opportunity Outlook:
14–24% growth

Environmental Conditions:
Inside

Physical Demands:
Sedentary—little or no lifting
Talking or hearing required
Seeing required

Temperaments:
Making decisions based upon facts
Dealing with people beyond giving and receving information

Vocational Preparation:
1/2–1 year

Tractor-Trailer Truck Driver

DOT = 904.383-010   GOE = 05.08.01

Drives gasoline or diesel tractor-trailer trucks, usually over long distances, to transport and deliver freight, livestock, and other materials.

Aptitudes:
Intelligence	Moderate
Verbal	Low
Numerical	Low
Spatial	High
Form Perception	Moderate
Clerical Perception	Moderate
Motor Coordination	Moderate
Finger Dexterity	Low
Manual Dexterity	Moderate
Eye-Hand-Foot Coordination	Moderate
Color Discrimination	Low

Data = Low   People = Low   Things = Mod

Salary Range:
$27,000 (average)

Opportunity Outlook:
14–24% growth

Environmental Conditions:
Inside and outside
Presence of loud noises and vibrations

Physical Demands:
Moderate—lifting of no more than 50 pounds required
Stooping, kneeling, crouching, or crawling required
Reaching, handling, fingering, or feeling required
Seeing required

Temperaments:
Working alone or apart from others
Performing repetitive tasks

Vocational Preparation:
3–6 months

Translator

DOT = 137.267-018   GOE = 11.08.04

Translates documents and other materials from one language to another.

Aptitudes:
Intelligence	High
Verbal	High
Numerical	Moderate
Spatial	Moderate
Form Perception	Low
Clerical Perception	Moderate
Motor Coordination	Low
Finger Dexterity	Low
Manual Dexterity	Low
Eye-Hand-Foot Coordination	Low
Color Discrimination	Low

Data = High   People = Low   Things = Low

Salary Range:
$18,000 (average)

Opportunity Outlook:
25–34% growth

Environmental Conditions:
Inside

Physical Demands:
Sedentary—little or no lifting
Reaching, handling, fingering, or feeling required
Seeing required

Temperaments:
Making decisions based upon senses and feelings
Making decisions based upon facts
Attempting to attain set limits

Vocational Preparation:
2–4 years

Transmission Tester (Telephone)

DOT = 822.361-026   GOE = 05.07.03

At telephone headquarters, tests and operates equipment that controls telephone lines extending between communities.

Aptitudes:
Intelligence	Moderate
Verbal	Moderate
Numerical	Moderate
Spatial	Moderate
Form Perception	High
Clerical Perception	Low
Motor Coordination	Low
Finger Dexterity	Moderate
Manual Dexterity	Moderate
Eye-Hand-Foot Coordination	Low
Color Discrimination	Low

Data = Mod   People = Low   Things = High

Salary Range:
$23,500 (average)

Opportunity Outlook:
14–24% growth

Environmental Conditions:
Inside

Physical Demands:
Light—lifting of no more than 20 pounds required
Reaching, handling, fingering, or feeling required
Seeing required

Temperaments:
Making decisions based upon facts
Attempting to attain set limits

Vocational Preparation:
2–4 years

Travel Agent

DOT = 252.157-010   GOE = 08.02.06

Plans the itinerary and arranges for hotel accommodations and other services for travelers; schedules airline tickets, use of rental car, and reservations at hotels and motels; may also point out places of interest to travelers.

Aptitudes:
  Intelligence   Moderate
  Verbal   Moderate
  Numerical   Moderate
  Spatial   Low
  Form Perception   Low
  Clerical Perception   High
  Motor Coordination   Low
  Finger Dexterity   Low
  Manual Dexterity   Low
  Eye-Hand-Foot Coordination   Low
  Color Discrimination   Low

Data = Mod   People = Mod   Things = Low

Salary Range:
  $12,000–$21,700

Opportunity Outlook:
  35% growth or more

Environmental Conditions:
  Inside

Physical Demands:
  Sedentary—little or no lifting
  Talking or hearing required
  Seeing required

Temperaments:
  Influencing the actions and beliefs of others
  Making decisions based upon senses and feelings
  Dealing with people beyond giving and receiving information

Vocational Preparation:
  3–6 months

Tree Planter

DOT = 452.687-018   GOE = 03.04.02

Plants seedling trees to reforest timber lands or for Christmas tree farms.

Aptitudes:
  Intelligence   Low
  Verbal   Low
  Numerical   Low
  Spatial   Low
  Form Perception   Low
  Clerical Perception   Low
  Motor Coordination   Moderate
  Finger Dexterity   Low
  Manual Dexterity   Moderate
  Eye-Hand-Foot Coordination   Low
  Color Discrimination   Low

Data = Low   People = Low   Things = Low

Salary Range:
  Varies

Opportunity Outlook:
  Not available

Environmental Conditions:
  Outside
  Wet and humid work environment

Physical Demands:
  Heavy—lifting of no more than 100 pounds required
  Climbing, or balancing required
  Stooping, kneeling, crouching, or crawling required
  Reaching, handling, fingering, or feeling required
  Seeing required

Temperaments:
  Performing repetitive tasks

Vocational Preparation:
  1–3 hours

Tree Pruner

DOT = 408.684-018   GOE = 03.04.05

Cuts away dead and excess branches from fruit, nut, and shade trees, using chain or handsaws, pruning hooks and shears, and long-handled clippers.

Aptitudes:
Intelligence	Moderate
Verbal	Moderate
Numerical	Low
Spatial	Moderate
Form Perception	Low
Clerical Perception	Low
Motor Coordination	Moderate
Finger Dexterity	Low
Manual Dexterity	Moderate
Eye-Hand-Foot Coordination	Moderate
Color Discrimination	Low

Data = Low   People = Low   Things = Mod

Salary Range:
Varies

Opportunity Outlook:
Not available

Environmental Conditions:
Outside
Presence of physical hazards

Physical Demands:
Moderate—lifting of no more than 50 pounds required
Climbing, or balancing required
Stooping, kneeling, crouching, or crawling required
Reaching, handling, fingering, or feeling required
Seeing required

Temperaments:
Performing repetitive tasks

Vocational Preparation:
3-6 months

Tree Surgeon

DOT = 408.181-010   GOE = 03.01.03

Using knowledge of tree and shrub biology, prunes and treats ornamental and shade trees and shrubs in yards and parks to improve their appearance, health, and value.

Aptitudes:
Intelligence	Moderate
Verbal	Moderate
Numerical	Low
Spatial	Moderate
Form Perception	Moderate
Clerical Perception	Low
Motor Coordination	Moderate
Finger Dexterity	Low
Manual Dexterity	Moderate
Eye-Hand-Foot Coordination	Moderate
Color Discrimination	Moderate

Data = Mod   People = Low   Things = High

Salary Range:
$8,000-$29,700

Opportunity Outlook:
14-24% growth

Environmental Conditions:
Outside
Wet and humid work environment
Presence of physical hazards
Presence of atmospheric dangers

Physical Demands:
Moderate—lifting of no more than 50 pounds
Climbing, or balancing required
Stooping, kneeling, crouching, or crawling required
Reaching, handling, fingering, or feeling required
Seeing required

Temperaments:
Making decisions based upon senses and feelings
Performing a variety of tasks

Vocational Preparation:
1-2 years

Trimming Machine Operator

DOT = 732.685-038   GOE = 06.04.05

Operates machines that trim ragged edges from various kinds of manufactured fabrics and similar materials.

Aptitudes:

Intelligence	Low
Verbal	Low
Numerical	Low
Spatial	Low
Form Perception	Low
Clerical Perception	Low
Motor Coordination	Moderate
Finger Dexterity	Low
Manual Dexterity	Moderate
Eye-Hand-Foot Coordination	Low
Color Discrimination	Low

Data = Low   People = Low   Things = Mod

Salary Range:
$12,000 (average)

Opportunity Outlook:
5–13% growth

Environmental Conditions:
Inside

Physical Demands:
Light—lifting of no more than 20 pounds required
Reaching, handling, fingering, or feeling required
Seeing required

Temperaments:
Performing repetitive tasks

Vocational Preparation:
1–30 days

Truck Driver (Light Deliveries)

DOT = 906.683-022   GOE = 05.08.01

Drives light-weight trucks to deliver materials from one location to another.

Aptitudes:

Intelligence	Moderate
Verbal	Low
Numerical	Low
Spatial	Moderate
Form Perception	Low
Clerical Perception	Low
Motor Coordination	Moderate
Finger Dexterity	Low
Manual Dexterity	Moderate
Eye-Hand-Foot Coordination	Moderate
Color Discrimination	Low

Data = Low   People = Low   Things = Low

Salary Range:
$16,000 (average)

Opportunity Outlook:
14–24% growth

Environmental Conditions:
Inside and outside

Physical Demands:
Moderate—lifting of no more than 50 pounds required
Stooping, kneeling, crouching, or crawling required
Reaching, handling, fingering, or feeling required
Seeing required

Temperaments:
Performing repetitive tasks

Vocational Preparation:
1–3 months

Truck Safety Inspector

DOT = 919.687-018 GOE = 05.07.01

Inspects diesel and gasoline trucks to insure they are equipped with safety accessories as prescribed by federal, state, and local laws.

Aptitudes:
Intelligence	Moderate
Verbal	Low
Numerical	Low
Spatial	Moderate
Form Perception	Moderate
Clerical Perception	Moderate
Motor Coordination	Moderate
Finger Dexterity	Low
Manual Dexterity	Moderate
Eye-Hand-Foot Coordination	Low
Color Discrimination	Low

Data = Mod   People = Low   Things = Low

Salary Range:
$18,200 (average)

Opportunity Outlook:
25-34% growth

Environmental Conditions:
Inside and outside

Physical Demands:
Light—lifting of no more than 20 pounds required
Stooping, kneeling, crouching, or crawling required
Reaching, handling, fingering, or feeling required
Seeing required

Temperaments:
Making decisions based upon facts
Attempting to attain set limits

Vocational Preparation:
3-6 months

Typist

DOT = 203.582-066 GOE = 07.06.02

Types letters, reports, stencils, forms, addresses, labels, and other documents from rough drafts or corrected copy as written by other individuals.

Aptitudes:
Intelligence	Moderate
Verbal	Moderate
Numerical	Low
Spatial	Low
Form Perception	Low
Clerical Perception	High
Motor Coordination	High
Finger Dexterity	High
Manual Dexterity	Moderate
Eye-Hand-Foot Coordination	Low
Color Discrimination	Low

Data = Low   People = Low   Things = Mod

Salary Range:
$12,300-$16,700

Opportunity Outlook:
0-4% growth or decline

Environmental Conditions:
Inside

Physical Demands:
Sedentary—little or no lifting
Reaching, handling, fingering, or feeling required
Seeing required

Temperaments:
Performing repetitive tasks

Vocational Preparation:
1-3 months

Ultrasound Technologist

DOT = 078.364-010   GOE = 02.04.01

Operates ultrasound equipment to produce two-dimensional pictures of a patient's internal organs for use by doctors and other health-care personnel in the diagnosis and treatment of illness and disease.

Aptitudes:
Intelligence	Moderate
Verbal	Moderate
Numerical	Moderate
Spatial	High
Form Perception	High
Clerical Perception	Moderate
Motor Coordination	Moderate
Finger Dexterity	Moderate
Manual Dexterity	Moderate
Eye-Hand-Foot Coordination	Low
Color Discrimination	Moderate

Data = Mod   People = Mod   Things = Mod

Salary Range:
  $27,800–$37,600

Opportunity Outlook:
  35% growth or more

Environmental Conditions:
  Inside

Physical Demands:
  Light—lifting of no more than 20 pounds required
  Reaching, handling, fingering, or feeling required
  Talking or hearing required
  Seeing required

Temperaments:
  Making decisions based upon facts
  Dealing with people beyond giving and receiving information
  Attempting to attain set limits

Vocational Preparation:
  2–4 years

Umpire

DOT = 153.267-018   GOE = 12.01.02

Officiates at an amateur or professional sporting event to ensure participants play the game fairly and within the bounds of established rules and regulations.

Aptitudes:
Intelligence	Moderate
Verbal	Moderate
Numerical	Moderate
Spatial	High
Form Perception	Moderate
Clerical Perception	Low
Motor Coordination	Low
Finger Dexterity	Low
Manual Dexterity	Low
Eye-Hand-Foot Coordination	Low
Color Discrimination	Moderate

Data = Mod   People = Low   Things = Low

Salary Range:
  $14,400–$100,000+

Opportunity Outlook:
  14–24% growth

Environmental Conditions:
  Inside and outside

Physical Demands:
  Light—lifting of no more than 20 pounds required
  Talking or hearing required
  Seeing required

Temperaments:
  Directing, controlling, or planning the work of others
  Making decisions based upon senses and feelings
  Making decisions based upon facts
  Performing under stressful conditions

Vocational Preparation:
  2–4 years

Urban Planner

DOT = 199.167-014   GOE = 11.03.02

Develops a comprehensive plan and programs for the best utilization of the land and physical facilities found within a city, county, or metropolitan area.

Aptitudes:

Intelligence	High
Verbal	High
Numerical	High
Spatial	High
Form Perception	High
Clerical Perception	Moderate
Motor Coordination	Low
Finger Dexterity	Moderate
Manual Dexterity	Low
Eye-Hand-Foot Coordination	Low
Color Discrimination	Low

Data = High   People = Mod   Things = Low

Salary Range:
$17,000–$48,000

Opportunity Outlook:
14–24% growth

Environmental Conditions:
Inside

Physical Demands:
Sedentary—little or no lifting
Talking or hearing required

Temperaments:
Making decisions based upon senses and feelings
Making decisions based upon facts
Dealing with people beyond giving and receiving information
Performing a variety of tasks

Vocational Preparation:
4–10 years

U.S. Special Agent

DOT = 375.167-042   GOE = 04.01.02

Investigates alleged or suspected criminal violations of federal laws to determine if evidence is sufficient to recommend arrest of suspected violators and prosecution in a court of law.

Aptitudes:

Intelligence	High
Verbal	High
Numerical	Moderate
Spatial	High
Form Perception	Moderate
Clerical Perception	Moderate
Motor Coordination	Moderate
Finger Dexterity	Low
Manual Dexterity	Moderate
Eye-Hand-Foot Coordination	Moderate
Color Discrimination	Low

Data = High   People = Mod   Things = Low

Salary Range:
$25,000–$58,500

Opportunity Outlook:
14–24% growth

Environmental Conditions:
Inside and outside
Presence of physical hazards

Physical Demands:
Moderate—lifting of no more than 50 pounds
Climbing, or balancing required
Stooping, kneeling, crouching, or crawling required
Talking or hearing required
Seeing required

Temperaments:
Making decisions based upon senses and feelings
Making decisions based upon facts
Dealing with people . . .
Performing under stressful conditions
Performing a variety of tasks

Vocational Preparation: 4–10 years

Vendor (Amusement/Sports Park)

DOT = 291.457-022   GOE = 08.03.01

Sells refreshments, programs, novelties, or similar merchandise at sports events, parades, parks, and other locations.

Aptitudes:
Intelligence	Low
Verbal	Low
Numerical	Low
Spatial	Low
Form Perception	Low
Clerical Perception	Moderate
Motor Coordination	Low
Finger Dexterity	Low
Manual Dexterity	Low
Eye-Hand-Foot Coordination	Low
Color Discrimination	Low

Data = Low   People = Low   Things = Low

Salary Range:
Varies

Opportunity Outlook:
25-34% growth

Environmental Conditions:
Inside and outside

Physical Demands:
Light—lifting of no more than 20 pounds required
Reaching, handling, fingering, or feeling required
Talking or hearing required
Seeing required

Temperaments:
Performing a variety of tasks

Vocational Preparation:
1-30 days

Veterinarian

DOT = 073.101-010   GOE = 02.03.03

Diagnoses and treats animals who are injured, ill, in labor, or who suffer from disease; may specialize in the care of certain animals, such as horses, domestic dogs and cats, or exotic animals.

Aptitudes:
Intelligence	High
Verbal	High
Numerical	Moderate
Spatial	High
Form Perception	High
Clerical Perception	Moderate
Motor Coordination	High
Finger Dexterity	Moderate
Manual Dexterity	High
Eye-Hand-Foot Coordination	Low
Color Discrimination	Moderate

Data = High   People = Mod   Things = High

Salary Range:
$27,000-$100,000

Opportunity Outlook:
25-34% growth

Environmental Conditions:
Inside and outside

Physical Demands:
Heavy—lifting of no more than 100 pounds required
Reaching, handling, fingering, or feeling required
Seeing required

Temperaments:
Making decisions based upon facts
Dealing with people beyond giving and receiving information
Attempting to attain set limits
Performing a variety of tasks

Vocational Preparation:
4-10 years

Vocational Rehabilitation Counselor

DOT = 045.107-042 GOE = 10.01.02

Counsels individuals who are physically, mentally, or emotionally challenged to help them train for, find, and secure employment; conducts assessment of each person's interests, abilities, and other factors to help clients determine appropriate educational and career goals.

Aptitudes:
Intelligence	High
Verbal	High
Numerical	Moderate
Spatial	Low
Form Perception	Low
Clerical Perception	Moderate
Motor Coordination	Low
Finger Dexterity	Low
Manual Dexterity	Low
Eye-Hand-Foot Coordination	Low
Color Discrimination	Low

Data = High   People = High   Things = Low

Salary Range:
$17,700–$49,300

Opportunity Outlook:
25–34% growth

Environmental Conditions:
Inside

Physical Demands:
Sedentary—little or no lifting
Talking or hearing required

Temperaments:
Directing, controlling, or planning the work of others
Making decisions based upon senses and feelings
Making decisions based upon facts
Performing a variety of tasks

Vocational Preparation:
4–10 years

Vocational Training Instructor

DOT = 097.227-014 GOE = 11.02.02

Teaches vocational training courses in specific trades to students enrolled in a public or private high school or college; may teach such courses as carpentry, electronics, auto mechanics, computer repair, and similar subjects.

Aptitudes:
Intelligence	High
Verbal	High
Numerical	High
Spatial	High
Form Perception	High
Clerical Perception	Moderate
Motor Coordination	Moderate
Finger Dexterity	Moderate
Manual Dexterity	Moderate
Eye-Hand-Foot Coordination	Moderate
Color Discrimination	Moderate

Data = High   People = High   Things = Low

Salary Range:
$12,000–$45,000+

Opportunity Outlook:
25–34% growth

Environmental Conditions:
Inside

Physical Demands:
Light—lifting of no more than 20 pounds required
Reaching, handling, fingering, or feeling required
Talking or hearing required
Seeing required

Temperaments:
Making decisions based upon senses and feelings
Making decision based upon facts
Dealing with people beyond giving and receiving information

Vocational Preparation:
4–10 years

Volunteer Services Supervisor

DOT = 187.137-014   GOE = 11.07.01

Supervises a team of volunteer workers who have donated their time and expertise to help carry out a community project; assigns duties and tasks to each worker, monitors the work progress, and arranges for needed materials and services.

Aptitudes:
Intelligence	Moderate
Verbal	Moderate
Numerical	Moderate
Spatial	Low
Form Perception	Low
Clerical Perception	Moderate
Motor Coordination	Low
Finger Dexterity	Low
Manual Dexterity	Low
Eye-Hand-Foot Coordination	Low
Color Discrimination	Low

Data = Mod   People = Mod   Things = Low

Salary Range:
$12,700–$18,500

Opportunity Outlook:
14–24% growth

Environmental Conditions:
Inside

Physical Demands:
Light—lifting of no more than 20 pounds required
Talking or hearing required

Temperaments:
Directing, controlling, or planning the work of others
Making decisions based upon senses and feelings
Performing a variety of tasks

Vocational Preparation:
2–4 years

Waiter (Bar)

DOT = 311.477-018   GOE = 09.04.01

Serves beverages to patrons seated at a bar or tables in a cocktail bar or restaurant; may also take orders for light meals and hors d'oeuvres; also collects bar and meal charges and makes change for customers.

Aptitudes:
Intelligence	Moderate
Verbal	Moderate
Numerical	Low
Spatial	Low
Form Perception	Low
Clerical Perception	Low
Motor Coordination	Moderate
Finger Dexterity	Low
Manual Dexterity	Moderate
Eye-Hand-Foot Coordination	Low
Color Discrimination	Low

Data = Low   People = Low   Things = Low

Salary Range:
$9,700–$22,300

Opportunity Outlook:
25–34% growth

Environmental Conditions:
Inside

Physical Demands:
Light—lifting of no more than 20 pounds required
Reaching, handling, fingering, or feeling required
Talking or hearing required
Seeing required

Temperaments:
Performing a variety of tasks

Vocational Preparation:
1–3 months

Warehouse Manager

DOT = 184.167-114   GOE = 11.11.03

Manages employees and activities of an industrial or commercial warehouse; determines operational procedures, verifies incoming and outgoing shipments, keeps accurate records of all materials and inventory, and performs similar activities.

Aptitudes:
Intelligence	High
Verbal	Moderate
Numerical	Moderate
Spatial	Moderate
Form Perception	Low
Clerical Perception	Moderate
Motor Coordination	Low
Finger Dexterity	Low
Manual Dexterity	Low
Eye-Hand-Foot Coordination	Low
Color Discrimination	Low

Data = Mod   People = Mod   Things = Low

Salary Range:
$19,200–$22,800

Opportunity Outlook:
5–13% growth

Environmental Conditions:
Inside

Physical Demands:
Sedentary—little or no lifting
Talking or hearing required

Temperaments:
Directing, controlling, or planning the work of others
Dealing with people beyond giving and receiving information
Performing a variety of tasks

Vocational Preparation:
2–4 years

Warehouse Supervisor

DOT = 929.137-022   GOE = 05.09.01

Supervises and coordinates activities of workers engaged in receiving, transporting, stacking, order filling, shipping, and maintenance of materials in a commercial or industrial warehouse.

Aptitudes:
Intelligence	Moderate
Verbal	Moderate
Numerical	Moderate
Spatial	Moderate
Form Perception	Low
Clerical Perception	Moderate
Motor Coordination	Low
Finger Dexterity	Low
Manual Dexterity	Low
Eye-Hand-Foot Coordination	Low
Color Discrimination	Low

Data = Mod   People = Mod   Things = Low

Salary Range:
$23,600 (average)

Opportunity Outlook:
5–13% growth

Environmental Conditions:
Inside

Physical Demands:
Light—lifting of no more than 20 pounds required
Reaching, handling, fingering, or feeling required
Talking or hearing required

Temperaments:
Directing, controlling, or planning the work of others
Dealing with people beyond giving and receiving information
Performing a variety of tasks

Vocational Preparation:
1–2 years

Water-Treatment Plant Operator

DOT = 954.382-014 GOE = 05.06.04

Operates and controls machines and equipment that purify and clarify water for human consumption or for commercial and industrial use.

Aptitudes:
Intelligence	Moderate
Verbal	Low
Numerical	Moderate
Spatial	Low
Form Perception	Moderate
Clerical Perception	Moderate
Motor Coordination	Moderate
Finger Dexterity	Low
Manual Dexterity	Moderate
Eye-Hand-Foot Coordination	Low
Color Discrimination	Low

Data = Low   People = Low   Things = Mod

Salary Range:
$14,100–$38,900

Opportunity Outlook:
25-34% growth

Environmental Conditions:
Inside and outside
Wet and humid work environment
Presence of loud noises and vibrations
Presence of physical hazards
Presence of atmospheric dangers

Physical Demands:
Moderate—lifting of no more than 50 pounds
Reaching, handling, fingering, or feeling required
Seeing required

Temperaments:
Making decisions based upon facts
Attempting to attain set limits

Vocational Preparation: 1/2–1 year

Weight Reduction Specialist

DOT = 359.367-014 GOE = 09.05.01

Counsels clients in devising and carrying out a weight-loss plan, using established dietary program, physical exercise routines, and positive reinforcement procedures.

Aptitudes:
Intelligence	Moderate
Verbal	Moderate
Numerical	Low
Spatial	Low
Form Perception	Low
Clerical Perception	Moderate
Motor Coordination	Low
Finger Dexterity	Low
Manual Dexterity	Low
Eye-Hand-Foot Coordination	Low
Color Discrimination	Low

Data = Mod   People = Mod   Things = Low

Salary Range:
$13,000 (average)

Opportunity Outlook:
25-34% growth

Environmental Conditions:
Inside

Physical Demands:
Light—lifting of no more than 20 pounds required
Reaching, handling, fingering, or feeling required
Talking or hearing required
Seeing required

Temperaments:
Making decisions based upon senses and feelings
Dealing with people beyond giving and receiving information

Vocational Preparation:
1-3 months

Welding Inspector

DOT = 819.687-010   GOE = 06.03.02

Inspects welded or soldered joints and seams for defects, such as cracks, cold welds, spatter, and undercuts; may inspect visually or with the use of x-ray machines.

Aptitudes:

Intelligence	Moderate
Verbal	Low
Numerical	Low
Spatial	Moderate
Form Perception	Moderate
Clerical Perception	Moderate
Motor Coordination	Low
Finger Dexterity	Low
Manual Dexterity	Moderate
Eye-Hand-Foot Coordination	Low
Color Discrimination	Low

Data = Mod   People = Low   Things = Low

Salary Range:
$13,000–$36,400

Opportunity Outlook:
0–4% growth or decline

Environmental Conditions:
Inside and outside
Presence of loud noises and vibrations

Physical Demands:
Light—lifting of no more than 20 pounds required
Reaching, handling, fingering, or feeling required
Seeing required

Temperaments:
Making decisions based upon facts
Attempting to attain set limits

Vocational Preparation:
3–6 months

Welfare Director

DOT = 188.117-126   GOE = 11.07.01

Directs and coordinates the activities of a public welfare program to aid individuals who are in need of medical care, food, clothing, shelter, or employment.

Aptitudes:

Intelligence	High
Verbal	High
Numerical	Moderate
Spatial	Low
Form Perception	Low
Clerical Perception	Moderate
Motor Coordination	Low
Finger Dexterity	Low
Manual Dexterity	Low
Eye-Hand-Foot Coordination	Low
Color Discrimination	Low

Data = High   People = Mod   Things = Low

Salary Range:
$28,500–$56,000

Opportunity Outlook:
5–13% growth

Environmental Conditions:
Inside

Physical Demands:
Sedentary—little or no lifting
Talking or hearing required

Temperaments:
Directing, controlling, or planning the work of others
Making decisions based upon senses and feelings
Making decisions based upon facts
Dealing with people beyond giving and receiving information
Performing a variety of tasks

Vocational Preparation:
4–10 years

Wildlife Control Agent

DOT = 379.267-010   GOE = 03.01.02

Monitors and controls the animal population of a national or state park; conducts surveys and research to determine kind and number of animals living in park and their food supply; may relocate animals that present danger to park visitors.

Aptitudes:
Intelligence	High
Verbal	Moderate
Numerical	Moderate
Spatial	Low
Form Perception	Moderate
Clerical Perception	Moderate
Motor Coordination	Moderate
Finger Dexterity	Moderate
Manual Dexterity	Moderate
Eye-Hand-Foot Coordination	Low
Color Discrimination	Low

Data = Mod   People = Low   Things = Low

Salary Range:
$22,000 (average)

Opportunity Outlook:
5–13% growth

Environmental Conditions:
Inside and outside
Presence of physical hazards

Physical Demands:
Moderate—lifting of no more than 50 pounds
Stooping, kneeling, crouching, or crawling required
Reaching, handling, fingering, or feeling required
Talking or hearing required
Seeing required

Temperaments:
Making decisions based upon facts
Performing under stressful conditions
Performing a variety of tasks

Vocational Preparation: 2–4 years

Word-Processing Machine Operator

DOT = 203.362-022   GOE = 07.06.02

Operates a word-processing machine to record, edit, store, and print reports, letters, forms, and other written materials in an office.

Aptitudes:
Intelligence	Moderate
Verbal	Moderate
Numerical	Low
Spatial	Low
Form Perception	Low
Clerical Perception	High
Motor Coordination	High
Finger Dexterity	High
Manual Dexterity	Moderate
Eye-Hand-Foot Coordination	Low
Color Discrimination	Low

Data = Mod   People = Low   Things = High

Salary Range:
$12,300–$16,700

Opportunity Outlook:
0–4% growth or decline

Environmental Conditions:
Inside

Physical Demands:
Sedentary—little or no lifting
Reaching, handling, fingering, or feeling required
Talking or hearing required
Seeing required

Temperaments:
Performing repetitive tasks
Attempting to attain set limits

Vocational Preparation:
3–6 months

Writer, Prose (Fiction & Nonfiction)

DOT = 131.067-046   GOE = 01.01.02

Writes original prose materials for publication, such as books, articles, and poems; may base works on personal experiences or interests, or may conduct research and interview people to gather information to help shape theme and content of written work.

Aptitudes:

Intelligence	High
Verbal	High
Numerical	Moderate
Spatial	Low
Form Perception	Low
Clerical Perception	Moderate
Motor Coordination	Low
Finger Dexterity	Low
Manual Dexterity	Low
Eye-Hand-Foot Coordination	Low
Color Discrimination	Low

Data = High   People = Low   Things = Low

Salary Range:
Varies

Opportunity Outlook:
25-34% growth

Environmental Conditions:
Inside

Physical Demands:
Sedentary—little or no lifting
Reaching, handling, fingering, or feeling required

Temperaments:
Interpreting the feelings and ideas of others
Making decisions based upon senses and feelings

Vocational Preparation:
4-10 years

X-Ray Equipment Tester

DOT = 729.281-046   GOE = 06.01.05

Tests X-ray machines and accessories to insure they operate effectively and safely; adjusts or repairs machinery if necessary.

Aptitudes:

Intelligence	Moderate
Verbal	Moderate
Numerical	High
Spatial	Moderate
Form Perception	High
Clerical Perception	Moderate
Motor Coordination	Low
Finger Dexterity	Moderate
Manual Dexterity	Moderate
Eye-Hand-Foot Coordination	Low
Color Discrimination	Low

Data = Mod   People = Low   Things = High

Salary Range:
$24,500 (average)

Opportunity Outlook:
25-34% growth

Environmental Conditions:
Inside
Presence of physical hazards

Physical Demands:
Light—lifting of no more than 20 pounds required
Reaching, handling, fingering, or feeling required
Seeing required

Temperaments:
Making decisions based upon facts
Performing a variety of tasks

Vocational Preparation:
1-2 years

Zoologist

DOT = 041.061-090   GOE = 02.02.01

Studies the origin, interrelationships, classification, life histories, habits, life processes, diseases, relation to environment, growth and development, genetics, and distribution of animals.

Aptitudes:

Intelligence	High
Verbal	High
Numerical	Moderate
Spatial	High
Form Perception	High
Clerical Perception	Moderate
Motor Coordination	Moderate
Finger Dexterity	Moderate
Manual Dexterity	Moderate
Eye-Hand-Foot Coordination	Low
Color Discrimination	Moderate

Data = High   People = Low   Things = Mod

Salary Range:
$13,100–$55,600

Opportunity Outlook:
25–34% growth

Environmental Conditions:
Inside and outside

Physical Demands:
Light—lifting of no more than 20 pounds required
Climbing, or balancing required
Stooping, kneeling, crouching, or crawling required
Reaching, handling, fingering, or feeling required
Seeing required

Temperaments:
Making decisions based upon senses and feelings
Dealing with people beyond giving and receiving information
Performing a variety of tasks

Vocational Preparation: 4–10 years

CHAPTER 6

Jobs of the Future

Before any discussion of the future can take place, we must define the phrase "Jobs of the Future." Occupations that are emerging (*i.e.*, just coming into our society for the first time) or that will be in much greater demand than other occupations may be described as "Jobs of the Future." If you wish to identify the best employment opportunities in the years ahead, you should examine both the new (emerging) occupations, and those existing ones that are predicted to be in most demand. The occupations found in this chapter reflect both emerging and in-demand occupations.

When we are speculating about jobs of the future, several preconditions must be understood so the predictions can be viewed in their proper context.

1. Predicting jobs of the future involves some science and art. Occupational forecasting is not an exact science based upon measurable and verifiable facts. Factual information is gathered and analyzed, but the interpretation of these facts and the projection of the status of the world to come is based upon professional guesswork.

2. Any prediction of the world to come is highly sensitive to and dependent upon the continuation of current factors, such as political, economic, social, environmental, educational, industrial, and technological conditions. Should any of these factors change dramatically in the years to come, then the job predictions upon which they are based can also be expected to change.

There are many factors and conditions that can determine which occupations will be in most demand in the future—too many to list here. However, the following represent some of the most important assumptions:

- Our labor force will continue to grow at its rapid pace.

- An increase in unemployment will continue.

- Changes in the labor force will continue (*i.e.* an increase in the number of women and immigrant workers).

- An increase in foreign trade will continue.

- Our negative trade balance will remain constant.

- Our nation's debtor status will continue.

- Computers and robots will continue to replace workers.

- A continual demand for more skilled workers will exist.

- A continuation of a friendly relationship with other superpowers in the world will exist for the United States.

3. Some of the occupations labeled as jobs of the future often offer, at first introduction, a relatively low number of employment opportunities. This is due to the fact that few of these positions exist when they first emerge. It may not be until the occupation is well established and widespread that substantial employment opportunities can be expected.

4. Far less information exists on jobs of the future than on contemporary occupations. Therefore, career planners and job seekers will have to invest more time and energy in learning about these new career options if they are to fully understand what opportunities do in fact exist.

With the above in mind, let us peer into the future and examine sixty emerging and in-demand occupations that are expected to exist in the near future. Included with each occupation is a brief rationale explaining why the occupation is emerging and/or in demand.

The Jobs

Actuaries
With an increase in the number of insurance policies (i.e. health, life, automotive), and with a growth in the number of people involved in financial investment activities, a greater demand will occur for actuaries, who will design, manage, and create insurance policies to meet the needs of insurance clients.

Alternate Energy Engineers
As our reserves of fossil fuels diminish, there will be a greater need for alternate energy engineers. These engineers will be responsible for finding and developing other sources of energy, such as solar, wind, ocean, thermal, and natural gas.

Artists
As our society becomes more technical (*i.e.*, more of the goods produced will be done by machine rather than by human hands), it is expected that an increase in the appreciation for art will occur.

An example of this attitude can be seen today in the growing interest in antiques. While our society can produce an unlimited number of factory-made furniture, more and more people are interested in buying antique furniture because they value the handiwork of our ancestors.

While computers can now produce unlimited artwork—equal in design to that of the human hand—the value of human-produced artwork continues to rise.

Bakers
As grocery store chains and restaurant franchise operations continue to expand across our land, a greater number of bakers will be hired to bake and prepare breads and other baked good products. This demand for bakers is due in large part to the growing demand by busy professionals for freshly baked products.

Bionic Implant Specialists
These highly trained physicians and surgeons will be called upon to remove defective human organs and skeletal parts (i.e. lungs, hearts, eyes, knee joints) and replace them with artificial replacements, which can extend and improve the normal functioning of the human body.

Biotechnology Engineers
Special biological scientists called biotechnology engineers will be called upon to develop new plant and animal life forms, engineer human genetic systems to improve health, and adapt organisms to better serve the technology needs of our industrial society.

CAD/CAM Design Engineers
Specially trained engineers armed with the most advanced computer systems will design a variety of manufactured goods using only their personal computers and then instruct the computer to control various machines that will in turn manufacture the goods. All this will be accomplished without creating a physical prototype of the products, in much less time, and at much lower costs than conventional means would require.

Computer Programmers
Continual improvements in the ease of use of personal computers, advances in software design, increases in telecommunications options, and a reduction in the cost of high-speed

computers with large storage capabilities will continue to automate more and more aspects of life, thus requiring more and better software programs.

Computer Security Officers

With the increased use of computers, many of which store valuable and sensitive business and government data, an increase in computer security officers will also occur. These specialists will design, develop, install, and maintain a variety of security measures to prevent unauthorized access to restricted data and information.

Computer System Analysts

As more and more computer software programs and hardware are developed, and as systems become more advanced and high-tech, computer systems analysts will be called upon to integrate these new systems into existing business and industrial operations to improve their overall productivity.

Computer Use Instructors/Trainers

As more Americans become dependent upon computers to conduct their daily business and personal affairs, a greater need for the services of a computer use instructor/trainer will occur. These specialized instructors will help users understand how to effectively use their computer system, software programs, and related equipment and services, such as computer online services.

Corporate Trainers

As the number of workers who arrive for work with less-than-adequate skills in language, math, and science continues to grow and limit the overall productivity of America companies, corporate trainers will be called upon to design and develop in-house and in-home training programs to resolve this problem.

Correctional Officers

As crime continues to increase and as more and more citizens demand tougher punishment of criminals, state and federal authorities will be forced to create more prison systems, thereby creating a greater need for more correctional officers.

Data Processing Equipment Technicians

As worldwide industries create more and more high-tech equipment (computers, televisions, multimedia stations, VCRs, etc.), the demand for highly skilled technicians who can repair this equipment will grow as well.

Electrical and Electronic Engineers

With business and industry constantly looking for ways to automate their systems to reduce their operating costs (necessary to compete in a worldwide market), electrical and electronic engineers will be called upon to design the next generation of equipment, machines, and systems, especially microelectronic equipment, to meet this need.

Electrical and Electronic Technicians and Technologists

As electrical and electronic engineers design more high-tech equipment, machines, and systems to meet our technological needs, electrical and electronic technicians and technologists will be called upon to test them, assist in their actual manufacture, and carry out their advanced installation and maintenance procedures.

Electronic Artists and Designers

Television stations, corporate communication departments, architects, fashion designers, real estate agents, building contractors, and other similar concerns will continue to demand more and better visual presentation of their ideas, services, and products in their advertising campaigns. Electronic artists and designers armed with high-tech computers and related multimedia equipment will be called upon to meet this demand.

Environmental Engineers

Abuses from hundreds of years of industrial growth have placed a critical demand on many of earth's natural life-supporting systems. Serious conditions exist in air, water, and land pollution, which must be addressed by environmental engineers worldwide.

Environmental (Hazardous) Waste Technicians

These highly skilled professionals will be called upon to help dispose of all forms of environmental waste products, including wastes that are hazardous to the health of people and animals and to the environment.

Ergonomics Engineers

Working in a branch of engineering that specializes in the understanding of how the human body functions, ergonomics engineers will be called upon to develop new machines, devices, equipment, and products that correspond to and operate in conjunction with the way the human body functions.

Farm Managers

As the population grows and as worldwide markets open for American food products, more farm managers will be needed to manage the high-tech and complex farming procedures necessary to meet this growing need.

Food Technologists

To meet the demands of busy professionals, food technologists will be called upon to create new food products and food preparation methods that are both high in nutritional value and quick and easy to prepare.

Health Care Cost Specialists

With the population of the United States aging, and with the cost of health care skyrocketing, health care cost specialists will be called upon to find ways to reduce the costs of health care to make it affordable to all Americans.

Health Care Technologists

To provide a high level of health care for all citizens, a variety of specially trained health care technologists will be required in such fields as ultrasound technology, nuclear medicine, biomedical computing, and CAT scan technology.

Housing Rehabilitation Specialists

Armed with information about carpentry, plumbing, electrical systems, and general construction techniques, housing rehabilitation specialists will advise home owners and building contractors on how to rehabilitate a home or building to bring it up to modern code conditions as a means of extending its life and usefulness.

Human Resource Managers

With the composition of the workforce changing (*i.e.*, the inclusion of more women, minorities, and foreign workers), with workers demanding more time to attend to their personal and social needs, with an increasingly mobile workforce, and with an aging work population, new policies need to be developed to keep workers happy and productive. Human resource managers will be called upon to accomplish this task.

Imaging Scientists
The demand to "see" more of our world will continue to create machines that can peer into the inner workings of the atom, view the inside of the human body without violating the skin, or outwards to the very ends of space. Imaging scientists will be called upon to create this new breed of imaging machines.

Industrial/Scientific Laserists
Engineers specially trained in the use of lasers will be called upon to work with industrial and scientific companies and organizations to apply the benefits to laser technology to the production of manufactured goods, the advancement of science and technology, improvements in telecommunication systems, and improved health care systems.

Information Officers
The use of personal computers by employees to carry out their daily work assignments will continue to grow, thereby requiring information officers to carefully determine and manage the computer systems and procedures used by employees.

Information Specialists
Much of what American companies produce is information. In all areas of life there is an abundance of information, and it is growing at an ever increasing rate. Information specialists will help companies and individuals alike sift through the volumes of information to find the data they need.

International Lawyers
As U.S. companies do more and more business abroad, the need for legal protection of their business concerns will produce an increase in the need for lawyers who are trained in international law and foreign customs and procedures, as well as in liability laws of distant lands.

Management Analysts
As businesses and industries attempt to reduce their overhead costs, especially salaries, to become more productive and competitive in a world market, they will increase the need for management analysts. These professionals will in turn find consultants who can provide business services to reduce their client's need for full-time employees.

Manufacturing Engineers
Facing worldwide market competition and an inadequate supply of well-trained employees at home, manufacturing engineers will be called upon to develop new manufacturing procedures and systems that can help to produce the products and materials needed to support the lifestyle of modern Americans.

Mediators
Increases in social problems have resulted in a dramatic increase in litigation cases—so many that most of our courts are backlogged for years. Mediation outside of a court room by professional mediators (trained lawyers and other professionals) will help to resolve this problem.

Medical and Scientific Equipment Technicians
As our medical and scientific equipment becomes more complex, a greater need will occur for trained technicians to install, repair, and maintain this equipment.

Medical Record Technicians
Changes in reimbursement policies recently enacted by medical insurance carriers will increase the need for medical record technicians in various kinds of health care facilities. Their main job will be to manage the overburdened record-keeping system.

Meteorologists
With millions of dollars lost each year to storm damage, more and more companies, governmental agencies, and insurance carriers are demanding up-to-date and accurate weather forecasts, thus resulting in a greater need for meteorologists.

Millwrights
As U.S. manufacturing concerns and industries upgrade their production equipment to compete in a modern, high-tech environment, additional millwrights will be required to install and maintain this new equipment.

Multimedia Programmers
Various types of programmers (some skilled in conventional languages and others skilled in the new Object Oriented Programming languages) will be called upon to develop a new line of multimedia programs. These programs will incorporate and integrate video and still images, sound clips, data and text, and graphics together into one program that can be run easily and viewed with a personal computer.

New Material Engineers
In every field imaginable, new materials that are lighter, stronger, more resistant to wear, and less expensive to manufacture are in strong demand. New material engineers, who create new materials from ceramics, petroleum and other resources, will lead the way in this area.

Numerical Tool Programmers
These specially trained computer programmers will develop the instructions (programming code) necessary to run the automated and robotic equipment and machines that will be found in tomorrow's industries and factories.

Ocean Mining Engineers
As human beings move farther into the oceans to find a new supply of minerals and natural resources, more ocean mining engineers will be called upon to find and manage the acquisition of these resources.

Operations Research Analysts
As business and industry attempt to modernize their equipment and procedures, operations research analysts will be called upon to determine how best this change can be introduced and managed.

Paralegals
Judges and lawyers, finding their time to be increasingly in demand, will depend more and more upon paralegal assistants to help them carry out their responsibilities.

Photographic Process Technicians

As modern technology advances, more photographs and video images will be used to enhance traditional print media (newspapers, magazines, books) and computer software programs. Many of these images will be created by individuals armed with a still camera, video camera, or personal computer. Photographic process technicians will be called upon to help process these photos and films.

Professional Athletes and Entertainers

With more leisure time and the general public's interest in athletic events and all forms of entertainment, professional athletes and entertainers will continue to be in great demand, with many earning exceptionally high salaries.

Recycling Consultants

As more and more Americans understand the need to recycle goods and materials, recycling consultants will be called upon by business and industry, city and local governments, and private organizations to design effective systems for recycling manufactured products.

Reproductive Endocrinologists

Millions of infertile couples desiring to have children will find greater success with medical advances made by reproductive endocrinologists. This new breed of scientists will be expert in ovulation, hormones, and various assisted reproductive technologies.

Robotic Engineers

Engineers skilled in the integration of computers and machines will continue to be in demand to help business and industry control its manufacturing costs to become more competitive in the growing world economy.

Security Systems Designers

To ensure that employees and home owners are safe from physical harm, security systems designers will be called upon to design new devices and systems that can keep criminals from inflicting physical harm on people and damage to their property.

Software Technicians

As more computer software programs are created, a greater demand will occur for software technicians who can debug the programs, update the programs when new information becomes available, convert them to other computer platforms and systems, and personalize the programs to meet specific customer needs and desires.

Soil Conservation Specialists

To overcome the damage caused by decades of misuse of pesticides and agricultural chemicals, soil conservation specialists will be in demand to help farmers extend the life and use of their soil to ensure its use by future generations.

Solar Systems Equipment Installers/Repairers

As advances in solar energy continues new systems will be created that can economically harness the energy of the sun to operate our homes and offices. Technologically trained solar systems equipment installers/repairers will be needed to install and maintain this new equipment.

Subway and Streetcar Operators

One of the solutions to our highway-congestion problem is the development of more mass transportation options, especially subway and streetcar systems. This movement to more dependency upon mass transportation will result in a need for more subway and streetcar operators.

Superconductivity Engineers

For engineers who are knowledgeable and capable of developing materials that do not resist the flow of electricity, the future will offer unlimited opportunities. These engineers are on the verge of developing new systems and machines that will revolutionize the fields of transportation, medical imaging, electronics, and energy production.

Surgical Technologists

Advances in medical technology and the demand for more and better health care will mean that many of the health care practices traditionally performed by physicians will soon be conducted by surgical technologists. These specially trained technicians will work under the care of an attending physician.

Telecommunication Integration Specialists

How a company or individual can integrate and best use computers, modems, fax machines, electronic database networks, and telephone systems to satisfy business and personal needs will be the main responsibility of a new breed of experts, called telecommunication integration specialists.

Telecommuting Specialists

As companies and workers better understand the disadvantages which exist when large populations of workers commute long distances to and from work, a growing need for telecommuting specialists will occur. These specialists will help companies and employees find electronic solutions to this problem. The main strategy employed by these specialists will be to link the employee's home electronically to the workplace via computers, phone modems, and fax machines to allow the employee to work from home.

Traveling Nurses

As the population of the United States continues to age, the traditional health care services will be unable to meet adequately the medical needs of this population. As a result, fewer beds will be available in hospitals and health care facilities. However, with advances in technology, more and more senior citizens will elect to convalesce at home and have their health care needs addressed by a traveling nurse armed with sophisticated medical devices electronically linked to a central medical facility.

Urban Redevelopment Planners

As Americans grasp the full impact of the movement to the suburbs that has occurred over the last few decades and the negative impact of this movement, urban redevelopment planners will be called upon to revitalize the inner cities to stem the decay of our urban centers.

Planning for Your Future

How can you determine if any of these occupations are right for you?

To determine which of these Jobs of the Future may be right for you, you should follow a procedure similar to the one as outlined earlier in Tasks 1, 2, and 3 of *Career Selector 2001*. The main difference here is the fact that little information exists on the Work Preferences (Task 2) of these future occupations. Therefore, rather than referring to this book for the information, you will have to gather it yourself from various sources.

If any of these occupations appeal to you, and if you would like to evaluate them in terms of a career goal, follow the procedure below:

1. Add the name(s) of any job of the future in which you are interested to your list of possible career options found at the end of Task 1.

2. Research your selected career option or options (using the suggested research strategies listed below) until you feel you have a strong understanding of the nature of each occupation. For each occupation, you should gather the following information:
   - The nature of the work
   - Entrance and training options
   - Typical salary and benefits
   - Positive and negative working conditions
   - Advancement opportunities
   - Required knowledge and skills
   - Special licenses, certifications, and degrees
   - Typical employers and places of employment
   - Future employment need
   - Lifestyle implications

   Use the worksheet found on page 311 to evaluate the appropriateness of each occupation.

3. As you locate information about each of the above factors, rate how desirable each factor is for you. For example, if you discover that your selected job of the future pays $45,000 per year and you were hoping to earn that amount, then you might want to enter 10 points to the typical salary and benefits row.

4. After all factors have been rated, determine a total score for your first occupation.

5. If you have selected more than one occupation from the list of jobs of the future, repeat the above procedure for each occupation. Then compare all total scores and determine which job of the future is most ideally suited to your needs and preferences.

6. Then compare the results of this exercise with the results of Tasks 1, 2, and 3. Which occupation do you now feel is the best one for you to pursue?

Where can you find additional information on any of these occupations?

Obtaining occupational information on jobs of the future can be more difficult (but not impossible) than finding information on other, more established occupations. The "occupational information gatherers" have simply not had time to collect information on these occupations because they are so new. You may have to spend a little more time hunting down the information.

Suggested Research Strategies

1. Ask a research librarian at a local public or college library for assistance. These professionals are trained to unearth this kind of information.

2. Conduct a periodical search (again with the help of a librarian) to find magazine articles, especially from industry trade journals, that describes these new occupations.

3. Contact several people working in your chosen occupation and/or personnel officers at companies that hire such individuals and ask them to share with you what they know about the occupation.

4. Contact several professional associations (check your library for their names and addresses) connected with your selected occupation to inquire about any information they have available.

5. Contact several futuristic associations and subscribe to their publications to keep abreast of the future. One example is the World Future Society, 4916 St. Elmo Avenue, Bethesda, MD, 20914 (301/656-8274).

6. Check your local bookstores for books and magazines that deal with the subject of the future.

7. Call your local colleges and universities and inquire about courses, workshops, and lectures available to the general public on the subject of future projections.

8. Subscribe to the *What's Next?* monthly newsletter offered by the Congressional Clearinghouse on the Future (555 House Annex #2, Washington, DC, 20515).

In short, dig, dig, dig! The more information you gather, the more knowledgeable you will become and the more likely you are to choose an enjoyable and rewarding career direction.

Jobs of the Future Evaluation Sheet

(This worksheet may be photocopied)

Occupational Title _____

Rating Scale: 10 = Very Desirable   5 = OK
                   7 = Desirable   0 = Undesirable

Factors	Rating Score
Nature of the work	[ ]
Entrance and training options	[ ]
Typical salary and benefits	[ ]
Positive/Negative working conditions	[ ]
Advancement opportunities	[ ]
Required knowledge & skills	[ ]
Special licenses, certifications, and degrees	[ ]
Typical employers and places of employment	[ ]
Future employment need	[ ]
Lifestyle implications	[ ]
Other	[ ]
Other	[ ]
Total Score	[ ]

Appendixes

	Page
A. Additional Resources A listing of materials and services designed to help you select a career direction and develop a plan for realizing your new career goal.	313
B. Alphabetical Index of Job Titles An alphabetical listing of all the occupational job titles found in *Career Selector 2001*.	323
C. How to Select a Career Counselor Suggestions on how to find and use a career counselor to help you select and plan for a new career direction.	329
D. How to Use the DOT, GOE, and OOH Directories Step-by-step directions for using the Dictionary of Occupational Titles (DOT), Guide for Occupational Exploration (GOE), and the Occupational Outlook Handbook (OOH) to find your career direction.	333

A. Additional Resources

No book, including *Career Selector 2001*, can be expected to resolve all the career guidance needs of its readers. Therefore, you may need to use other resources to help you select and plan you career direction. Listed in this section are selected resources that may be useful. It is important to stress that the resources listed here are only a sampling of the many resources that exists. It is simply impossible to list them all. Also, the resources found here are mainly related to career selection and planning, not to other career development tasks, such as job hunting and placement. If you do not find a resource listed here that suits your needs, you can ask a librarian or a guidance professional in your area for additional recommendations. The resources are listed by category to aid you in quickly identifying materials useful to your needs.

Where can you obtain these materials?

You can generally find these materials in a commercial bookstore, public or school library, school or college counseling office, or through a career guidance catalog service, such as those found in the *Directories of Career Guidance Information and Assistance* section below. Also, in most cases, you can obtain the resources listed from the publisher or distributor.

Career Selection and Planning

The resources are designed to help you select a career direction or develop a plan for reaching your chosen career goal. Some of these materials, such as *The Career Finder*, follow strategies similar to those found in *Career Selector 2001*. Other materials incorporate a different guidance strategy.

The Career Finder
Dr. Lester Schwartz & Irv Brechner
Ballantine Books
Division of Random House, Inc.
New York, NY
(212) 751-2600

A book incorporating a system whereby you first determine your interests and work preferences, and then compare those factors to over 1500 entry-level occupations to determine a career goal. Excellent book for high school and soon-to-be college graduates who are involved in selecting their first career goal.

How to Create a Picture of Your Ideal Job or Next Career
Richard N. Bolles
Ten Speed Press
Box 1723
Berkeley, CA 94707
(415) 845-8414

Exerpted from *What Color is Your Parachute?* (see below). Includes various workbook exercises to help you identify your preference of various factors, such as physical, spiritual, and emotional work settings; skills; and types of people; then guides you in identifying occupations that may be related.

The New Quick Job Hunting Map
Richard N. Bolles
Ten Speed Press
Box 1723
Berkeley, CA 94707
(415) 845-8414

Exerpted from *What Color is Your Parachute?* (see below). Guides you in identifying your skills and relating them to occupational goals.

What Color is Your Parachute?
Richard N. Bolles
Ten Speed Press
Box 1723
Berkeley, CA 94707
(415) 845-8414

One of the most popular self-help career guidance books on the market today. Guides you in identifying information about yourself, such as interest, skills, values, desired work environments, etc. Then suggests ways to identify matching occupations. Excellent suggestions for conducting a job search, as well as a listing of career development resources and services.

Working for America
James C. Gonyea
Barron's Educational Series, Inc.
250 Wireless Blvd.
Hauppauge, NY 11788
(516) 434-3311

Specifically written to help students and adults select and secure a career with the federal government. Extensive information on over 160 federal departments and agencies, with step-by-step directions for finding, applying to, and securing employment with the federal government. Includes a Career Interest Survey, Job Titles Index, and College Majors Index to help readers identify federal occupations matching their interests, employment, and educational experiences.

Computerized Career Guidance and Information Programs

These software programs are designed to enable you to enter information about yourself (*i.e.*, interests, skills, work preferences) and then obtain a listing of occupations that match. Some of these programs also offer extensive information of occupations, educational programs to study and institutions, and sources of financial assistance. Some programs are very comprehensive, while others offer only basic guidance and information. Most of these programs can be found in school, college, and private guidance offices. Some may be found in computer software stores. Those items marked with an asterisk (*) are expensive. It is recommended that you use these programs at a local high school or college rather than purchase them for your private use.

Career Design
Career Design Software
PO Box 95624
Atlanta, GA 30347
(404) 321-6100

*Career Options**
Peterson's Guides, Inc.
PO Box 2123
Princeton, NJ 08543
(800) 338-3282

*Choices**
STM Systems Corp./Careerware
810 Proctor Avenue
Industrial Park Building #3
Ogdensburg, NY 13669
(800) 267-1544

*C-LECT**
Chronicle Guidance Publications, Inc.
Aurora Street
Moravia, NY 13118
(800) 622-7284

*DISCOVER**
Amercian College Testing Center
230 Schilling Circle
Hunt Valley, MD 21301
(301) 628-8000

Federal Occupational and Career Information System (FOCIS)
National Technical Information Service
5285 Port Royal Road
Springfield, VA 22161
(703) 487-4650

*Sigi Plus**
Educational Testing Service
Princeton, NJ 08541
(800) 257-7444

*The Job Search System**
West Virginia Research and Training Center
West Virginia University
806 Allen Hall
PO Box 6122
Morgantown, WV 26506
(304) 293-5313

Computerized Career Guidance Services

The following services provide career guidance and information via the mail to help students and adults identify occupations matching their interests, skills, and personality style.

Career Analysis Service (CAS)
Gonyea and Associates, Inc.
45 Whig Drive
Manchester, NH 03104
(603) 622-5587   Fax (603) 622-5587
Cost: $39.95

CAS compares your interests, skills, and work preferences to more than 13,500 occupations as a means of identifying appropriate career goals. The process involves two steps. First you complete a questionnaire at home and return your answers for processing. An Interpretation Guide and listing of occupational suggestions are then returned to you. CAS is based upon information gathered by the U.S. Department of Labor.

GuidePak
Behaviordyne, Inc.
994 San Antonia Road
PO Box 10994
Palo Alto, CA 94303
(800) 627-2673
Cost: $25

GuidePak is a service whereby you complete an interest and personality inventory at home and return your answer sheets for scoring. A personalized report and workbook are returned to you listing occupations found to match your interests and personality characteristics. The service incorporates two widely used instruments, the Strong-Campbell Interest Inventory and the California Psychological Inventory. Your interest areas are compared to approximately 160 major occupational groups and professions.

Computer Online Guidance Services

AMERICA ONLINE (AOL) CAREER CENTER
America Online Computer Network, Inc.
8619 Westwood Center Drive
Vienna, VA 22182
(800) 827-6364

America Online is one of the top three computer telecommunication networks in the United States. It is a subscription service that anyone may subscribe to and access with a personal computer and a modem. The Career Center offers a wide variety of information and guidance services to help with educational and career planning (including federal career planning), job hunting and placement, and starting and running a small business from your home. Personal, professional, career counseling is available online from a staff of career counselors.

System requirements: A personal computer (IBM, IBM-compatible, Apple IIe/IIc/IIGS or Macintosh), modem (2400-baud recommended), and communication software (free of charge from AOL).

Cost/ordering instructions: Subscription to the AOL network is $5.95 per month, plus connect charges that range from approximately 16 cents/minute during daytime hours to 8 cents/minute during evening and weekend hours.

Directories of Career Guidance Information and Assistance

These directories provide information on a wide variety of resources helpful to individuals who are involved in the process of career development. Resources typically cover such topics as personal assessment, occupational exploration, career planning, job seeking, employment interviewing, and self-employment. The address and telephone number where you may obtain any resource is usually included for each item listed in each of these directories. In the case of *JIST Works* and the *Whole Work Catalog*, you may order any item listed in their directories directly from them.

JUST JIST Catalog
JIST Works, Inc.
720 North Park Avenue
Indianapolis, IN 46202
(800) 648-JIST

The Whole Career Sourcebook
Robbie Miller Kaplan
American Management Association
135 West 50th Street
New York, NY 10020
(212) 586-8100

The Whole Work Catalog
The New Career Center
1515 23rd Street
PO Box 339-ST
Boulder, CO 80306
(800) 634-9024

Miscellaneous Publications

From College to Career
Nancy Schuman and Adele Lewis
Barron's Educational Series Inc.
250 Wireless Blvd
Hauppauge, NY 11788
(516) 434-3311

Advice on job searching and examples of resumes and cover letters.

Information Interviewing: What It Is and How to Use It in Your Career
Martha Stoodley
Garrett Park Press
Garrett Park, MD 20896
(301) 946-2553

An excellent guide for learning how to conduct informational interviews for use in gaining information on career options and employment.

New Emerging Careers: Today, Tomorrow, and in the 21st Century
S. Norman Feingold & Maxine H. Atwater
Garrett Park Press
Garrett Park, MD 20896
(301) 946-2553

Information on future career opportunities in a wide variety of occupational areas.

The Career Connection
A Guide to College Majors and Their Related Careers
Fred A. Rowe
JIST Works, Inc.
720 North Park Avenue
Indianapolis, IN 46202
(800) 648-JIST

A listing of 100 college majors and 1000 related occupations.

The Career Connection II
A Guide to Technical Majors and Their Related Careers
Fred A. Rowe
JIST Works, Inc.
720 North Park Avenue
Indianapolis, IN 46202
(800) 648-JIST

A listing of 70 technical majors and 450 related occupations.

Occupational Information

These resources provide detailed information on hundreds of occupations. Typically, each resource provides information on the nature of the occupation, entrance qualifications, training options, salary and benefits, future employment outlook, related occupations, sources of additional information, and other general information. Those items coded with an asterisk (*) are expensive. You may want to use them at a local high school or college rather than purchase them for your private use.

The American Almanac of Jobs and Salaries
(1990-1991 Edition)
John W. Wright & Edward J. Dwyer
Avon Books
1350 Avenue of the Americas
New York, NY 10019
(800) 238-0658
$16.00

A comprehensive listing of occupations with information on salaries. Excellent resource for determining the value of a particular occupation in today's market.

The Dictionary of Occupational Titles
Fourth Edition, Revised 1991
U.S. Department of Labor
Employment and Training Administration
Superintendent of Documents
U.S. Government Printing Office
Washington, DC 20402
(202) 783-3238
$40.00

The largest collection of job titles and (brief) descriptions available in print. An excellent source of information for people who want a quick description of a particular occupation.

The Enhanced Guide for Occupational Exploration
Compiled by Marilyn Maze
Based upon information from the U.S. Department of Labor
JIST Works, Inc.
720 North Park Avenue
Indianapolis, IN 46202
(800) 648-JIST
$29.95

An excellent directory listing 2500 of the most common occupations found in the United States. Occupations are arranged by twelve interest categories for easy identification of occupations related to interests. This publication has fewer occupational listings than the regular GOE (see below), but provides more information on each occupation.

Encyclopedia of Careers and Vocational Guidance
Edited by William E. Hopke
J.G. Fergusen Publishing Company
200 West Monroe Street
Chicago, IL 60606
(312) 580-5480

An extensive collection in four volumes of information on hundreds of occupations.

The Guide for Occupational Exploration
Original Publisher: U.S. Department of Labor
Edited by Thomas F. Harrington & Arthur J. O'Shea
American Guidance Service
Publishers' Building
Circle Pines, MN 55014
(800) 328-2560
$38.50

An extensive listing of more than 13,500 occupations found in the United States. Occupations are arranged by twelve major interest categories for easy identification of occupations related to one's interests.

Occu-Facts
Careers, Inc.
PO Box 135
Largo, FL 34649
(800) 726-0441
$38.00

Profiles on more than 550 occupations.

Occupational Brief Library
Chronical Guidance Publications, Inc.
Aurora Street
Moravia, NY 13118
(800) 622-7284

An extensive library of more than 1000 occupational profiles with detailed information on each.

Occupational Outlook Handbook
1992-1993 Edition
U.S. Department of Labor
Bureau of Labor Statistics
Superintendent of Documents
U.S. Government Printing Office
Washington, DC 20402
(202) 783-3238
$26.00

A widely used directory of occupational information. Provides detailed information on approximately 250 occupations.

Occupational Outlook Quarterly
U.S. Department of Labor
Bureau of Labor Statistics
Superintendent of Documents
U.S. Government Printing Office
Washington, DC 20402
(202) 783-3238
$6.50

A magazine that quarterly updates the *Occupational Outlook Handbook* with information on new occupations and trends.

Occupational Projections and Training Data
1992 Edition
U.S. Department of Labor
Bureau of Labor Statistics
Superintendent of Documents
U.S. Government Printing Office
Washington, DC 20402
(202) 783-3238
$5.50

Detailed occupational projections (of future need) for hundreds of occupations.

Vocational Biographies
Vocational Biographies, Inc.
PO Box 31
Sauk Centre, MN 56378
(800) 255-0752

An extensive library of nearly 1000 occupational profiles with detailed information on each. Each profile includes information obtained from someone working in the actual career field for a "personal touch."

Vocational/Career Assessment Instruments

These instruments, often referred to as inventories or tests, are designed to help you gather information about yourself (interests, abilities, values, personality characteristics), and then to relate your findings to matching occupations. These instruments are normally administered and interpreted by a trained career counselor or psychologist and, therefore, are not normally available to the general public. If you wish to use any of these instruments, you should contact a local career counselor.

Interest Inventories Some inventories are in paper format, while others are available as a computer software program. Some inventories are self-scoring and self-interpreting, while others need to be scored and interpreted by a counselor.

California Occupational Preference System (COPS)
Edits, Inc.
PO Box 7234
San Diego, CA 92167
(619) 222-1666

Career Quest
Chronical Guidance Publications
Aurora Street
Moravia, NY 13118
(800) 622-7284

Self-Directed Search
Psychological Assessment Resources, Inc.
Box 998
Odessa, FL 33556
(800) 331-TEST

Strong Interest Inventory
Consulting Psychologists Press, Inc.
3803 East Bayshore Road
Box 10096
Palo Alto, CA 94303
(800) 624-1765

Ability or Aptitude Test Such tests help you measure your abilities or your potential for certain skills and identify related occupations. These instruments usually need to be administered, scored, and interpreted by a trained counselor.

Career Ability Placement Survey (CAPS)
Edits, Inc.
PO Box 7234
San Diego, CA 92167
(619) 222-1666

Eureka Skills Inventory
The California Career Information System
130 33rd Street, Room 408
Richmond, CA 94804
(415) 235-3883

General Aptitude Test Battery (GATB)
(Contact your local State Employment Office)

Values Inventories These measure your personal values and needs, and in some cases, identify related occupations.

Career Orientation Placement and Evaluation Survey (COPES)
Edits, Inc.
PO Box 7234
San Diego, CA 92167
(619) 222-1666

Hall Occupational Orientation Inventory
Scholastic Testing Service, Inc.
480 Meyer Road
PO Box 1056
Bensenville, IL 60106
(800) 642-6787

Personality Inventories These measure your personality characteristics and, with assistance of a career counselor, can be used to identify related occupations.

California Psychological Inventory
Consulting Psychologists Press, Inc.
3803 East Bayshore Road
Box 10096
Palo Alto, CA 94303
(800) 624-1765

Myers-Briggs Type Indicator
Consulting Psychologists Press, Inc.
3803 East Bayshore Road
Box 10096
Palo Alto, CA 94303
(800) 624-1765

B. Alphabetical Index of Job Titles

Job Title	Page
Account Executive	49
Accountant	49
Acquisitions Librarian	50
Acrobat	50
Actor	51
Actuary	51
Acupuncturist	52
Adding Machine Operator	52
Advertising Manager	53
Aerial Photographer	53
Aeronautical Research Engineer	54
Agricultural Shipping Inspector	54
Agronomist	55
Air-Conditioning Installer	55
Air-Traffic Control Specialist	56
Airbrush Painter	56
Airline Crew Scheduler	57
Airplane Flight Attendant	57
Ambulance Driver	58
Amusement Park Entertainer	58
Anesthesiologist	59
Animal Breeder	59
Animal Caretaker	60
Animal Scientist	60
Animal Trainer	61
Animal Trapper	61
Antenna Installer	62
Anthropologist	62
Apartment Manager	63
Appliance Service Supervisor	63
Aquarist	64
Aquatic Performer	64
Arbitrator	65
Archaeologist	65
Architect	66
Architectural Drafter	66
Art Appraiser	67
Art Teacher	67
Art Therapist	68
Artists' Model	68
Association Executive	69
Astronomer	69
Athletic Director	70
Athletic Manager	70
Auctioneer	71
Audiometrist	71
Audiovisual Technician	72
Auditor	72
Auto Club Travel Counselor	73
Automobile Body Repairer	73
Automobile-Laboratory Technician	74
Automobile Racer	74
Automobile Rental Clerk	75
Automobile Repair Service Estimator	75
Ballistics Expert	76
Bank Collection Clerk	76
Bank Loan Counselor	77
Bank President	77
Bank Proof Machine Operator	78
Bank Teller	78
Barber	79
Bartender	79
Bell Captain	80
Bibliographer	80
Bill Collector	81
Billing Clerk	81
Biochemist	82
Biographer	82
Biologist	83
Biomedical Equipment Technician	83
Blaster	84
Blood Laboratory Assistant	84
Bodyguard	85
Boiler Operator	85
Bookkeeper	86
Botanist	86
Bricklayer	87
Bridge Inspector	87
Budget Analyst	88
Building Inspector	88
Bulldozer Operator	89
Bus Driver	89
Business Manager (College/University)	90
Buyer	90
Cable Maintainer (Light/Heat/Power)	91
Cafeteria Attendant	91
Car Rental Vehicle Deliverer	92
Cardiopulmonary Technologist	92
Cargo Agent	93
Carpenter	93
Carpet & Rug Weaver	94
Cashier (Gambling Casino)	94
Casting Director	95

	Page		Page
Cemetery Supervisor	95	Critic	118
Chauffeur	96	Customs Inspector	119
Check Cashier	96	Customs Patrol Officer	119
Chemical-Laboratory Technician	97	Dairy Farm Supervisor	120
Chemical Processing Supervisor	97	Dance Studio Manager	120
Chemical Test Engineer	98	Dancer	121
Chemist	98	Dancing Instructor	121
Chief Bank Examiner	99	Deaf Interpreter	122
Chief Deputy Sheriff	99	Dealer (Gambling Establishment)	122
Children's Librarian	100	Dean of Students (College)	123
Chiropractor	100	Delivery Person (In-town)	123
Choral Director	101	Demonstrator	124
Choreographer	101	Dental Assistant	124
City Manager	102	Dental Hygienist	125
Civil Engineer	102	Dentist	125
Claim Examiner	103	Department Manager	126
Classified Ad Clerk	103	Detective	126
Clergy Member	104	Dialysis Technician	127
Clerk-Typist	104	Director of Admissions	127
Clinical Psychologist	105	Director of Placement (College)	128
Clothes Designer	105	Disk Jockey	128
Clothes Model	106	District Attorney	129
Coin-Machine Collector	106	Diver (Amusement)	129
Comedian	107	Dog Groomer	130
Commercial Airplane Pilot	107	Double (Film/TV)	130
Composer	108	Dramatic Coach	131
Computer Operator	108	Drill Press Operator	131
Computer Software Technician	109	Driving Instructor	132
Computer Subassembly Supervisor	109	Dust Sampler (Mining)	132
Concrete-Mixing Truck Driver	110	Economist	133
Concrete-Paving Machine Operator	110	Editor, Dictionary	133
		Editor, Film	134
Construction Drill Operator	111	Editor, News	134
Construction-Maintenance Inspector	111	Editor, Publications	135
		Editorial Assistant	135
Construction Worker	112	Electrical Appliance Repairer	136
Consumer Affairs Director	112	Electrical Equipment Tester	136
Contract Administrator	113	Electrician	137
Contractor (Construction)	113	Electrologist	137
Cook	114	Electronic Typeset Machine Operator	138
Copy Writer	114		
Correctional Officer	115	Electronics Research Engineer	138
Corrosion Prevention Metal Sprayer	115	Elevator Operator	139
		Emergency Medical Technician	139
Cosmetologist	116	Engineering Analyst	140
Counselor (Professional)	116	Environmental Analyst	140
County Agricultural Agent	117	Equal Opportunity Representative	141
Credit Analyst	117	Equestrian	141
Criminalist	118	Exhaust Emissions Inspector	142

Appendixes

	Page		Page
Exhibit Artist (Museum)	142	Hospital Administrator	166
Exhibit Builder (Museum)	143	Hospital Admitting Clerk	166
Extra (Film/Stage/TV)	143	Hospital Orderly	167
Faculty Member (College/University)	144	Host	167
Farm Machine Operator	144	Hotel Clerk	168
Farmer	145	Hotel/Motel Manager	168
Fashion Coordinator	145	Hunting & Fishing Guide	169
Fast-Foods Worker	146	Hydroelectric Station Operator	169
Ferryboat Captain	146	Illustrator (Commercial)	170
Final Inspector, Musical Instruments	147	Incinerator Plant Supervisor	170
Financial Aid Officer	147	Industrial Engineer	171
Financial Analyst	148	Information Scientist	171
Finished Carpet Inspector	148	Injection-Molding Machine Offbearer	172
Finishing Machine Operator	149	Insect/Disease Inspection Supervisor	172
Fire Fighter	149	Insurance Claim Examiner (Clerk)	173
Fire Marshall	150	Insurance Estate Planner	173
Fish Farmer	150	Insurance Sales Agent	174
Fishing Vessel Captain	151	Insurance Underwriter	174
Floral Designer	151	Intelligence Specialist	175
Flying Instructor	152	Interior Designer	175
Food & Drug Inspector	152	Interpreter	176
Food Technologist	153	Inventory Clerk	176
Foreign Service Officer	153	Investigator (Utility Bill Complaints)	177
Forest Fire Fighter	154	Investigator	177
Forest Fire Ranger	154	Ironworker Machine Operator	178
Forest Nursery Supervisor	155	Janitor	178
Forester	155	Jeweler	179
Forester Aide	156	Job Analyst	179
Front-End Loader Operator	156	Jockey	180
Fund Raiser	157	Judge	180
Funeral Attendant	157	Laboratory Assistant (Zoo)	181
Funeral Director	158	Landscape Gardener	181
Gas Dispatcher (Light/Heat/Power)	158	Landscape Laborer	182
Geographer	159	Lawn Service Worker	182
Geologist (Petroleum)	159	Lawn/Tree Spray Service Supervisor	183
Glass Inspector	160	Lawyer	183
Golf Club Manager	160	Librarian	184
Graphologist	161	Library Technical Assistant	184
Grip (Film/TV)	161	Lifeguard	185
Hair Stylist	162	Literary Agent	185
Hand Engraver	162	Livestock Farm Worker	186
Helicopter Pilot	163	Livestock Rancher	186
Highway Maintenance Worker	163	Lobbyist	187
Historian	164	Locomotive Engineer	187
Home Economist	164	Log Loader	188
Home Housekeeper	165	Logging Operations Inspector	188
Horse Trainer	165		

	Page
Machine Operator	189
Machine Setup Worker	189
Machinist	190
Magician	190
Mail Carrier	191
Mailroom Supervisor	191
Maintenance Superintendent	192
Make-Up Artist (Film/TV)	192
Manicurist	193
Manufacturers' Representative	193
Masseur	194
Material Coordinator	194
Mathematician	195
Mechanical Shovel Operator	195
Media Director	196
Medical Equipment Repairer	196
Membership Director	197
Membership Solicitor	197
Mental Retardation Aide	198
Meteorologist	198
Microfilm Document Preparer	199
Mine Superintendent	199
Modeling Instructor	200
Mortgage Accounting Clerk	200
Motorboat Operator	201
Museum Curator	201
Music Director (Film/Radio/TV)	202
Music Teacher	202
Musician	203
Narrator	203
Navigator	204
Net Fisher	204
News Assistant (Radio/TV)	205
Newswriter	205
Nuclear Engineer	206
Numerical-Control Lathe Operator	206
Nurse (General Duty)	207
Nurse (Licensed Practical)	207
Nurse's Aide	208
Nursery School Attendant	208
Occupational Therapist	209
Office File Clerk	209
Office Files Supervisor	210
Office Manager	210
Offset Press Operator	211
Optometric Assistant	211
Orchestra Conductor	212
Outdoor Advertising Leasing Agent	212

	Page
Packing Materials Inspector	213
Painter	213
Paperhanger	214
Paralegal Assistant	214
Park Ranger	215
Park Superintendent	215
Parking Lot Supervisor	216
Parts Manager	216
Patent Agent	217
Pawnbroker	217
Payroll Clerk	218
Perfusionist	218
Personal Shopper	219
Personnel Recruiter	219
Petroleum Field Engineer	220
Petroleum Inspector	220
Photographer	221
Photographers' Model	221
Physical Education Instructor	222
Physical Therapist	222
Physician (General Practitioner)	223
Physicist	223
Plant Guide	224
Playwright	224
Plumber	225
Police Chief	225
Police Officer	226
Political Scientist	226
Pollution Control Engineer	227
Pollution Control Technician	227
Post Office Clerk	228
Poultry Farm Supervisor	228
Precision Lens Grinder	229
Probation & Parole Officer	229
Production Coordinator	230
Production Engine Repairer	230
Production Superintendent	231
Professional Athlete	231
Professional Athletic Coach	232
Professional Sports Scout	232
Programmer (Business)	233
Programmer (Engineering/Science)	233
Programmer (Information Systems)	234
Promotion Manager	234
Prop Maker (Film/Stage/TV)	235
Property Manager	235
Property Utilization Officer	236
Psychiatrist	236

Appendixes

	Page		Page
Psychologist (Educational)	237	Shipping & Receiving Clerk	260
Psychologist (Industrial)	237	Sightseeing Guide	260
Public Health Educator	238	Sign Painter	261
Public Service Director	238	Silversmith	261
Public Works Commissioner	239	Singer	262
Purchasing Agent	239	Skip Tracer	262
Quality Control Food Technician	240	Social Director	263
Radial-Arm Saw Operator	240	Social Service Caseworker	263
Radiation Therapy Technologist	241	Sociologist	264
Radio Dispatcher (Fire Service)	241	Solar-Energy Systems Designer	264
Radiographer	242	Solid-Waste Disposal Manager	265
Radiologic Technologist	242	Special Effects Specialist	265
Real Estate Sales Agent	243	Speech Pathologist	266
Receptionist	243	Spinning Lathe Operator	266
Records Analyst Manager	244	Sports Instructor	267
Recreational Leader	244	Stage Director	267
Reducing Salon Attendant	245	Stationary Engineer	268
Reporter	245	Statistician	268
Reservations Agent (Airline)	246	Steam-Cleaning Machine Operator	269
Respiratory Therapist	246	Stock Clerk	269
Risk & Insurance Manager	247	Storage Facility Rental Clerk	270
Riveter	247	Store Cashier Checker	270
Rodeo Performer	248	Story Editor (Film/Radio/TV)	271
Rotary Oil Drill Operator	248	Streetcar Operator	271
Safety Coordinator	249	Stunt Performer	272
Sales Agent (Financial Services)	249	Surgical Dressing Maker	272
Sales Manager	250	Tax Attorney	273
Sales Rep (Chemicals & Drugs)	250	Taxi Driver	273
Sales Rep (Computers)	251	Taxidermist	274
Sales Rep (Data Processing Services)	251	Teacher (Adult Education)	274
Sales Rep (Dental/Medical Supplies)	252	Teacher (Elementary)	275
Sales Rep (Livestock)	252	Teacher (Kindergarten)	275
Sales Route Driver	253	Teacher (Preschool)	276
Salesperson (General Merchandise)	253	Teacher (Secondary)	276
		Teacher (Special Needs Students)	277
Salesperson (Household Appliances)	254	Technical Director (Radio/TV)	277
Sanitation Superintendent	254	Technical Writer	278
School Attendance Officer	255	Telephone Communication Consultant	278
School Psychologist	255	Telephone Operator (Central Office)	279
School Social Worker	256	Test Pilot	279
Screen Writer	256	Theater Manager	280
Sculptor	257	Threading Machine Operator	280
Secretary	257	Ticket Agent	281
Securities Sales Agent	258	Title Examiner	281
Security Guard	258	Toll Collector	282
Sewing Machine Operator	259	Tool & Equipment Rental Clerk	282
Ship Pilot	259	Town Clerk	283

	Page
Tractor-Trailer Truck Driver	283
Translator	284
Transmission Tester (Telephone)	284
Travel Agent	285
Tree Planter	285
Tree Pruner	286
Tree Surgeon	286
Trimming Machine Operator	287
Truck Driver (Light Deliveries)	287
Truck Safety Inspector	288
Typist	288
Ultrasound Technologist	289
Umpire	289
Urban Planner	290
U.S. Special Agent	290
Vendor (Amusement/Sports Park)	291
Veterinarian	291

	Page
Vocational Rehabilitation Counselor	292
Vocational Training Instructor	292
Volunteer Services Supervisor	293
Waiter (Bar)	293
Warehouse Manager	294
Warehouse Supervisor	294
Water-Treatment Plant Operator	295
Weight Reduction Specialist	295
Welding Inspector	296
Welfare Director	296
Wildlife Control Agent	297
Word-Processing Machine Operator	297
Writer, Prose (Fiction & Nonfiction)	298
X-Ray Equipment Tester	298
Zoologist	299

C. How to Select a Career Counselor

If you're reading this section, then it is likely that you are still uncertain as to which career direction to pursue. You may have religiously completed all the exercises contained in *Career Selector 2001* and still you find yourself confused about a career goal.

Or perhaps you have made a decision regarding a career goal, but have several important, but unanswered, questions regarding how to reach your objective. And without a clear plan you are reluctant to take the first step.

If either of the above two scenarios is true for you, do not become alarmed, or depressed. It's normal for some people to experience confusion or uncertainty at this point in the program. Such symptoms as confusion and a reluctance to forge ahead are really emotional signs telling you that additional information may be needed before you are ready to advance your career planning. It is at this point that the services of a professional career counselor can be most helpful.

As in all professions, there are good career counselors and then there are those you want to stay away from at all costs. Considering your emotional state at this point (*i.e.*, you're probably desperate for some good advice), the last thing you want or need is someone giving you bad information or guidance.

So how do you select a good career counselor? This task is just as difficult as selecting any other professional, such as a doctor, lawyer, accountant, or dentist. Approach this task as you would approach hiring an employee—first do some research to find potential candidates and then interview several before deciding whose services you will use. The operative word here is "interview"! Remember, you are interviewing counselors, not the other way around. It is your job to pick the person best suited to help you, and you are totally in control of this process. This is no simple task, and I have no magic formula to offer. However, if you are willing to invest a little of your time and follow the suggestions below, you are much more likely to find a counselor who can make a positive difference in your career development.

Where to look for a counselor

Listed below are several places you should investigate. Use your telephone at first to identify counselors who might be appropriate. Then, arrange with each person a time, date, and location where you can conduct your interview. If possible, avoid paying a fee for an interview session. Many counselors are willing to meet with you for a few minutes free of charge to answer questions about their counseling service.

1. **High School Guidance Offices** Call several high school guidance counselors and ask them if they can recommend any good career counselors in your area. While most high school guidance counselors do not specialize in career guidance, they often know colleagues who do. In some cases, they themselves may be interested in working with you.

2. **College Counseling Offices (or Offices of Career Planning and Placement)** Often counselors working on the college level are specialists in career planning. Call several to inquire if they provide services to the general public.

3. **Counselors in Private Practice** Check your telephone yellow pages for the names of counselors and psychologists who specialize in career guidance.

4. **State Employment Office** While these professionals usually specialize in employment placement, rather than in career planning, they may know of other career guidance services available in your community. In some cases, these people may be able to provide you with certain career guidance information and assistance.

5. **Social Service Agencies** Check your telephone yellow and white pages for the number of your local Department of Social Services. Sometimes a social service counselor is trained in career guidance, in addition to their normal training in personal, social, and family counseling.

6. **Charitable Agencies** Some charitable agencies offer assistance to help people with career concerns. Check with such agencies as the United Way and Catholic Charities.

7. **Computer Online Services** Fast becoming one of the easiest ways in which to obtain information and assistance, services such as America Online, CompuServe, and Prodigy now offer a wide variety of information and, in some cases, personal assistance to help you with your career development. If you have access to a personal computer equipped with a telephone modem, you can obtain personal counseling and information from the comfort of your home or office. For further information on subscribing to any of the following computer online services, call the number listed:

   America Online   800-227-6364—offers counseling via your computer
   CompuServe   800-848-8199
   GEnie   800-638-9636
   Prodigy   800-776-3460 ext 888

8. **Professional Association Referrals** Two professional associations exist that can provide you with information on career counseling services in your area. For further information on their referral services, contact:

   International Association of Counseling Services
   5999 Stevenson Avenue
   Alexandria, VA 22304
   (703) 823-9840

   National Board of Certified Counselors, Inc.
   3-D Terrace Way
   Greensboro, NC 27403
   (919) 547-0607

Guidelines for selecting a career counselor

Once you have identified several career counselors who are willing to meet with you to discuss your career needs and their services, your next step is to evaluate each counselor. The following suggestions can help you determine which counselor is right for you.

1. **Interview several** Talk to at least three counselors about what they can do for you before you select one to work with. Don't accept help from the first counselor you meet. A comparison of several counselors can reveal the relative strengths—and weaknesses—of each person. Only then can you determine which counselor is best for you.

2. **Go with experience** Becoming proficient in career guidance strategies takes time. While this is bad news for entry-level career guidance practitioners, you're best bet is to find someone who has at least three to five years of practical, hands-on experience guiding people in career decision-making and planning.

3. **Ask about their strategy** Ask them to state what procedures and steps they will take you through and what materials they will use to help you resolve your confusion or indecision. It is generally accepted by many career counselors that inherent in the process of career guidance are the following activities: personal assessment (learning about yourself), occupational exploration (learning about occupations available in our society),

decision-making (learning how to evaluate occupations to determine which one or ones are best for you), and career planning (learning how to develop a plan for reaching your career goal).

Avoid counselors who build their entire guidance procedure around only one task—an interest inventory. Collecting information about your personality style involves much more than the use of an interest inventory. Ideally, a good career counselor will incorporate several strategies for collecting information about your personality style, such as self-assessment (where you contribute information about who you believe you are), peer-assessment (where friends, coworkers, and relatives provide information about you), counseling (where the counselor, through questioning, offers an opinion regarding your personality), and testing (where standard assessment instruments, such as interest inventories, ability tests, and personality surveys are used to gather information).

If a counselor is not able to clearly articulate the guidance strategy, or is unwilling to do so, run—don't walk—out of the office. It is wise to ask counselors to provide a thumbnail sketch of their strategy in writing (to protect you in the event you do not get the services you desire).

4. **Ask for references** Ask for the names of several clients the counselor has worked with in the last six months whom you may call for a recommendation. Call those individuals to ask how helpful they found the counselor to be. If the counselor cannot provide you with any clients, be suspicious.

5. **Ask to see credentials** While good career counselors are not necessarily trained by completing a college degree program, it is wise to ask for evidence of any formal training the counselor has completed. Ideally, a career counselor should have some formal training in education, guidance, or counseling, as well as specific training in career counseling. If you are offered no evidence of training in any of these areas, be suspicious.

Ask if the counselor has written anything (i.e. articles and books) on the subject of career planning. While not all counselors should be expected to be published, this is a good sign that the counselor has thought the guidance process through carefully.

6. **Avoid guarantees** If any counselor guarantees you that you will have a clear idea of a career direction once you have completed the counseling program, get up and leave immediately. The best any counselor should hope for is to help you better understand your career options, and what might be involved in attempting to reach any option. There are no guarantees possible in this business.

7. **Don't pay too much** It's not uncommon to find counselors charging anywhere from a few hundred dollars to over several thousand dollars to help you select a career direction. You don't automatically get more help if you pay more money. Fees of $30–$100 per hour for career counseling are reasonable. You can sometimes find top quality, professional career counseling available free of charge at many community colleges, four year colleges, and universities.

Some counselors will insist that you sign a contract, which includes a clause about their fee, before they will work with you. While not all contracts are bad in themselves, and while not all counselors who insist on a contract should be avoided, there are plenty of horror stories of people who have been forced to pay exorbitant fees for less than satisfactory service simply because they signed a legal document.

Working with a career counselor who charges by the hour is recommended because you have the option of quitting any time you think you have received the help you desired, or are not getting the service you need, without owing any additional money.

8. **Who will do what?** Make sure you ask each counselor to indicate clearly what responsibilities you and the counselor will have in completing the various work assignments inherent in the guidance strategy. Again, ask for this in writing.

9. **Ask about the competition** Ask the counselor to evaluate some of the standard guidance programs (strategies) that are available and generally accepted by career counselors today, such as *What Color is Your Parachute?* (by Richard Bolles) or *Where Do I Go From Here With My Life?* (by John Crystal and Richard Bolles). A counselor who is unable to talk intelligently about any of these landmark publications may not be well schooled in the process of career guidance. Be suspicious.

10. **Go with your instincts** Lastly, after taking in all the above suggestions, you must trust your instincts about which counselor is right for you. Your internal voice will guide you in selecting the counselor with whom you have the most rapport, as well as the one you feel most comfortable with talking about yourself and your career aspirations. Trust your own judgment.

D. How to Use the DOT, GOE, and OOH Directories

This appendix contains information regarding three of the most commonly used publications for identifying occupations related to your interests. These publications include:

- *Dictionary of Occupational Titles (DOT)*
- *Guide for Occupational Exploration (GOE) and Expanded Guide for Occupational Exploration (EGOE)*
- *Occupational Outlook Handbook (OOH)*

If, after completing Task 1 in *Career Selector 2001*, you want to explore even more career options before moving on to Task 2, you may wish to use these directories. Using these materials will require some research time on your part, usually conducted in a local school or college guidance office or library or public library. If you prefer not to conduct the research yourself and would like to use a computerized occupational research service, see Appendix A for information on the Career Analysis Service.

About the directories

As its title implies, the *Dictionary of Occupational Titles (DOT)* is a dictionary of occupational titles. It contains brief descriptions of the main work functions for more than 13,500 occupations. It is an excellent source of information when you want a quick description of a particular occupation.

The *Guide for Occupational Exploration (GOE)* contains the same listing of occupations found in the DOT but arranges them into twelve major interest areas, which are subdivided into a total of sixty-six work groups (the same work groups found in Task 1 of *Career Selector 2001*). The GOE does not provide descriptive information on occupations, but is ideally suited for identifying occupations (by job title) that match a particular interest.

The *Expanded Guide for Occupational Exploration (EGOE)* is a spin-off of the GOE. There are two main differences between the EGOE and the regular GOE. The EGOE contains a listing of only 2500 occupations—those that offer the best employment opportunities in the near future. In addition, for the 2500 occupations listed, the EGOE provides far more descriptive information than in the GOE.

The *Occupational Outlook Handbook (OOH)* contains detailed information on 225 occupations. While it contains fewer job titles than the above directories, it provides the most in-depth information of all the above directories on each occupation listed.

How to identify occupations related to your interests

To find occupations related to your interests, use the GOE (or EGOE). Refer to the master listing of twelve Interest Areas found at the beginning of each directory. Note the page number of those areas that match your interests. Then flip to the pages you have identified and review the listing of occupations. Whenever you find an occupation you would like to consider as a career goal, add it to your list of possible career options.

If you want a brief description of any occupation, refer to the DOT or OOH. Cross-referencing from the GOE (or EGOE) to the DOT is simple. Each occupation in the GOE (and EGOE) is coded two ways:

- by GOE number   Example: Lawyer 11.04.02
- by DOT number   Example: Lawyer 110.107-010

Once you have found an occupation in the GOE (or EGOE) that you are interested in exploring, note its DOT number. Next, refer to the DOT and find the page with the same number.

Pages are arranged numerically from 001.061-010 to 979.687-022. On the page with the same number as your occupation, you will find a description of your occupation. In this way, you can easily flip back and forth from the GOE (or EGOE) to the DOT as you identify occupations worthy of consideration.

The meaning of the DOT code number

The DOT number is a unique nine-digit number assigned to each occupation by the federal government. No two occupations have the same DOT number. The DOT number refers to a classification system (i.e. a method of organizing occupations according to various criteria) that is no longer widely used by career seekers and changers or professional counselors. The DOT classification system has become somewhat archaic due to its rather complex structure and, therefore, has been replaced by other classification systems, such as the GOE arrangement.

Its meaning is of questionable value and, therefore, not necessary to define at this point, but the use of the DOT numbering system is still helpful. You should keep track of the DOT number for each occupation you are interested in exploring. By doing so, you can easily cross-reference to many occupational directories, such as the GOE and OOH. Other occupational directories using the DOT system can be found in Appendix A.

The meaning of the GOE code number

The GOE number is a unique six-digit number assigned to each occupation by the federal government. As in the DOT system no two occupations have the same number. Each number represents a group of occupations that are similar in nature, so the numbering system makes it easy for you to find occupations that match your interests.

The first two digits refer to a particular interest area, of which there are twelve:

01 Artistic
02 Scientific
03 Plants and Animals
04 Protective
05 Mechanical
06 Industrial
07 Business Detail
08 Selling
09 Accommodating
10 Humanitarian
11 Leading and Influencing
12 Physical Performing

For example, lawyer (11.04.02) belongs to the Leading and Influencing interest area.

The second set of two digits refers to the work group within a particular interest area. There are a total of sixty-six work groups found in all twelve interest areas. For example, lawyer belongs to the fourth work group (Law) found in the Leading and Influencing interest area.

Finally, the third set of two digits refers to a particular subgroup within a work group. In the case of lawyer, it belongs to the second subgroup (Legal Practice) in the Law work group.

The real value of using the GOE numbering system is in finding related occupations. For example, assume you were once interested in the occupation of Biologist (02.02.03). However, you also wish to explore occupations that are similar in nature. Using the GOE, you could find occupations in the 02 Interest Area that would be somewhat similar. However, in the 02.02 Work Group you would find occupations that are even more similar. Finally, the most similar occupations could be found in the 02.02.03 Subgroup.

Where to find these directories

Although you can buy any of these four publications for your own personal use, you may prefer to borrow these materials from a local high school or college guidance office or from a public or school library.

About the Author

With more than twenty years of professional experience, James C. Gonyea is a nationally recognized expert in the field of career guidance. He has counseled thousands of students and adults in educational and career planning, employment placement, and small-business development. He is the author of several career guidance interest inventories, software programs, and career and planning guides which have been used by thousands of students and adults nationwide. Mr. Gonyea is also the president of Gonyea and Associates, Inc., a southern New Hampshire company specializing in the creation of educational, career, and business development materials.

Mr. Gonyea is the founder and director of the nation's first and only electronic career guidance agency—the Career Center—available on the America On Line computer network. The Career Center offers career development information and assistance to more than 220,000 people nationwide.

Mr. Gonyea has also written *Working for America* for Barron's Educational Series. He lives in Manchester, New Hampshire with his wife Pamela and daughter Korie.

Notes

Notes

TITLES THAT GENERATE SUCCESS!

Business Success Series

Fifteen titles comprise Barron's innovative series designed to help the business person succeed! All offer advice and facts on how to master job techniques that will generate success. Each book: Paperback, $4.95, Canada $6.50, 96 pp., 4 3/16" × 7"

Conduct Better Job Interviews (4580-7)
Conquering Stress (4837-7)
Creative Problem Solving (1461-8)
Delegating Authority (4958-6)
How To Negotiate a Bigger Raise (4604-8)
Make Presentations With Confidence (4588-2)
Maximizing Your Memory Power (4799-0)
Motivating People (4673-0)
Projecting a Positive Image (1455-3)
Running a Meeting That Works (4640-4)
Speed Reading (1845-1)
Time Management (4792-3)
Using the Telephone More Effectively (4672-2)
Winning With Difficult People (4583-1)
Writing Effective Letters and Memos (4674-9)

Books may be purchased at your bookstore, or by mail from Barron's. Enclose check or money order for total amount plus sales tax where applicable and add 10% for postage and handling (minimum charge $3.75, Canada $4.00). All books are paperback editions. Prices subject to change without notice.

ISBN PREFIX: 0-8120

Barron's Educational Series, Inc.
250 Wireless Boulevard, Hauppauge, NY 11788
In Canada: Georgetown Book Warehouse
34 Armstrong Avenue, Georgetown, Ont. L7G 4R9

(#53) R 2/96

From The Leading Publisher Of Test Prep books, With Over 10 Million Sold *The Most Famous Name In Educational Guidance*

BUSINESS

HOW TO PREPARE FOR THE GRADUATE MANAGEMENT ADMISSION TEST (GMAT), *10th Edition, Jaffe & Hilbert.* Over half a million copies have already been sold of this collection of six complete practice tests with all answers thoroughly explained. 672 pp. $12.95, Can. $16.95 (1920-2)

HOW TO PREPARE FOR THE GRADUATE RECORD EXAMINATION (GRE), *11th Edition, Brownstein, Weiner & Weiner Green.* Here's a 3,500-word vocabulary builder and six model exams with answers explained. 672 pp., $12.95, Can. $16.95 (1939-3)

Also Available:
HOW TO PREPARE FOR THE GRE—BIOLOGY TEST, *3rd Edition, Snyder & Rodgers.* 304 pp., $12.95, Can. $16.95 (4199-2).
HOW TO PREPARE FOR THE GRE—PSYCHOLOGY TEST, *3rd Edition, Palmer.* 288 pp., $11.95, Can. $15.50 (4192-5)

BARRON'S GUIDE TO GRADUATE BUSINESS SCHOOLS, *9th Edition, Miller.* Detailed descriptions of master's programs at nearly 700 business schools across America are accompanied by tips on school selection, application procedures, financing, and more. 704 pp., $14.95, Can. $19.95 (1753-6)

HOW TO PREPARE FOR THE MILLER ANALOGIES TEST (MAT) *6th Edition, Sternberg.* Over 1,100 sample analogies—with answers explained—reflect every type of analogy found on the exam. All analogies are categorized by content. 176 pp., $11.95, Can. $15.95 (1776-5)

LAW

HOW TO PREPARE FOR THE LAW SCHOOL ADMISSION TEST (LSAT), *Revised 8th Edition, Bobrow.* Recommended by LSAT study programs, this book contains a diagnostic test and six comprehensive model exams with all answers explained. 512 pp., $13.95, Can. $17.95 (9348-8)

BARRON'S GUIDE TO LAW SCHOOLS, *11th Edition, Barron's College Division.* Along with comprehensive profiles of over 200 law schools approved by the American Bar Association, this book provides a solid preparation and practice for the LSAT. 384 pp., $14.95, Can. $19.95 (1754-4)

MEDICAL AND DENTAL

HOW TO PREPARE FOR THE MEDICAL COLLEGE ADMISSION TEST (MCAT), *Revised 7th Edition Seibel & Guyer.* The most comprehensive MCAT review available, here are four complete model exams with all answers provided. 480 pp., $12.95, Can. $16.95 (4646-3)

BARRON'S GUIDE TO MEDICAL AND DENTAL SCHOOLS, *7th Edition, Wischnitzer.* Here are current profiles on U.S. and Canadian medical schools accredited by the American Medical Association, as well as on dental schools in both countries. 320 pp., $16.95, Can. $21.95 (9052-7)

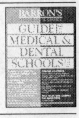

CAREER PREPARATION

HOW TO PREPARE FOR THE CERTIFIED PUBLIC ACCOUNTANT EXAMINATION (CPA), *Revised 5th Edition, Person & Dauber.* Written by experts who have successfully prepared over 75,000 CPA candidates, this guide includes the two most recent exams, diagnostic tests, and study tips. 640 pp., $18.95, Can. $24.95 (2865-1)

HOW TO PREPARE FOR PRAXIS, *Postman.* This book reflects the complete revision of NTE (National Teach Examination) format and their replacement by the Praxis test series. Book comes with 60-minute listening comprehension cassette. 700 pp. $18.95, Can. $24.95 (8225-7)

BARRON'S EDUCATIONAL SERIES, INC.
250 Wireless Boulevard, Hauppauge, New York 11788
In Canada: Georgetown Book Warehouse
34 Armstrong Avenue, Georgetown, Ontario L7G 4R9

ISBN Prefix: 0-8120
Prices subject to change without notice Books may be purchase at your bookstore or by mail from Barron's. Enclose check Or money order for total amount plus sales tax where applicable and 10%. for postage and handling (minimum charge of $3.75, Can. $4.00). All books are paperback editions.